The Human Capital Index 2020 UPDATE

The Human Capital Index 2020 UPDATE

Human Capital in the Time of COVID-19

© 2021 International Bank for Reconstruction and Development / The World Bank

1818 H Street NW, Washington, DC 20433
Telephone: 202-473-1000; Internet: www.worldbank.org
Some rights reserved
1 2 3 4 24 23 22 21

This work is a product of the staff of The World Bank with external contributions. The findings, interpretations, and conclusions expressed in this work do not necessarily reflect the views of The World Bank, its Board of Executive Directors, or the governments they represent. The World Bank does not guarantee the accuracy of the data included in this work. The boundaries, colors, denominations, and other information shown on any map in this work do not imply any judgment on the part of The World Bank concerning the legal status of any territory or the endorsement or acceptance of such boundaries. Nothing herein shall constitute or be considered to be a limitation upon or waiver of the privileges and immunities of The World Bank, all of which are specifically reserved.

Rights and Permissions

This work is available under the Creative Commons Attribution 3.0 IGO license (CC BY 3.0 IGO) http://creativecommons.org/licenses/by/3.0/igo. Under the Creative Commons Attribution license, you are free to copy, distribute, transmit, and adapt this work, including for commercial purposes, under the following conditions:

Attribution—Please cite the work as follows: World Bank. 2021. *The Human Capital Index 2020 Update: Human Capital in the Time of COVID-19.* Washington, DC: World Bank. doi:10.1596/978-1-4648-1552-2. License: Creative Commons Attribution CC BY 3.0 IGO.

Translations—If you create a translation of this work, please add the following disclaimer along with the attribution: *This translation was not created by The World Bank and should not be considered an official World Bank translation. The World Bank shall not be liable for any content or error in this translation.*

Adaptations—If you create an adaptation of this work, please add the following disclaimer along with the attribution: *This is an adaptation of an original work by The World Bank. Views and opinions expressed in the adaptation are the sole responsibility of the author or authors of the adaptation and are not endorsed by The World Bank.*

Third-party content—The World Bank does not necessarily own each component of the content contained within the work. The World Bank therefore does not warrant that the use of any third-party-owned individual component or part contained in the work will not infringe on the rights of those third parties. The risk of claims resulting from such infringement rests solely with you. If you wish to reuse a component of the work, it is your responsibility to determine whether permission is needed for that reuse and to obtain permission from the copyright owner. Examples of components can include, but are not limited to, tables, figures, or images.

All queries on rights and licenses should be addressed to World Bank Publications, The World Bank Group, 1818 H Street NW, Washington, DC 20433, USA; e-mail: pubrights@worldbank.org.

ISBN (paper): 978-1-4648-1552-2
ISBN (electronic): 978-1-4648-1647-5
DOI: 10.1596/978-1-4648-1552-2

Cover and interior design: Jihane El Khoury Roederer, World Bank

Library of Congress Control Number: 2020951890

Contents

Boxes

Figures

Map

Tables

Acknowledgments

The Human Capital Index is a collaboration between the Chief Economist offices of the Human Development Practice Group and of the Development Economics Group in the World Bank. The 2020 update was led by Roberta Gatti and Aart Kraay and produced by Paul Corral, Nicola Dehnen, Ritika D'Souza, and Juan Mejalenko. Noam Angrist, Syedah Aroob Iqbal, and Harry Patrinos updated the harmonized test score outcomes. We are grateful to Pablo Ariel Acosta, Rita Kullberg Almeida, D. H. C. Aturupane, Anne Margreth Bakilana, Tekabe Ayalew Belay, Paolo Belli, Livia M. Benavides, Kamel Braham, Fadila Caillaud, Carine Clert, Jorge Coarasa, Gabriel Demombynes, Heba Elgazzar, Sameh El-Saharty, Stefan Emblad, Lire Ersado, Antonio Giuffrida, Inaam Ul Haq, Susanna Hayrapetyan, Samira Ahmed Hillis, Camilla Holmemo, Keiko Inoue, Timothy Johnston, Pierre Joseph Kamano, Olga Khan, Christophe Lemiere, Yasuhiko Matsuda, Muna Meky, Sophie Naudeau, Dorota Agata Nowak, Emre Ozaltin, Aleksandra Posarac, Maria Laura Sanchez Puerta, Hnin Hnin Pyne, Jamele P. Rigolini, Rafael Rofman, Cristina Isabel Panasco Santos, Aparnaa Somanathan, Lars Sondergaard, Michel Welmond, William Wiseman, Ruslan Yemtsov, and Xiaoqing Yu for careful data review. We are also grateful to Luis Eduardo San Martin and Luiza Andrade from the DIME Analytics team for a thorough code review.

This report was written by a core team led by Roberta Gatti and including Paul Corral, Nicola Dehnen, Ritika D'Souza, and Juan Mejalenko. Steven Pennings wrote the chapter on human capital utilization. This report benefited from Aart Kraay's advice and from analytical inputs by Daniel Halim (gender analysis); Amer Hasan and Fiona Mackintosh (case studies narrative); Jigyasa Sharma (fragile contexts); Joao Pedro de Azevedo and Diana Goldemberg (COVID-19 impact on learning-adjusted years of schooling); Dina Abu-Ghaida and Mohamed Audah (schooling in Syria); Alejandro de la Fuente (schooling in Sierra Leone); Chloé Desjonquères (learning progress in Ceará); Alina Sava and Lars Sondergaard (schooling in Romania); Utz Pape (rapid response phone surveys); Halsey Rogers (challenges in test-score comparison over time); Saskia de Pee, Cecilia Garzón, and Naveed Akbar (nutrition interventions in Pakistan); and Emanuela Galasso, Lisa Saldanha, Meera Shekar, Marie-Chantal Uwanyiligira, and Kavita Watsa (cross-sectoral approaches to combat stunting). We are grateful to Diego Angel-Urdinola, Aneesa Arur, Salman Asim, Anne Margreth Bakilana, Livia Benavides, Catalina Castillo Castro, Carine Clert, Verónica Díaz Hinostroza, Sameh El-Saharty, Karlene Francis, Laura Gregory, Timothy Johnston, Amira Kazem, Flora Kelmendi, Igor Kheyfets, Sophie Naudeau, Jamele Rigolini, Hiroshi Saeki, Maria Laura Sanchez Puerta, Emmanuel Skoufias, Aparnaa Somanathan, Ryoko Tomita, and Inaam Ul Haq for providing country-level insights into changes in human capital outcomes over time.

The team is indebted to David Weil for his overarching guidance. We are grateful to our peer reviewers Shubham Chaudhuri, Rachel Glennerster, William Maloney, and David Weil for their insightful views and to Deon Filmer for his detailed comments on earlier versions of this draft. We thank Kathleen Beegle, Hana Brixi, Emanuela Galasso, Ramesh Govindaraj, Ambar Narayan, Meera Shekar, Sharad Tandon, Tara Vishwanath, and Michael Weber for thoughtful comments and conversations. We are grateful to Alex Irwin and Nora Mara for their outstanding editing touch; to Chloé Desjonquères, Nicola Dehnen, and Mary Fisk for efficiently managing the report's production process; and to Ruben Conner, Sebastian Insfran, and Andres Yi Chang for their careful read of the report.

This Human Capital Index update was developed under the strategic guidance of Mari Pangestu, Annette Dixon, and Mamta Murthi and benefited from the views of Nadir Mohammed and Alberto Rodriguez.

September 2020

About the Authors

Roberta Gatti, the Task Team Leader for this report, is the Chief Economist of the Human Development Practice Group at the World Bank. In this capacity, she co-leads the conceptualization and release of the Human Capital Index (HCI) and oversees the Service Delivery Indicators surveys initiative. After joining the World Bank as a Young Professional, she has worked in the Development Research Macro Group and in the Social Protection and Jobs units in the Middle East and North Africa and in Europe and Central Asia, based in Washington, DC, and in Bulgaria and Poland. She has also served as the World Bank Global Lead for Labor Policies. Roberta's research includes theoretical and empirical contributions on labor and household economics, political economy, growth, and social inclusion, and is published in top field journals. She is also the author of numerous World Bank flagship reports on jobs, informality, the Roma inclusion agenda, and the economics of human capital. She has taught at Georgetown University and Johns Hopkins University. An Italian national, Roberta holds a bachelor of arts degree from Università Bocconi and a PhD in economics from Harvard University.

Paul Corral is a Senior Economist in the World Bank's Chief Economist Office for Human Development. He previously worked in the World Bank's Poverty and Equity Global Practice and was part of the global unit working on just-in-time microsimulation models and small area estimation methods and applications. He led the work on small area estimation, which has revamped the institution's tools used for poverty mapping. He has published peer-reviewed articles on agricultural development and is the author of multiple Stata commands. An Ecuadorian national, he holds a PhD in economics from American University and a master of science degree in agricultural economics from the University of Hohenheim.

Nicola Dehnen is a Research Analyst in the World Bank's Chief Economist Office for Human Development. She works on the Human Capital Index (HCI) and the Human Capital Project. Her research covers topics in education, health, labor markets, and social protection. Previously, she worked on early learning programs in the World Bank's Education Global Practice and on social safety nets in the Social Protection, Labor, and Jobs division for West Africa. Before joining the World Bank, Nicola worked at the Inter-American Development Bank, the Leibniz Centre for European Economic Research, and the German Institute for Economic Research. She holds a graduate diploma in economics from the University of Nottingham and a master of science degree in economics from University College London.

Ritika D'Souza is a Research Analyst in the World Bank's Chief Economist Office for Human Development. She works on the Human Capital Index (HCI) and related analytics, including methodologies for the socioeconomic and spatial disaggregation of the HCI. Previously, she worked in the South Asia Chief Economist's Office, where her research covered the areas of nutrition, education, gender, and jobs. She has also managed the field implementation of impact evaluations of agriculture, food security, and nutrition projects in Nepal and Rwanda with the World Bank's Development Impact Evaluation (DIME) group. She holds a master's degree in public administration from the School of International and Public Affairs, Columbia University.

Juan Mejalenko is a PhD student at the University of Chicago Booth School of Business and has previously worked in the World Bank's Chief Economist Office for Human Development. Before joining the World Bank, he worked at the Inter-American Development Bank as a Research Analyst in the Office of Strategic Planning and Development Effectiveness, as well as in the Labor Markets division. An Argentinian national, he holds a bachelor's degree and master of science degree in economics from San Andrés University, Argentina.

Steven Pennings is an Economist in the Macroeconomics and Growth Team of the World Bank's Development Research Group. His research covers a variety of topics in macroeconomics, development, and political economy, including monetary policy, fiscal multipliers and rules, exchange rate pass-through, the determinants of conflict, and the growth contributions of national leaders. He also co-leads the World Bank's Long-Term Growth Model project. Before joining the World Bank, he worked at the Reserve Bank of Australia and at Save the Children in Vietnam. He has spent time at the International Monetary Fund, the Federal Reserve Board, and the Asian Development Bank. An Australian national, he holds a PhD from New York University and a bachelor of economics degree from the Australian National University.

Abbreviations

4Ps	Pantawid Pamilyang Pilipino Program (the Philippines)
ANER	adjusted net enrollment rate
BER	better employment rate
COVID-19	coronavirus disease 2019
DHS	Demographic and Health Surveys
EGRA	Early Grade Reading Assessment
EYS	expected years of school
FCS	fragile and conflict-affected situations
FQSE	Free Quality School Education (program in Sierra Leone)
GAML	Global Alliance to Monitor Learning
GBD	Global Burden of Disease (project)
GCFF	Global Concessional Financing Facility
GDP	gross domestic product
GER	gross enrollment rate
GNI	gross national income
GSFP	Ghana School Feeding Program
HCI	Human Capital Index
HTS	harmonized test score
IGME	United Nations Interagency Group for Child Mortality Estimation
IHME	Institute of Health Metrics and Evaluation
ILO	International Labour Organization
JME	Joint Child Malnutrition Estimates (database)
JOIN	Global Jobs Indicators Database (World Bank)
LAYS	learning-adjusted years of schooling
LLECE	Latin American Laboratory for Assessment of the Quality of Education
MICS	Multiple Indicator Cluster Surveys
NER	net enrollment rate
NHIS	National Health Insurance Scheme (Ghana)
PASEC	Program for the Analysis of Education Systems
PILNA	Pacific Island Learning and Numeracy Assessment
PIRLS	Progress in International Reading Literacy Study
PISA	Programme for International Student Assessment
PISA-D	PISA for Development
PPP	purchasing power parity
RBF	results-based financing
RRPS	rapid response phone survey

SACMEQ	The Southern and Eastern Africa Consortium for Monitoring Educational Quality
SDI	service delivery indicators
SEBJ	share of employment in better jobs
SNF	specialized nutritious food
TIMSS	Trends in International Mathematics and Science Study
TNER	total net enrollment rate
UHCI	Utilization-Adjusted Human Capital Index
UIS	United Nations Educational, Scientific, and Cultural Organization's Institute of Statistics
UNICEF	United Nations Children's Fund
UNPD	United Nations Population Division
WHO	World Health Organization

INTRODUCTION

The Human Capital Index (HCI) is an international metric that benchmarks key components of human capital across economies. The HCI was launched in 2018 as part of the Human Capital Project, a global effort to accelerate progress toward a world where all children can achieve their full potential. Measuring the human capital that a child born today can expect to attain by her 18th birthday, the HCI highlights how current health and education outcomes shape the productivity of the next generation of workers. In this way, it underscores the importance for governments and societies of investing in the human capital of their citizens.

Over the past decade, many economies have made important progress in improving human capital. Today, however, the COVID-19 (coronavirus) pandemic threatens to reverse many of those gains. Urgent action is needed to protect hard-won advances in human capital, particularly among the poor and vulnerable. Designing the needed interventions, targeting them to achieve the highest effectiveness, and navigating difficult trade-offs in times of reduced fiscal space make investing in better measurement of human capital now more important than ever.

Human capital consists of the knowledge, skills, and health that people accumulate over their lives. People's health and education have undeniable intrinsic value, and human capital also enables people to realize their potential as productive members of society. More human capital is associated with higher earnings for people, higher income for countries, and stronger cohesion in societies. It is a central driver of sustainable growth and poverty reduction.

This report accompanies the release of 2020 data on the HCI. Building on momentum from the first edition in 2018, the 2020 issue updates the index using new and expanded data for each of the HCI components through March 2020. As such, the report provides a snapshot of the state of human capital before COVID-19 and a baseline to track its impact.

COVID-19 struck at a time when the world was healthier and more educated than ever. Yet data presented in this report reveal that substantial human capital shortfalls and equity gaps existed before the crisis. Worldwide, a child born just before the advent of COVID-19 could expect to achieve on average just 56 percent of her potential productivity as a future worker. Gaps in human capital remain especially deep in low-income economies and those affected by violence, armed conflict, and institutional fragility. Expanded sex-disaggregated data show that girls currently enjoy a slight edge over boys in human capital accumulation in most economies, reflecting in part a female biological advantage early in life. Women continue to be at a substantial disadvantage, however, in many dimensions of human capital that are not captured by the HCI's components, including participation in economic life.

In addition to describing HCI data and methodology, this report documents the evolution of human capital over the last decade. Human capital outcomes progressed in almost all economies by about 4 percent on average during this period, thanks primarily to better health and increased access to schooling. Many economies, however, struggled to improve learning outcomes, because educational quality often failed to keep pace with gains in enrollment. The various dimensions of human capital improved with economic development, and they did so at a surprisingly similar pace across country groups. Progress was only slightly faster in low-income economies, which are further away from the frontier of full health and education.

The trajectories of individual economies differed considerably, including in how human capital gains were distributed across the socioeconomic spectrum within each economy. In some contexts, the most disadvantaged groups achieved the greatest gains. In others, poorer and richer families benefited equally. Along with economic development, specific policies contributed to some economies' progress in human capital. Effective policies included expanding the population coverage of health services, notably for maternal and child health; bolstering nutrition and access to sanitation; making school more affordable; and providing financial support to vulnerable families through mechanisms such as cash transfer programs and insurance. Strong gains were more likely in economies that maintained commitment to reform across political cycles and adopted an evidence-based, whole-of-society approach to policy making.

These same elements will be essential to protect human capital in the face of the COVID-19 crisis. Although data on COVID-19's impacts on human capital outcomes are only beginning to emerge, simulations conducted for this report suggest that school closures combined with family hardship are significantly affecting the accumulation of human capital for the current generation of school-age children. These impacts appear comparable in magnitude to the gains that many economies achieved during the previous decade, suggesting that the pandemic may roll back many years' worth of human capital progress. In parallel, COVID-19's disruption of health services, losses in income, and worsened nutrition are expected to increase child mortality and stunting, with effects that will be felt for decades to come.

The HCI can be a useful tool to track such losses and guide policy to counter them, because the index is based on robust markers for key stages of human capital accumulation in the growth trajectory of a child. But the five components of the HCI do not cover all the important aspects of the accumulation and productive use of human capital. In particular, the index is silent on the opportunities to use accumulated human capital in adulthood through meaningful work. In many economies, a sizable fraction of today's young people may not be employed when they become adults. Even if they find employment, they may not hold jobs in which they can use their skills and cognitive abilities to increase their productivity. Recognizing the salience of such patterns for how human capital gains are translated into economic progress and shared prosperity, this report analyzes two measures that augment the HCI to account for the utilization of human capital. These measures provide insight on further margins that economies can explore to boost their long-term growth and productivity. Both utilization measures suggest that human capital is particularly underutilized in middle-income economies. A key message is that human capital is also strikingly underutilized for women in many settings: the gender gap in employment rates (a basic measure of utilization) is 20 percentage points on average worldwide, but it exceeds 40 percentage points in South Asia and in the Middle East and North Africa.

By bringing salience to the productivity implications of shortfalls in health and education, the HCI has not only clarified the importance of investing in human capital but also highlighted the role that measurement can play in catalyzing consensus for reform. Better measurement enables policy makers to design effective interventions and target support to those who are most in need, which is often where interventions yield the highest payoffs. Investing in better measurement and data use now is a necessity, not a luxury. In the immediate term, it will guide pandemic containment strategies and support for the most affected. In the medium term, better curation and use of administrative, survey, and identification data will be essential to guide policy choices in an environment of limited fiscal space and competing priorities.

Today, hard-won human capital gains in many economies are at risk. But economies can do more than just work to recover the lost ground. Ambitious, evidence-driven policy measures in health, education, and social protection can pave the way for today's children to surpass the human capital achievements and quality of life of the generations that preceded them.

Protecting and extending earlier human capital gains will require, among others, expanding health service coverage and quality among marginalized communities, boosting learning outcomes together with school enrollments, and supporting vulnerable families with social protection measures adapted to the scale of the COVID-19 crisis. Informed by rigorous measurement, bold policies can drive a resilient recovery from the pandemic and open a future in which rising generations will be able to develop their full potential and tackle the vast challenges that still lie ahead: from ending poverty to preventing armed conflict to controlling climate change. COVID-19 has underscored the shared vulnerability and common responsibility that today link all nations. Fully realizing the creative promise embodied in each child has never been more important.

OVERVIEW

The Human Capital Index (HCI) measures the human capital that a child born today can expect to attain by her 18th birthday, given the risks of poor health and poor education prevailing in her country.[1] The index incorporates measures of different dimensions of human capital: health (child survival, stunting, and adult survival rates) and the quantity and quality of schooling (expected years of school and international test scores). Human capital has intrinsic value that is undeniably important but difficult to quantify, making it a challenge to combine the different components of human capital into a single measure. The HCI uses global estimates of the economic returns to education and health to create an integrated index that captures the expected productivity of a child born today as a future worker, relative to a benchmark—the same for all countries—of complete education and full health.

THE HCI 2020 UPDATE

The 2020 update of the HCI incorporates the most recent available data to report scores for 174 economies, 17 more than the 2018 edition. The 2020 update uses new and expanded data for each of the HCI components, available as of March 2020. As in the previous issue, data were obtained from official sources and underwent a careful process of review and curation. Given the timing of data collection, this update can serve as a benchmark of the levels of human capital accumulation that existed immediately before the onset of the COVID-19 (coronavirus) pandemic.

Globally, the HCI 2020 shows that, before the pandemic struck, a child could expect to attain an average of 56 percent of her potential productivity as a future worker. This global average masks considerable variation across regions and economies. For instance, a child born in a low-income economy could expect to be 37 percent as productive as if she had full education and full health. For a child born in a high-income economy, this figure is 70 percent.

INCOME ALONE DOES NOT EXPLAIN CROSS-COUNTRY DIFFERENCES IN HUMAN CAPITAL

What explains these variations in human capital outcomes? Despite a strong correlation between the HCI and gross domestic product per capita, human capital does not always move in lockstep with economic development. Economies like Burundi, Estonia, the Kyrgyz Republic, Uzbekistan, and Vietnam have human capital outcomes that are higher than predicted by their gross domestic product per capita. Conversely, in a number of economies, human capital is lower than per capita income would suggest. Among these are several resource-rich economies in which human capital development has not yet matched the potential that one would anticipate, given these economies' wealth.

Differences in the quantity and quality of schooling account for the largest part of HCI differences across country income groups. Of the 33-percentage-point difference between the scores of the average low- and high-income economy, almost 25 percentage points are accounted for by the differences in learning-adjusted years of schooling, a measure that combines expected years of school with learning as measured by harmonized test scores (that is, test scores that are made comparable across countries).

Although education drives HCI differences across country income groups, education's contribution to gaps within these groups varies. For instance, education accounts for roughly 90 percent of the difference between high and low performers in the high-income economy group but for only 60 percent within the group of low-income economies. In contrast, differences in child survival rates account for less of the difference in HCI scores among high-income economies. The same is true for health, which explains a lower share of differences in the HCI as one moves from low- to high-income groups, because health outcomes tend to be uniformly better as economies get richer.[2]

Human capital outcomes also vary for girls and boys. A disaggregation of the HCI by sex—now available for 153 of the 174 economies—shows that on average girls have a slight advantage over boys. Girls are not only catching up to but also outperforming boys in expected years of school and learning outcomes in some regions. For example, in the Middle East and North Africa, girls can expect to complete more than half of an additional learning-adjusted year of schooling compared with boys. In Sub-Saharan Africa and in South Asia, however, the reverse is true.

Investing in human capital enhances social cohesion and equity while strengthening people's trust in institutions. Nowhere is this more important than in countries grappling with fragility and conflict. External shocks such as armed conflict and natural disasters have destructive impacts both on countries' existing human capital stock and on the process of building new human capital. Evidence increasingly suggests that, for armed conflict as well as famine, these negative effects can persist for decades and even across generations, weakening the core of sustainable and equitable economic development.

Unfortunately, yet unsurprisingly, the HCI 2020 indicates that, on average, economies affected by fragility, conflict, and violence have lower HCI values compared to the rest of the world. In particular, the seven economies with the lowest HCI 2020 scores are all classified by the World Bank as fragile or conflict affected. This situation adds to the urgency of addressing human capital gaps in such settings. Only by preserving and rebuilding human capital can countries durably escape cycles of fragility and underdevelopment.

MOST ECONOMIES ACHIEVED HUMAN CAPITAL GAINS IN THE DECADE BEFORE COVID-19

Because this is the first update of the HCI, the 2020 release presents an opportunity to assess the evolution of human capital over time, as measured here by the index in the last decade. The HCI is based on outcomes that typically change slowly from year to year. Some of them—such as stunting and educational test scores—are measured infrequently, every three to five years. As a result, changes in the HCI over a short period are small and may simply reflect updates to some components that are measured sporadically.

To provide more reliable insights on economies' human capital trajectories over time, this report focuses on changes in the index over the past decade. To this end, a (circa) 2010 version of the HCI is constructed with data carefully curated to maximize comparability with the 2020 results. In particular, only those economies for which learning scores were measured by the same international assessment program in 2010 and 2020 enter the comparison.[3] The resulting sample for the 2010 HCI includes 103 economies.[4]

As measured by the HCI, human capital progressed in the vast majority of economies in this sample. On average, between 2010 and 2020, the HCI improved by 2.6 percentage points, about 4 percent of its average value in 2010.[5] One economy in four that experienced a rise in the index recorded gains of more than five percentage points—a substantial achievement. Economies starting from lower levels of human capital improved by larger amounts. Better health (child and adult survival, and reduction of stunting) accounts for about half of the HCI's changes. Increased enrollments—especially at preprimary and secondary school levels—account for the rest. In contrast, progress on learning outcomes has proved difficult, because test scores failed to keep pace with enrollment gains in many settings.

In the human capital dimensions captured by the index, girls and boys made similar progress over time, with only a handful of economies reporting opposite trends. In the 90 economies for which sex-disaggregated data are available and comparisons with 2010 are possible, the average gender ratio is similar in 2010 and 2020, at about 1.06 in favor of girls. Around 2010, the HCI was uniformly larger among girls than among boys, with the exception of seven economies. Over the last decade, the girl-to-boy ratio improved, approaching or surpassing gender parity, in all of these economies.

THE EXTENT TO WHICH DISADVANTAGED HOUSEHOLDS BENEFITED FROM HUMAN CAPITAL GAINS OVER TIME VARIES ACROSS ECONOMIES

National averages mask differential trends in human capital between richer and poorer households. Using household data from Demographic and Health Surveys and Multiple Indicator Cluster Surveys, it is possible to calculate a version of the HCI disaggregated by socioeconomic status for a number of low- and middle-income economies. There is substantial variability in how gains in human capital outcomes are distributed across the population.[6] For instance, Haiti, Malawi, and Senegal all improved their child survival rates over the last decade; however, the gap between rich and poor households in Haiti remained constant but decreased in Malawi and Senegal.[7] Similarly, the years of schooling a child could expect in Bangladesh, Burkina Faso, and India increased significantly. But in Burkina Faso the six-year gap in expected years of school between rich and poor households stayed constant over the past 10 years, whereas, in the same period, Bangladesh and India—although starting from different levels—were able to halve the gap between their richest and poorest households. Côte d'Ivoire's 25-percentage-point gap between stunting rates for rich and for poor households remained unchanged, notwithstanding a significant average reduction in stunting. Conversely, between 2000 and 2016, Uganda was able to narrow this gap from a difference of 20 percentage points to a difference of 16 percentage points. Addressing such rich–poor gaps in human capital must remain a priority for governments committed to equitable growth, not least because the returns to investment in human capital are often highest for disadvantaged groups, especially for measures that act early in life.

Human capital is a central driver of sustainable growth and poverty reduction. Even for governments that recognize the importance of investing in the human capital of their citizens, however, the benefits of designing policy and building institutions that foster human capital accumulation can take years or even decades to fully materialize. This slow process is evidenced in the relatively modest progress measured for the average economy on the HCI over the past decade. Adopting a longer time frame can help identify many forms of government action that can improve human capital. For that purpose, this report incorporates insights from case studies to better understand the trajectories of economies that have made notable improvements in various dimensions of human capital. Sustained political commitment spanning election cycles, coordination across the many programs and agencies that may influence human capital, and using a robust evidence base to inform policy choices emerge as key elements contributing to successful policies for human capital.[8]

HCI SIMULATIONS REVEAL COVID-19'S LARGE IMPACT ON HUMAN CAPITAL

COVID-19 threatens countries' hard-won human capital gains. A lesson from past pandemics and crises is that their effects are not only felt by those directly impacted, but often ripple across populations and, in many cases, across generations. This lesson underscores the urgent need to protect and rebuild human capital to foster recovery in the short and longer terms.

Setbacks during certain life stages—chiefly early childhood—can have especially damaging and long-lasting effects on human capital accumulation. During childhood, the link between parental income and child health is particularly strong (see Almond 2006). In previous crises, poorer nutrition and reduced well-being among pregnant mothers led to permanent losses in their children's cognitive attainment, as well as to higher chronic disease rates when the children became adults (see Almond and Currie 2011). In this crisis, human capital impacts associated with economic shocks come atop reductions in care linked to service disruptions during the pandemic's acute phase. As such, the pandemic, even if transitory, may have repercussions for years to come. Children in disadvantaged families will be disproportionately vulnerable to all these effects, thus deepening existing inequalities.

The HCI methodology can be used to quantify some of the potential impacts of COVID-19 on the future human capital of children and youth. For young children—those born during the pandemic or who are currently under the age of five—disruptions to health systems, reduced access to care, and family income losses will materialize as increased child mortality, malnutrition, and stunting. Because stunting and educational outcomes are closely intertwined, the pandemic risks durably setting back these children's learning. According to HCI-based simulations, in low-income economies, young children today can expect their human capital to be up to 1 percent lower than it would have been in the absence of COVID-19.

At the height of the pandemic, close to 1.6 billion children worldwide were out of school. For school-age children today, the pandemic has meant that formal teaching and learning no longer happen face to face. Because the ability to roll out distance learning differs across—and even within—economies, considerable losses in schooling and learning can be anticipated. The income shocks associated with COVID-19 will also force many children to drop out of school. Putting these effects together suggests that the pandemic could reduce global average learning-adjusted years of schooling by half a year. Translated into HCI units, this loss means a drop of almost 4.5 percent in the HCI of the current cohort of children. For an economy with an HCI of 0.5, this signifies a drop of 0.0225 or 2.25 HCI points, a reduction of the same order of magnitude as the HCI increase that many economies have achieved over the past decade.

Without a strong policy response now, the pandemic's negative human capital effects will likely continue to reduce economies' productivity and growth prospects for decades. In 20 years, roughly 46 percent of the typical economy's workforce (people aged 20 to 65 years) will be composed of individuals who were either in school or under the age of 5 during the COVID-19 pandemic. The human capital losses of today's children will translate into a drop of a full HCI point (0.01) for this future workforce. That is, even if the pandemic is brought under control relatively rapidly, the COVID-19 shock could still leave current cohorts of children behind for the rest of their lives. No society can afford to let that happen.

A MEASURE OF UTILIZATION OF HUMAN CAPITAL HIGHLIGHTS SIGNIFICANT GENDER GAPS

The HCI is based on reasonably directly measured markers for key stages of human capital in the growth trajectory of a child. The five components of the index, however, do not cover all the important aspects of the accumulation and productive use of human capital. When today's child becomes a worker in the future, in many countries she may not be able to find a job; even if she can, it might not be a job in which she can fully use her skills and cognitive abilities to increase her productivity. In these cases, her human capital can be considered *underutilized*.

Recognizing the importance of this pattern both for individuals and for policy, this report analyzes two simple extensions of the HCI that adjust it for labor market underutilization of human capital. Both Utilization-Adjusted Human Capital Indexes (UHCIs) can be calculated for more than 160 economies. Both have the same simple form—the HCI multiplied by a utilization rate—and represent the long-run income gains if an economy moves to the frontier where human capital is complete and completely utilized.[9] Given their different purposes, the UHCIs are meant to complement, not replace, the HCI.

The two UHCIs take different approaches to measuring utilization. In the *basic* UHCI, utilization is measured as the fraction of the working-age population that is employed. Although this measure is simple and intuitive, it cannot capture the fact that a large share of employment in developing countries is in jobs for which workers may not be able to fully use their human capital to increase their productivity. The *full* UHCI adjusts for this shortcoming by introducing the concept of *better employment*, which represents the types of jobs (for nonagricultural employees and employers) that are common in high-productivity economies. The full utilization rate depends on the fraction of an economy's working-age population in better employment. Because they have more human capital to underutilize, economies with higher HCI scores also face larger utilization penalties if they show low rates of better employment.

Although the different methodologies produce different scores for some individual economies, the basic and full measures yield broadly similar utilization rates across country income groups and regions, and in general. Utilization rates average about 0.6, but they follow U-shaped curves when plotted against per capita income across economies, and are lowest over a wider range of lower-middle-income economies. The analysis of underutilization suggests that moving to a world with complete human capital and complete utilization of that human capital could almost triple long-run per capita incomes.

Both UHCIs reveal starkly different gender gaps from those calculated using the HCI. Whereas the HCI is roughly equal for boys and girls, with a slight advantage for girls on average, UHCIs are lower for females than males, driven by lower utilization rates. Basic utilization (employment) rates are 20 percentage points lower for women than for men in general, with a gap of more than 40 percentage points in the Middle East and North Africa and in South Asia. Female employment rates follow strongly U-shaped curves when plotted against economies' levels of income, whereas male employment rates are much flatter, and with less dispersion across economies. The gender gap is also present in the full utilization rate, though it is smaller. These results suggest that, although gender gaps in human capital in childhood and adolescence have closed in the last two decades (especially for education), major challenges remain to translate these gains into opportunities for women.

BETTER MEASUREMENT ENABLES BETTER POLICY

As the COVID-19 crisis continues to unfold, data and measurement are more vital than ever to shape governments' immediate response and to guide future policy choices toward (cost-) effective solutions. Better measurement and data use are investments that pay off, a consideration that is particularly important now as countries face dwindling fiscal space and many competing demands.

By generating a shared understanding among diverse actors, measurement can shine a light on constraints that limit progress in human capital. In the same way, effective measurement can facilitate political consensus based on facts and help muster support for reforms. Measurement also enables policy makers to target support to those who are most in need, which is often where interventions yield the highest payoffs. As policy implementation moves forward, measurement provides feedback to guide course corrections.

In the context of a pandemic, governments that use relevant data in real time are better able to monitor the evolution of disease transmission and continuously update containment strategies, while responding to the immediate and long-term effects of the economic crisis on households and communities. At all times, data are especially important in countries affected by fragility or conflict, though measurement is far more difficult in these settings.

The HCI offers a high-level view of human capital across economies that can help catalyze new conversations with key stakeholders. At the same time, much greater depth in measurement and research is needed to better understand the dynamics of human capital accumulation, including across socioeconomic groups and geography, and how policies can affect it. Some key measurement improvements—such as leveraging phone surveys and making better use of administrative data—can be achieved in the short term. Other improvements will demand a more sustained effort from economies and development partners. These longer-range efforts include rethinking the architecture of country data systems to connect different administrative data sources and fielding surveys to better understand the needs and behavior of teachers and health providers.

The COVID-19 crisis threatens gains in human capital that countries have achieved through decades of effort. A renewed, society-wide commitment is needed to protect human capital in the short run and to remediate the looming losses in the longer run. Challenges range from crafting context-sensitive school reopening protocols to deeper reforms that will promote children's learning at all stages: starting from cognitive stimulation in the early years, then continuing to nurture relevant skills throughout childhood and adolescence. Building blocks for success will include better-prepared teachers, better-managed schools, and incentives that are aligned across the many stakeholders in education reform.

Support to households will be essential not only to buffer income losses but also to sustain the demand side of schooling and health care. Such support can come through cash transfers and through interventions aimed at reconnecting workers to jobs. Strengthening disease surveillance and a renewed commitment to universal health coverage will be critical to build resilient health systems that offer affordable, quality care to all. Investments in water, sanitation, and—increasingly—digitalization are important complements to sustain human capital accumulation. Current deepening inequalities in human capital outcomes make it imperative to target interventions to children from the most disadvantaged families.

With fiscal space shrinking as competing priorities multiply, policy makers face hard choices. Proven strategies include engaging the whole of society, identifying cross-sectoral synergies, and using data to select cost-effective interventions and track their effective implementation. These approaches will not make tough policy trade-offs painless. But they will enable leaders to choose the options that have the highest probability of success. Applying these tools, governments can go far toward protecting and rebuilding human capital in the wake of COVID-19. And that is not all. Strong, evidence-driven human capital investments now can do far more than restore what has been lost. Health, education, social protection, and other complementary policies informed by rigorous measurement can take countries' human capital beyond the levels previously achieved, opening the way to a more prosperous and inclusive future.

NOTES

1. The HCI was introduced in World Bank (2018a, 2018b), and the methodology of the HCI is detailed in Kraay (2018).
2. Stunting and adult survival are here considered together for easy comparison.
3. As described in chapter 2, this rule is relaxed for only five economies, which are included in the sample with learning scores from different international assessments (Trends in International Mathematics and Science Study [TIMMS]/Progress in International Reading Literacy Study [PIRLS] in 2010 and the Programme for International Student Assessment [PISA] in 2020). To increase comparability, only scores for secondary schooling are considered for 2010.
4. This sample is, unsurprisingly, skewed toward richer economies for which data tend to be more complete and of better quality.
5. Richer economies are closer to the frontier of full schooling and health and would naturally display slower change in their human capital. With the 2010–20 sample skewed toward richer economies, the human capital pace of change is likely underestimated.
6. The analysis of HCI outcomes disaggregated by socioeconomic status is based on D'Souza, Gatti, and Kraay (2019).
7. It is important to note the dramatic increase in child mortality that occurred in Haiti in 2010 in the aftermath of the country's catastrophic January 2010 earthquake.
8. This approach informs the work of the World Bank's Human Capital Project (HCP).
9. Specifically, long-run gross domestic product per capita is 1/UHCI times higher in a world with complete human capital and complete utilization than under the status quo. This rate is a generalization of the interpretation of the HCI. See Pennings (2020) for details.

REFERENCES

Almond, D. 2006. "Is the 1918 Influenza Pandemic Over? Long-Term Effects of In Utero Influenza Exposure in the Post-1940 US Population." *Journal of Political Economy* 114 (4): 672–712.

Almond, D., and J. Currie. 2011. "Killing Me Softly: The Fetal Origins Hypothesis." *Journal of Economic Perspectives* 25 (3): 153–72.

D'Souza, R., R. Gatti, and A. Kraay. 2019. "A Socioeconomic Disaggregation of the World Bank Human Capital Index." Policy Research Working Paper 9020, World Bank, Washington, DC.

Kraay, A. 2018. "Methodology for a World Bank Human Capital Index." Policy Research Working Paper 8593, World Bank, Washington, DC.

Pennings, S. 2020. "The Utilization-Adjusted Human Capital Index (UHCI)." Policy Research Working Paper 9375, World Bank, Washington, DC.

World Bank. 2018a. *World Development Report 2018: Learning to Realize Education's Promise*. Washington, DC: World Bank.

World Bank. 2018b. "The Human Capital Project." World Bank, Washington, DC.

1 The Human Capital Index 2020 UPDATE

At the organization's 2018 Annual Meetings, the World Bank Group launched the Human Capital Project, an unprecedented global effort to support human capital development as a core element of countries' overall strategies to increase productivity and growth. The main objective of the project was rapid progress toward a world in which all children can achieve their full potential. For that to happen, children need to reach school well-nourished and ready to learn, attain real learning in the classroom, and enter the job market as healthy, skilled, and productive adults.

Central to this effort has been the Human Capital Index (HCI), a cross-country metric measuring the human capital that a child born today can expect to attain by her 18th birthday, given the risks of poor health and poor education prevailing in her country.[1] The HCI brings together measures of different dimensions of human capital: health (child survival, stunting, and adult survival rates) and the quantity and quality of schooling (expected years of school and international test scores). Using estimates of the economic returns to education and health, the components are combined into an index that captures the expected productivity of a child born today as a future worker, relative to a benchmark of complete education and full health.

The HCI ranges from 0 to 1, so that an HCI value of, for instance, 0.5 implies that a child born today will be only half as productive as a future worker as she would be if she enjoyed complete education and full health. By benchmarking shortfalls in future worker productivity deriving from gaps in human capital across countries, the HCI underscores the urgency of improving human capital outcomes for children today.

In response to the call for governments to invest in the human capital of their citizens, 78 economies across the world are now part of the Human Capital Project. These economies have affirmed building, protecting, and employing human capital as a national priority and have undertaken difficult reforms, sometimes in very challenging contexts. With a view to maintaining this momentum, the 2020 update of the HCI incorporates the most recent data to report HCI scores for 174 economies, adding 17 new economies to the index relative to the 2018 edition.

This update uses new and expanded data for each of the HCI components, with a cut-off date of March 2020. Computed using data collected before COVID-19 (coronavirus) had impact on a global scale, the HCI 2020 provides a useful benchmark to track the evolution of human capital and its key components in the wake of the pandemic.

The next three sections of this chapter outline the HCI methodology and describe the main features of the HCI 2020 and its components. The subsequent sections discuss gender differences across countries and regions, and highlight the unique human capital challenges that arise in states grappling with fragility, conflict, and violence. The final section provides the HCI 2020 scores for 174 economies and an explanation of the discontinued use of rankings.

1.1 THE HCI METHODOLOGY

The HCI is designed to highlight how improvements in current health and education outcomes shape the productivity of the next generation of workers, assuming that children born today experience over the next 18 years the same educational opportunities and health risks as children currently in this age range.

The HCI captures key stages of a child's trajectory from birth to adulthood. In the poorest countries in the world, there is a significant risk that a child will not survive to her fifth birthday. Even if she does reach school age, there is a further risk that she will not start school, let alone complete the full cycle of 14 years of schooling, from preschool to grade 12, which is the norm in high-income countries. The time she does spend in school may translate unevenly into learning, depending on a variety of factors including the quality of teachers and schools that she experiences. When she turns 18, she carries with her the lasting effects of poor health and nutrition during childhood that limit her physical and cognitive abilities as she moves into adulthood.

Several criteria have guided the design of the HCI. First, the HCI is outcome- rather than inputs-based, focusing the conversation on what matters—results. This focus provides incentives for countries not only to invest more but also to invest better in human capital, without concerns that the HCI might be susceptible to gaming. The likelihood that a cross-country benchmarking exercise can spur policy action is strongly influenced by the over-time and cross-country coverage of the metric. Aiming for good coverage limits the choice of components to data that are systematically collected for a large number of economies over time. Further, for the index to promote change, the components of the HCI should be responsive to policy action in the short to medium term. The need to produce such a metric has oriented the index toward measuring the human capital of the next generation, rather than measuring the stock of human capital of the current workforce, which largely reflects policy choices made decades ago, when the current workforce was of school age.[2] The resulting HCI quantitatively illustrates the key stages in a child's human capital trajectory and their consequences for the productivity of the next generation of workers, with three components:

Component 1: Survival from birth to school age, measured using under-5 mortality rates.

Component 2: Expected years of learning-adjusted school, combining information on the quantity and quality of education. The quantity of education is measured as the number of years of school a child can expect to obtain by age 18 given the prevailing pattern of enrollment rates across grades. The quality of education reflects work undertaken at the World Bank to harmonize test scores from major international student achievement testing programs (Patrinos and Angrist 2018). These two measures are combined into a measure of learning-adjusted years of schooling as proposed in Filmer et al. (2018) (see box 1.1).

Component 3: Health. In the absence of a single broadly accepted, directly measured, and widely available metric, the overall health environment is captured by two proxies: (1) adult survival rates, defined as the fraction of 15-year-olds who survive until age 60, and (2) the rate of stunting for children under age 5. Adult survival rates can be interpreted as a proxy for the range of fatal and nonfatal health outcomes that a child born today would experience as an adult, if current conditions prevail into the future. Stunting is broadly accepted as a proxy for the prenatal, infant, and early childhood health environments, and so summarizes the risks to good health that children born today are likely to experience in their early years—with important consequences for health and well-being in adulthood.

The health and education components of human capital have intrinsic value that is undeniably

Box 1.1: Learning-adjusted years of schooling

The knowledge and skills that an individual acquires through schooling form an important part of her human capital. The standard summary measure for education used in aggregate-level contexts—the average number of years of schooling in a population—is an imprecise proxy for education, however, because a given number of years in school leads to much more learning in some settings than in others. As recent research shows, students in different countries who have completed the same number of years of school often have vastly different learning outcomes.[a]

Learning-adjusted years of schooling (LAYS), a measure described in Filmer et al. (2018), addresses this concern by combining information on the quantity and quality of schooling into a single easy-to-understand metric of progress. It is calculated as the product of average years of school and a particular measure of learning relative to a numeraire:

$$LAYS_c = S_c \times R_c^n \qquad \text{(B1.1.1)}$$

where S_c is a measure of the average years of schooling acquired by a relevant cohort of the population of country c, and R_c^n is a measure of learning for a relevant cohort of students in country c, relative to a numeraire (or benchmark). For the Human Capital Index, expected years of school, *EYS*, measures the quantity of education. Harmonized test scores, *HTS*, from the 2020 update of the Global Dataset on Education Quality, provide information on education quality relative to a benchmark score of 625, which corresponds to the Trends in International Mathematics and Science Study (TIMSS) standard of advanced achievement:

$$LAYS_c = EYS_c \times \frac{HTS_c}{625} \qquad \text{(B1.1.2)}$$

By adjusting years of school for quality, LAYS reflects the reality that children in some countries learn far less than those in other countries, despite being in school for a similar amount of time. The simplicity and transparency of its construction make LAYS a compelling summary measure of education to use in policy dialogue.[b] Filmer et al. (2018) also find that LAYS improves upon the standard metric of average years of schooling as a predictor of economic growth.

Source: Filmer et al. 2018.

a. In Nigeria, for example, 19 percent of young adults who have completed primary education are able to read; by contrast, 80 percent of Tanzanians with the same level of schooling are literate (Kaffenberger and Pritchett 2017, as reproduced in World Bank 2018d).

b. Like all aggregate measures, LAYS should be used with caution. Because there are standard errors around test measures, any LAYS measure will also have some error band around it. This means that it is important not to overinterpret small cross-country differences or small changes over time.

important but difficult to quantify. This makes it challenging to combine the different components into a single index. Rather than relying on ad hoc aggregation with arbitrary weights, the HCI uses the estimated earnings associated with an additional unit of health and education to translate them into contributions to worker productivity, relative to a benchmark of complete education and full health (see box 1.2).[3] The resulting index ranges between 0 and 1. A country in which a child born today can expect to achieve full health (no stunting and 100 percent adult

Table 1.1: Human Capital Index 2020, averages by World Bank region

Indicator	East Asia and Pacific	Europe and Central Asia	Latin America and Caribbean	Middle East and North Africa	North America	South Asia	Sub-Saharan Africa
HCI Component 1: Survival							
Probability of Survival to Age 5	0.98	0.99	0.98	0.98	0.99	0.96	0.93
HCI Component 2: School							
Expected Years of School	11.9	13.1	12.1	11.6	13.3	10.8	8.3
Harmonized Test Scores	432	479	405	407	523	374	374
HCI Component 3: Health							
Survival Rate from Age 15 to 60	0.86	0.90	0.86	0.91	0.91	0.84	0.74
Fraction of Children Under 5 Not Stunted	0.76	0.90	0.85	0.82	—	0.69	0.69
Human Capital Index (HCI) 2020	**0.59**	**0.69**	**0.56**	**0.57**	**0.75**	**0.48**	**0.40**

Source: World Bank calculations based on the 2020 update of the Human Capital Index (HCI).

Note: The table reports averages of the index components and the overall Human Capital Index (HCI) by World Bank Group regions. — = not available.

survival) and full education potential (14 years of high-quality school by age 18) would score a value of 1. Therefore, a score of 0.70 indicates that the productivity as a future worker of a child born today is 30 percent below what could have been achieved with complete education and full health. Because the theoretical underpinnings of the HCI are in the development accounting literature, the index is linked to real differences in how much income a country can generate in the long run (see box 1.3 for limitations of the HCI). If a country has a score of 0.50, then the gross domestic product (GDP) per worker could be twice as high if the country reached the benchmark of complete education and full health (see appendix A for a detailed discussion of the HCI methodology).

1.2 THE HCI 2020

The HCI 2020 scores for 174 economies are reported in the final section of this chapter (see table 1.2). Economies' scores are sorted from lowest to highest. Next to the HCI score, lower and upper bounds for the estimates are reported. Unlike the HCI 2018 launch, economies' rankings are not reported, for reasons that are detailed in box 1.6.

The sobering reality is that, as measured by the HCI 2020, worldwide, a child born today would expect to achieve on average only 56 percent of her full productivity as a future worker. And this estimate does not account for any impact that may have resulted from the COVID-19 pandemic. Clearly there is considerable heterogeneity around the 56 percent figure. Importantly, the HCI is lower in low-income economies than in high-income economies by a substantial margin. In the poorest economies in the world, a child born today will grow up to be only 30 percent as productive as she could be; in the richest economies, the corresponding figure is 80 percent or more (see figure 1.1, which plots the HCI 2020 on the vertical axis against log GDP per capita at purchasing power parity on the horizontal axis). Compared to a child in Europe and Central Asia, a child born in Sub-Saharan Africa can expect to be only 58 percent as productive (see table 1.1).

Box 1.2: The Human Capital Index's aggregation methodology

The components of the Human Capital Index (HCI) are combined into a single index by first converting them into contributions to productivity relative to a benchmark of complete education and full health. Multiplying these contributions to productivity together gives the overall HCI:

$$HCI = Survival \times School \times Health \quad \text{(B1.2.1)}$$

In the case of survival, the relative productivity interpretation is stark: children who do not survive childhood never become productive adults. As a result, expected productivity as a future worker of a child born today is reduced by a factor equal to the survival rate, relative to the benchmark in which all children survive.

$$Survival = \frac{1 - \text{Under-5 Mortality Rate}}{1} \quad \text{(B1.2.2)}$$

The benchmark of complete high-quality education corresponds to 14 years of school and a harmonized test score of 625. The relative productivity interpretation for education is anchored in the large empirical literature measuring the returns to education at the individual level. A rough consensus from this literature is that an additional year of school raises earnings by about 8 percent. The parameter $\phi = 0.08$ measures the returns to an additional year of school and is used to convert differences in learning-adjusted years of school across countries into differences in worker productivity.

$$School = e^{\phi\,(\text{Expected Years of School} \times \frac{\text{Harmonized Test Score}}{625} - 14)} \quad \text{(B1.2.3)}$$

Compared with a benchmark in which all children obtain a full 14 years of school by age 18, a child who obtains only 10 years of education can expect to be 32 percent less productive as an adult (a gap of 4 years of education, multiplied by 8 percent per year).

In the case of health, the relative productivity interpretation is based on the empirical literature measuring the economic returns to better health at the individual level. The key challenge in this literature is the lack of any unique, directly measured summary indicator of the various aspects of health that matter for productivity. This microeconometric literature often uses proxy indicators for health, such as adult height, because adult height can be measured directly and reflects the accumulation of shocks to health through childhood and adolescence. A rough consensus drawn from this literature is that an improvement in health associated with a one-centimeter increase in adult height raises productivity by 3.4 percent.

Converting this evidence on the returns to one proxy for health (adult height) into the other proxies for health used in the HCI (stunting and adult survival) requires information on the relationships between these different proxies:

- For stunting, a direct relationship exists between stunting in childhood and future adult height, because growth deficits in childhood persist to a large extent into adulthood, together with the associated health and cognitive deficits. Available evidence suggests that a reduction in stunting rates of 10 percentage points increases attained adult height by approximately one centimeter, which increases productivity by (10.2 × 0.1 × 3.4) percent, or 3.5 percent.

(continued next page)

Box 1.2: The Human Capital Index's aggregation methodology *(Continued)*

- For adult survival, the empirical evidence suggests that, if overall health improves, both adult height and adult survival rates increase in such a way that adult height rises by 1.9 centimeters for every 10-percentage-point improvement in adult survival. This implies that an improvement in health that leads to an increase in adult survival rates of 10 percentage points is associated with an improvement in worker productivity of (1.9 × 3.4) percent, or 6.5 percent.

In the HCI, the estimated contributions of health to worker productivity based on these two alternative proxies are averaged together, if both are available, and are used individually if only one of the two is available. The contribution of health to productivity is expressed relative to the benchmark of full health, defined as the absence of stunting, and a 100 percent adult survival rate.

$$Health = e^{(\gamma_{ASR} \times (Adult\ Survival\ Rate - 1) + \gamma_{Stunting} \times (Not\ Stunted\ Rate - 1))/2} \quad (B1.2.4)$$

For example, compared with a benchmark of no stunting, in a country where the stunting rate is 30 percent, poor health reduces worker productivity by (30 × 0.34) percent, or 10.2 percent.

Compared with the benchmark of 100 percent adult survival, poor health reduces worker productivity by (30 × 0.65) percent, or 19.5 percent, in a country where the adult survival rate is 70 percent. The average of the two estimates of the effect of health on productivity is used in the HCI.

These parameters used to convert the components of the index into their contributions to productivity (ϕ= 0.08 for school, γ_{ASR} = 0.65 for adult survival, and $\gamma_{Stunting}$ = 0.35 for stunting) serve as weights in the construction of the HCI. The weights are chosen to be the same across countries, so that cross-country differences in the HCI reflect only cross-country differences in the component variables. This facilitates the interpretation of the index. This is also a pragmatic choice, because estimating country-specific returns to education and health for all countries included in the HCI is not feasible.

Source: Kraay (2018).

Despite the high correlation between the HCI and GDP per capita, some economies perform significantly better than their income levels might suggest. These economies include Estonia, Kyrgyz Republic, Vietnam, and West Bank and Gaza. Conversely, in a number of economies, human capital is lower than per capita income would suggest. Among them are a few resource-rich economies, where human capital has not yet matched the potential that one would envisage given these economies' development.

The correlation between poverty and low HCI scores is also high. Given that better education and health translate to improved productivity for people, and that human capital is often the only asset the poor have, the World Bank's twin goals of promoting shared prosperity and eradicating extreme poverty are unlikely to be met without human capital improvements. The world's extreme poor are disproportionately found in economies with the lowest HCI scores; 30 percent of the world's poor reside in the 10 economies with the lowest HCI values, although these 10 economies are home to only 5 percent of the total global population (figure 1.2). In fact, 80 percent of the world's extreme poor reside in economies with an HCI value under 0.5. If prosperity is to be shared, growth must be inclusive for those at the bottom of the distribution, and inclusive growth necessitates strong investments in human capital.

Figure 1.1: The Human Capital Index 2020

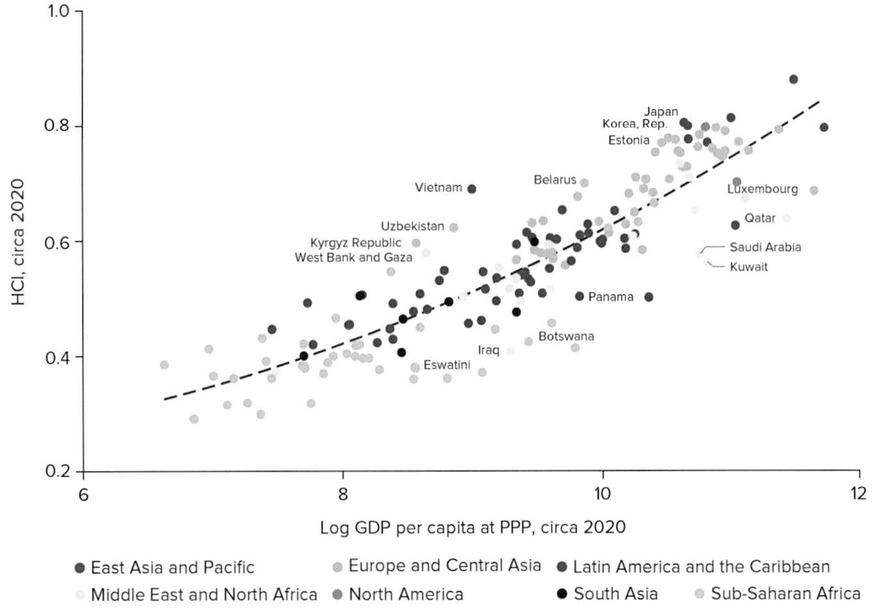

HCI, circa 2020

Japan
Korea, Rep.
Estonia
Vietnam
Belarus
Luxembourg
Uzbekistan
Qatar
Kyrgyz Republic
West Bank and Gaza
Saudi Arabia
Kuwait
Panama
Botswana
Iraq
Eswatini

Log GDP per capita at PPP, circa 2020

● East Asia and Pacific ● Europe and Central Asia ● Latin America and the Caribbean
● Middle East and North Africa ● North America ● South Asia ● Sub-Saharan Africa

Source: World Bank calculations based on the 2020 update of the Human Capital Index (HCI) for HCI data and the World Development Indicators and Penn World Tables 9.1 for per capita GDP data.

Note: The figure plots country-level HCI on the y-axis and GDP per capita in PPP on the x-axis, in constant 2011 dollars, for most recently available data as of 2019. Per capita GDP data for South Sudan are not available. The dashed line illustrates the fitted regression line between GDP per capita and the HCI 2020. Scatter points above (below) the fitted regression line illustrate economies that perform better (worse) in the HCI than their level of GDP would predict. Economies above the 95th and below the 5th percentile in distance to the regression fitted line are labeled. HCI = Human Capital Index; PPP = purchasing power parity.

Figure 1.2: Concentration of the extreme poor in economies sorted by their Human Capital Index scores

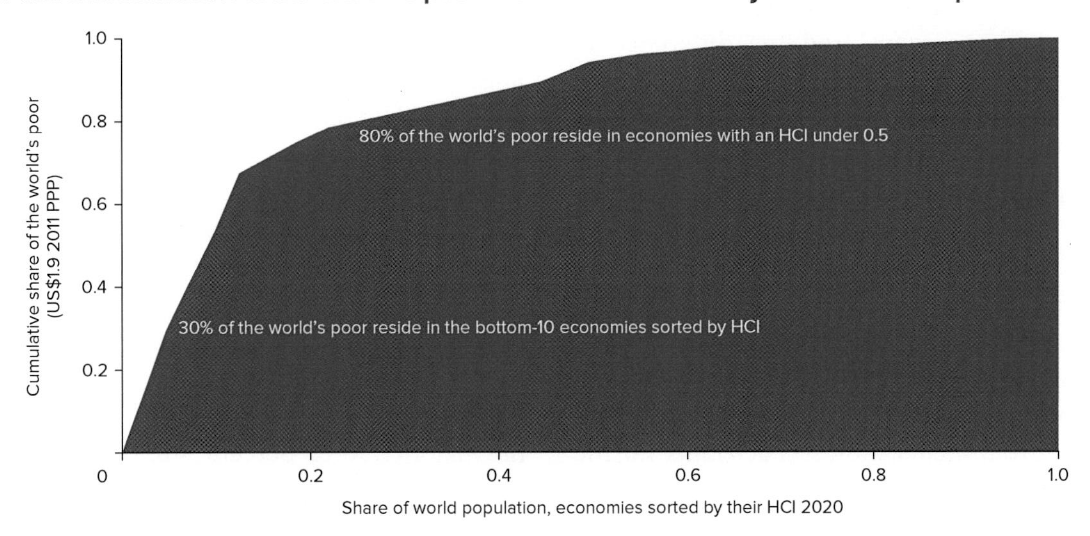

Source: World Bank calculations based on the 2020 update of the Human Capital Index (HCI). Poverty values come from Corral et al. (2020) and are calculated before COVID-19.

Note: The horizontal axis represents the share of the global population accounted for by the countries sorted by their HCI value. HCI = Human Capital Index; PPP = purchasing power parity

Two elements help explain how different dimensions of human capital contribute to differences in the HCI scores. The first are the weights of the health and education components of the HCI, reflecting the empirical literature on the contribution of health and education to earnings (box 1.2 and appendix A). Second, the components have different distributions, globally and by country income groupings, according to the World Bank's most recent classification. For example, the variation of child survival is nine times larger among low-income than among high-income economies, where child survival is uniformly close to 100 percent (figure 1.3).

A simple decomposition exercise can help account for differences in the HCI across country income groups.[4] Consider the HCI difference between the typical low-income and high-income economy, which is about 0.33 (figure 1.4). Of these 33 HCI points, almost 25 are accounted for by the differences in expected years of school (EYS) and harmonized test scores. Overall, differences in the quality and quantity of schooling account for the largest share of index differences across country income groups, ranging from 65 to 85 percent.

There is also considerable heterogeneity within country income groups, and the difference in HCI between the economy with the lowest HCI and the economy with the highest HCI in each income group rivals the difference between income groups and, in some cases, exceeds it. For example, the difference in the HCI between the top and bottom performers among high-income economies is roughly 0.38, or 38 HCI points, which compares with a difference of 33 points between the average HCI values of high- and low-income economies. Overall, both within and across all groups, education still accounts for the largest share of the differences observed between top and bottom performers (figure 1.5); however, education accounts for a smaller share as one moves down income groups, falling from roughly 90 percent among high-income to 60 percent among low-income economies. In contrast, differences in child survival rates account for less of the difference in HCI scores among high-income economies, largely because economies in this group are close to universal child survival. The same is true for the health component, with stunting and adult survival taken together for easy comparison. Health differences explain a lower share of HCI differences as one moves from low- to high-income economies, because health outcomes tend to be uniformly better as economies get richer.[5] These results reflect the fact that, within the high-income group, values for health and survival components in most economies are close to the frontier, whereas there is still considerable variation in test scores (see the box plots in figure 1.3).

Gaps in human capital outcomes between rich and poor people within economies can be quite large. A socioeconomic disaggregation of the HCI, constructed using comparable survey data for 50 low- and middle-income economies, reveals that differences across socioeconomic quintiles within economies account for nearly one-third of the total variation in human capital (D'Souza, Gatti, and Kraay 2019). Outcomes can also vary across rural-urban status, as in the case of Romania. Some of that country's counties have urban areas with learning outcomes as high as top performers in Europe, whereas some rural areas rank at par with economies in the bottom third of the HCI distribution (World Bank 2020a). Some of these within-country differences align with ethnic divides. For example, in Vietnam, survey data from 2014 disaggregated by ethnic group show that ethnic minorities have an HCI score of 0.62, compared with a score of 0.75 for the ethnic majority. At 32 percent, stunting rates are two times larger among ethnic minorities than among the majority. School enrollment also lags among ethnic minorities relative to their majority peers by 30 percentage points (World Bank 2019b).

Box 1.3: Limitations of the Human Capital Index

Like all cross-country benchmarking exercises, the Human Capital Index (HCI) has limitations. Components of the HCI such as stunting and test scores are measured only infrequently in some economies and not at all in others. Data on test scores come from different international testing programs and need to be converted into common units, and the age of test-takers and the subjects covered vary across testing programs. Moreover, test scores may not accurately reflect the quality of the whole education system in an economy, to the extent that test-takers are not representative of the population of all students. Reliable measures of the quality of tertiary education that are comparable across most economies of the world do not yet exist, despite the importance of higher education for human capital in a rapidly changing world. The data on enrollment rates needed to estimate expected years of school often have many gaps and are reported with significant lags. Socioemotional skills are not explicitly captured. In terms of health, child and adult survival rates are imprecisely estimated in economies where vital registries are incomplete or nonexistent. These limitations have implications not only for the construction of the 2020 update but also for the comparison of the index over time.

One objective of the HCI is to call attention to these data shortcomings and to galvanize action to remedy them. Improving data will take time. In the interim and in recognition of these limitations, the HCI should be interpreted with caution. The HCI provides rough estimates of how current education and health will shape the productivity of future workers, but it is not a finely graduated measurement that can distinguish small differences between economies. Naturally, because the HCI captures outcomes, it is not a checklist of policy actions, and the proper type and scale of interventions to build human capital will be different in different economies. Although the HCI combines education and health into a single measure, it is too blunt a tool to inform the cost-effectiveness of policy interventions in these areas, which should instead be assessed through careful cost-benefit analysis and impact assessments of specific programs. Because the HCI uses common estimates of the economic returns to health and education for all economies, it does not capture cross-country differences in how well economies are able to productively deploy the human capital they have. Finally, the HCI is not a measure of welfare, nor is it a summary of the intrinsic values of health and education; rather, it is simply a measure of the contribution of current health and education outcomes to the productivity of future workers.

1.3 HCI 2020: INDEX COMPONENTS

1.3.1 HCI components and data sources

The components of the HCI are built using publicly available official data, primarily from administrative sources. The data are subject to a careful vetting process with World Bank country teams and, at the discretion of country teams, with line ministry counterparts. These data and the relevant definitions are described in the text that follows and in more in detail in appendix C.

Child survival

The probability of survival to age 5 is calculated as the complement of the under-5 mortality rate. The under-5 mortality rate is the probability that a child born in a specified year will die before reaching the age of 5 if subject to current age-specific mortality rates. It is frequently expressed as a rate per 1,000 live births, in which case it must be divided by 1,000 to obtain the probability of dying before age 5. Under-5 mortality rates are calculated by the United

Figure 1.3: Human Capital Index 2020 components, distribution by country income group

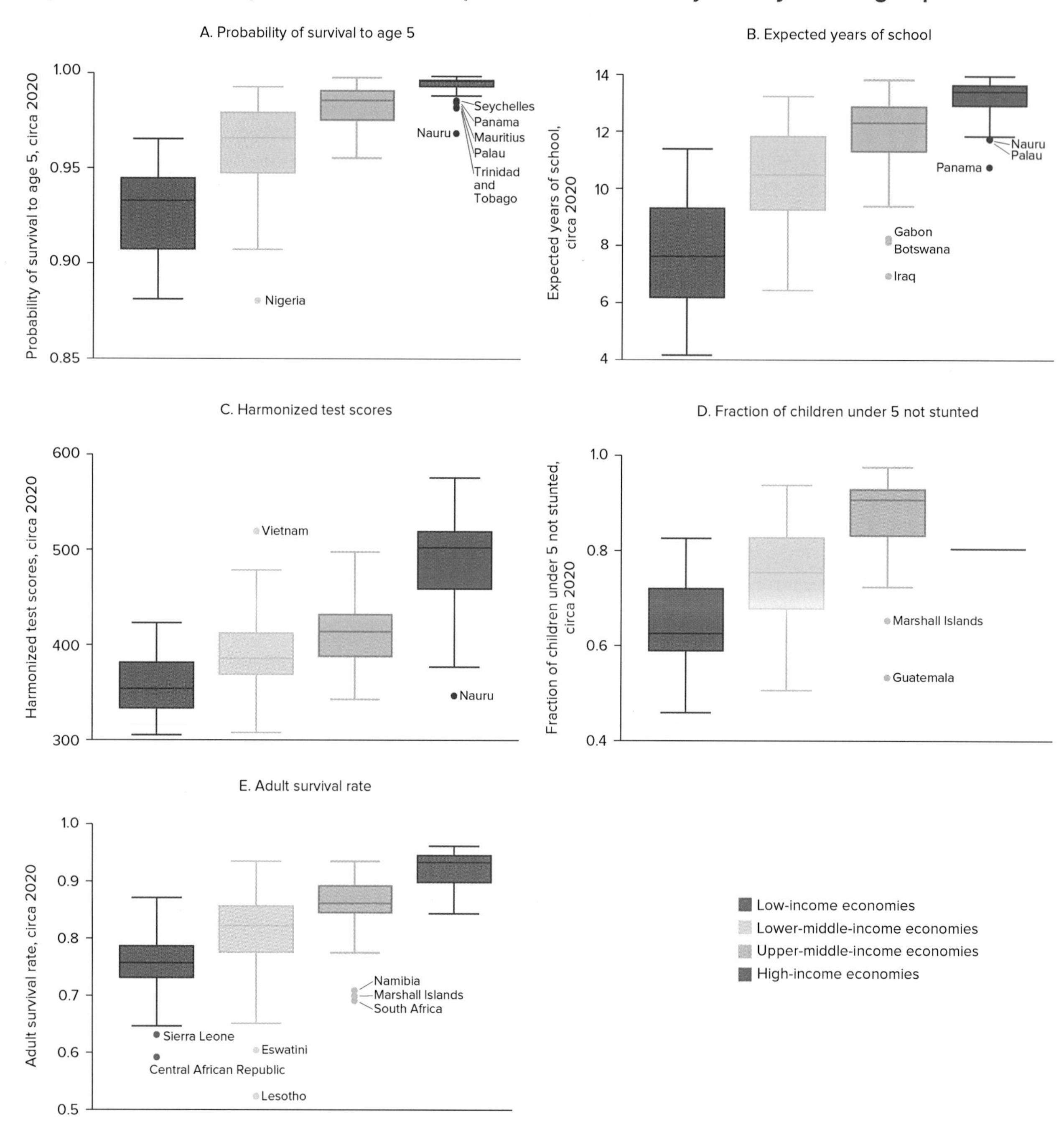

Source: World Bank calculations based on the 2020 update of the Human Capital Index (HCI).

Note: Each box spans the interquartile range with the upper and lower end of the boxes illustrating the 25th and 75th percentile values. The horizontal lines in the inner boxes represent the median value. Outer horizontal lines show maximum and minimum values excluding outliers. Thinner box plots indicate less dispersion in values.

Figure 1.4: Decomposition of observed mean HCI differences between selected country income groups

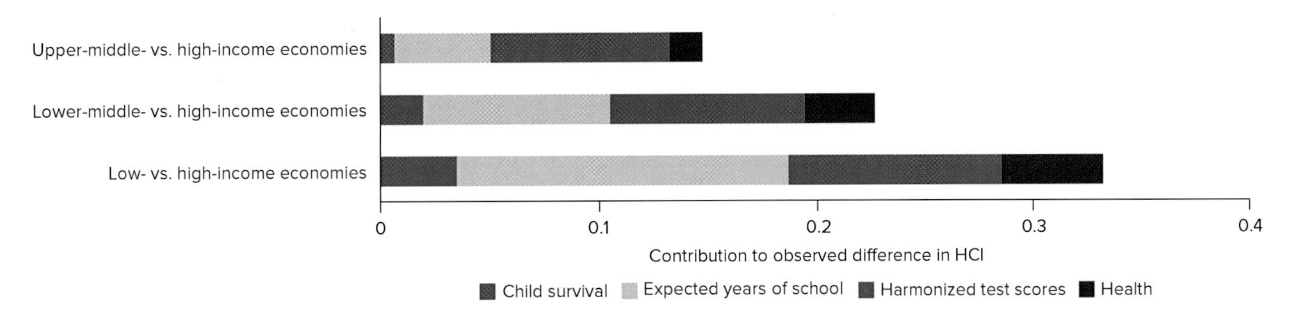

Source: World Bank calculations based on the 2020 update of the Human Capital Index (HCI).

Note: The figure plots the contribution to observed HCI differences between country income groups.

Figure 1.5: Differences between the top and bottom Human Capital Index performers within each country income group

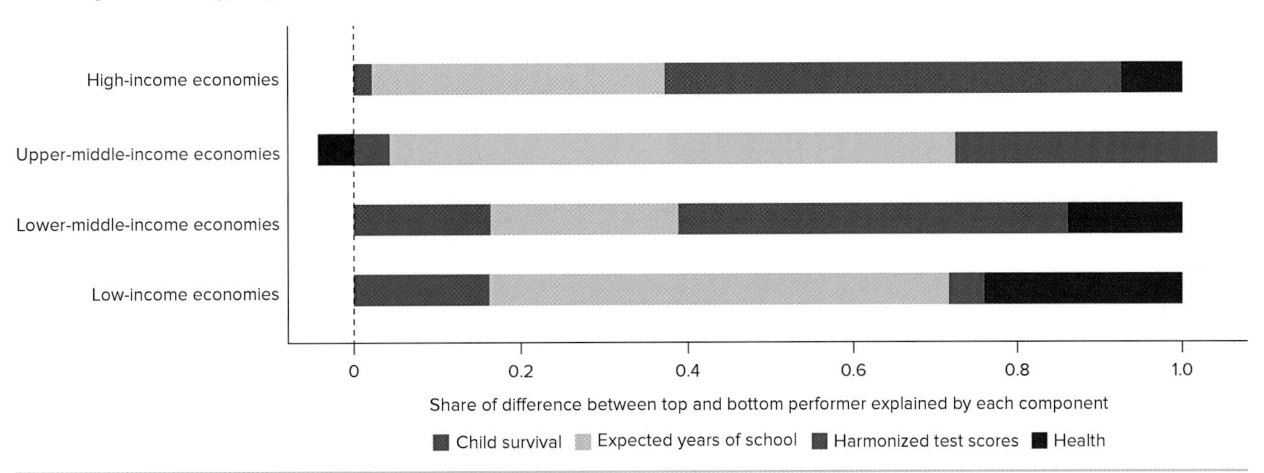

Source: World Bank calculations based on the 2020 update of the Human Capital Index (HCI).

Note: The figure plots the share of the observed HCI differences between selected economies by component. Comparison economies for the high-income group are Singapore and Panama; for the upper-middle-income group, Belarus and Iraq; for lower-middle-income economies, Nigeria and Vietnam; and, for low-income economies, the Central African Republic and Tajikistan.

Nations Interagency Group for Child Mortality Estimation (IGME) using mortality as recorded in household surveys and vital registries. For the 2020 update of the HCI, under-5 mortality rates come from the September 2019 update of the IGME estimates and are available on the IGME website.[6]

Expected years of school

The EYS component of the HCI captures the number of years of school a child born today can expect to obtain by age 18, given the prevailing pattern of enrollment rates in her economy. Conceptually, EYS is the sum of enrollment rates by age from ages 4 to 17. Because age-specific enrollment rates are neither broadly nor systematically available, data on enrollment rates by level of school are used to approximate enrollment rates in different age brackets. Preprimary enrollment rates approximate the enrollment rates for 4- and 5-year-olds, primary enrollment rates approximate the rates for 6- to 11-year-olds, lower-secondary rates approximate for 12- to 14-year-olds, and upper-secondary rates approximate for 15- to 17-year-olds. Cross-country definitions in school starting ages and the duration of the various levels of school imply that these rates will only be approximations of the number of years of school a child can expect to complete by age 18. Enrollment rates for 2020 for each school level and for different enrollment rate types are obtained from the United Nations Educational, Scientific and Cultural Organization's Institute for Statistics.[7] These data are then complemented with inputs from World Bank teams working on specific countries to validate the data and provide more recent values when available.[8]

Harmonized test scores

The school quality indicator is based on a large-scale effort to harmonize international student achievement tests from several multicountry testing programs to produce the Global Dataset on Education Quality. A detailed description of the test score harmonization exercise is provided in Patrinos and Angrist (2018), and the HCI draws on an updated version of this dataset as of January 2020. The dataset harmonizes scores from three major international testing programs: the Trends in International Mathematics and Science Study (TIMSS), the Progress in International Reading Literacy Study (PIRLS), and the Programme for International Student Assessment (PISA). It further includes four major regional testing programs: the Southern and Eastern Africa Consortium for Monitoring Educational Quality (SACMEQ), the Program for the Analysis of Education Systems (PASEC), the Latin American Laboratory for Assessment of the Quality of Education (LLECE), and the Pacific Island Learning and Numeracy Assessment (PILNA). It also incorporates Early Grade Reading Assessments (EGRAs) coordinated by the United States Agency for International Development. The 2020 update of the Global Dataset on Education Quality extends the database to 184 economies from 2000 to 2019, drawing on a large-scale effort by the World Bank to collect global learning data. Updates to the database come from new data from PISA 2018, PISA for Development (PISA-D),[9] PILNA, and EGRA. The database adds 20 new economies,[10] bringing the percentage of the global school-age population represented by the database to 98.7 percent. In addition, more recent data points have been added for 94 economies.[11] Since the launch of the HCI in 2018, a complementary measure has been created to address foundational skills and to help economies prioritize their response to HCI and learning-adjusted years of schooling (LAYS) scores: Learning Poverty represents the share of 10-year-olds who cannot read and understand a simple text (see box 1.4). The correlation between Learning Poverty and LAYS is high, in the range of −0.90. The Learning Poverty measure is available for 113 of the economies in the HCI 2020.

Fraction of children under 5 not stunted

The fraction of children under 5 not stunted is calculated as the complement of the under-5 stunting rate. The stunting rate is defined as the share of children under the age of 5 whose height is more than two reference standard deviations below the median for their ages. The median and standard deviations are set by the World Health Organization (WHO) for normal healthy child development (World Health Organization 2009). Child-level stunting prevalence is averaged across the relevant 0–5 age range to arrive at an overall under-5 stunting rate. The stunting rate is used, in addition to the adult survival rate, as a proxy for latent health of the population in economies where stunting data are available, as discussed in the next section. Stunting rates for this edition of the HCI come from the March 2020 update of the

Box 1.4: Measuring Learning Poverty

The World Bank collaborated with the United Nations Educational, Scientific and Cultural Organization Institute for Statistics (UIS) to create a measure of Learning Poverty—the share of 10-year-olds who cannot read and understand a simple text.

According to this measure, the World Bank estimates that 53 percent of children in low- and middle-income economies suffer from Learning Poverty. In the poorest economies, the share is often more than 80 percent. Such high levels of Learning Poverty are an early warning sign that the learning-adjusted years of schooling (LAYS) indicator, which measures quantity and quality of education that 18-year-olds have benefited from, will be unacceptably low for that cohort of children. In better-performing systems, virtually all children learn to read with comprehension by age 10. Although it may take decades to build up the high-quality education systems that lead to the highest scores on the LAYS indicator of the Human Capital Index (HCI), teaching children to reach a minimum proficiency in reading requires much less time.

Why measure reading? Children need to learn to read so that they can read to learn. Those who do not become proficient in reading by the end of primary school often cannot catch up later, because the curriculum of every school system assumes that secondary school students can learn through reading. Reading is, in other words, a gateway to all types of academic learning. This is not to say that reading is the only skill that matters. Reading proficiency can serve as a proxy or warning indicator for foundational learning in other areas that are also essential, like mathematics and reasoning abilities. Education systems that enable all children to read are likely to succeed in helping them learn other subjects as well. Across economies and schools, the data show that proficiency rates in reading are highly correlated with proficiency in other subjects.

How is Learning Poverty calculated? Conceptually similar to the LAYS indicator in the HCI for youth, the Learning Poverty measure combines learning with enrollment, to emphasize the importance of learning for all children and not just those currently in school. The learning component captures enrolled students who cannot read with comprehension, whereas the participation component corresponds to the out-of-school rate. "Reading with comprehension" is defined here as reaching the global minimum proficiency in literacy. UIS leads the Global Alliance to Monitor Learning (GAML), which agreed to a common definition of minimum proficiency in literacy for the purposes of monitoring Sustainable Development Goal 4. With this definition, several cross-national and some national assessments were harmonized by applying GAML's definition of reading proficiency as a common benchmark. Unlike the HCI, Learning Poverty relies only on assessments targeting children from grades 4 to 6. For each assessment incorporated into the database, the harmonization process looks at the definitions of each level of proficiency for that exam and selects the one that maps most clearly to the GAML definition. The harmonization process allows much greater coverage of countries than does relying on a single assessment like the Progress in International Reading Literacy Study (PIRLS)—an excellent assessment for measuring Learning Poverty, but one in which relatively few low- and middle-income countries participate. The high correlation between students' performance on different assessments increased confidence that this harmonization method is valid. Once the share of children below minimum proficiency is calculated, the final step in calculating Learning Poverty is to adjust this share for out-of-school children of primary school age who are considered nonproficient in reading.

The HCI, LAYS, and Learning Poverty, each with its own unique mandate and methodology, are synthetic indicators intended to build political commitment and galvanize action.

Source: World Bank Education Global Practice, World Bank (2019a).

Joint Malnutrition Estimates (JME) database (see UNICEF, WHO, and World Bank Group 2020). This latest release of the database allows an update of stunting rates for 54 economies, and adds stunting rates for Argentina, Bulgaria, and Uzbekistan, which did not have a rate in the previous iteration of the HCI.

Adult survival rates

The adult survival rate is calculated as the complement of the mortality rate for 15- to 60-year-olds. The mortality rate for 15- to 60-year-olds is the probability that a 15-year-old in a specified year will die before reaching the age of 60 if subject to current age-specific mortality rates. The mortality rate is frequently expressed as a rate per 1,000 alive at 15, in which case it must be divided by 1,000 to obtain the probability that a 15-year-old will die before age 60. Adult mortality rates for the 2020 update of the HCI come from the 2019 update of the United Nations Population Division (UNPD) World Population Prospects estimates.[12] Because UNPD does not individually report adult mortality rates for economies with fewer than 90,000 inhabitants, UNPD data are supplemented with adult mortality rates from the Global Burden of Disease (GBD) project, managed by the Institute of Health Metrics and Evaluation (IHME). Data from this source are used for Dominica and the Marshall Islands. Data for Nauru, Palau, San Marino, St. Kitts and Nevis, and Tuvalu come from WHO. The GBD data for the HCI 2020 come from the GBD 2017 update and can be retrieved from the IHME data visualization site.[13] The WHO data are located on the United Nations data platform, UNData.[14]

1.3.2 Index components across economies

All five components of the index increase with income, though at a different pace (figure 1.6). Child survival rates range from 0.998 (2 deaths per 1,000 live births) in the richest economies to about 0.880 (120 deaths per 1,000 live births) in the poorest economies, reflecting the disproportionate burden of child mortality that low-income economies continue to face. Child survival rates also vary significantly by region, with economies in the Europe and Central Asia region bundled at the top of the distribution and the lowest rates in Sub-Saharan Africa, in economies like Chad, Nigeria, and Sierra Leone; however, in a number of economies in Sub-Saharan Africa, including Burundi, Malawi, or Rwanda, child survival rates are significantly higher than those economies' level of GDP would predict (figure 1.6).

Although internationally comparable stunting measures are primarily collected in low- and middle-income economies, the share of stunted children decreases as economies get richer. But income and stunting rates do not always go in lockstep, including across socioeconomic groups within economies (de Onis and Branca 2016). For example, in economies such as Burundi, Niger, and Tanzania, the gap in stunting rates between the first and the fourth socioeconomic quintiles is smaller than the gap between stunting rates in the fourth and fifth quintiles (the richest households), reflecting the interaction of environmental, economic, and cultural factors that can contribute to slower physical development in children (World Bank 2019b). In economies such as Guatemala, Papua New Guinea, and Timor-Leste, more than 45 percent of children are stunted. On the other end of the spectrum are economies like Moldova, Samoa, Tonga, and West Bank and Gaza, where the stunting rate is below 10 percent, and significantly lower than their levels of GDP would predict. The second proxy for health—adult survival—is lowest in the Central African Republic, Eswatini, and Lesotho, where the chances of surviving from age 15 to age 60 are at 60 percent or lower.

Quantity of schooling—as measured by EYS—increases as economies get richer. High-income economies are bundled at the top of the distribution, and low-income economies are at the bottom. In economies like the Kyrgyz Republic, Malawi, Nepal, and Zimbabwe, EYS are higher than those economies' levels of GDP would

Figure 1.6: Human Capital Index 2020: Index components

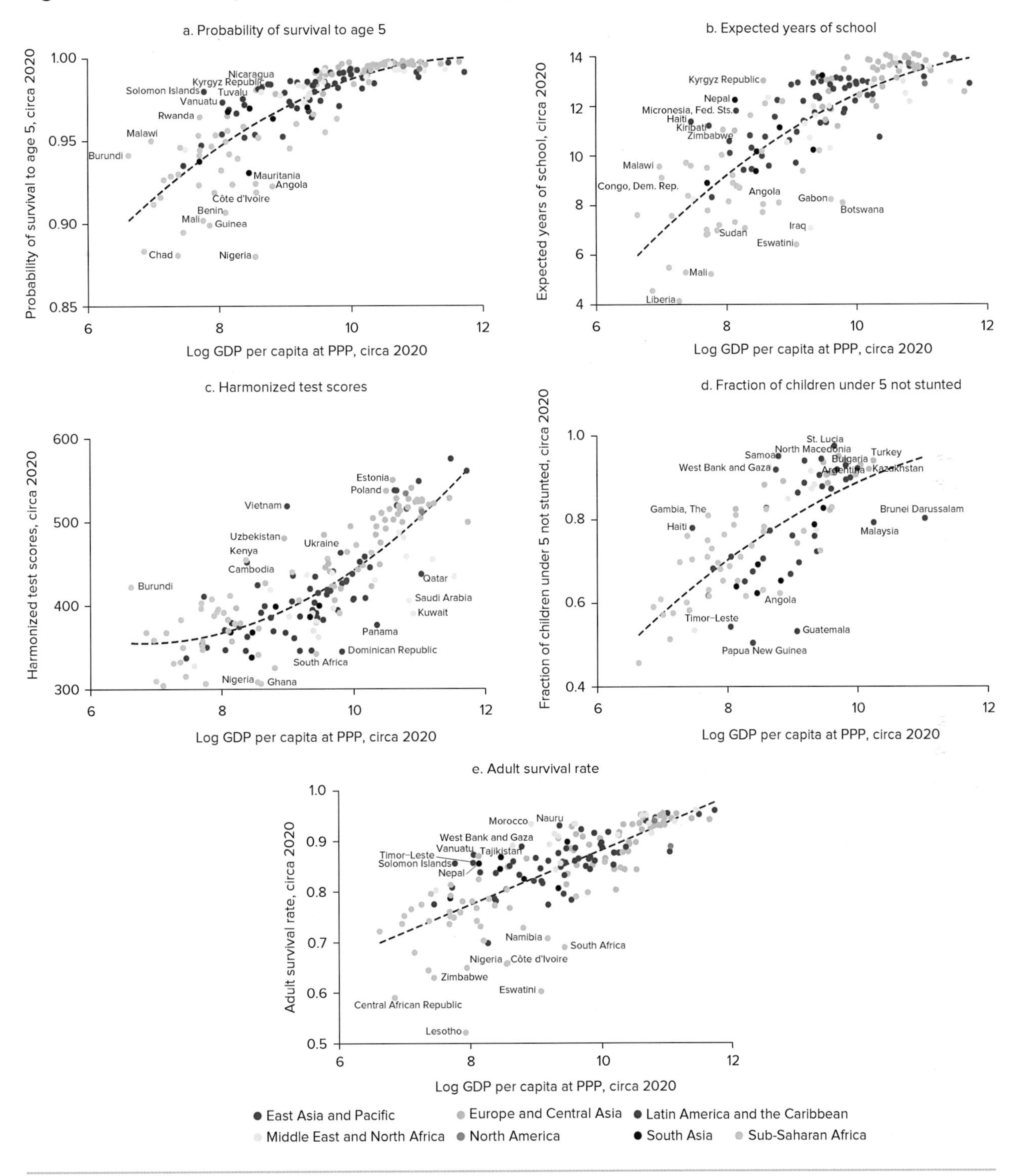

Source: World Bank calculations based on the 2020 update of the Human Capital Index (HCI).

Note: The figure reports the most recent cross-section of 174 economies for the five HCI components (child survival, expected years of school, harmonized test scores, fraction of children under 5 not stunted, and adult survival), as used to calculate the 2020 HCI. Each panel plots the country-level averages for each component on the y-axis and GDP per capita in PPP on the x-axis. The dashed line illustrates the fitted regression line between GDP per capita and the respective component. Scatter points above (below) the fitted regression line illustrate economies that perform better (worse) in the outcome variable than their level of GDP would predict. Countries above the 95th and below the 5th percentile in distance to the fitted regression line are labeled.

predict, reflecting the progress these economies have made in improving access to schooling (figure 1.6). Outliers for which the quantity of schooling is about 2.5 to 5.3 years below what their level of GDP would predict include economies such as Iraq, Liberia, and Mali, which are characterized by different levels of institutional fragility and conflict.

Quality of schooling—as measured by harmonized test scores (HTSs)—increases with income, too, though seemingly faster than years of education. The HTS ranges from a score of about 305 in the poorest economies to a score of about 575 in the richest economies (figure 1.6). To interpret the units of the HTS, note that 400 corresponds to the benchmark of "low proficiency" in TIMSS at the student level, whereas 625 corresponds to "advanced proficiency." Accounting for the level of GDP, economies such as Vietnam, Ukraine, and Uzbekistan, as well as Cambodia and Kenya, performed particularly well in learning. Vietnam reaches an HTS of 519, a level similar to economies like the Netherlands, New Zealand, and Sweden, which are significantly richer.[15] Economies for which learning is below what their income per capita would predict include high-income economies such as Kuwait, Qatar, and Saudi Arabia. Their relatively disappointing performance in learning may result in part from a traditional emphasis on investing in school infrastructure rather than in other factors that are also necessary to improve educational outcomes. These factors include governance and accountability, effective monitoring mechanisms, information sharing with parents and students, and school systems geared toward inclusive learning (Galal et al. 2008). Education systems in these economies may also be reacting to the pull from labor markets, where pervasive informality generates low returns to schooling, and the lure of public employment that puts more emphasis on diplomas than on skills (El-Kogali and Krafft 2020; World Bank 2013). As a consequence, learning lags behind the progress that economies in this region have achieved in access to schooling and gender parity.

1.4 HCI MEASURES OF GENDER GAPS IN HUMAN CAPITAL

Globally, the average HCI is slightly higher for girls (0.59) than for boys (0.56).[16] This pattern can be observed across all HCI components (figure 1.7). Although the gap between boys and girls has closed in these early-life outcomes, boys and girls both remain far from the frontier of complete education and full health. The gap in human capital compared to full potential far exceeds any gender gap in HCI in most economies. Boys and girls are, respectively, 2.6 and 2.5 years of schooling away from completing upper-secondary education. Large shares of boys and girls are stunted—24 and 21 percent, respectively. Far too many boys and girls do not survive beyond their fifth birthday—2.8 and 2.4 percent, respectively. Conditional on making it to age 15, only 83 percent of boys and 89 percent of girls are expected to survive to age 60.

The global HCI average, however, masks important regional and income group differences with respect to gender (figure 1.8). Although girls still surpass boys in the HCI value overall, with lower stunting and lower child and adult mortality rates in all regions and income groups, advantages for girls are more prominent in some regions and muted in others. For example, the gap in stunting rates between girls and boys is as high as 4.6 percentage points in Sub-Saharan Africa, with boys having a higher stunting rate.

With regard to EYS, girls are still disadvantaged compared to boys in South Asia and Sub-Saharan Africa, where girls and boys experience 0.45 and 0.15 years of school disadvantage, respectively (figure 1.8). In settings affected by fragility, conflict, and violence, girls on average complete 0.14 years less schooling than boys. In low-income economies, aside from completing less schooling, girls also have lower HTSs, with a 0.8 percent deficit.

The gender gap in the HCI varies quite widely across economies, with a difference in the score

Figure 1.7: Sex-disaggregated Human Capital Index and its components

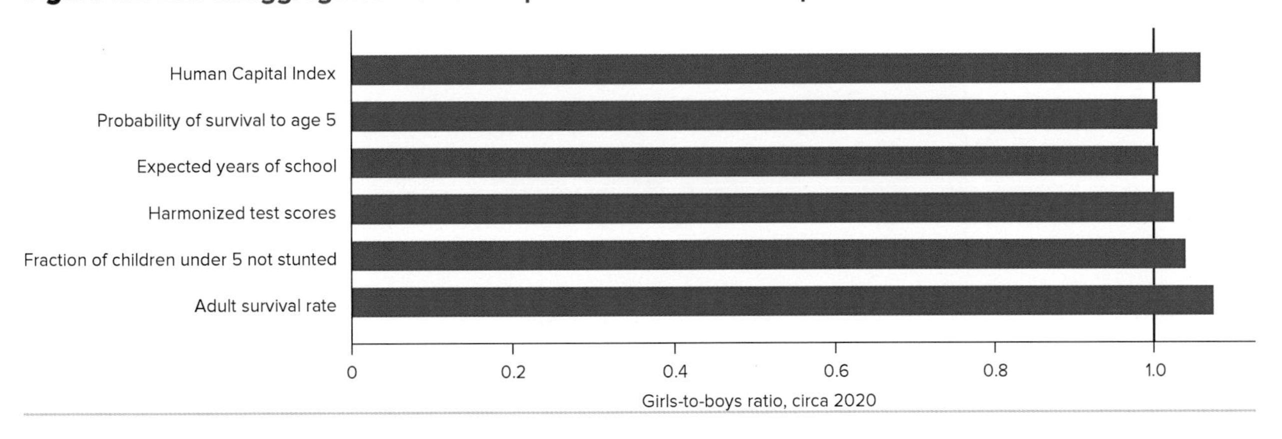

Source: World Bank calculations based on the 2020 update of the Human Capital Index (HCI).

Note: The red vertical line indicates gender parity for each component. Simple averages are computed without population weights.

between boys and girls ranging from a low of −0.043 in Afghanistan to a high of 0.096 in Lithuania (figure 1.9). Overall, girls are outperforming boys in 140 of the 153 economies for which sex-disaggregated data are available.

Gender gaps in EYS and HTSs show similar patterns. The gender gap in EYS favors boys in 46 economies (30 percent of all economies with a sex-disaggregated HCI; figure 1.9). In learning outcomes, boys are favored in 31 economies (20 percent). Although EYS are higher for girls than for boys in most economies, the magnitude of the resulting gender disparity is larger in those economies where boys have an advantage over girls with respect to schooling. For example, in Kiribati, St. Vincent and the Grenadines, and Tunisia, girls on average complete more than one extra year of school compared to boys, whereas, in Angola and Afghanistan, boys on average complete 2.3 to 2.7 more years of school than girls. The top-five economies where girls outperform boys in learning outcomes are Nauru, Qatar, Oman, Bahrain, and Samoa, three of which are in the Middle East and North Africa region. Conversely, 6 in 10 economies where boys have higher learning outcomes than girls are in Sub-Saharan Africa. In high- and middle-income economies, girls outperform boys in enrollment and learning outcomes (Bossavie and Kanninen 2018). For example, in Guyana, girls are expected to complete one-fifth of a year more schooling than boys, with 5 percent higher learning outcomes. This reverse gap in enrollment begins in lower-secondary education and widens in upper-secondary, where girls are 11 percent more likely to be enrolled than boys.

In survival and health outcomes, girls are generally better off than boys. Girls have higher adult survival rates in all of the 153 economies for which sex disaggregation is available in the HCI 2020. In all but two economies—India and Tonga—child survival rates are higher for girls than for boys. Meanwhile, girls are more likely to be stunted than boys in just 5 of 85 economies: Bhutan, Iraq, Kazakhstan, Moldova, and Tunisia.[17]

Overall, out of the 13 economies where boys have a higher HCI score than girls, 8 are in Sub-Saharan Africa, 2 in South Asia, 1 in the East Asia and Pacific region, 1 in Latin America and the Caribbean, and 1 in the Middle East and North Africa region. Seven of those economies are low-income, 5 are lower-middle-income, and 1

Figure 1.8: Regional and income-group variations in education gaps between boys and girls

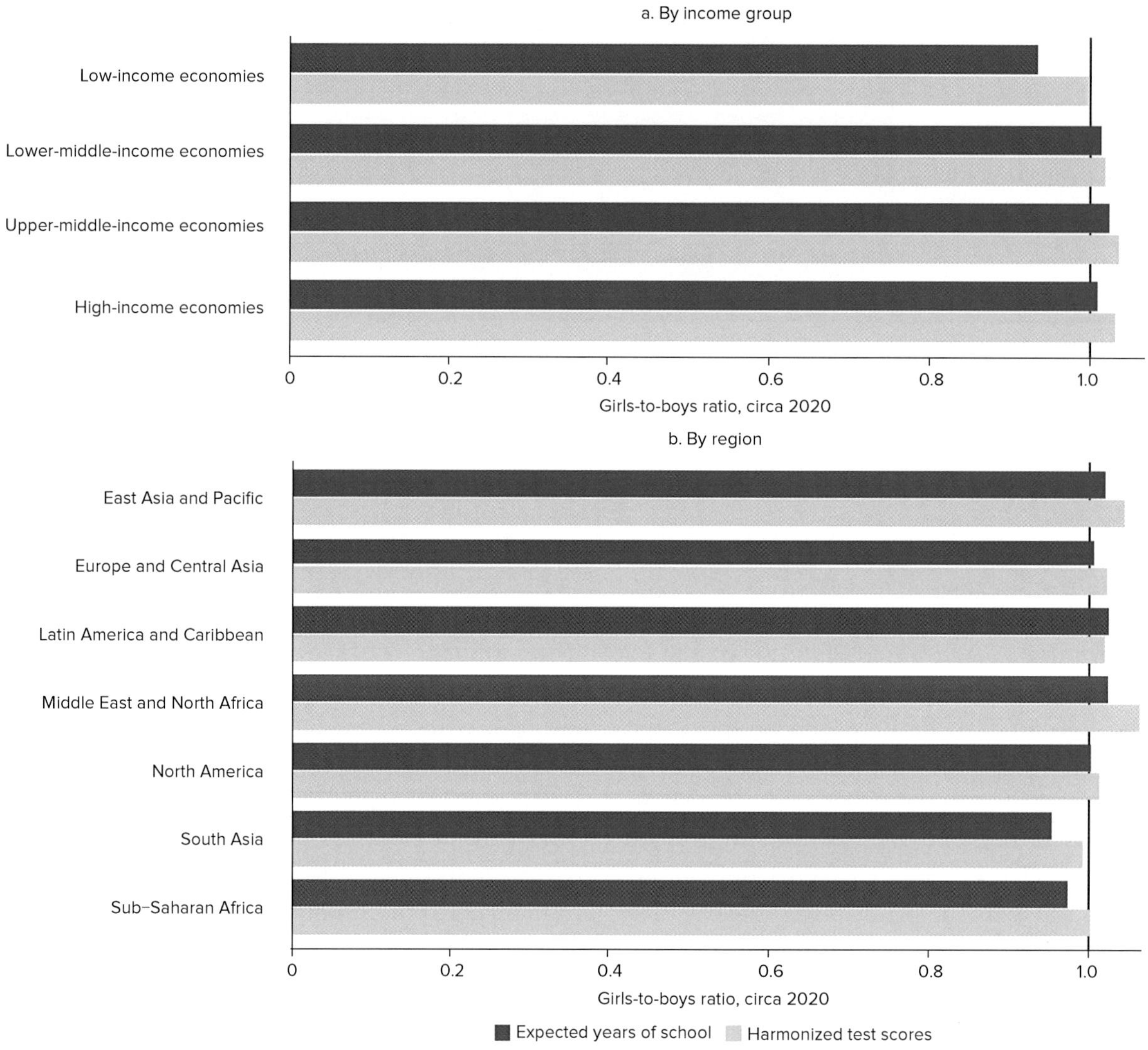

a. By income group

Low-income economies
Lower-middle-income economies
Upper-middle-income economies
High-income economies

0 0.2 0.4 0.6 0.8 1.0
Girls-to-boys ratio, circa 2020

b. By region

East Asia and Pacific
Europe and Central Asia
Latin America and Caribbean
Middle East and North Africa
North America
South Asia
Sub-Saharan Africa

0 0.2 0.4 0.6 0.8 1.0
Girls-to-boys ratio, circa 2020

Expected years of school Harmonized test scores

Source: World Bank calculations based on the 2020 update of the Human Capital Index (HCI).

is upper-middle-income. In all 13 economies, EYS for boys are higher than for girls, ranging from a quarter year in Peru to almost three full years in Afghanistan. On average, boys have a 10-percentage-point higher likelihood of completing primary education, a 12-percentage-point higher likelihood of completing lower-secondary education, and a 13-percentage-point higher likelihood of completing upper-secondary education. Boys also have better learning outcomes than girls in 9 of these 13 economies. In Chad and Guinea, this difference reaches more than 14 percent in favor of boys.

Human capital accumulation is a complex process. This complexity is especially clear when looking at the HCI to understand gender gaps. Women, girls, men, and boys face different challenges at different stages of the life cycle. The HCI focuses on specific life-cycle stages in which girls have slight

Figure 1.9: Global variation in gender gaps, Human Capital Index and education components

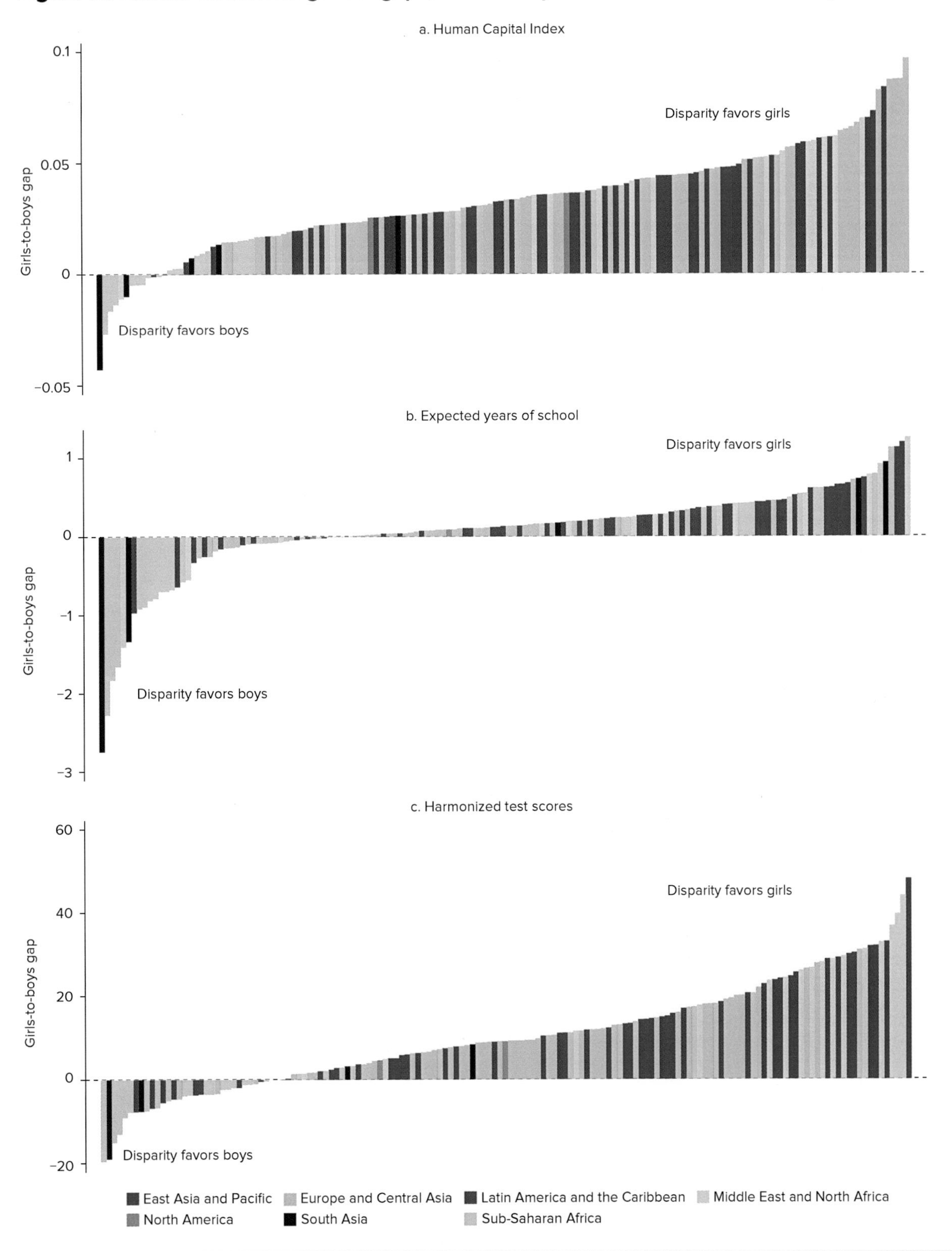

Source: World Bank calculations based on the 2020 update of the Human Capital Index (HCI).

Note: The x-axis show economies ranked by girls-to-boys gap in the variable in question. The y-axes are on the 0-1 scale for the HCI, years of schooling for EYS, and HTS points for Harmonized Test Scores.

biological advantages over boys in child and adult survival rates (Crimmins et al. 2019; United Nations 2011). As with any indicator, the components of the index are not perfect proxies of human capital and try to balance accuracy and data availability. For example, the index does not capture gender bias in terms of sex-selective abortions (what might be called prebirth survival).[18] Moreover, health is proxied by adult mortality rates, but some evidence shows that, although women live longer than men, they are not necessarily in better health (Bora and Saikia 2018; Guerra, Alvarado, and Zunzunegui 2008). As a measure of the human capital potential of children today, the index does not capture gender gaps in human capital among the current population of adults. These caveats are important backdrops to any analysis of gender gaps using the HCI. Finally, the index implicitly assumes that a child born today will be absorbed into the labor market to use her human capital potential in terms of income generation, when, in fact, female labor participation rates, globally, are 27 percentage points lower than male labor participation rates.[19] Chapter 4 on human capital utilization delves into this disparity, by proposing an adjustment of the HCI that captures labor outcomes. These outcomes reflect one of many ways human capital is utilized to improve well-being and overall economic development.

Equal access to education and health is far from realized. Despite progress, girls continue to face greater challenges. Child marriage, household responsibilities, teenage pregnancies, and gender-based violence in schools pose challenges to keeping girls enrolled, especially, but not only, in low-income settings.

1.5 HUMAN CAPITAL IN FRAGILE AND CONFLICT-AFFECTED CONTEXTS

Human capital accumulation requires a sustained political commitment, an adequate and timely resource mobilization, a whole-of-society approach, and effective use of data and measurement. These features, however, are not typical of economies that are grappling with fragility, conflict, and violence. By definition, such settings are plagued with high levels of institutional and social fragility, often with deteriorating governance capacity. In many cases, these economies are experiencing prolonged political crises or are undergoing a gradual but delicate reform and recovery process. Such circumstances complicate the process of consensus building and resource mobilization across political cycles and therefore pose a unique set of challenges in improving human capital (World Bank 2020b).

The importance of investing in human capital extends beyond the gains it promises in labor productivity and in ensuring that growth is inclusive and sustainable. Human capital is also a cornerstone of social cohesion, equity, and trust in institutions (Kim 2018). The seven economies scoring lowest on the HCI in 2020 are all on the World Bank's current annual list of fragile and conflict-affected situations (FCS).[20] Compared with the rest of the world, economies affected by conflict and violence are, on average, significantly further away from reaching the productivity frontier.

Shocks, such as armed conflict or natural disasters, have a lasting impact on human capital. Some pathways for this impact are obvious, including the destruction of human potential through combat deaths and casualties of natural calamities; damage to critical infrastructure and institutions, such as hospitals and schools; and the loss of skills resulting from mass displacement. But the impacts of these shocks on human capital reach farther. For instance, emerging evidence shows that the destructive impacts of armed conflict on health and education outcomes persist long after the fighting stops—extending to future generations not yet born when the conflict occurred (Corral et al. 2020).

Classic studies of conflict and human capital have given central attention to health impacts on children exposed to conflict settings. The link between violent conflict and a range of negative health outcomes among children has been established causally. For example, physical development was stunted in children who were exposed to the 2002–07 civil conflict in Côte d'Ivoire, and this negative impact increased with the length of exposure to the conflict (Minoiu and Shemyakina 2014). The impact of conflict on human capital increases with increasing conflict severity. Children living in areas of Nigeria that were heavily affected by the Boko Haram insurgency had lower weight-for-age and weight-for-height z-scores and higher probability of wasting than children living in less-affected areas.[21]

The intensity of conflict also determines the extent of human capital depletion. For instance, at aggregate level, the distance from the HCI frontier (an HCI score of 1) increases with the intensity of conflict, even among economies in FCS. Those economies with high-intensity conflict, defined as having at least 10 conflict deaths per 100,000 people, with a minimum of 150 casualties, have consistently scored lower on all components of the index, compared with other FCS and non-FCS economies (figure 1.10).

Conflict can have adverse effects on human capital across generations. Well-being and health outcomes among women in Nepal exposed as children to the country's post-1996 civil war were significantly worse than for those women and children who were not exposed to conflict. Not only did the first-generation victims show significant reductions in final adult height, but, when the conflict-exposed victims had children of their own, those children also suffered reduced weight-for-height and body mass index z-scores, on average. Women exposed to the conflict during childhood had more children and lived in poorer households as adults. The combination of these two factors may decrease parents' ability to invest in their children's human capital during critical phases of physical and cognitive development and therefore may propagate these impacts intergenerationally (Phadera 2019).

Human capital depletion in economies in FCS also happens through reduced and unequal access to education and through poor learning outcomes among those who do have access. Refugee and internally displaced children embody the losses of educational human capital associated with armed conflict. Conflict in the Syrian Arab Republic, for example, has led to disruptions in education for millions of children, including over a million who have been forced to flee to neighboring countries (Sieverding et al. 2018). Jordan hosts one of the largest populations of Syrian refuges and has made concerted efforts to provide access to education for refugee children. Despite those efforts, Syrian refugee children in Jordan experience delayed entry into school and early exit, with enrollment rates dropping sharply from around age 12, when refugee children come under pressure to work and help support their families (box 1.5; see also Tiltnes, Zhang, and Pedersen 2019).

Globally, refugees access education at much lower rates than other children do. In 2016, only 61 percent of refugee children attended primary school, compared to 91 percent of all children. At the secondary level, 23 percent of refugee children were enrolled, versus 84 percent of eligible young people worldwide (UNHCR 2017). These shortfalls are especially concerning because the number of refugees and displaced people worldwide has risen steadily through the past decade and now stands at its highest level since World War II.

The intergenerational impact of conflict and violence extends to losses in educational attainment for children not even born when fighting took place. For example, in utero exposure to the Rwandan genocide decreased educational attainment by 0.3 years and the likelihood of completing primary school by 8 percent (Bundervoet and Fransen 2018). The impact on years of schooling was stronger for females and for individuals exposed to the genocide in the first trimester of gestation. Each additional month of exposure in utero decreased educational attainment by 0.21 years of schooling.

Figure 1.10: Human capital and severity of conflict

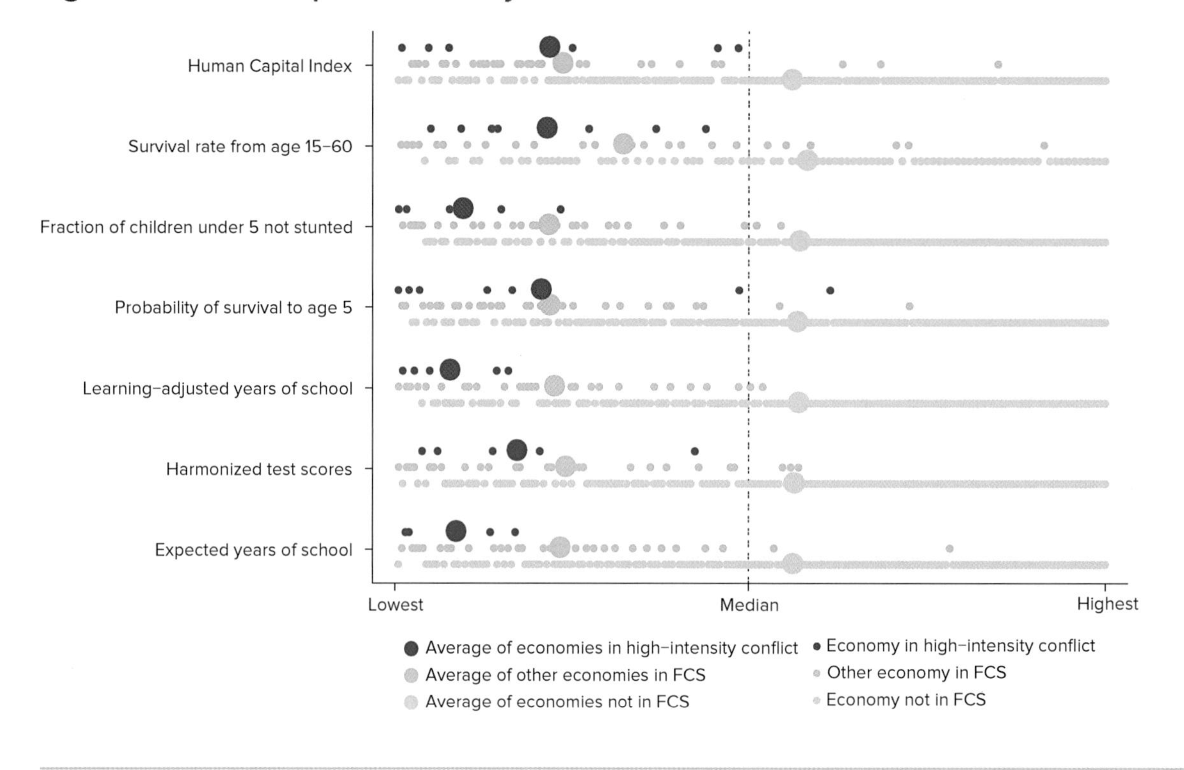

Source: Corral et al. 2020 with updated Human Capital Index (HCI) data for 2020.

Note: Economies in high-intensity conflict are defined as having at least 10 conflict deaths per 100,000 people according to the Armed Conflict and Event Data Project (ACLED) and the Uppsala Conflict Data Program (UCDP), while also experiencing a total of more than 250 conflict deaths according to ACLED, or more than 150 conflict deaths according to UCDP. FCS = fragile and conflict-affected situations.

Through in utero exposure, conflict-related disruptions of fetal cognitive development may affect children's subsequent cognitive capacities, educational outcomes, and earning power as adults.

How can fragile countries and development partners confront the losses of human capital driven by conflict? The best solution is to prevent fragility, conflict, and violence from engulfing countries in the first place. But, when conflict does erupt, effective delivery of health and education services tailored to economies in FCS is vital. Only the preservation and rebuilding of human capital can enable countries to durably escape cycles of fragility and violence.

The delivery of health and education services in FCS poses daunting challenges, not least because of the extreme diversity of FCS contexts. Much has recently been learned, however, from the experiences of various countries. In Afghanistan, for example, following the withdrawal of the Taliban in 2001, the Ministry of Public Health had to provide emergency relief services to address the grave health situation throughout the country. Yet the health system was in ruins after decades of warfare and neglect. As they rolled out emergency health services, including in many areas still subject to conflict, health officials had to plan for the future, which included rebuilding and sustaining a functional national health system. Acknowledging its capacity limitations and with technical assistance from the international community, the Ministry of Public Health led the creation of an innovative public-private partnership framework for health service delivery in Afghanistan (Newbrander, Waldman, and Shepherd-Banigan 2011). This delivery model has improved key health

Box 1.5: Schooling for Syrian refugee children in Jordan

The government of Jordan has adopted a policy of offering refugee children tuition-free access to the public education system, while also providing accredited schools in refugee camps. As a result, overcrowding has occurred in schools in some locations. Despite these measures, access to school for refugee children is still limited. Only about 152,000 of the estimated 236,000 Syrian refugee children present in Jordan are enrolled (64 percent). Figure B1.5.1 paints a stark picture of the enrollment decline by age among refugees. It shows that enrollment significantly tails off after age 11, more so for boys than for girls. This decline is driven by several factors, including poverty (because most families cannot cover the auxiliary costs of education, such as transportation and school materials); early marriage (which is also evident in recent household surveys); and increased opportunity cost of education (because many children start working early to support their families).

Reports suggest that bullying at schools and the absence of a safe learning space impede learning for Jordanian boys as well as for Syrian refugees, and the Jordanian government is taking measures to address this issue. In addition, important reforms such as ensuring universal enrollment for 5-year-olds in preprimary education apply to all inhabitants of Jordan, including Syrian refugee children.

Figure B1.5.1: Net enrollment rate of Syrian refugees in formal education in Jordan

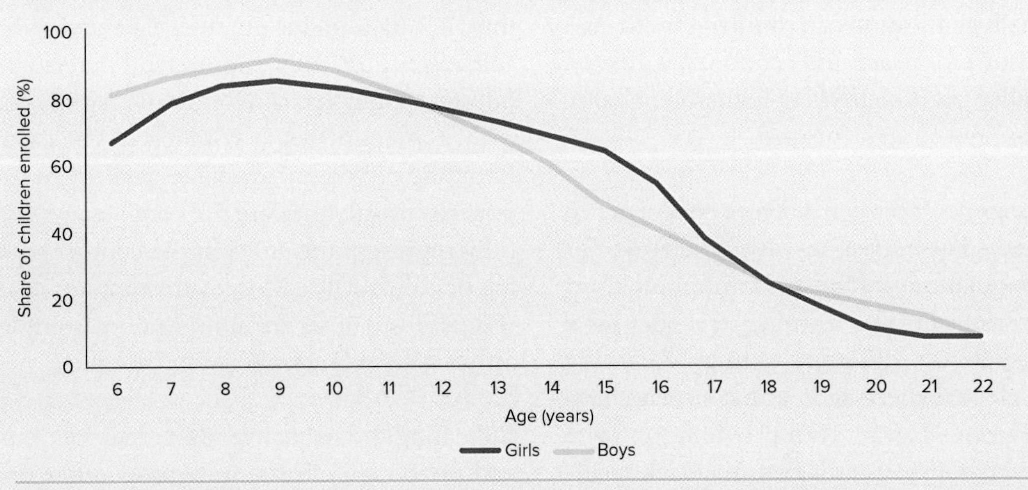

Source: Krafft et al. 2018.

Note: Data include only refugees registered with the United Nations High Commissioner for Refugees.

indicators under highly challenging conditions and has been recognized as an example for other post-conflict countries (World Bank 2018c).

Without adequate health financing, health service delivery simply will not happen. The ongoing Syrian crisis has underscored that country authorities, donors, and international partners must coordinate their efforts to ensure that health and other essential services for refugees can be sustainably paid for. An important resource to facilitate such durable support came with the 2016 launch of the Global Concessional Financing Facility (GCFF). Led jointly by the World Bank, the United Nations, and the Islamic Development Bank, the GCFF is a global platform designed to deliver concessional funding to middle-income countries that provide a global public good by hosting large numbers of refugees. GCFF resources enable governments in host countries to offer expanded services to refugees while continuing to meet the needs of their own citizens. Early GCFF concessional loans reduced the acute financial burden on Lebanon and Jordan, two countries on the front lines of the Syrian refugee response. Subsequently, the GCFF has worked to smooth the transition from humanitarian assistance to development by providing medium- and long-term concessional finance.

Even more than other countries, those in FCS need education systems that can promote learning, life skills, and social cohesion. Only by securing broad dissemination of these capacities in the population through quality education can countries build lasting foundations for peace and economic recovery. But the challenges in delivering equitable, quality education are not straightforward.

Some of the greatest service delivery challenges in conflict-affected countries involve education for displaced populations and host communities. Over the years, various flexible learning strategies have been fielded across different settings. Learning from these global experiences, host countries have consistently moved away from providing refugee education in parallel systems that may lack qualified teachers, consistent funding, ability to provide diplomas, and quality control. Ethiopia's Refugee Proclamation, for example, gives refugees access to national schools and gives host children access to refugee schools. The Islamic Republic of Iran decreed in 2015 that schools accept all Afghan children regardless of documentation. Turkey has committed to include all Syrian refugee children in its national education system by 2020 (UNESCO 2019). The inclusion of refugees in national education systems dramatically expands educational opportunities for refugees. But the process remains fraught with challenges related to system capacities, persistent access barriers, quality, and resources.

Furthermore, the lack of timely, reliable, and actionable data and of a robust measurement agenda also hinders progress in human capital accumulation in FCS. Although high-quality data are critical for diagnosing deficiencies and formulating targeted policies and programs to enhance human capital, such data are not readily available across many economies that are in the midst of, or are recovering from, fragility and conflict. For instance, the HCI score cannot be calculated for some of the economies that are considered FCS according to the World Bank 2020 classification, often because data informing various HCI components either do not exist or are outdated. Even when the index can be calculated compatibly with the HCI data inclusion rules (see appendix C), it still might not fully capture the deterioration of human capital that can follow the rapidly changing reality of countries in conflict. In the case of the Republic of Yemen, available data for index components mostly predate the conflict and might not fully represent the effect of the conflict on schooling or child health. Moreover, comparable data for refugees and hosts are almost nonexistent in economies afflicted by fragility and conflict.

Collecting high-quality data requires sustained and deliberate efforts. In light of other pressures in situations of violence and conflict, measurement is rarely a priority; however, collecting high-quality data is feasible in these settings. For instance, mobile phone interviews were used for data collection during the Ebola crisis in Sierra Leone and to inform a response to drought in Nigeria, Somalia, South Sudan, and the Republic of Yemen (Hoogeveen and Pape 2020). Likewise, satellite images and machine learning algorithms were employed to address the lack of a sampling frame in the Democratic Republic of Congo and in Somalia. When data collection is hampered by security concerns for enumerators, locally recruited resident enumerators make it possible to collect relevant, reliable, and timely evidence that can shed light on the plight of the most vulnerable populations. These efforts can move the needle on addressing persistent data deprivation in FCS.

Protecting and rebuilding human capital in settings of fragility and conflict are crucial to restore hope in these countries. They are also critical for reaching global poverty goals. Over recent decades, poverty has become steadily more concentrated in economies in FCS. Fragility and conflict deplete human capital, yet societies must rely heavily on human capital to recover from fragility and conflict. This paradox underscores the importance of health and education services in FCS settings. Delivering these services lays the foundations that will enable countries to emerge from cycles of violence and return to peace, stability, and development. Overcoming systemic barriers will simultaneously require careful coordination between humanitarian and development partners and a whole-of-society approach.

1.6 THE HCI 2020 UPDATE

Table 1.2 presents the overall HCI 2020 for 174 economies. The index ranges from 0 to 1 and is measured in terms of the productivity of the next generation of workers relative to the benchmark of complete education and full health. An economy in which a child born today can expect to achieve complete education and full health will score a value of 1 on the index. All of the components of the HCI are measured with some error, and this uncertainty naturally has implications for the precision of the overall HCI. To capture this imprecision, the HCI estimates for each economy are accompanied by upper and lower bounds that reflect the uncertainty in the measurement of the components of the HCI. These bounds are constructed by recalculating the HCI using lower- and upper-bound estimates of the components of the HCI and are also reported in table 1.2.[22] This is intended to help move the discussion away from small differences in economy ranks on the HCI and toward more useful discussions around the level of the HCI and what this implies for the productivity of future workers (see box 1.6).

Box 1.6: Where did the HCI rankings go?

The 2020 update does not report rankings for the 174 economies with an HCI score. There are four reasons for this change.

First, coverage of the index has increased by 17 economies, from 157 economies in the inaugural 2018 HCI to 174 economies in 2020. Therefore, a rank of 37 out of 157, for instance, cannot be compared with a rank of 37 out of 174. Given the change in HCI coverage between 2018 and 2020, simple comparisons of rankings as an indication of an economy's progress over time are meaningless.

Second, even if comparisons were restricted to the set of economies included in both the 2018 and the 2020 versions of the index, rankings artificially inflate small differences in HCI scores. For example, eight economies are clustered between HCI scores of 0.60 and 0.61; if one of those economies at 0.60 improves by just 0.01, it would move up eight places in the ranking. By contrast, only two economies have scores between 0.70 and 0.71; if one of those two economies were to improve its score by 0.01, it would move up only one rank.[a]

(continued next page)

Box 1.6: Where did the HCI rankings go? *(Continued)*

Third, rankings suppress information on the absolute gains and losses economies have made on the HCI. Consider for example the comparison of HCI 2020 and HCI 2010, which is graphed in panel a of figure B1.6.1.[b] Most economies have improved their human capital outcomes, reflected by the fact that they are above the 45-degree line in the figure. Rankings cannot convey these gains (or losses), because they present only the positions of economies relative to each other, as illustrated in panel b of figure B1.6.1, which plots the same information for 2020 versus 2010 but in rank terms. Even economies that have made gains in human capital accumulation may fall below the 45-degree line simply because of their position relative to other economies. In addition, points in panel b are more spread out than those in panel a, illustrating how ranks artificially magnify small changes.

Figure B1.6.1: Changes in Human Capital Index scores and ranks, 2010 vs. 2020

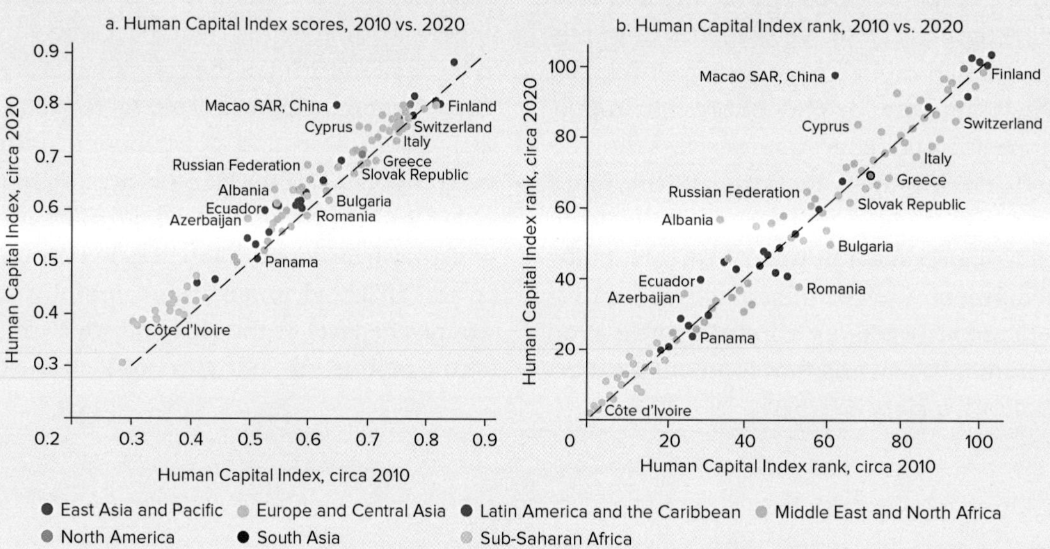

Source: World Bank calculations based on the 2020 update of the Human Capital Index (HCI).
Note: This figure compares HCI data for 2020 and 2010. The construction of an HCI for 2010 is described in chapter 2. The sample for 2010 does not include any South Asian countries since they are missing learning data for 2010 from a comparable representative international assessment.

Fourth, and most important, there is no need to focus on rankings because the index itself is expressed in meaningful units. Because the HCI is measured in terms of the productivity of the next generation of workers relative to the benchmark of complete education and full health, the units of the index have a natural interpretation: a value of 0.50 for an economy means that the productivity as a future worker of a child born in a given year in that economy is only half of what it could be under the benchmark. Rankings place an inordinately large focus on the fact that an economy with an HCI of 0.51 is ahead of an economy with an HCI of 0.50. This interpretation misses the more critical issue, which is that in both economies children born today will grow up with half their human capital potential unfulfilled. This information is vastly more important than whether one economy is "ahead of" another.

[a] This problem is amplified by the fact that the components of the HCI are measured with some error, and this uncertainty naturally has implications for the precision of the overall HCI. To capture this imprecision, the HCI estimates for each economy are accompanied by upper and lower bounds that reflect the uncertainty in the measurement of HCI components. In cases where these intervals overlap for two economies, it indicates that the differences in the HCI estimates for these two economies should not be overinterpreted, because they are small relative to the uncertainty around the value of the index itself. Rankings further amplify these minor differences.

[b] The construction of an HCI for 2010 is described in the following chapter.

Table 1.2: The Human Capital Index (HCI), 2020

Economy	Lower Bound	Value	Upper Bound	Economy	Lower Bound	Value	Upper Bound	Economy	Lower Bound	Value	Upper Bound
Central African Republic	0.26	**0.29**	0.32	India	0.49	**0.49**	0.50	Mauritius	0.60	**0.62**	0.64
Chad	0.28	**0.30**	0.32	Egypt, Arab Rep.	0.48	**0.49**	0.51	Uzbekistan	0.60	**0.62**	0.64
South Sudan	0.27	**0.31**	0.33	Guyana	0.48	**0.50**	0.51	Brunei Darussalam	0.62	**0.63**	0.63
Niger	0.29	**0.32**	0.33	Panama	0.49	**0.50**	0.51	Kazakhstan	0.62	**0.63**	0.63
Mali	0.31	**0.32**	0.33	Dominican Republic	0.49	**0.50**	0.52	Costa Rica	0.62	**0.63**	0.64
Liberia	0.30	**0.32**	0.33	Morocco	0.49	**0.50**	0.51	Ukraine	0.62	**0.63**	0.64
Nigeria	0.33	**0.36**	0.38	Tajikistan	0.48	**0.50**	0.53	Seychelles	0.61	**0.63**	0.66
Mozambique	0.34	**0.36**	0.38	Nepal	0.49	**0.50**	0.52	Montenegro	0.62	**0.63**	0.64
Angola	0.33	**0.36**	0.39	Micronesia, Fed. Sts.	0.47	**0.51**	0.53	Albania	0.62	**0.63**	0.64
Sierra Leone	0.35	**0.36**	0.38	Nicaragua	0.50	**0.51**	0.52	Qatar	0.63	**0.64**	0.64
Congo, Dem. Rep.	0.34	**0.37**	0.38	Nauru	0.49	**0.51**	0.53	Turkey	0.64	**0.65**	0.66
Guinea	0.35	**0.37**	0.39	Fiji	0.50	**0.51**	0.52	Chile	0.64	**0.65**	0.66
Eswatini	0.35	**0.37**	0.39	Lebanon	0.50	**0.52**	0.52	Bahrain	0.64	**0.65**	0.66
Yemen, Rep.	0.35	**0.37**	0.39	Philippines	0.50	**0.52**	0.53	China	0.64	**0.65**	0.67
Sudan	0.36	**0.38**	0.39	Tunisia	0.51	**0.52**	0.52	Slovak Republic	0.66	**0.66**	0.67
Rwanda	0.36	**0.38**	0.39	Paraguay	0.51	**0.53**	0.54	United Arab Emirates	0.66	**0.67**	0.68
Côte d'Ivoire	0.36	**0.38**	0.40	Tonga	0.51	**0.53**	0.55	Serbia	0.67	**0.68**	0.69
Mauritania	0.35	**0.38**	0.41	St. Vincent and the Grenadines	0.52	**0.53**	0.54	Russian Federation	0.67	**0.68**	0.69
Ethiopia	0.37	**0.38**	0.39	Algeria	0.53	**0.53**	0.54	Hungary	0.67	**0.68**	0.69
Burkina Faso	0.36	**0.38**	0.40	Jamaica	0.52	**0.53**	0.55	Luxembourg	0.68	**0.69**	0.69
Uganda	0.37	**0.38**	0.40	Indonesia	0.53	**0.54**	0.55	Vietnam	0.67	**0.69**	0.71
Burundi	0.36	**0.39**	0.41	Dominica	0.53	**0.54**	0.56	Greece	0.68	**0.69**	0.70
Tanzania	0.38	**0.39**	0.40	El Salvador	0.53	**0.55**	0.56	Belarus	0.69	**0.70**	0.71
Madagascar	0.37	**0.39**	0.41	Kenya	0.53	**0.55**	0.56	United States	0.69	**0.70**	0.71
Zambia	0.38	**0.40**	0.41	Samoa	0.54	**0.55**	0.56	Lithuania	0.70	**0.71**	0.72
Cameroon	0.38	**0.40**	0.42	Brazil	0.55	**0.55**	0.56	Latvia	0.69	**0.71**	0.72
Afghanistan	0.39	**0.40**	0.41	Jordan	0.54	**0.55**	0.56	Malta	0.70	**0.71**	0.72
Benin	0.38	**0.40**	0.42	North Macedonia	0.55	**0.56**	0.56	Croatia	0.70	**0.71**	0.72
Lesotho	0.38	**0.40**	0.42	Kuwait	0.55	**0.56**	0.57	Italy	0.72	**0.73**	0.74
Comoros	0.36	**0.40**	0.43	Grenada	0.55	**0.57**	0.58	Spain	0.72	**0.73**	0.73
Pakistan	0.39	**0.41**	0.42	Kosovo	0.56	**0.57**	0.57	Israel	0.72	**0.73**	0.74
Iraq	0.40	**0.41**	0.41	Georgia	0.56	**0.57**	0.58	Iceland	0.74	**0.75**	0.75
Malawi	0.40	**0.41**	0.43	Saudi Arabia	0.56	**0.58**	0.59	Austria	0.74	**0.75**	0.76
Botswana	0.39	**0.41**	0.43	Azerbaijan	0.56	**0.58**	0.59	Germany	0.74	**0.75**	0.76
Congo, Rep.	0.39	**0.42**	0.44	Armenia	0.57	**0.58**	0.59	Czech Republic	0.74	**0.75**	0.76
Solomon Islands	0.41	**0.42**	0.43	Bosnia and Herzegovina	0.57	**0.58**	0.59	Poland	0.74	**0.75**	0.76
Senegal	0.40	**0.42**	0.43	West Bank and Gaza	0.57	**0.58**	0.59	Denmark	0.75	**0.76**	0.76
Gambia, The	0.39	**0.42**	0.44	Moldova	0.57	**0.58**	0.59	Cyprus	0.75	**0.76**	0.76
Marshall Islands	0.40	**0.42**	0.44	Romania	0.57	**0.58**	0.60	Switzerland	0.75	**0.76**	0.77
South Africa	0.41	**0.43**	0.44	St. Kitts and Nevis	0.57	**0.59**	0.60	Belgium	0.75	**0.76**	0.77
Papua New Guinea	0.41	**0.43**	0.44	Palau	0.57	**0.59**	0.61	France	0.75	**0.76**	0.77
Togo	0.41	**0.43**	0.45	Iran, Islamic Rep.	0.58	**0.59**	0.60	Portugal	0.76	**0.77**	0.78
Namibia	0.42	**0.45**	0.47	Ecuador	0.59	**0.59**	0.60	Australia	0.76	**0.77**	0.78
Haiti	0.43	**0.45**	0.46	Antigua and Barbuda	0.58	**0.60**	0.61	Norway	0.76	**0.77**	0.78
Tuvalu	0.43	**0.45**	0.46	Kyrgyz Republic	0.59	**0.60**	0.61	Slovenia	0.77	**0.77**	0.78
Ghana	0.44	**0.45**	0.46	Sri Lanka	0.59	**0.60**	0.60	New Zealand	0.77	**0.78**	0.78
Timor-Leste	0.43	**0.45**	0.47	Uruguay	0.59	**0.60**	0.61	Estonia	0.77	**0.78**	0.79
Vanuatu	0.44	**0.45**	0.47	Argentina	0.59	**0.60**	0.61	United Kingdom	0.77	**0.78**	0.79
Lao PDR	0.44	**0.46**	0.47	St. Lucia	0.59	**0.60**	0.62	Netherlands	0.78	**0.79**	0.80
Gabon	0.43	**0.46**	0.48	Trinidad and Tobago	0.57	**0.60**	0.62	Ireland	0.78	**0.79**	0.80
Guatemala	0.45	**0.46**	0.47	Colombia	0.59	**0.60**	0.62	Sweden	0.79	**0.80**	0.81
Bangladesh	0.46	**0.46**	0.47	Peru	0.59	**0.61**	0.62	Macao SAR, China	0.79	**0.80**	0.80
Zimbabwe	0.44	**0.47**	0.49	Oman	0.60	**0.61**	0.62	Finland	0.79	**0.80**	0.80
Bhutan	0.45	**0.48**	0.50	Thailand	0.60	**0.61**	0.62	Canada	0.79	**0.80**	0.81
Myanmar	0.46	**0.48**	0.49	Malaysia	0.60	**0.61**	0.62	Korea, Rep.	0.79	**0.80**	0.81
Honduras	0.47	**0.48**	0.49	Mexico	0.60	**0.61**	0.62	Japan	0.80	**0.80**	0.81
Cambodia	0.47	**0.49**	0.51	Bulgaria	0.60	**0.61**	0.62	Hong Kong SAR, China	0.80	**0.81**	0.82
Kiribati	0.46	**0.49**	0.52	Mongolia	0.60	**0.61**	0.63	Singapore	0.87	**0.88**	0.89

HCI < 0.40 | 0.40 ≤ HCI < 0.50 | 0.50 ≤ HCI < 0.60 | 0.60 ≤ HCI < 0.70 | 0.70 ≤ HCI < 0.80 | 0.80 ≤ HCI

Source: World Bank calculations based on the 2020 update of the Human Capital Index (HCI).

Note: The Human Capital Index (HCI) ranges between 0 and 1. The index is measured in terms of the productivity of the next generation of workers relative to the benchmark of complete education and full health. An economy in which a child born today can expect to achieve complete education and full health will score a value of 1 on the index. Lower and upper bounds indicate the range of uncertainty around the value of the HCI for each economy.

NOTES

1. The HCI was introduced in World Bank (2018a, 2018b), and its methodology is detailed in Kraay (2018).
2. As a result of the criteria for its construction, the index measures dimensions of human capital that are important, but it does not include all of the important dimensions of human capital.
3. The literature has recognized the usefulness of moving from "a large and eclectic dashboard" to a single summary metric (Stiglitz, Sen, and Fitoussi 2009). Doing so, however, requires a coherent aggregation method, in contrast with "mashup indicators of development" that combine different components in arbitrary ways (Ravallion 2010). The HCI is constructed by transforming its components into contributions to productivity, anchored in microeconometric evidence on the effects of education and health on worker productivity, consistent with the large literature on development accounting (see, for example, Caselli 2005).
4. The decomposition of the group averages is obtained via a Shapley decomposition. For an application see Azevedo, Inchauste, and Sanfelice 2013.
5. Among upper-middle-income economies, the health component value of the bottom performer is higher than that of the top performer, and thus it accounts for a negative share of the difference.
6. For more information, see the IGME website, http://www.childmortality.org/.
7. For Institute for Statistics data, see http://data.uis.unesco.org/. See also appendix C for the description of different enrollment rates: gross, net, adjusted net, and total net enrollment rates.
8. For the 2020 update, this review process was conducted between January and May 2020 in collaboration with the country units of the World Bank.
9. PISA-D results are used only for Bhutan.
10. For the 20 new economies included in the Global Dataset on Education Quality, 8 are updated using EGRAs, 8 using PILNA, 3 using PISA and PISA-D, and 1 using a national TIMSS-equivalent assessment.
11. Of the 94 economies with updated test scores in the Global Dataset on Education Quality, 75 use scores from PISA 2018, 7 from PISA-D, 5 from EGRAs, and 7 from PILNA.
12. See the UNPD website, https://population.un.org/wpp/.
13. See the IHME website, http://www.healthdata.org/results/data-visualizations.
14. See https://data.un.org/.
15. Note that Vietnam enters the HCI 2020 with its 2015 PISA score, because 2018 PISA scores are not reported for the country. Although Vietnam participated in the 2018 round of PISA using paper-based instruments, the Organisation for Economic Co-operation and Development's country note states that the international comparability of the country's performance in reading, mathematics, and science could not be fully ensured (OECD 2019).
16. This difference is statistically significant at the 5 percent level.
17. Stunting rates are calculated using survey data, and differences in average rates between girls and boys may not be statistically significant.
18. The number of "missing women" was estimated to be 126 million in 2010 (Bongaarts and Guilmoto 2015). This term refers to the deficit of females relative to males, compared to the figures that would have been observed had all female fetuses been allowed to be born.
19. Data from ILOSTAT, the International Labour Organization's labor statistics database. Retrieved from World Bank Gender Data Portal, https://datatopics.worldbank.org/gender/.

20. These economies are the Central African Republic, Chad, Liberia, Mali, Niger, Nigeria, and South Sudan.
21. A *z-score* is a measure of how many standard deviations below or above the population mean a raw score is. See Ekhator-Mobayode and Abebe Asfaw (2019).
22. The upper and lower bounds of the HCI are a tool to highlight to users that the estimated HCI values for all countries are subject to uncertainty, reflecting the corresponding uncertainty in the components. In cases where these intervals overlap for two countries, this indicates that the differences in the HCI estimates for these two countries should not be overinterpreted because they are small relative to the uncertainty around the value of the index itself.

REFERENCES

Azevedo, J. P., G. Inchaust, and V. Sanfelice. 2013. "Decomposing the Recent Inequality Decline in Latin America." Policy Research Working Paper 6715, World Bank, Washington, DC.

Bongaarts, J., and C. Guilmoto. 2015. "How Many More Missing Women? Excess Female Mortality and Prenatal Sex Selection, 1970–2050." *Population and Development Review* 41 (2): 241–69.

Bora, J. K., and N. Saikia. 2018. "Neonatal and Under-Five Mortality Rate in Indian Districts with Reference to Sustainable Development Goal 3: An Analysis of the National Family Health Survey of India (NFHS), 2015–2016." *PLoS ONE* 13 (7): e0201125.

Bossavie, L., and O. Kanninen. 2018. "What Explains the Gender Gap Reversal in Educational Attainment?" Policy Research Working Paper 8303, World Bank, Washington, DC.

Bundervoet, T., and S. Fransen. 2018. "The Educational Impact of Shocks in Utero: Evidence from Rwanda." *Economics & Human Biology* 29 (C): 88–101.

Caselli, F. 2005. "Accounting for Cross-Country Income Differences." In *Handbook of Economic Growth*, 1st ed., vol. 1, edited by P. Aghion and S. Durlauf, 679–741. Elsevier.

Corral, P., A. Irwin, N. Krishnan, D. G. Mahler, and T. Vishwanath. 2020. *Fragility and Conflict: On the Front Lines of the Fight against Poverty.* Washington, DC: World Bank.

Crimmins, E., H. Shim, Y. S. Zhang, and J. Kim. 2019. "Differences between Men and Women in Mortality and the Health Dimensions of the Morbidity Process." *Clinical Chemistry* 65 (1): 135–45.

de Onis, M., and F. Branca. 2016. "Childhood Stunting: A Global Perspective." *Maternal & Child Nutrition* 12 Suppl 1 (Suppl 1): 12–26.

D'Souza, R., R. Gatti, and A. Kraay. 2019. "A Socioeconomic Disaggregation of the World Bank Human Capital Index." Policy Research Working Paper 9020, World Bank, Washington, DC.

Ekhator-Mobayode, U. E., and A. Abebe Asfaw. 2019. "The Child Health Effects of Terrorism: Evidence from the Boko Haram Insurgency in Nigeria." *Applied Economics* 51 (6): 624–38.

El-Kogali, S., and C. Krafft. 2020. *Expectations and Aspirations: A New Framework for Education in the Middle East and North Africa*. Washington, DC: World Bank.

Filmer, D., H. Rogers, N. Angrist, and S. Sabarwal. 2018. "Learning-Adjusted Years of Schooling (LAYS): Defining a New Macro Measure of Education." Policy Research Working Paper 8591, World Bank, Washington, DC.

Galal, A., M. Welmond, M. Carnoy, S. Nellemann, J. Keller, J. Wahba, and I. Yamasaki. 2008. "The Road Not Traveled: Education Reform in the Middle East and North Africa." MENA Development Report, World Bank, Washington, DC.

Guerra, R. O., B. E. Alvarado, and M. V. Zunzunegui. 2008. "Life Course, Gender and Ethnic Inequalities in Functional Disability in a Brazilian Urban Elderly Population." *Aging Clinical and Experimental Research* 20 (1): 53–61.

Hoogeveen, J., and U. Pape, eds. 2020. *Data Collection in Fragile States: Innovations from Africa and Beyond*. Washington, DC: World Bank.

Kaffenberger, M., and L. Pritchett. 2017. "More School or More Learning? Evidence from Learning Profiles from the Financial Inclusion Insights Data." Background paper, *World Development Report 2018: Learning to Realize Education's Promise,* World Bank, Washington, DC.

Kim, J. 2018. "The Human Capital Gap: Getting Governments to Invest in People." *ForeignAffairs* July/August 2018. https://www.foreignaffairs.com/articles/2018-06-14/human-capital-gap.

Kraay, A. 2018. "Methodology for a World Bank Human Capital Index." Policy Research Working Paper 8593, World Bank, Washington, DC.

Krafft, C., M. Sieverding, C. Keo, and C. Salemi. 2018. "Syrian Refugees in Jordan: Demographics, Livelihoods, Education, and Health." Working Paper 1184, Economic Research Forum, Giza, Egypt.

Minoiu, C., and O. N. Shemyakina. 2014. "Armed Conflict, Household Victimization, and Child Health in Côte d'Ivoire." *Journal of Development Economics* 108 (C): 237–55.

Newbrander, W., R. Waldman, and M. Shepherd-Banigan. 2011. "Rebuilding and Strengthening Health Systems and Providing Basic Health Services in Fragile States." *Disasters* 35: 639–60.

OECD (Organisation for Economic Co-operation and Development). 2019. "Viet Nam Country Note—PISA 2018 Results." Programme for International Student Assessment (PISA), OECD.

Patrinos, H. A. and Angrist, N. 2018. "Global Dataset on Education Quality: A Review and Update (2000–2017)." Policy Research Working Paper 8592, World Bank, Washington, DC.

Phadera, L. 2019. "Unfortunate Moms and Unfortunate Children: Impact of the Nepali Civil War on Women's Stature and Intergenerational Health." Policy Research Working Paper 8927, World Bank, Washington, DC.

Ravallion, M. 2010. "Mashup Indices of Development." Policy Research Working Paper 5432, World Bank, Washington, DC.

Sieverding, M., C. Krafft, N. Berri, C. Keo, and M. Sharpless. 2018. "Education Interrupted: Enrollment, Attainment, and Dropout of Syrian Refugees in Jordan." Working Paper 1261, Economic Research Forum, Giza, Egypt.

Stiglitz, J., A. Sen, and J.-P. Fitoussi. 2009. "The Measurement of Economic Performance and Social Progress Revisited: Reflections and Overview." Sciences Po, Publications 2009-33, Paris Institute of Political Studies.

Tiltnes, A., H. Zhang, and J. Pedersen. 2019. *The Living Conditions of Syrian Refugees in Jordan: Results from the 2017–2018 Survey of Syrian Refugees Inside and Outside Camps*. Oslo: Fafo Institute for Labour and Social Research.

UNESCO (United Nations Educational, Scientific and Cultural Organization). 2019. *Global Education Monitoring Report 2019: Migration, Displacement and Education: Building Bridges, not Walls*. Paris: UNESCO.

UNHCR (United Nations High Commissioner for Refugees). 2017. "Left Behind: Refugee Education in Crisis." UNHCR, Geneva.

UNICEF (United Nations Children's Fund), WHO (World Health Organization), and World Bank Group. 2020. *Levels and Trends in Child Mortality: Key Findings of the 2020 Edition*. UNICEF, WHO, and World Bank Group.

United Nations. 2011. "Sex Differentials in Childhood Mortality." Department of Economic and Social Affairs, Population Division, United Nations, New York.

World Bank. 2013. *Jobs for Shared Prosperity: Time for Action in the Middle East and North Africa*. Washington, DC: World Bank.

World Bank. 2018a. "The Human Capital Project." World Bank, Washington, DC.

World Bank. 2018b. "Human Capital: A Project for the World." Development Committee, World Bank, Washington, DC.

World Bank. 2018c. "Progress in the Face of Insecurity: Improving Health Outcomes in Afghanistan." World Bank, Washington, DC.

World Bank. 2018d. *World Development Report 2018: Learning to Realize Education's Promise*. Washington, DC: World Bank.

World Bank. 2019a. "Ending Learning Poverty: What Will It Take?" World Bank, Washington, DC.

World Bank. 2019b. "Insights from Disaggregating the Human Capital Index." World Bank, Washington, DC.

World Bank. 2020a. *Markets and People: Romania Country Economic Memorandum*. Washington, DC: World Bank.

World Bank. 2020b. "World Bank Group Strategy for Fragility, Conflict, and Violence 2020–2025." World Bank, Washington, DC.

World Health Organization. 2009. "The WHO Multicentre Growth Reference Study (MGRS)." World Health Organization, Geneva.

2 Human Capital Accumulation OVER TIME

As the first update of the Human Capital Index (HCI), the 2020 release is an opportunity to look at the evolution of human capital outcomes, as measured by the HCI, across economies over time.

Unlike indexes that aggregate laws or regulation, which can be modified by swift government legislative or regulatory action, the HCI is based on outcomes that typically change slowly from year to year. Some of them—such as stunting and educational test scores—are measured infrequently, every three to five years. As a result, changes in the HCI over a short period are small and might simply reflect updates to components that are measured sporadically. In contrast, the analysis of longer-term trends has a more solid basis, given the scope for smoothing out short-run idiosyncrasies.

This chapter examines trends in human capital over time. The first section discusses the construction of an HCI for 2010 and the evolution of the HCI between 2010 and 2020. The following section unpacks these dynamics by looking at changes in the components of the HCI. The final section provides a policy focus. Drawing lessons from case studies, it shows that a longer-run perspective on country trajectories can highlight promising policies, including the role that a whole-of-government approach, steady political commitment, domestic resource mobilization, and evidence-based policies can play in human capital progress.

2.1 HUMAN CAPITAL ACCUMULATION OVER THE PAST DECADE

To track progress over the past decade, a version of the HCI has been calculated for 103 economies using component data from or near 2010. Data used to populate the 2010 HCI have been carefully selected to maximize comparability with the 2020 HCI. In particular, only those economies for which learning scores were measured by the same international assessment in 2010 and 2020 enter the comparison (see box 2.1). Requiring test scores from the same testing program proved the main constraint to building large and representative coverage, and the resulting 2010 sample is, unsurprisingly, skewed toward richer economies that tend to have more complete and better-quality data. For example, the sample does not cover South Asia, because none of the seven economies in the region with an HCI in 2020 has learning data for 2010 from the same representative international test assessment as for 2020. The average 2020 HCI is 0.56 for the 174 economies in the overall sample, compared to 0.62 for the 103 economies that are part of the comparison-over-time sample (table 2.1). The potential bias is largest in the East Asia and Pacific region: the average 2020 HCI for the region is 20 percent higher in economies also included in the 2010 HCI compared to the overall 2020 sample (gross domestic product [GDP] per capita is 88 percent higher).

As measured by the HCI, human capital improved in most economies in the last decade. Figure 2.1

Box 2.1: Ensuring comparability across time in the Human Capital Index

The 2020 update of the Human Capital Index (HCI) also reports a version of the HCI calculated for 2010, offering an opportunity to track progress on human capital outcomes. The outcome measures that are used to calculate the HCI typically register only small changes from one year to the next. A time frame of 10 years allows the index to track real underlying change in human capital outcomes over a longer period, smoothing out short-run idiosyncrasies. The HCI for 2010 is calculated for 103 economies for which comparable data are available, and it provides a benchmark year for economies to measure changes over time as well as the pace of their progress.

The data used to populate the 2010 HCI are selected to be "near" 2010 and to maximize comparability with 2020. This comparison is straightforward in the case of child survival rates that are updated annually and adult survival rates that are updated every two years.[a] Although enrollment rates used to calculate the expected years of school are reported annually for some economies, others may have significant gaps in their time series. In the case of gaps in enrollment for 2010, data are imputed using an annualized growth rate derived from available enrollment data for the economy.[b]

In the case of more sporadically reported stunting and test scores data, the surveys and tests used to populate the two time periods are typically selected to be at least five years apart and as close as possible to 2010 and 2020. In the case of test scores, an additional requirement that both data points come from the same testing assessment program ensures comparability over time—with five exceptions to that requirement. For Algeria, harmonized test scores from the Trends in International Mathematics and Science Study (TIMSS) in 2007 are used to populate the 2010 HCI, whereas harmonized test scores based on the Programme for International Student Assessment (PISA) in 2015 are used to populate the 2020 HCI. For North Macedonia and Ukraine, harmonized test scores from TIMSS in 2011 are used to populate the 2010 HCI, whereas harmonized test scores based on PISA in 2018 are used to populate the 2020 HCI. For Morocco and Saudi Arabia an average of test data from the 2011 TIMSS and 2011 Progress in International Reading Literacy Study (PIRLS) are used for the 2010 HCI, and data from the 2018 PISA are used for the 2020 HCI. To maximize comparability with PISA, only secondary-level scores from TIMSS and PIRLS are used to calculate the 2010 harmonized test scores for these five economies.

Finally, although child survival, expected years of school, and harmonized test scores are essential to calculating an HCI, the fraction of children not stunted and the adult survival rate both act as proxies for latent health. Consequently, the HCI can be calculated using either one of these proxies if both are not available.[c] To ensure comparability in HCI scores over time, the same health proxies are used to calculate both the 2010 and 2020 scores. This means that, if data for stunting are unavailable in 2010, they are not used to calculate the HCI for 2020, and vice versa.

[a] Adult survival rates are the complement of mortality rates for 15- through 60-year-olds, reported for five-year periods by the United Nations Population Division. These data are linearly interpolated to produce the annual estimates for economies used to calculate the HCI. See the section on adult survival rates in appendix C for more details.

[b] The methodology to fill in gaps in enrollment data is described in detail in the expected years of school section of appendix C.

[c] See appendix A for a detailed description of how HCI components are aggregated to calculate the final index.

Table 2.1: Regional coverage of the Human Capital Index over-time sample

REGION	ECONOMIES WITH A 2020 HCI			ECONOMIES WITH A 2020 HCI AND A 2010 HCI		
	HCI 2020	Real GDP per capita	Number of economies	HCI 2020	Real GDP per capita	Number of economies
East Asia and Pacific	0.59	23,376	31	0.71	43,977	12
Europe and Central Asia	0.69	35,278	48	0.71	39,479	41
Latin America and the Caribbean	0.56	15,572	26	0.58	18,444	13
Middle East and North Africa	0.57	28,437	18	0.60	34202	14
North America	0.75	55,857	2	0.75	55,857	2
South Asia	0.48	6,605	7	—	—	—
Sub-Saharan Africa	0.40	5,125[a]	42	0.42	6,586	21
Average, total	**0.56**	**21,403[a]**	**174**	**0.62**	**30,243**	**103**

Source: World Bank calculations based on the 2020 update of the Human Capital Index (HCI) for HCI data and the World Development Indicators and Penn World Tables 9.1 for per capita GDP data.

Note: The table uses real GDP per capita at purchasing power parity, in constant 2011 US dollars, for most recently available data as of 2019. — = not available.

[a]Per capita GDP data for South Sudan are not available.

Figure 2.1: Changes in the Human Capital Index, circa 2010 vs. circa 2020

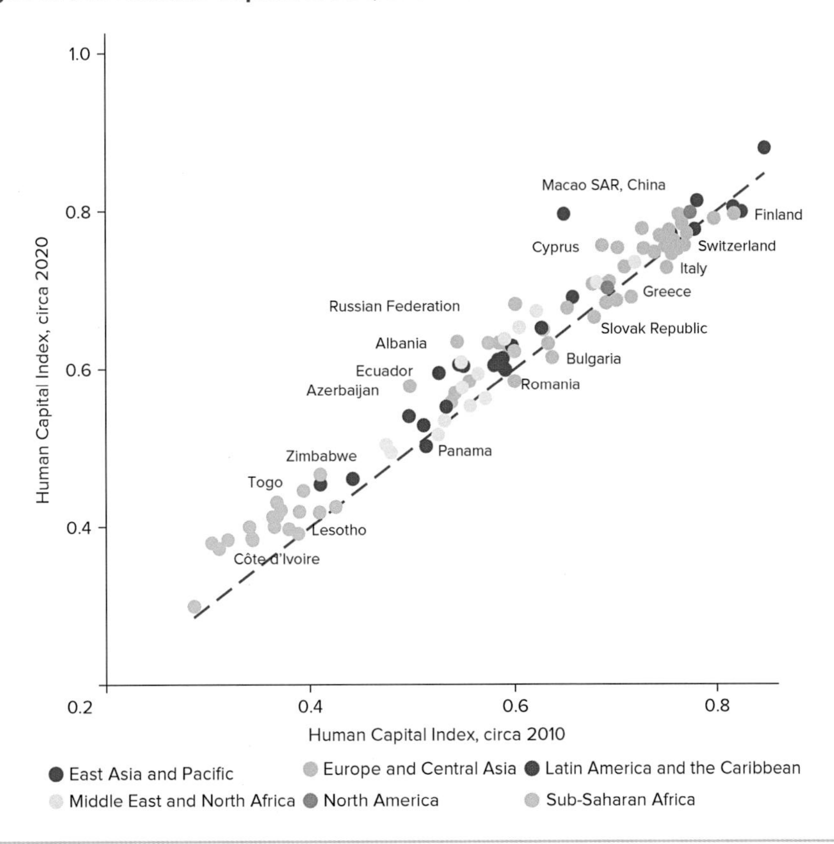

Source: World Bank calculations based on the 2020 update of the Human Capital Index (HCI).

Note: The figure plots the 2020 HCI (on the vertical axis) against the 2010 HCI (on the horizontal axis) for 103 economies for which data are available for both 2010 and 2020. The dashed line is a 45-degree line. Points above (below) represent an increase (decrease) in the HCI between 2010 and 2020.

plots HCI 2020 scores against HCI 2010 scores, likely reflecting underlying secular trends in various dimensions of human capital. On average, the HCI increased by 2.6 HCI points (or 0.026) between 2010 and 2020. For economies in which the HCI scores improved—about 80 percent of the sample, depicted above the 45-degree line in figure 2.1—scores increased by an average of 3.5 HCI points. One economy in four that experienced a rise in the index had increases above 5.0 HCI points. This means that, in those economies, the productivity of future workers approached the frontier by 5 percentage points—a substantial progress. Over time, there is convergence in the HCI. That is, in economies starting at lower values of the HCI in 2010, human capital improved more rapidly than in economies for which the HCI was higher to begin with, even after accounting for initial GDP per capita.[1]

The economies with the largest gains include Macao SAR, China; Albania; the Russian Federation; Azerbaijan; and Côte d'Ivoire, listed in order of the size of their gain. Various factors account for these improvements: improved learning as measured by higher test scores (Albania and Macao SAR, China), better health (in the case of Russia, specifically improvements in adult survival, marking a rebound from the drop in life expectancies in the post-Soviet era; see Smith and Nguyen 2013), and school enrollment (at the preprimary level in Azerbaijan; at the primary level in Côte d'Ivoire and Macao SAR, China; and at the secondary level in Russia).

Some economies experienced modest declines in the index. They include the Republic of Korea, Greece, Bulgaria, and Italy, listed in order of the size of their decline, where the index fell by about 2 or more HCI points. Among the 10 economies with the largest drops, 8 are European, and only 1 is not a high-income economy. These decreases in the HCI can be traced back mainly to drops in test scores.

As incomes increase, on average, human capital improves. Panels a and b of figure 2.2 indicate the direction of change of the HCI from 2010 to 2020, denoted, respectively, by the dots and the arrow points. The slopes of the arrows signal the rate at which rising per capita income is associated with more human capital. The pace is quite uniform across country income groups. In low-income economies, however, human capital improved slightly more quickly relative to GDP per capita. With health accounting for an important share of improvement in the index, especially in low-income economies (see the next section of this chapter), a steeper slope in the HCI–GDP relationship likely reflects global gains in health, such as better and less expensive treatments and improved technology, which benefited all economies but brought about larger advances in poorer ones.

Regional and income group averages mask different individual economy trajectories, which are depicted in figure 2.2, panel c. For example, in Azerbaijan, human capital outcomes increased by 0.08 (from 0.50 to 0.58), but there was almost no change in the country's GDP per capita. By contrast, Lithuania experienced only a small increase in the HCI despite a significant increase in per capita income.

Looking back over the last decade shows that both girls and boys have made strides in improving human capital. Sex-disaggregated data are available for 90 economies in the comparison over time sample (figure 2.3). The average gender ratio is similar in circa 2010 and circa 2020, at about 1.06 in favor of girls. This stable average, however, conceals considerable differences at the economy level. Around 2010, in all but seven economies, the HCI was higher among girls than among boys. Among those seven economies, the girl-to-boy ratio improved in Cameroon, Chad, and Côte d'Ivoire approaching full gender parity in the last decade. These are the countries in the lower left quadrant of figure 2.3, above the 45-degree line

Figure 2.2: Human capital and GDP per capita: Changes over time

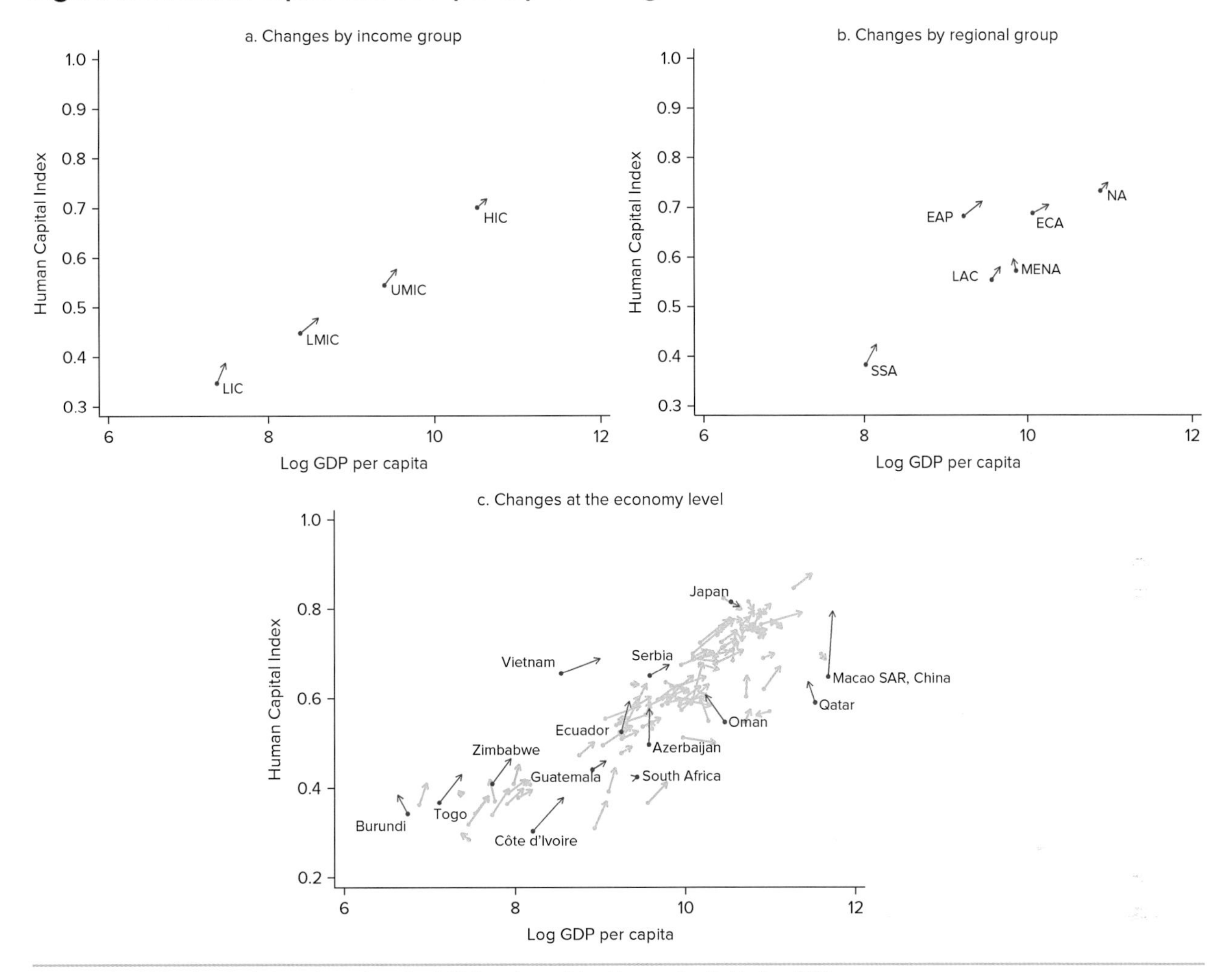

Source: World Bank calculations based on the 2020 update of the Human Capital Index (HCI).

Note: Panel a (panel b) plots the average HCI for income groups (regional groups) using the World Bank Group classification (on the vertical axis) against log real GDP per capita (on the horizontal axis) for 103 economies for which data are available for both 2010 and 2020. The 2010 HCI is denoted by dots, and the HCI 2020 is denoted by arrow points. Panel c plots economy-level data for HCI 2010 and HCI 2020 (on the vertical axis), represented by dots and arrow points, respectively, against log real GDP per capita (on the horizontal axis) for the 103 economies for which data are available for both 2010 and 2020. EAP = East Asia and Pacific; ECA = Europe and Central Asia; HIC = high-income countries; LAC = Latin America and the Caribbean; LIC = low-income countries; LMIC = lower-middle-income countries; MENA = Middle East and North Africa; NA = North America; SSA = Sub-Saharan Africa; UMIC = upper-middle-income countries.

and below the horizontal dashed line. Meanwhile, in Benin, Burkina Faso, and Morocco, girls fully caught up with boys, even surpassing them in the latter two economies.[2] Among the 83 economies in which the HCI was higher for girls in 2010, the ratio in favor of girls widened in 34 economies; however, a favorable girl-to-boy ratio in the HCI does not capture gaps in other areas of human capital development, such as labor force participation. In many countries, women participate in the labor force at far lower rates than men. This point is taken up further in chapter 4, which discusses an extension of the HCI capturing labor market utilization.

Figure 2.3: Girl-to-boy ratio, HCI 2010 vs. HCI 2020

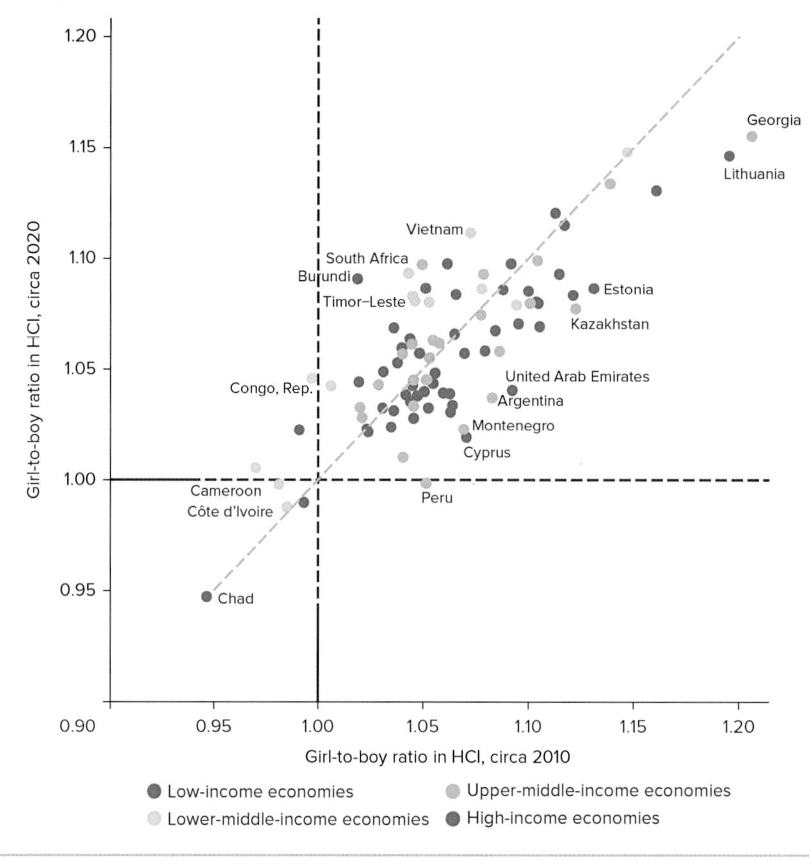

Source: World Bank calculations based on the 2020 update of the Human Capital Index (HCI).

Note: The figure plots the gender ratio (girl to boy) of the 2020 HCI (on the vertical axis) against the 2010 HCI (on the horizontal axis) for 90 economies for which sex-disaggregated data are available for both 2010 and 2020. The light blue dashed line is a 45-degree line; points above (below) represent an increase (decrease) in the HCI gender ratio between 2010 and 2020. The dashed horizontal (vertical) line indicates gender parity in the HCI in 2020 (2010).

2.2 CHANGES IN KEY HUMAN CAPITAL DIMENSIONS OVER THE PAST DECADE

2.2.1 Component contributions to changes in the HCI

The evolution of the HCI reflects changes in the components of the index. There are considerable differences in the pace of change across components and in the extent to which they contribute to changes in the overall HCI. Similar to the analysis for the HCI 2020 cross-section, a decomposition[3] suggests that almost one-third of changes in the HCI over the past decade are due to gains in health, as proxied by reductions in stunting and improvements in adult survival. Considered together, progress in child survival, stunting, and adult survival accounts for close to half the increase in the HCI; the remainder is explained by changes in education—namely, enrollment and, to a limited extent, learning (figure 2.4).

Although economies in every income group experienced an increase in their HCI, the factors that contributed to these improvements differ across income groups, reflecting both economies' initial conditions and their development trajectories. Low-income economies in the sample experienced considerable gains in child survival rates (which, on average, rose from 90.6 percent in 2010 to 93.4 percent in 2020). Low-income economies also registered growth in enrollment rates in preprimary education (from 26.6 to 42.5 percent) and at the primary level (from 82.3 to 89.6 percent). These gains were offset in some economies by declines in measured learning. In high-income economies, which were already closer to the frontier for most components, increases in the HCI are mostly explained by gains in upper-secondary enrollment and improvements in health, as proxied by adult survival (figure 2.5).

Figure 2.4: Component contribution to Human Capital Index gains, 2010–20

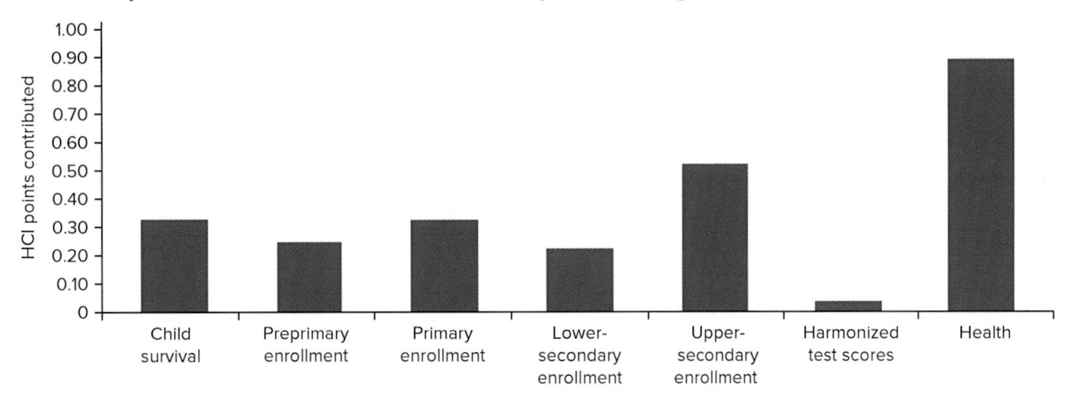

Source: World Bank calculations based on the 2020 update of the Human Capital Index (HCI). Note that 2 HCI points corresponds to 0.02 in the HCI 0-1 scale.

Note: This figure reports a decomposition computed for 103 economies for which data are available for both 2010 and 2020.

Figure 2.5: Contribution to changes in the Human Capital Index, by country income group, 2010–20

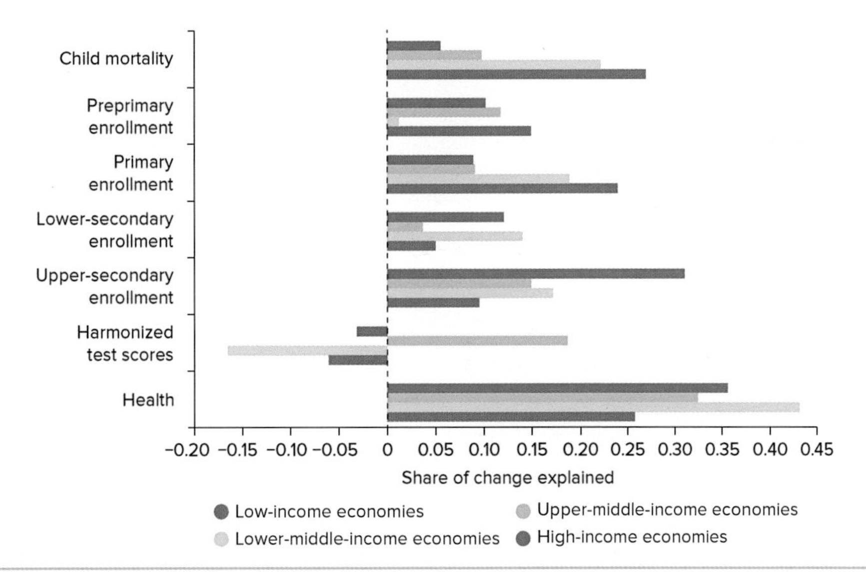

Source: World Bank calculations based on the 2020 update of the Human Capital Index (HCI).

Note: This figure reports a decomposition computed for 103 economies for which data are available for both 2010 and 2020.

2.2.2 Changes in index components over time

The analysis in this subsection considers the evolution of components of the HCI over the last decade. On average, there has been progress on most components of the HCI, as illustrated in table 2.2, which looks at the sample of economies with an index in both 2010 and 2020.

Although the HCI comparison between 2010 and 2020 is possible for only 103 economies, comparisons between these two points in time for individual HCI components are possible for a larger (and variable) number of economies. The following analysis includes all economies for which data are available, in order to provide a comprehensive picture of changes in the different dimensions of human capital. The specific trajectories of individual components are discussed below.

Child survival

Progress in child survival over the past decade has been substantial in many economies, improving in 136 of the 173 economies for which data are available, as depicted in figure 2.6.[4] On average, the child survival rate rose from 0.96 to 0.97, which translates to 10 fewer deaths per 1,000 live births.[5] At an average of 3.6 percentage points, improvements have been most significant among low-income economies, which started out with lower rates. In economies such as Angola, Malawi, Niger, Sierra Leone, and Zimbabwe, improvements in child survival meant between 39 and 58 fewer deaths per 1,000 live births.[6]

This progress is the result of global improvements in health but also of a combination of greater extension of health coverage, better maternal and childcare, and better sanitation. For example, Malawi, where child survival rates increased from 91 to 95 percent in the last decade, adopted several evidence-based policies financed by the government and development partners to improve child health, including the Accelerated Child Survival and Development Strategy, Child Health Strategy, Integrated Management of Childhood Illness, and a road map to accelerate maternal and newborn survival. These policies and interventions have led to improved coverage of essential child health services and practices across the country, including immunizations (at 93 percent in 2014), exclusive breastfeeding (from 44 percent in 2000 to 70 percent in 2014), prevention of mother-to-child HIV transmission, and oral rehydration

Table 2.2: Changes in Human Capital Index components, 2010–20

Component	Global	East Asia and Pacific	Europe and Central Asia	Latin America and the Caribbean	Middle East and North Africa	North America	Sub-Saharan Africa
Child survival rate (percentage point difference)	0.007	0.004	0.002	0.004	0.003	0.001	0.022
Expected years of school (year difference)	0.437	0.651	0.176	0.351	0.458	0.440	0.862
Harmonized test scores (score difference)	−0.110	−3.659	1.002	8.001	0.443	−5.769	−5.106
Fraction of children under 5 not stunted (percentage point difference)	0.056	0.048	0.048	0.051	0.034	—	0.070
Adult survival rate (percentage point difference)	0.030	0.013	0.020	0.013	0.015	0.002	0.082

Source: World Bank calculations based on the 2020 update of the Human Capital Index (HCI).

Note: This table reports changes in regional averages (as defined by the World Bank Group regional classification), computed for 103 economies for which data are available for both 2010 and 2020.

— = not available.

Figure 2.6: Changes in probability of survival to age 5, circa 2010 vs. circa 2020

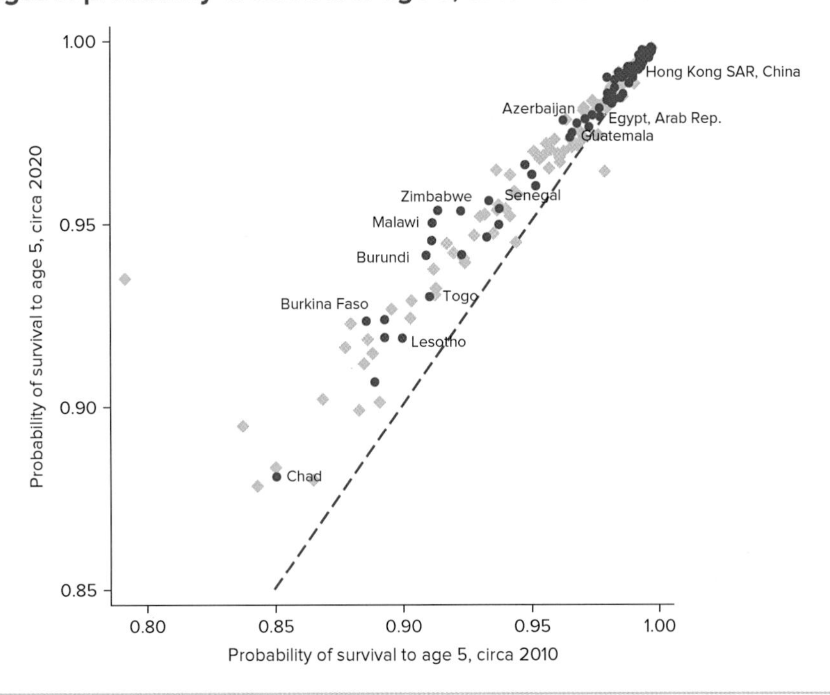

Source: World Bank calculations based on the 2020 update of the Human Capital Index (HCI).

Note: The figure plots the probability of survival to age 5, circa 2020 HCI (on the vertical axis), against the probability of survival to age 5, circa 2010 (on the horizontal axis), for 173 economies for which child survival data are available for both 2010 and 2020. The dashed line is a 45-degree line; points above (below) represent an increase (decrease) in the probability of survival to age 5 between 2010 and 2020. Yellow diamonds in the panels indicate economies for which data are available for both 2010 and 2020, but that are not part of the sample used for the HCI analysis of changes over time because they are missing 2010 comparator data for one of the HCI components. The outlier (yellow diamond at far left) is Haiti, where the probability of survival to age 5 was significantly affected by the 2010 earthquake.

for diarrhea (up from 48 percent in 2000 to 64 percent in 2014), that have in turn contributed to improve child survival rates (CD2015 2015).

Fraction of children under 5 not stunted

Advances in health over time are also reflected in decreases in stunting rates for children under 5, though declines have been modest, on average. The fraction of children under 5 not stunted is available for comparison between 2010 and 2020 for 91 economies, of which 42 are in the 2010–20 HCI comparison sample. Across these economies, depicted in figure 2.7, the fraction of children not stunted increased by about 8 percentage points, on average. The economies with the largest improvements are Côte d'Ivoire (from 61 to 78 percent, an increase of 17 percentage points), Sierra Leone (from 56 to 71 percent, a 15-percentage-point increase), Eswatini (from 60 to 74 percent, a 14-percentage-point increase), and India (from 52 to 65 percent, a 13-percentage-point increase). The fraction of children not stunted declined in only a small group of countries: Angola (with a decline from 71 to 62 percent), Malaysia (from 83 to 79 percent), Niger (from 56 to 52 percent), Papua New Guinea (from 56 to 51 percent), South Africa (from 75 to 73 percent), and Vanuatu (from 74 to 71 percent).

The overall trend in stunting between 2010 and 2020 is consistent with its worldwide decline over the past decades. Progress resulted from a variety of factors—not only from overall economic development but also from health and nutrition

Figure 2.7: Changes in fraction of children under 5 not stunted, circa 2010 vs. circa 2020

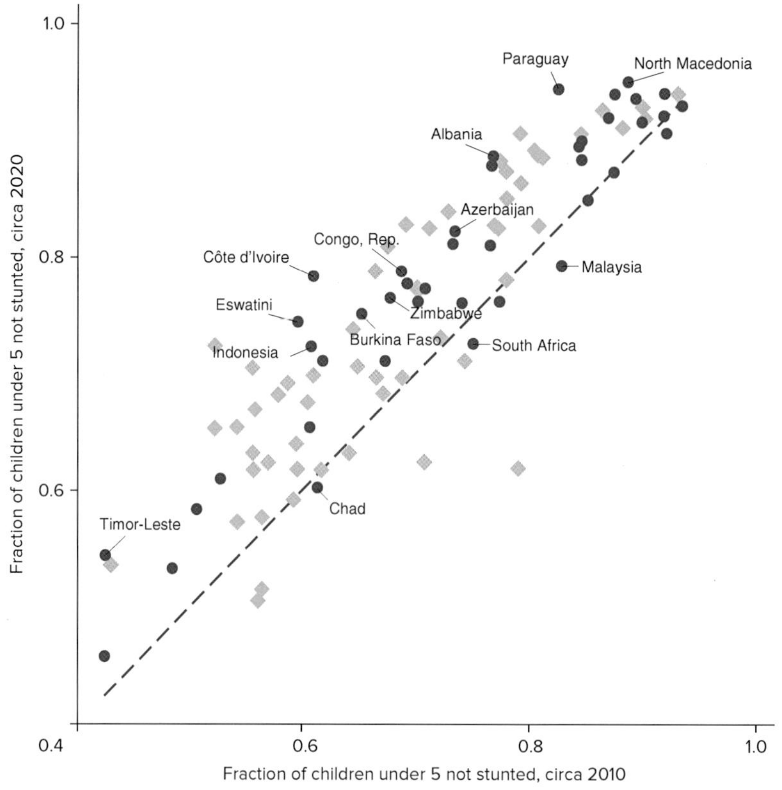

Source: World Bank calculations based on the 2020 update of the Human Capital Index (HCI).

Note: The figure plots the fraction of children under 5 not stunted, circa 2020 HCI (on the vertical axis), against the fraction of children under 5 not stunted, circa 2010 (on the horizontal axis), for 91 economies for which data are available for both 2010 and 2020. The dashed line is a 45-degree line; points above (below) represent an increase (decrease) in the fraction of children under 5 not stunted between 2010 and 2020. Yellow diamonds in the panels indicate economies for which data are available for both 2010 and 2020, but that are not part of the sample used for the analysis of changes over time because they are missing 2010 comparator data for one of the HCI components.

interventions, maternal education and nutrition, maternal and newborn care, reductions in fertility or reduced interpregnancy, and improved sanitation. Given the multiple determinants of stunting, multisectoral solutions are necessary. Some examples are described in box 2.2 (see also Bhutta et al. 2020). Of the economies for which stunting data are available, 25 are classified as fragile and conflict-affected situations (FCS). Although stunting decreased on average in these economies too, improvements in economies in FCS were on the order of 3.6 percentage points; in nonfragile economies they were on the order of 6.1 percentage points.[7]

Adult survival

Adult survival rates have been improving steadily over the last decade. In 2010, 82 percent of 15-year-olds were expected to survive to age 60, compared with 85 percent in 2020. Figure 2.8 illustrates the improvement in adult survival rates over the last 10 years; most economies are above the 45-degree line. Economies with the greatest improvements include Eswatini, where survival rates increased—although from an extremely low base—by close to 25 percentage points from 35 to 60 percent, and Zimbabwe, where rates increased from 47 percent to 65 percent. Although most of the economies with large improvements in adult

Box 2.2: Cross-sectoral interventions to address stunting

Through its effects on health and cognitive development, undernutrition early in life stunts children's development and prevents them from reaching their full potential, in school and during adulthood. According to Bhutta et al. (2020), interventions that target nutrition both from within and outside the health sector—through improvements in maternal education and nutrition, maternal and newborn care, reductions in fertility, or extending interpregnancy intervals—can be effective in reducing stunting in a variety of contexts. The following examples illustrate cross-sectoral engagements designed to accelerate stunting reduction.

Madagascar. With rates as high as 60 percent in some regions, stunting is one of the most serious impediments to Madagascar's socioeconomic development. The World Bank, with cofinancing from The Power of Nutrition, is supporting the government of Madagascar's efforts to reduce stunting through the Multiphase Programmatic Approach to Improve Nutrition Outcomes (World Bank 2018). This intervention aims to reach 75 percent of children in Madagascar over the next 10 years with a high-impact package of services delivered through a strengthened integrated nutrition and health platform. The program evolves on the basis of lessons learned from the field and on scaling up successful and cost-effective interventions. Madagascar's social safety net programs also play an important role in addressing child malnutrition and development. The Fiavota safety net program in the drought-affected areas of Southern Madagascar had positive impacts on acute malnutrition, and the Human Development Cash Transfer program has had positive impacts on food security as well as on young children's socio-cognitive development, including language learning and social skills.

Rwanda. Over the past two decades, Rwanda has registered strong progress on poverty reduction and human development. Its child stunting rate, however, remains high at 38 percent, particularly among poorer and larger households. The government has been taking evidence-based action to combat stunting and invest in child development across multiple sectors. Social protection has been central to this effort, striking at the nexus between poverty, vulnerability, and child malnutrition. Rwanda's flagship social safety net, the Vision 2020 Umurenge program, has received sustained World Bank support over the years, providing over a million poor and vulnerable people with income support and accompanying measures. In recent years, child- and gender-sensitive safety net interventions were introduced in the Vision 2020 Umurenge program and are now being expanded. They include Nutrition-Sensitive Direct Support and a Co-responsibility Cash Transfer, which targets the poorest households with pregnant women, with children under age 2, or with both, incentivizing them to access essential health and nutrition services. Rwanda's game plan also includes strengthening high-impact health and nutrition interventions on the supply side, as well as agriculture interventions that improve food security and increase dietary diversity, and preprimary level education interventions.

Pakistan. Fill the Nutrient Gap, an innovative analysis by the World Food Programme, identifies the bottlenecks that drive malnutrition across the food system, with a special emphasis on the availability, cost, and affordability of a nutritious diet. Using the Cost of the Diet software developed by Save the Children UK, Fill the Nutrient Gap estimates the minimum cost of a nutritious diet using locally available foods. By comparing this cost to household food expenditure data, the proportion of households unable to afford a nutritious diet is estimated. In Punjab, this exercise highlighted that two-thirds of the population could not afford a nutritious diet, with the largest gap for the poorest 20 percent who are also targeted by the Benazir Income Support Program. The government of

(continued next page)

Box 2.2: Cross-sectoral interventions to address stunting *(Continued)*

Pakistan and the World Food Programme jointly evaluated options to complement a cash transfer with nutrition-specific interventions, comparing the impact of market-based interventions with a free provision of Specialized Nutritious Foods (SNF), and SNF provision in combination with a fresh food voucher. Locally produced SNF could be an effective way to reduce the nutrient intake gap caused by nonaffordability (World Food Programme 2017, 2019). For instance, research among pregnant and lactating women and children under 2 by Aga Khan University has found effects on some nutritional indicators. On the basis of this finding, the government of Pakistan, together with development partners, designed a nutrition-sensitive conditional cash transfer program targeting pregnant and lactating women (until 6 months after delivery) and children up to 24 months old. The program included a combination of antenatal care checkups, immunization, growth monitoring and nutrition education, SNF for women and for children, a small cash transfer to encourage the uptake of the services, and a condition of one child per household enrolled at a time to encourage birth spacing. The program will be piloted before a nationwide rollout. The World Bank will support an impact evaluation to determine cost-effectiveness of interventions. Other initiatives are already ongoing, including a nutrition-sensitive conditional cash transfer program supported by the World Bank in the Federal territories, Punjab Province, and the merged districts of Khyber Pakhtunkhwa province, as is increasing multisectoral collaboration between the federal government and provincial governments to improve nutrition in Pakistan.

survival are in Sub-Saharan Africa, survival also improved substantially in three economies in Eastern Europe and Central Asia: Belarus (from 79 to 84 percent), Kazakhstan (from 76 to 84 percent), and Russia (from 75 to 80 percent).

Many factors drive these trends. In Zimbabwe, improvements were fueled by a combination of increased resources allocated to the health sector and a progressive focus on results. This focus included the implementation of results-based financing (RBF) approaches in health centers and district hospitals, increasing from 2 rural districts in 2011 to 18 rural districts in 2013, and eventually reaching 60 districts. The RBF in Zimbabwe initially focused on reproductive, maternal, newborn, and child health indicators and later expanded to include HIV/AIDS, tuberculosis, malaria, and noncommunicable diseases. The early indications of positive performance under RBF, marked by increased coverage and quality of key maternal and child health services (a 13-percentage-point increase in institutional deliveries in RBF-implementation districts, for instance), led to the scale-up of RBF implementation across the country (World Bank 2016). Maternal mortality also saw declines through the improved coverage of maternal health services facilitated by urban and rural voucher schemes providing care to pregnant women (World Bank 2019). Another potential contributing factor is the decrease in HIV/AIDS prevalence and reduction in HIV/AIDS-related mortality due to the improved coverage of antiretroviral treatment.[8]

Eswatini also witnessed some of the largest improvements in adult survival rates during the decade. Still, however, it has the second-lowest adult survival rate among non-FCS economies in the sample, which reflects the high prevalence of HIV/AIDS, the leading cause of deaths in the country (CDC 2019). Eswatini continues to experience the highest rate of HIV/AIDS prevalence globally, affecting 27 percent of 15- to

Figure 2.8: Changes in adult survival rates, circa 2010 vs. circa 2020

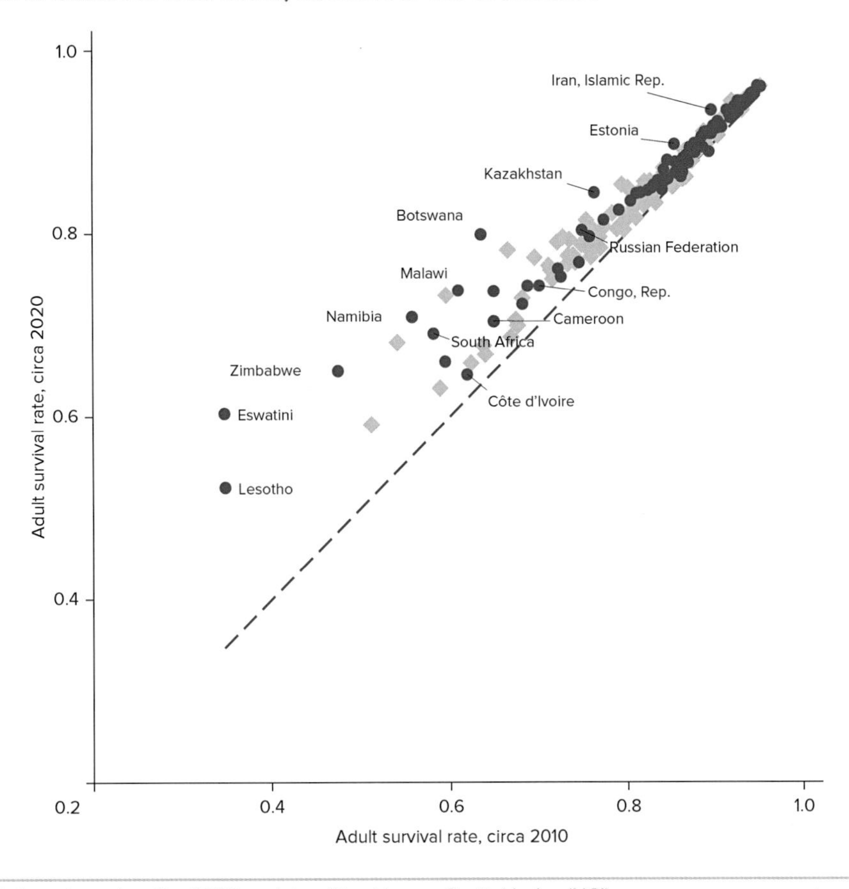

Source: World Bank calculations based on the 2020 update of the Human Capital Index (HCI).

Note: The figure plots adult survival rates circa 2020 HCI (on the vertical axis) against adult survival rates circa 2010 (on the horizontal axis) for 169 economies for which adult survival data are available for both 2010 and 2020. The dashed line is a 45-degree line; points above (below) represent an increase (decrease) in adult survival rates between 2010 and 2020. Yellow diamonds in the panels indicate economies for which data are available for both 2010 and 2020, but that are not part of the sample used for the HCI analysis of changes over time because they are missing 2010 comparator data for one of the HCI components.

49-year-olds.[9] The rate of new infections is also the highest in the world, with young women ages 15–24 years five times more likely to be infected with HIV than their male counterparts.[10] Although the crisis is far from resolved, the country has made enormous progress in reducing the number of AIDS-related deaths, with a 35 percent reduction between 2010 and 2018.[11]

Adult survival rates declined in only a handful of economies, among which Jamaica experienced the largest decline (less than 1 percentage point). The United States, where adult mortality rose from 106 to 110 deaths per 1,000 15-year-olds, is the richest economy among this group. In 2020, the adult survival rate for the United States was significantly below the level that would have been predicted on the basis of income.[12]

Unsurprisingly, child and adult survival improved together, reflecting a broad improvement in the underlying health status of populations.

Expected years of school

Quantity of schooling, as measured by expected years of school (EYS), increased by about a half year of schooling (0.47 years to be precise) over the past decade in the 119 economies for which schooling data are available in 2010 and 2020 (figure 2.9).[13] These gains materialized across all levels of income (figure 2.10). Low-income economies had the largest improvement, 0.90 years, mostly due to higher enrollment rates in preprimary and primary education. In lower-middle-income economies, EYS have risen by an average of 0.81 years, and most of this increase derives from higher enrollment rates in primary and upper-secondary education. Upper-middle- and high-income economies, which had the highest EYS values at the start of the period, experienced the smallest increases since 2010. Among high-income economies, about 50 percent of the rise can be explained by an increase in upper-secondary enrollment; among upper-middle-income economies, the rise stems from preprimary and upper-secondary enrollment.

Economies that have experienced a significant increase in EYS over the past decade include Bangladesh; Burkina Faso; Côte d'Ivoire; Macao SAR, China; and Togo. In Bangladesh, EYS rose from 8.2 years in 2010 to 10.2 years in 2020. Although many elements account for this success, the government's sustained effort to reduce fertility likely provided incentives to invest more in children's schooling. Girls' participation in secondary school was also stimulated by the Bangladesh Female Stipend Program, which has helped the country to achieve one of its Millennium Development Goals, gender parity in education (see Gribble and Voss 2009; Rob et al. 1987).

Of the 103 economies with an HCI in 2010 and 2020, 21 exhibit lower EYS in 2020 than in 2010. Among these 21 economies, the median economy lost 0.09

Figure 2.9: Changes in expected years of school, circa 2010 vs. circa 2020

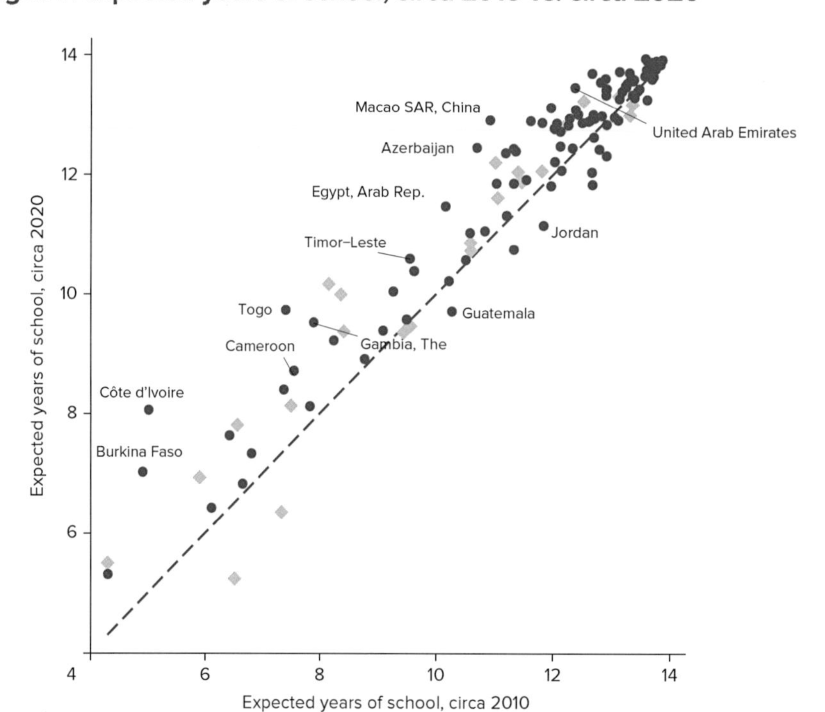

Source: World Bank calculations based on the 2020 update of the Human Capital Index (HCI).

Note: The figure plots expected years of school circa 2020 HCI (on the vertical axis) against expected years of school, circa 2010 (on the horizontal axis) for 119 economies for which enrollment data are available for both 2010 and 2020. The dashed line is a 45-degree line; points above (below) represent an increase (decrease) in expected years of school between 2010 and 2020. Yellow diamonds in the panels indicate economies for which data are available for both 2010 and 2020, but that are not part of the sample used for the analysis of changes over time because they are missing 2010 comparator data for one of the HCI components.

Figure 2.10: Contribution to change in expected years of school, by country income group, 2010–20

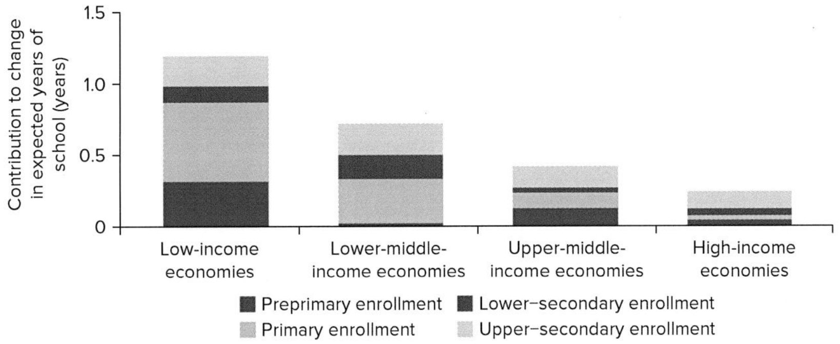

Contribution to change in expected years of school (years)
1.5
1.0
0.5
0
Low-income economies
Lower-middle-income economies
Upper-middle-income economies
High-income economies
Preprimary enrollment
Lower–secondary enrollment
Primary enrollment
Upper–secondary enrollment

Source: World Bank calculations based on the 2020 update of the Human Capital Index (HCI).

Note: Based on 103 economies with an HCI for 2010 and 2020. Results are the outcome of a Shapley decomposition at the economy level and averaged by income group.

years of school. Enrollment rates have declined in some of the richer economies, including Bulgaria, Luxembourg, Italy, Romania, and Ukraine. In Romania, between 2010 and 2020, EYS fell by 0.8 years, largely driven by decreases in primary and upper-secondary enrollment (see box 2.3).

Learning

Progress in learning outcomes as measured by harmonized test scores has been modest over the past decade. Despite challenges in comparing test scores over time (see box 2.4), harmonized test score data from comparable testing programs are available for 103 economies circa 2010 and circa 2020. The average test score from this sample remained virtually unchanged, at 452 (figure 2.11); however, underlying this stable average are substantial improvements and declines in different economies over the past decade. Of these 103 economies, roughly half (49) saw a drop in test scores (appearing below the 45-degree line in figure 2.11), whereas the other half saw small increases. Among economies with improvements in test scores, Ecuador's harmonized test score based on the Latin American Laboratory for Assessment of the Quality of Education (LLECE) test went up by 47 points from 373 to 420, and Cyprus and Qatar recorded gains of about 40 points in harmonized test scores based on Trends in International Mathematics and Science Study (TIMSS)/Progress in International Reading Literacy Study (PIRLS) and Programme for International Student Assessment (PISA) tests, respectively (also see box 2.5 for reforms that vastly improved learning outcomes in the state of Ceará in Brazil). Meanwhile, the Arab Republic of Egypt and Lebanon saw their harmonized test scores based on TIMSS/PIRLS decline by about 40 points (from 399 to 356 and 428 to 390, respectively). In Sub-Saharan Africa, test scores in Cameroon, Chad, and Madagascar dropped significantly between the two rounds of the Program for the Analysis of Education Systems (PASEC).

Albania witnessed one of the largest improvements in learning outcomes, with harmonized test scores increasing from 397 (based on PISA 2009) to 434 (based on PISA 2018). Albania's PISA score improvements coincide with the launch of intensive reform efforts in its education sector. The government launched the National Education Strategy in 2004, which was the first attempt to develop a long-term road map for the sector. The National Education Strategy served as a catalyst for a range of reforms that continued to be implemented through the Pre-University Education Strategy launched in 2014. These reforms include improved teacher recruitment, compensation, and management; a revised curriculum for basic and general

Box 2.3: Why have expected years of school decreased in Romania?

Three main factors explain why the expected years of school (EYS) in Romania have declined in the past decade (from 12.7 to 11.8 years). First, in the wake of the financial crisis of 2008–09, Arts and Crafts Schools, which offered a vocational path as part of upper-secondary education, were closed. Enrollment in these schools dropped without a corresponding rise in enrollment in other types of upper-secondary education. (see figure B2.3.1). Although the resident population of school-age children fell by only 7 percent during the decade, net upper-secondary enrollment rates fell by 10 percent (from 86 percent to 77 percent in 2010–18). In short, the young people who would have enrolled in the vocational schools never enrolled in other schools. In 2015, the three-year vocational path was reintroduced, subsequently helping the system to recover.

Second, the number of out-of-school children, including those children of primary school age, has continued to increase during the past decade. Specifically, the number of out-of-school children ages 6–10 more than doubled between 2009 and 2018, from 43,000 to 98,000. The underlying reasons include persistent underfunding of the sector. Government spending on preprimary and primary education is the lowest among European Union countries (see figure B2.3.2). Moreover, Romania still lacks an early warning system to alert authorities about children who are at risk of dropping out. With the help of the European Commission and the World Bank, work is under way to implement such a system (European Commission and World Bank 2018).

Figure B2.3.1: Dynamics in enrollment numbers in upper-secondary education, Romania (index, 2009 = 100)

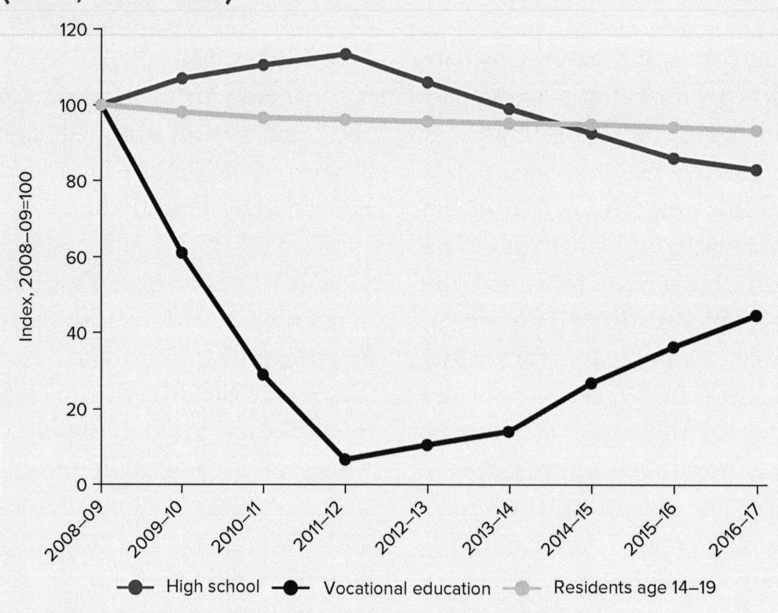

Source: National Institute of Statistics, Romania 2018.

(continued next page)

Box 2.3: Why have expected years of school decreased in Romania? *(Continued)*

Third, in 2012, the government introduced an additional compulsory year of "preparatory" schooling for children reaching the age of 6 before the beginning of the school year (Romanian National Education Law No. 1/2011, article 29, paragraph 2). In 2018, six years after the implementation of the new law, some parents were still postponing enrolling their young children in the preparatory school year. These children also added to the count of out-of-school children in Romania.

Figure B2.3.2: Spending on preprimary and primary education, European Union

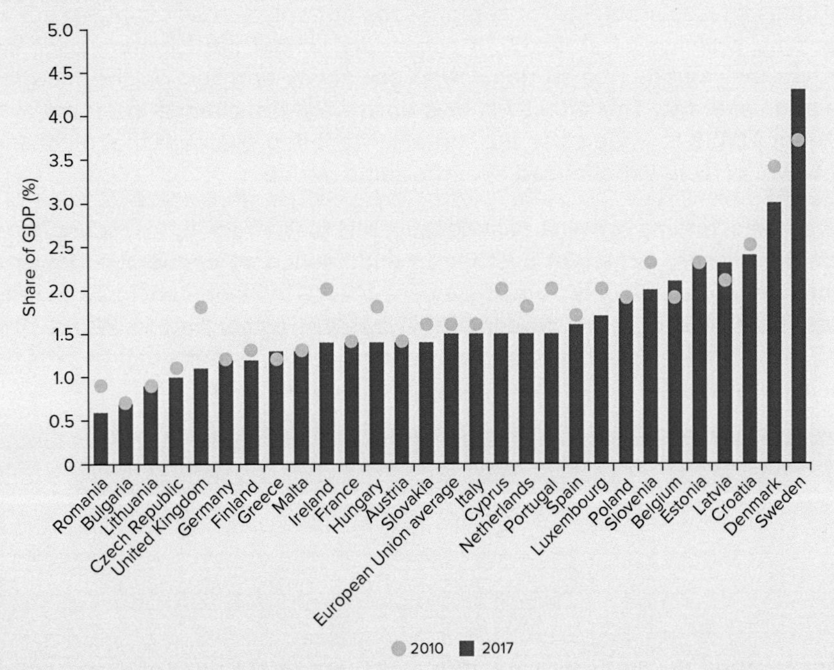

Source of figure: "General Government Expenditure by Function," https://ec.europa.eu/eurostat/data/database.

Source: Contributed by Alina Sava and Lars Sondergaard.

upper-secondary education focused on competencies; enhanced transparency and accountability through reform of the Matura (grade 12 exam), the national student assessment; reduced price and improved textbook quality through a reformed procurement process; provision of textbook subsidies to the poorest households; a stronger focus on inclusive education; and expansion of enrollment in preprimary and upper-secondary education (Ministry of Education and Science, Republic of Albania 2005).

A question that is often part of policy discussions is whether improvements in school access are associated with drops in learning. This sample shows no clear correlation between changes in years of education and test scores; however, changes in learning and in years of education appear to be positively

Box 2.4: Challenges in test score comparison over time

Using the Programme for International Student Assessment (PISA) or the Trends in International Mathematics and Science Study (TIMSS) to compare performance of secondary school students at two points in time may be more complicated in a middle- or low-income economy than in a high-income economy. In settings where secondary school completion is far from universal, selection bias can affect the results, because assessments like PISA and TIMSS test only enrolled students. Youth who are still enrolled in school at age 15 (PISA) or in grade 8 (TIMSS) are generally those from better-off, better-educated households or who have higher ability—which is likely to bias test scores upward (Hanushek and Woessmann 2011). This bias causes problems for comparisons not only across countries but also potentially over time (Glewwe et al. 2017). If secondary school participation rises significantly between two test rounds, the students who are newly enrolled on the margin will likely score lower on average. This effect will bias downward the change in scores, which would cause PISA or TIMSS to understate the actual system improvement that a constant sample of students would have experienced over the same period.

For the average economy over the past decade, this bias affecting test score improvements was probably not very large. On average in middle-income economies, lower-secondary completion rates increased only from 76 percent in 2010 to 79 percent in 2018; in low-income economies, they rose from 36 percent to 41 percent (according to World Development Indicators). Nevertheless, the bias could matter over longer periods of time or for economies that have increased secondary school participation more rapidly.

Source: Contributed by Halsey Rogers.

correlated in upper-middle- and high-income economies and (albeit very weakly) negatively correlated in lower-middle- and lower-income economies.[14] Although this evidence is suggestive at best, it points to the need to understand more clearly how education systems can be strengthened in poorer countries to achieve high-quality learning while they expand access.

2.2.3 Dimensions of human capital and economic development

Much like the overall HCI, changes in individual measures of human capital do not happen in a vacuum and are correlated with changes in income. Using a similar visualization as in the previous section (see figure 2.2), figure 2.12 illustrates the average improvements in the index components as per capita income rises. For example, in panel a, child survival rates are plotted against log real GDP per capita. A line connects the solid dots indicating the country-group average in 2010 to the arrow points indicating the average in 2020. The lines all slope upward, reflecting the pattern of improved child survival globally. The lines also become shorter as they approach the top of the panel, because there is less room for improvement. The gradient of the lines is also of interest, reflecting the rate at which outcomes improved with changes in per capita GDP. The steep lines, such as those for low-income economies and Sub-Saharan Africa, showcase large increases in child survival rates despite relatively small gains in per capita GDP. This pattern is likely a reflection of improvements in global health, such as better and

Figure 2.11: Changes in harmonized test scores, circa 2010 vs. circa 2020

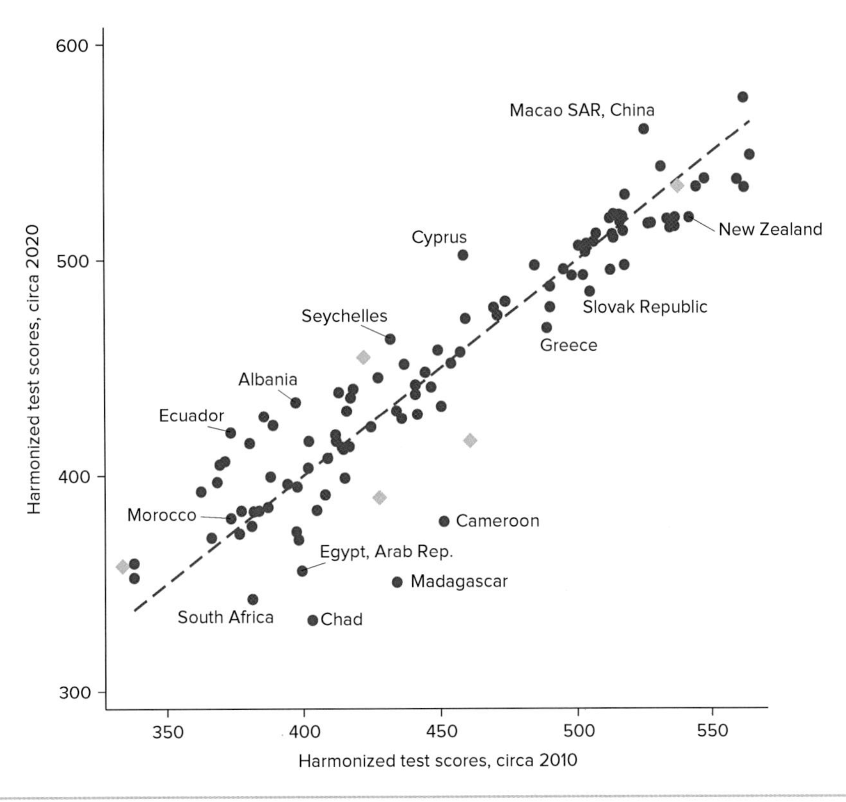

Source: World Bank calculations based on the 2020 update of the Human Capital Index (HCI).

Note: The figure plots harmonized test scores circa 2020 HCI (on the vertical axis) against harmonized test scores circa 2010 (on the horizontal axis) for 103 economies for which harmonized test score data are available for both 2010 and 2020. The dashed line is a 45-degree line; points above (below) represent an increase (decrease) in harmonized test scores between 2010 and 2020. Yellow diamonds indicate economies for which data are available for both 2010 and 2020, but that are not part of the sample used for the HCI analysis of changes over time because they are missing 2010 comparator data for one of the HCI components.

Box 2.5: Transforming a low-performing education system into the best school network in Brazil

Ceará is a northeastern state in Brazil that improved its education outcomes much faster than the rest of Brazil, in just over a decade. Home to 9 million people (4 percent of the population of Brazil) and with the fifth-lowest gross domestic product per capita in the country, almost all of Ceará's 184 municipalities had low levels of quality in teaching and had very limited resources, spending about one-third less in per-student education than wealthier Brazilian states such as São Paulo.

Among these municipalities is Sobral (with 200,000 inhabitants), which in the late 1990s suffered from a highly fragmented school system, with many poorly maintained small schools, most in rural areas and with multigrade classes. Despite a reorganization of the school network, a 2005 diagnostic found that 40 percent of grade 3 children were not able to read; 32 and

(continued next page)

Box 2.5: Transforming a low-performing education system into Brazil's best school network *(Continued)*

74 percent of students in primary and lower-secondary schools, respectively, were over grade-appropriate ages; and 21 percent of lower-secondary school students dropped out. Between 2005 and 2015, Sobral managed to achieve remarkable progress in educational outcomes. In 2005, Sobral ranked 1,366th in education among Brazilian municipalities.[a] A decade later, it ranked first among 5,570 municipalities in the country in both primary and lower-secondary education, achieving learning outcomes comparable to world-class education systems as measured by the Programme for International Student Assessment (PISA). Today, although its per capita gross domestic product amounts to little over half the national average,[b] Ceará has the lowest rate of learning poverty in Brazil, and Sobral has some of the country's best primary schools. Education outcomes in both the region and the municipality exceed all expectations, given the socioeconomic context in which students live and learn: Sobral's student-to-teacher ratio is relatively high, at 28.9, compared with 21.0 in Ceará and 20.3 on average in Brazil as a whole. These points suggest a high efficiency of the education system.

Ceará's approach was driven by a mix of the following elements, whose effectiveness is supported by international evidence: the provision of fiscal and nonmonetary incentives for municipalities to achieve education outcomes; technical assistance to municipal school networks to enhance teacher effectiveness and achieve age-appropriate learning; the regular use of a robust monitoring and evaluation system, followed by adequate action; and giving municipalities autonomy and accountability to achieve learning. In Ceará, unlike the rest of Brazil, municipalities are responsible for the entirety of the education provided, from preprimary to lower-secondary school (Loureiro, di Gropello, and Arias 2020).

A key factor enabling Ceará to emerge as one of Brazil's top performers in education has been the capacity of state political leaders to insulate education from partisan politics. This has contributed to strong, sustained political leadership committed to improving the quality of education. Sobral organized its education policy under four pillars: continuous use of student assessments, a focused curriculum with a clear learning sequence and prioritization of foundational skills, a pool of well-prepared and motivated teachers, and a system of autonomous and accountable school management with school principals appointed through a meritocratic technical selection process (Loureiro, di Gropello, and Arias 2020). The municipality's goal was to achieve the universal completion of lower-secondary education at the right age with appropriate learning. The results obtained show the effectiveness of goal setting and the importance of political leadership for education outcomes.

The COVID-19 (coronavirus) pandemic threatens the progress made by Ceará. A recent study shows that two to three weeks of school closures in São Paulo during the previous H1N1 (novel influenza A virus) pandemic resulted in an estimated two months in learning loss. Using this as a proxy for the COVID-19 pandemic, the paper concludes that an estimated two to three months' school closure could induce a learning loss equivalent to a half-semester of a school year in Brazil (World Bank 2020). Ceará's progress and the pillars that led it there, however, should help the region tackle the tough job that lies ahead once the pandemic subsides.

Source: Based on Cruz and Loureiro 2020; World Bank 2020.

[a] According to Brazil's Basic Education Development Index, IDEB.

[b] Ceará's per capita gross domestic product was $8,068 in 2019, compared with $10,666 in Sobral and $15,662 in Brazil (all in purchasing power parity US dollars).

Figure 2.12: Changes in income and Human Capital Index components, 2010–20

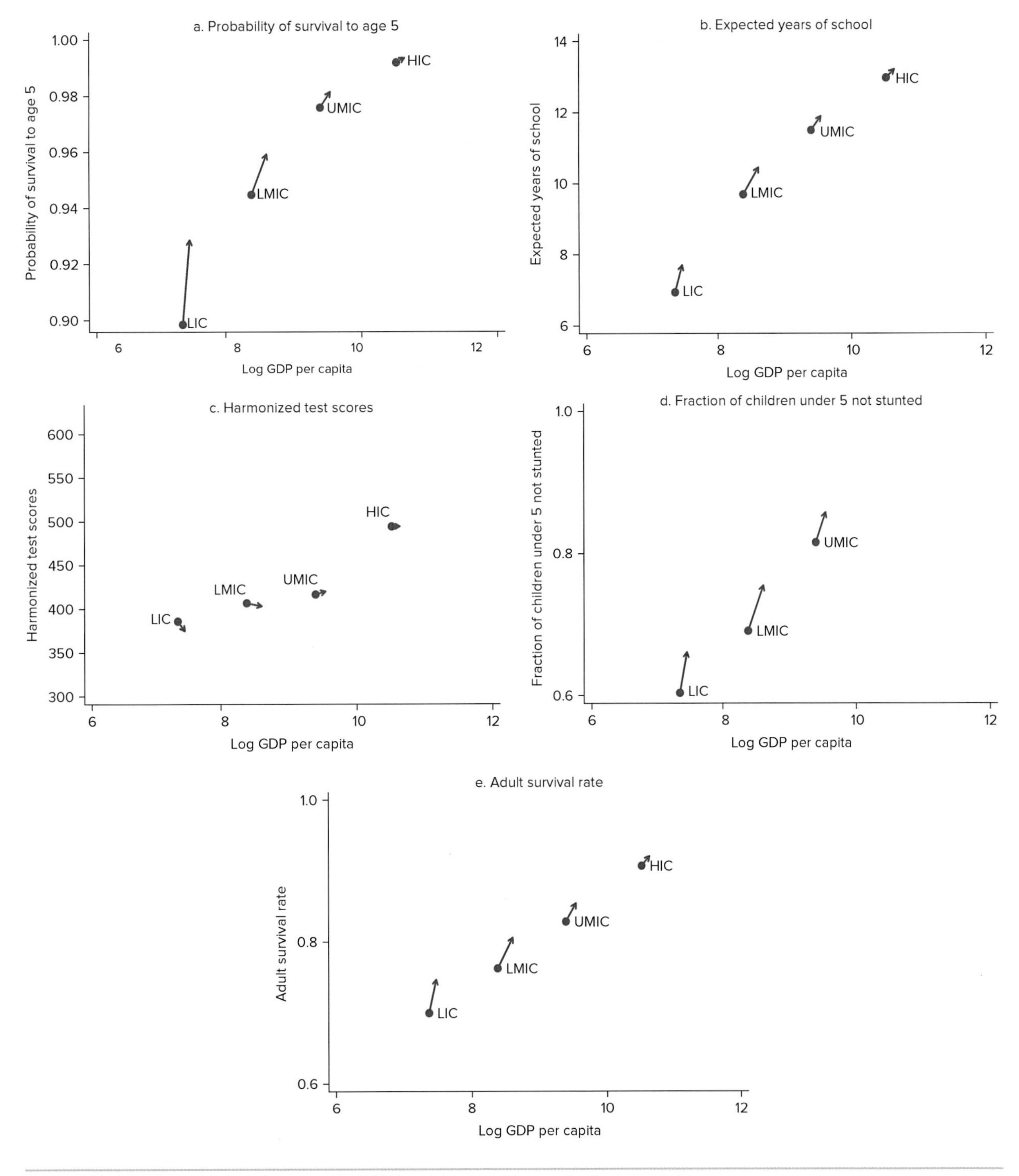

Source: World Bank calculations based on the 2020 update of the Human Capital Index (HCI).

Note: Each panel plots the component average for income groups using the World Bank Group classification (on the vertical axis) against log real GDP per capita (on the horizontal axis) for economies for which data are available for both 2010 and 2020. The 2010 HCI is denoted by dots and the HCI 2020 is denoted by an arrow point. Panel a shows income group averages for the probability of survival to age 5 for 173 economies for which data were available. Panel b shows income group averages for expected years of school for 119 economies for which data were available. Panel c shows income group averages for harmonized test scores for 103 economies for which data were available. Panel d shows income group averages for the fraction of children under 5 not stunted for 91 economies for which data were available. Panel e shows income group averages for adult survival rates for 169 economies for which data were available. HIC = high-income countries; LIC = low-income countries; LMIC = lower-middle-income countries; UMIC = upper-middle-income countries.

cheaper technologies.[15] Conversely, flatter slopes in high-income economies, Europe and Central Asia, and North America suggest smaller gains in the outcome relative to increases in per capita GDP. The lines are also shorter, because these countries were already near full child survival in 2010.

The patterns are similar (upward sloping with decreasing slopes as income increases) for adult survival and the absence of stunting across these income groups, though adult survival and child survival rates share the feature of steeper improvements at low income levels. Learning in low-income economies dropped marginally with respect to relatively small increases in GDP. It stayed virtually unchanged for middle- and high-income economies.

Reconstructing this picture at the economy level in figure 2.13 reveals significant heterogeneity, including dramatic improvements in outcomes despite little improvement in income (this is the case, for example, of survival in Eswatini). No economy, however, showed large GDP improvement without at least some improvement in some human capital dimension.

2.2.4 Socioeconomic differences and progress in human capital

Regional and national averages provide important insights into development trajectories over time. They also, however, mask the differential trends in human capital across socioeconomic groups within economies, particularly between richer and poorer households. The HCI relies on component data from administrative sources that cannot readily be disaggregated by socioeconomic status. Survey data—particularly from Demographic and Health Surveys and Multiple Indicator Cluster Surveys—also measure child survival rates, enrollment rates, and stunting rates disaggregated by quintiles of socioeconomic status. Although these survey estimates are not always directly comparable with administrative data, they can provide insights into the rates of change in outcomes for the richest and poorest households within economies.

This subsection discusses child survival, enrollment, and fraction of children not stunted disaggregated by socioeconomic status, using data from Demographic and Health Surveys and Multiple Indicator Cluster Surveys for selected economies with large changes in outcomes in the HCI dataset.[16] Because these surveys are fielded predominantly in low- and lower-middle-income economies, the examples come from these economies. Figure 2.14 reports human capital outcomes over time, disaggregated by socioeconomic status against log GDP per capita. Panel a shows child survival rates, panel b shows EYS, and panel c shows the fraction of children under 5 not stunted. Each panel depicts the average outcomes for each economy over time, the outcomes for the richest quintile, and the rates in the poorest quintile.

In the case of child survival, Haiti made massive strides between 2000 and 2012, increasing survival rates from 86 to 91 percent. Between 2000 and 2015, survival rates in Malawi rose from 80 to 93 percent. In Senegal, rates increased from 87 to 94 percent between 2005 and 2015. Although each country showed declines in child mortality, the composition of these changes was quite different. In Malawi and Senegal, the length of the bars, that is, the gap between rich and poor households, shortened over time because the increase in the average child survival rate was driven by improvements in outcomes among the poorest households. In Haiti, average rates improved, but the size of the gap between the rich and poor remained virtually constant.[17]

Trends in EYS show similar variation.[18] Burkina Faso raised the EYS by two years, but the gap between rich and poor households was maintained at six years. In contrast, Bangladesh increased the average EYS and also cut the gap between the richest and poorest households in half, from four to two years, between 2004 and 2016. Azerbaijan improved the EYS by one year, but the gap between rich and poor households rose from 0.5 years to 1.0 year. Box 2.6 offers an example from

Figure 2.13: Changes in Human Capital Index components and per capita income, circa 2010 vs. circa 2020, cross-country trajectories

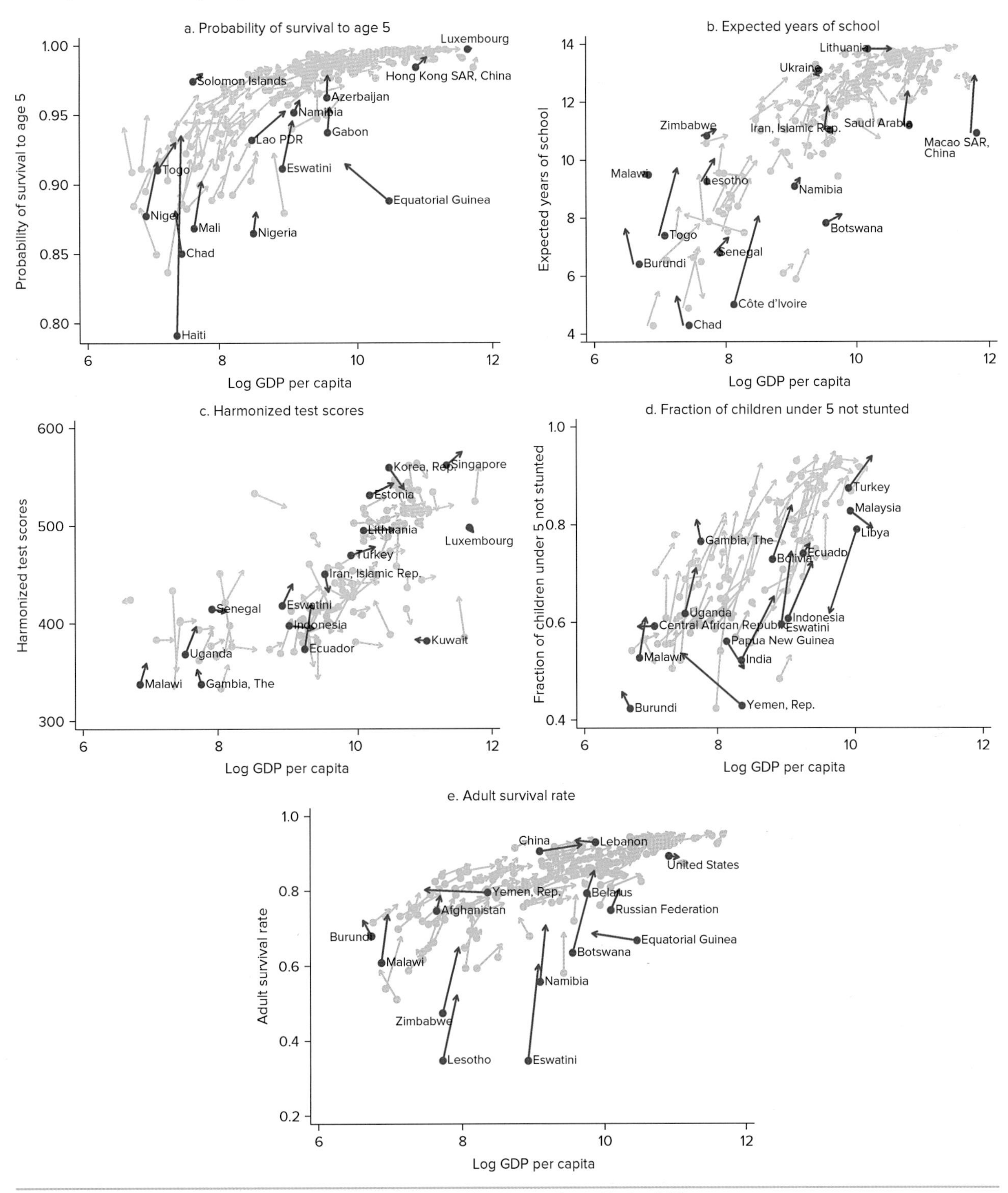

Source: World Bank calculations based on the 2020 update of the Human Capital Index (HCI).

Note: Each panel plots the economy-level averages for each component (on the vertical axis) against log real GDP per capita (on the horizontal axis) for economies for which data are available for both 2010 and 2020. The 2010 HCI is denoted by dots and the HCI 2020 is denoted by an arrow point. Panel a shows the probability of survival to age 5 for 173 economies for which data were available. Panel b shows expected years of school for 119 economies for which data were available. Panel c shows harmonized test scores for 103 economies for which data were available. Panel d shows the fraction of children under 5 not stunted for 91 economies for which data were available. Panel e shows adult survival rates for 169 economies for which data were available.

Sierra Leone of how a well-designed intervention can contribute to improve education outcomes for the most disadvantaged.

The fraction of children under 5 not stunted also increased in most countries in the last decade, as in the cases of Côte d'Ivoire, the Republic of Congo, and Uganda. In Côte d'Ivoire, the average fraction of children not stunted increased from 72 percent to 80 percent between 2011 and 2016, but the 25-percentage-point gap between rates for rich and poor households remained unchanged.

Figure 2.14: Evolution of Human Capital Index components, disaggregated by socioeconomic status

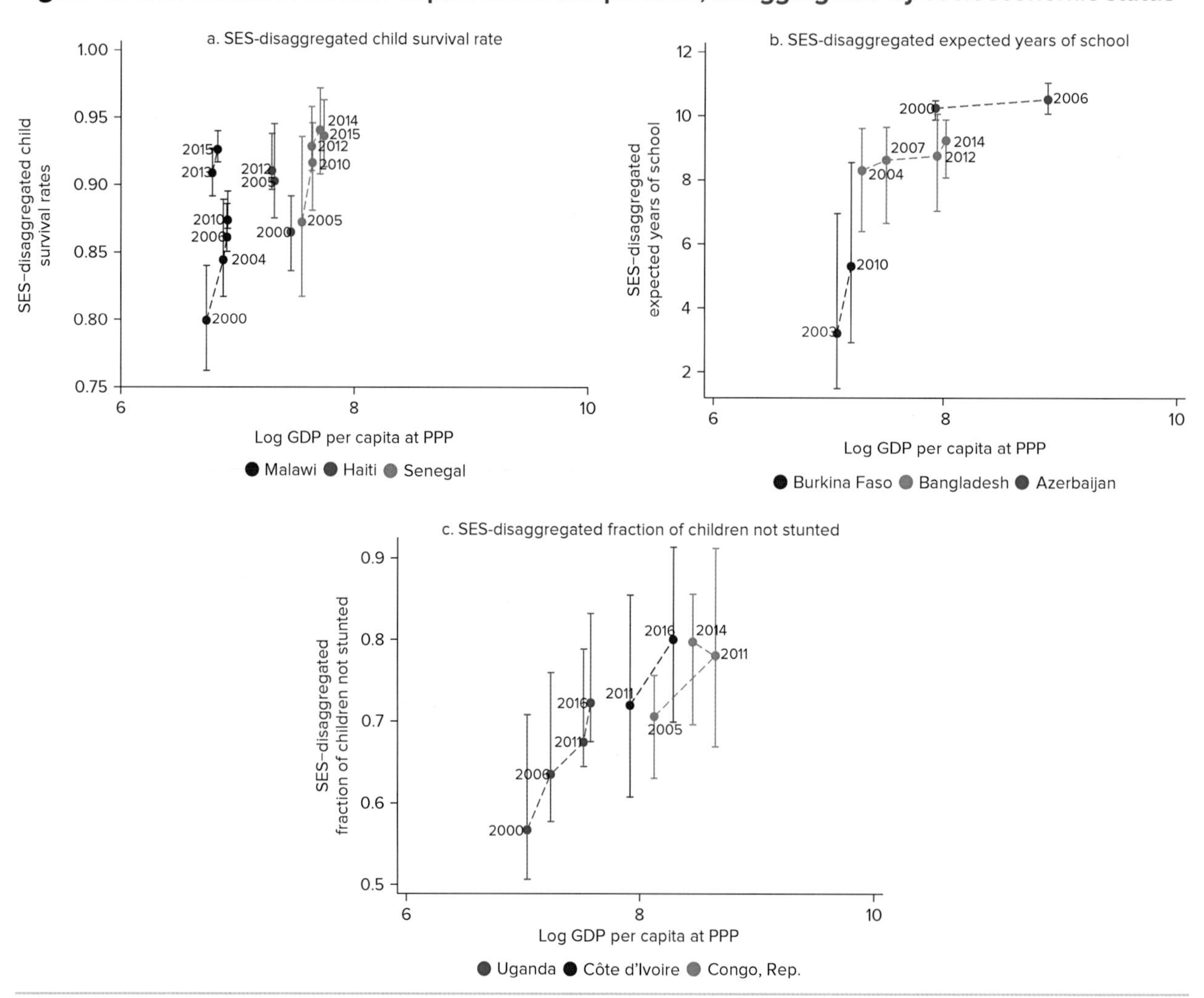

Source: World Bank calculations based on Demographic and Health Survey/Multiple Indicator Cluster Survey data as reported in Wagstaff et al. 2019 (for child survival rates and fraction of children under 5 not stunted) and Filmer and Pritchett 1998 and subsequent updates (for expected years of school).

Note: The figure plots selected Human Capital Index components disaggregated by quintile of socioeconomic status (vertical axis) against log real GDP per capita (horizontal axis). The solid dot indicates the average across quintiles, and the top (bottom) end of the vertical bar indicates the value for the top (bottom) quintile. Colored bars show the spread of components over time. Panel a shows SES-disaggregated child survival rates for Haiti, Malawi, and Senegal. Panel b shows SES-disaggregated expected years of school for Azerbaijan, Bangladesh, and Burkina Faso. Panel c shows SES-disaggregated fraction of children under 5 not stunted for Côte d'Ivoire, the Republic of Congo, and Uganda. PPP = purchasing power parity; SES = socioeconomic status.

Box 2.6: The immediate effects of providing free education in Sierra Leone

Although most children in Sierra Leone start school, few successfully complete their secondary education. As a result, Sierra Leone's learning outcomes are among the lowest in the world, contributing to a significant human capital gap. The reason most often cited for why children drop out of school is not poor quality, however, but cost. Although out-of-pocket expenditures on education are fairly low, both in absolute terms and as a percent of household expenditure (about 3 percent across income groups), they can still represent a significant barrier for poor families, especially given that school fees are due in September, at the height of the lean season.

The government's flagship program is the Free Quality School Education (FQSE) program, which was launched in September 2018. It provides selected public schools with block grants (calculated on a per-pupil basis) and school materials, such as textbooks, and it mandates that recipient schools not charge fees. The program seeks to reduce out-of-pocket household spending on education (the "free" component in the program's name) by eliminating or at least reducing school fees. It also seeks to raise the quality of education (the "quality" component) through the provision of textbooks and other measures. Public messaging around the program has also emphasized the importance of enrolling children in school.

Data collected in February and March 2019 allow for an assessment of the effects of free schooling on out-of-pocket household expenditures and enrollment in the first term of the program, because over 4,000 households that had been interviewed for the 2018 Sierra Leone Integrated Household Survey were reinterviewed then. For each child, the specific school attended for the 2017–18 and 2018–19 school years was recorded and linked to the Annual School Census to determine whether the school benefited from the FQSE program in the first term of 2018–19.

The main impact of the FQSE program in the first term appears to have been a substantial reduction in out-of-pocket education expenditures by households. Over 90 percent of students at public primary and secondary schools receiving the block grants report that they do not pay school fees, up from about one-third of primary school students and almost no secondary school students in the prior school year. In addition, about two-thirds of students at public schools not yet supported under the program also report that they do not pay school fees. The financial benefits of the program are shared fairly evenly across the welfare distribution, although the poorest 20 percent of households receive the largest benefit as a percentage of total consumption.

Administrative data show a large increase in the number of students, but data collected from households reveal no significant change in net or gross enrollment rates. This discrepancy is not unexpected: a young and growing population like Sierra Leone's will naturally see an increase in the number of school-age students each year, and the way the program is structured gives schools an incentive to maximize their reported enrollment. Increases in secondary school enrollment can only come over time as more students successfully reach this level. There has been a small rise in the percent of 5- to 7-year-olds who start school for the first time; this increase is concentrated among the poorest households.

Although the FQSE project has reduced out-of-pocket expenditures, the most keenly felt barrier to education for households, follow-up research will be needed to see whether such reductions will eventually result in higher enrollment rates at the secondary level and higher levels of secondary school completion, and whether the program will be successful in improving the quality of education these students receive.

Source: Contributed by Alejandro de la Fuente based on de la Fuente, Foster, and Jacoby (forthcoming).

By contrast, Uganda reduced stunting while also modestly closing the rich–poor gap, which narrowed from a difference of 20 to 16 percentage points between 2000 and 2016. In the Republic of Congo, the rich–poor gap initially increased, with the fraction of children not stunted increasing from 71 percent to 78 percent between 2005 and 2011. The country was able to maintain momentum, however, in reducing stunting while also reducing the difference between rich and poor households from 24 to 16 percentage points between 2011 and 2014.

This analysis highlights that countries vary significantly in the extent to which gains in human capital outcomes are distributed across the population. Addressing these rich–poor gaps in human capital must remain a priority for governments because, in many cases, the returns to investment in the human capital of disadvantaged groups, especially early in life, are the highest. Related evidence, however, shows that, among low- and middle-income economies, government redistributive policies do, on average, as good a job of reducing human capital inequality as does increased national income (D'Souza, Gatti, and Kraay 2019). At the same time, the experiences of countries like Bangladesh, Senegal, and Uganda show that countries can sometimes decouple children's human capital outcomes from the income differences among their households.

The following section takes an in-depth look at the experiences of a selected set of economies to understand how concerted government action can deliver marked improvements in national outcomes linked to human capital over time and also reduce rich–poor gaps within countries to achieve greater equity.

2.3 A LONGER-RUN VIEW OF COUNTRY PROGRESS

Human capital is a central driver of sustainable growth and poverty reduction.[19] Even for governments that recognize the importance of investing in the human capital of their citizens, however, the process of designing policy and building institutions that foster human capital accumulation can be complex, with the benefits taking years and even decades to materialize. This is evident in, among others, the relatively modest average progress in human capital in the past decade, as measured by the HCI.

A comprehensive understanding of how countries can improve their human capital outcomes requires an analysis that adopts a longer time frame and identifies the many aspects of government intervention that can lead to positive change. By allowing a richer appreciation of countries' development trajectories, identifying the policies and institutions that proved critical to improving outcomes, and documenting the challenges involved in maintaining momentum, a comparative case study approach offers this depth of information.

This section presents the experiences of four countries that have made notable improvements in their key human capital indicators over roughly the last decade: Ghana, Morocco, the Philippines, and Singapore. The case studies illustrate how policies, programs, and processes that the governments of these countries adopted improved human capital outcomes, documenting three interrelated aspects of the countries' trajectories: continuity—sustaining effort over many political cycles; coordination—ensuring that programs and agencies work together; and evidence—building an evidence base to improve and update human capital strategies.[20]

The four countries featured in this section were selected because they have all prioritized investments in key dimensions of human capital in recent years. They vary considerably, however, in their levels of development, their choice of policies and programs to develop human capital, and the outcomes they achieved.

With a score of 0.88, the Southeast Asian island state of Singapore is one of the top performers on the HCI. It has a population of 5.7 million and a per capita GDP at 2011 purchasing power parity (PPP) of US$96,477,[21] making it the richest of the four countries studied here. Singapore has built a world-class education system with an increasing emphasis on analytical skills, teamwork, and creativity. The success of these efforts is evident in the increase of mean years of schooling from 4.7 in 1980 to over 11.2 in 2019.[22] In the health sector, Singapore's life expectancy at birth increased from 67 years in 1965 to 83 years in 2017, and infant mortality has been on a downward slope, from 27 deaths per 1,000 live births in 1965 to 2 per 1,000 in 2017.[23] Despite this enviable position, the country's prime minister has stated that "the job is never done," identifying healthy longevity and early childhood education as areas for improvement (The Straits Times 2020).

The Philippines, with a population of 104.9 million, is the eighth most populous country in Asia (and the most populous country included in this analysis) and has a per capita GDP at 2011 PPP of US$8,123. The country's HCI score of 0.52 means that children born in the country today will only achieve half their potential. The importance that governments in the 1970s accorded to mass education in the country jump-started an expansion in school enrollment, with primary gross enrollment rates at about 100 percent and rates nearing 90 percent at the secondary level in 2017.[24] Although access has increased, quality remains an issue, with 15-year-old Philippine students scoring lower than students in nearly all other participating economies in the latest round of PISA in 2018.

Morocco, located in the Maghreb region of Africa, has a population of 35.7 million and a per capita GDP at 2011 PPP of US$7,641. The country's commitment to human capital development has led to remarkable gains in the health of its citizens. The government has launched efforts to combat child and maternal mortality while controlling fertility rates through intensive, sustained family planning programs. A diligent immunization policy has meant that 91 percent of Moroccan children are now fully immunized.[25] These efforts have improved human capital outcomes for the country, reflected in an HCI score that increased from 0.45 in 2010 to 0.50 in 2020.[26]

Finally, Ghana in West Africa has a population of 28.8 million and a per capita GDP of US$5,194 at 2011 PPP, making it the country with the lowest income in this sample. Despite limited fiscal space, Ghana's commitment to improving human capital and its innovative policies have led to marked improvements in the outcomes of its citizens. Since the government introduced education reforms after a major national economic crisis in 1983, primary enrollment rates have increased substantially, for example, from 67 percent to 95 percent between 2000 and 2017. Increasing school enrollments and increased access to education have led to an influx of students who are more likely to come from disadvantaged families. Despite this influx, Ghana's harmonized test scores have not declined. Stunting in children under the age of 5 has fallen significantly, from 22.7 percent in 2011 to 17.5 percent in 2017 (UNICEF, WHO, and World Bank Group 2020).

The trajectories of policies in these countries indicate a strong focus on continuity of government support across political cycles, coordination between sectoral programs and among different levels and branches of government, and evidence-based policies. Although all four countries did not implement all of these policy directions, the case studies point to the whole-of-government approach as having enormous potential to build human capital in a wide variety of development contexts.

2.3.1 Sustaining political commitment to human capital development

Continuity of commitment and effort over successive governments is key to reaching any long-term goals, but especially in growing human capital, which can take decades and even generations. Although not all politically stable economies were able to maintain a sustained focus on human capital, ensuring this continuity is easier if the economy in question enjoys political stability, as in the cases of Ghana and Singapore, the former characterized by a stable, multiparty democracy since 1992.

By contrast, a consistent approach to building human capital has been harder to achieve in Morocco, where political commitment to education across successive governments did not extend to other policies critical to improving human capital outcomes. In the Philippines, although several successive political administrations have adopted and sustained robust strategies to build the human capital of the population, they have not succeeded in growing sufficiently the capacity and good governance needed to implement these efforts on the ground.

In addition to political commitment, human capital development requires adequate and sustainable funding. In particular, domestic resources are central to achieving development objectives. Economies can enhance the quality and foster the legitimacy of tax systems by strengthening the operational capacity of tax administrations. Doing so can be a challenge for developing economies with limited resources, but some economies have found innovative ways to finance the necessary policies (Junquera-Varela et al. 2017).

For example, the Singapore government has mobilized domestic resources through the Central Provident Fund, which has played a critical role in financing infrastructure, housing, and other vital investments. Each individual and his or her employer make monthly contributions to the Central Provident Fund, which are distributed among three accounts owned by the individual: (1) an ordinary account for housing and retirement purposes; (2) a special account that is primarily for retirement; and (3) a Medisave account that is used to cover medical expenses. The government supplements the contributions of low-income earners through a workfare scheme and adds to Medisave savings of senior citizens. The Central Provident Fund has also underpinned health care financing through Medisave and has fostered citizens' responsibility for their own welfare. Thus, policy makers have managed to contain the cost of providing the country's entire population with affordable, high-quality primary health care by tailoring subsidies to the patient's age and ability to pay and charging users high copayments financed from mandatory health savings accounts. Regulation and bulk buying of drugs have also kept pharmacy costs in check.

Levels of funding are crucial, but so is using resources efficiently. The government of Singapore has set a high standard in this respect by ensuring that expenditures are tightly managed, including by imposing severe sanctions for corrupt practices.

Although successive governments in the Philippines have enacted human capital development laws that reflect principles similar to those espoused by more successful economies, they have generally failed to provide adequate financing to ensure effective implementation. The Philippines spends 4.4 percent of its GDP on its health programs and 3.5 percent on education programs, compared with an average of 6.5 percent and 4.5 percent, respectively, for an average economy at the same income level. This low expenditure has resulted in understaffed and overcrowded clinics and schools, underpaid providers, inadequate infrastructure, and a lack of administrative and technical capacity, especially at local schools and health facilities. The absence of adequate funding has also hampered efforts to improve governance. Widespread fraud in the distribution of textbooks, theft of funds or supplies, and ghost workers (workers who are paid but do not carry out their jobs) in municipal health facilities are all reflected in the country's outcomes. In the PISA 2018 exam, about four-fifths of students (81 percent) achieved lower than a minimum level of proficiency in reading, and a similarly high percentage of students performed below the minimum level of proficiency in mathematics.

The lack of adequate financing—resulting in understaffed facilities, underpaid providers, and overcrowded clinics and schools—has particularly affected the country's low-income households and more remote regions, which now lag behind the rest of the country in terms of access to services. By contrast, Ghana's innovative funding mechanism—the National Health Insurance Scheme (NHIS)—was designed to expand primary care coverage while also reducing inequity in access to health care by exempting the poor from premiums.[27] The NHIS is funded mainly by a 2.5 percent value added tax on selected goods and services, 2.5 percent from the Social Security and National Insurance Trust (largely paid by formal sector workers), and the payment of premiums. These funds enable the NHIS to provide prenatal and postnatal care, maternal health care, vaccinations, and health and nutrition education, all of which may have helped reduce stunting rates in Ghana. As a result of the NHIS, the government has been able to devote a high percentage of its spending to the health budget (10.6 percent as of 2013), which has helped bring down the rate of childhood stunting in Ghana in both absolute and relative terms.

2.3.2 Collecting and using evidence to inform policy making

Collecting data to inform policy implementation and design is easier in a compact city-state like Singapore than in a sprawling island nation like the Philippines, but digital technologies are making it easier for all economies to collect and analyze data and to use the resulting evidence when making policies and decisions. Singapore's public agencies and statutory boards, state-of-the-art digital technology, tech-savvy administrators, and experienced teachers form a robust data-collection infrastructure that feeds critical information to policy makers in real time. Policy makers use these data to assess school and student performance, control costs, help managers and teachers make decisions at every level, and conduct workforce planning. For example, the Ministry of Education has installed an information-gathering mechanism that helps school administrators assess the strengths and weaknesses of their own institution and track student performance (using a Pupil Data Bank). The system has enabled the ministry to keep closer tabs on how individual schools are faring.

In Ghana, the government used data to effectively retarget school feeding efforts under the Ghana School Feeding Program (GSFP) after it found that the targeted population (the poor) was not being reached. Data from national poverty statistics and a food security and vulnerability analysis were combined to refine targeting and reduce leakages (Drake et al. 2016; World Food Programme 2013). After the retargeting exercise was completed, as of 2013, about 70 to 80 percent of the GFSP was being received by the poorest communities (World Food Programme 2013). In Morocco, by contrast, a paucity of data has stymied improvements to the country's Tayssir conditional cash transfer program. The Audit Office of Morocco explicitly stated in its 2016–17 report that "no quantifiable indicators are available to monitor the different programs and prepare annual progress and financial reports that enable evaluation of the performance of these programs" (as cited in Benkassmi and Abdelkhalek 2020, 15–16)

2.3.3 "Whole-of-government" approaches: Adopting coordinated, multisectoral strategies

Multisectoral strategies are most likely to effectively address the complex underlying determinants of human capital outcomes. Policies that cut across sectors and lines of authority can also be especially beneficial to economies such as the Philippines that have limited resources and technical and administrative capacity. In the last 40 years, successive governments in the Philippines have adopted policies that involved more than one sector, promoted integrated approaches, and encouraged greater participation by stakeholders in service delivery. In addition, many policies reflect the fact that factors beyond the social sectors affect human capital development, such as clean air, a safe water supply, and the provision of sanitation services.

The country has several programs that are organized on multisectoral lines. An example is the Pantawid Pamilyang Pilipino Program (4Ps), which provides cash to chronically poor households living in poor areas and with children between 0 and 14 years old.[28] In return, the beneficiary households are required to undertake certain activities aimed at improving their children's health and education, such as taking them to health centers regularly, sending them to school, and going to prenatal checkups in the case of pregnant women. Thus, 4Ps integrates human capital development with poverty reduction efforts. The Department of Social Welfare and Development was charged with leading the program's implementation, and worked with the Department of Health, the Department of Education, the Department of the Interior and Local Government, and the government-owned Land Bank of the Philippines. In addition, 4Ps actively involved local service providers (such as school principals and midwives) in implementation by tasking them with verifying that households were fully complying with the prerequisite conditions for the cash transfers.[29]

Impact evaluation studies show that the program is resulting in improved education and health outcomes among beneficiaries, including enhanced food security, community participation, and women's empowerment. Specifically, it has helped reduce short-term poverty and food poverty at the national scale by up to 1.4 percentage points each—a substantial reduction, given that pre-4Ps rates were 26.4 percent for total poverty and 12.5 percent for food poverty (Acosta and Velarde 2015).

Ghana's progress in decreasing stunting rates has also been due in large part to the multisectoral approach taken by policy makers (Gelli et al. 2019). For example, the GSFP links school feeding programs with agriculture development, especially smallholder production, thus helping create new markets for locally grown food (Sumberg and Sabates-Wheeler 2011; World Bank 2012). Thus, the GSFP spans three different sectors—agriculture, education, and health.[30] Also, initiatives aimed at improving water sanitation and hygiene in schools have helped increase access to water and sanitation, which is a proven factor in improving health and education indicators.

The experiences of the four countries examined here highlight the importance of sustained effort to improve human capital outcomes across political cycles, sufficient resource mobilization and effective allocation across programs, data and measurement to inform and design, and multisectoral strategies that address the complex underlying determinants of human capital. These best practices are likely to assume an even greater significance in the wake of the COVID-19 pandemic, as economies attempt to mitigate its negative effects on human capital outcomes.

NOTES

1. All the components of the HCI, and the HCI itself, are bounded above. For example, adult and child survival rates cannot be larger than 100 percent, and the maximum number of learning-adjusted years of schooling between ages 4 and 17 is fixed at 14. This means that the absolute size of improvements become smaller as countries get closer to the upper bound.

2. In Togo, the gender gap in HCI slightly widened in favor of boys. Both boys' and girls' outcomes improved during this time period. The widening gender gap is driven by different rates of improvement among boys and girls. In expected years of school, girls' outcomes improved but by slightly less than those of boys. Meanwhile, in child survival and stunting, boys are catching up to girls, closing the gender gaps toward parity.
3. This decomposition is implemented as a Shapley decomposition. For a description of the method see Azevedo, Sanfelice, and Nguyen (2012).
4. Although most economies experienced declines in child (under-5) mortality, the rates rose in Grenada, Mauritius, Fiji, Brunei, and Dominica, reported here in ascending order of the increase.
5. For more information, see the United Nations Interagency Group for Child Mortality Estimation website, http://www.childmortality.org/.
6. Although most economies experienced modest changes in child survival rates, a unique case is Haiti, where the child survival rate dropped massively and abruptly to 79 percent (79 of 100 children survive) in 2010 from 92 percent in 2009, following a major earthquake. Survival rates have since rebounded to 94 per 100 children.
7. This differential persists even when the initial level of stunting and GDP per capita are factored in.
8. Data from the UNAIDS Zimbabwe country profile at https://www.unaids.org/en/regionscountries/countries/zimbabwe.
9. Data from the UNAIDS Eswatini country profile at https://www.unaids.org/en/regionscountries/countries/swaziland.
10. Data from the United Nations Children's Fund HIV/AIDS web page, https://www.unicef.org/eswatini/hivaids.
11. Data from the Joint United Nations Programme on HIV/AIDS Eswatini country profile, https://www.unaids.org/en/regionscountries/countries/swaziland.
12. Case and Deaton (2020) connect the decrease in life expectancy in the United States to the "deaths of despair" phenomenon.
13. Refer to appendix C for more details on this calculation and for details on how enrollment data are imputed when missing.
14. Test scores and years of schooling series are negatively correlated within Latin America and the Caribbean (correlation of −0.16), the Middle East and North Africa (−0.28), and Sub-Saharan Africa (−0.14).
15. For the role of technology in the progress in child survival, see Jamison, Murphy, and Sandbuc (2016).
16. School enrollment data by age disaggregated by socioeconomic status are based on the latest update to the household wealth and educational attainment dataset first described in Filmer and Pritchett (1998). The latest version of their dataset contains 345 Demographic and Health Surveys and Multiple Indicator Cluster Surveys, with enrollment rates for 99 countries over 1990–2017. The child (under-5) mortality rates and stunting rates disaggregated by socioeconomic status come from the latest edition of the Health Equity and Financial Protection Indicators database described in Wagstaff et al. (2019). Both datasets calculate the socioeconomic status index in the same way, using principal component analysis to aggregate responses to questions on asset ownership and housing characteristics into a household-level socioeconomic status index.
17. Notably, the increase in child mortality in 2010 in the aftermath of the earthquake in Haiti was massive.
18. The EYS data used to calculate the HCI rely on administrative data on preprimary through

upper-secondary enrollment, covering the 4–17 age range for a maximum of 14 years of school. By contrast, Demographic and Health Surveys and Multiple Indicator Cluster Surveys collected enrollment data for children ages 6–17 for a maximum of 12 years of school. As a result, the EYS reported in the HCI, calculated using administrative data, cannot be compared to the EYS reported in this section, computed using survey data.

19. The analysis in this section is based on four country case studies produced as part of a series titled Building Human Capital: Lessons from Country Experiences (see Benkassmi and Abdelkhalek 2020; Blunch 2020; King 2020; Yusuf 2020).
20. This approach is based on that used in the World Bank's Human Capital Project (HCP), taking a whole-of-government approach.
21. Based on World Bank national accounts data, and Organisation for Economic Co-operation and Development National Accounts data files.
22. Data from Statistics Singapore; see https://www.tablebuilder.singstat.gov.sg/publicfacing/displayChart.action.
23. Data from the World Development Indicators.
24. Based on data from the World Bank dataset, https://data.worldbank.org/indicator/SH.STA.STNT.ZS?locations=PH-1W-Z4; https://data.worldbank.org/indicator/SE.PRM.NENR?locations=PH-1W-Z4.
25. Data from Enquête Nationale sur la Population et la Santé Familiale (ENPSF), 2011 and 2018.
26. Note, however, that, as indicated in appendix C, comparisons for learning in Morocco, as in a handful of other economies, refer to different international testing programs.
27. Not everybody has to pay the NHIS premium. Pregnant women are exempt, as are people under 18 years of age, people age 70 and above, and individuals employed in the formal sector who contribute to the Social Security and National Insurance Trust. Additionally, individuals considered too poor to pay are also exempt from paying the premium. They include beneficiaries of the Livelihood Empowerment Against Poverty program.
28. Eligible households received between 500 pesos and 1,400 pesos (US$11.00–US$32.00) per month, depending on the number of eligible children in the household (King 2020).
29. In 2009, the Department of Social Welfare and Development institutionalized the system as the National Household Targeting System for Poverty Reduction, and by 2011 it had shared the database with the Philippine Health Insurance Corporation, Department of Agriculture, and Department of Health to help those agencies better target the benefits of their own programs (Fernandez and Olfindo 2011).
30. The GSFP is run by the Ghana School Feeding Program Secretariat under the direct supervision of the Ministry of Local Government and Rural Development. Other public partners directly involved include the Ministry of Education, the Ministry of Food and Agriculture, the Ministry of Health, the Ministry of Women and Children's Affairs, the Ministry of Finance and Economic Planning, and the District Assemblies.

REFERENCES

Acosta, P., and R. Velarde. 2015. "An Update of the Philippine Conditional Cash Transfer's Implementation Performance." Philippine Social Protection Note No. 8, World Bank, Washington, DC.

Azevedo, J. P., V. Sanfelice, M. and Nguyen. 2012. "Shapley Decomposition by Components of a Welfare Aggregate." MPRA Paper No. 85584, Munich Personal RePEc Archive. https://mpra.ub.uni-muenchen.de/85584/.

Benkassmi, M., and T. Abdelkhalek. 2020. "Building Human Capital: Lessons from

Country Experiences—Morocco." World Bank, Washington, DC.

Bhutta, Z., N. Akseer, E. Keats, T. Vaivada, S. Baker, S. Horton, J. Katz, P. Menon, E. Piwoz, M. Shekar, C. Victora, and R. Black. 2020. "How Countries Can Reduce Child Stunting at Scale: Lessons from Exemplar Countries." *American Journal of Clinical Nutrition* 112 (2): 894S–904S.

Blunch, N.-H. 2020. "Building Human Capital: Lessons from Country Experiences—Ghana." World Bank, Washington, DC.

Case, A., and A. Deaton. 2020. Deaths of Despair and the Future of Capitalism. Princeton, NJ: Princeton University Press.

CD2015 (Countdown to 2015). 2015. "Malawi: Understanding Progress on Child Survival." Countdown Country Case Study, CD2015, July. https://www.countdown2015mnch.org/documents/CD_Malawi_July2015_2logos_FINAL2.pdf.

CDC (Centers for Disease Control and Prevention). 2019. "CDC in Eswatini Factsheet." CDC, Atlanta. https://www.cdc.gov/globalhealth/countries/eswatini/pdf/eswatini-factsheet.pdf.

Cruz, R., and L. Loureiro. 2020. "Achieving World-Class Education in Adverse Socioeconomic Conditions: The Case of Sobral in Brazil." World Bank, Washington, DC.

de la Fuente, A., E. Foster, and H. Jacoby. Forthcoming. "The Immediate Effects of the Free Quality Education Program in Sierra Leone." World Bank, Washington, DC.

Drake, L., A. Woolnough, C. Burbano, and D. Bundy. 2016. *Global School Feeding Sourcebook: Lessons from 14 Countries*. London: Imperial College Press.

D'Souza, R., R. Gatti, and A. Kraay. 2019. "A Socioeconomic Disaggregation of the World Bank Human Capital Index." *Policy Research Working Paper* 9020, World Bank, Washington, DC.

European Commission and World Bank. 2018. "A Proposed Early Warning Mechanism for Early School Leaving Prevention and Proposed Action Plan for Implementation." Administration Agreement SRSS/S2018/063, European Commission, Brussels; World Bank, Washington, DC.

Fernandez, L., and R. Olfindo. 2011. "Overview of the Philippines' Conditional Cash Transfer Program: The Pantawid Pamilyang Pilipino Program." Social Protection Discussion Papers and Notes 62879, World Bank, Washington, DC.

Filmer, D., and L. H. Pritchett. 1998. "Estimating Wealth Effects without Expenditure Data—or Tears: With an Application to Educational Enrollments in States of India." Policy Research Working Paper 1994, World Bank, Washington, DC.

Gelli, A., E. Aurino, G. Folson, D. Arhinful, C. Adamba, I. Osei-Akoto, E. Masset, K. Watkins, M. Fernandes, L. Drake, L., and H. Alderman. 2019. "A School Meals Program Implemented at Scale in Ghana Increases Height-for-Age during Midchildhood in Girls and in Children from Poor Households: A Cluster Randomized Trial." *Journal of Nutrition* 149 (8): 1434–42.

Glewwe, Paul, Jongwook Lee, Khoa Vu, and Hai Anh Dang. 2017. "What Explains Vietnam's Exceptional Performance in Education Relative to Other Countries? Analysis of the 2012 PISA Data." RISE Annual Conference, Center for Global Development, Washington, DC.

Gribble, J., and M. L. Voss. 2009. "Family Planning and Economic Well-Being: New Evidence from Bangladesh." Policy Brief, Population Reference Bureau, Washington, DC, May.

Hanushek, Eric A., and Ludger Woessmann. 2011. "Sample Selectivity and the Validity of International Student Achievement Tests in Economic Research." *Economics Letters* 110 (2): 79–82.

Jamison, D. T., S. M. Murphy, and M. E. Sandbuc. 2016. "Why Has Under-5 Mortality Decreased at Such Different Rates in Different Countries?" *Journal of Health Economics* 48 (July): 16–25.

Junquera-Varela, R. F., M. Verhoeven, G. P. Shukla, B. Haven, R. Awasthi, and B. Moreno-Dodson. 2017. *Strengthening Domestic Resource Mobilization Moving from Theory to Practice in Low- and Middle-Income Countries*. Directions in Development. Washington, DC: World Bank.

King, E. 2020. "Building Human Capital: Lessons from Country Experiences—Philippines." World Bank, Washington, DC.

Loureiro, A., E. di Gropello, and O. Arias. 2020. "There Is No Magic: The Formula for Brazil's Ceará and Sobral Success to Reduce Learning Poverty." *Education for Global Development* (blog), July 9, 2020. https://blogs.worldbank.org/education/there-no-magic-formula-brazils-ceara-and-sobral-success-reduce-learning-poverty?token=53176c4095d917916aa31ea735b5ceaa.

Ministry of Education and Science, Republic of Albania. 2005. "National Education Strategy 2004–2015." Ministry of Education and Science, Tirana. https://planipolis.iiep.unesco.org/sites/planipolis/files/ressources/albania-education-strategy-2004-2015.pdf.

National Institute of Statistics, Romania. 2018. *Statistical Yearbook 2017*. Bucharest: INS.

Rob, U., J. F. Phillips, J. Chakraborty, and M. A. Koenig. 1987. "The Use Effectiveness of the Copper T-200 in Matlab." *International Journal of Gynecology and Obstetrics* 25 (4): 315–22.

Smith, O., and S. Nguyen. 2013. *Getting Better: Improving Health System Outcomes in Europe and Central Asia*. Washington, DC: World Bank.

Sumberg, J., and R. Sabates-Wheeler. 2011. "Linking Agricultural Development to School Feeding in Sub-Saharan Africa: Theoretical Perspectives." *Food Policy* 36 (3): 341–49.

The Straits Times. 2020. "World Bank Ranks Singapore Tops in Human Capital Index." *Straits Times*, October 15, 2020. *https://www.straitstimes.com/singapore/world-bank-ranks-singapore-tops-in-human-capital-index*.

UNICEF (United Nations Children's Fund), WHO (World Health Organization), and World Bank Group. 2020. *Levels and Trends in Child Malnutrition: Key Findings of the 2020 Edition*. UNICEF, WHO, and World Bank Group.

Wagstaff, A., P. Eozenou, S. Neelsen, and M.-F. Smitz. 2019. "Introducing the World Bank's 2018 Health Equity and Financial Protection Indicators Database." *Lancet Global Health* 7 (1): E22–E23.

World Bank. 2012. "What Matters Most for School Health and School Feeding: A Framework Paper." SABER Working Paper 3, Systems Approach for Better Education Results, World Bank, Washington, DC.

World Bank. 2016. "Rewarding Provider Performance to Improve Quality and Coverage of Maternal and Child Health Outcomes: Zimbabwe Results-Based Financing Pilot Program." World Bank, Washington, DC.

World Bank. 2018. "Reducing Childhood Stunting with a New Adaptive Approach." World Bank, Washington, DC, September 28. https://www.worldbank.org/en/news/immersive-story/2018/09/28/reducing-childhood-stunting-with-a-new-adaptive-approach.

World Bank. 2019. "Improving Access to Maternal Health for Zimbabwe's Expectant Mothers." Feature Story, January 10, 2019. World Bank, Washington, DC. https://www.worldbank.org/en/news/feature/2019/01/10/improving-access-to-maternal-health-for-zimbabwes-expectant-mothers.

World Bank. 2020. "The Effect of the H1N1 Pandemic on Learning. What to Expect with Covid-19?" World Bank, Washington, DC.

World Food Programme. 2013. "State of School Feeding Worldwide 2013." World Food Programme, Rome.

World Food Programme. 2017. "Fill the Nutrient Gap: Pakistan. Summary Report." World Food Programme, Rome.

World Food Programme. 2019. "Cost-Effective & Sector-Specific Recommendations for Improving Nutrition Outcomes in Pakistan: Evidence from the Fill the Nutrient Gap Analysis." World Food Programme, Rome.

Yusuf, S. 2020. "How Singapore Does It." Building Human Capital: Lessons from Country Experiences, World Bank, Washington, DC.

3 Accumulation Interrupted? COVID-19 and HUMAN CAPITAL

COVID-19 (coronavirus) is exacting a heavy toll in illness and lost lives, and on the economy. Lacking a vaccine or effective pharmaceutical treatment against SARS-CoV-2, the novel coronavirus responsible for COVID-19, many countries initially resorted to large-scale nonpharmaceutical interventions to slow the virus's spread. Such interventions resulted in economywide lockdowns of different levels of restrictiveness. These measures further amplified the disruptions that COVID-19 brought to supply chains and global trade, adding to the already-dramatic economic dimension of the health crisis. A baseline forecast for gross domestic product (GDP) in 2020 predicts a global drop of 5.2 percent (World Bank 2020), the worst recession in eight decades, which is likely to push 100 million more people into poverty (Mahler et al. 2020b).

A lesson from past pandemics and crises is that their effects not only are felt by those directly impacted, but also often ripple across populations and in many cases across generations. COVID-19 is no exception. Both the health and economic effects of the disease and its control measures have significant consequences for people's human capital. In many health systems, the fight against the pandemic has crowded out other essential health services. At the same time, people's fear of infection has led many to choose not to seek treatment, possibly derailing years of gains against diseases like tuberculosis, HIV, and malaria.

Lockdowns translated into school closures with a shift to remote learning in some form, which can in many cases worsen learning gaps between children with a more affluent background and those who are less well-off. It can also lead to widening gaps between countries, because many may not have the infrastructure in place for digital connection. Adding to people's hardship are household income losses due to unemployment and reduced remittances, with effects that might be quite different across developed and developing countries.[1]

Despite tremendous uncertainty still on the overall impact of the pandemic on human capital, it is clear that both direct and indirect pathways will matter. Those who were most vulnerable to begin with are likely to be the worst hit, and many dimensions of inequality are likely to increase. The next two sections of this chapter discuss channels of impact from COVID-19 to human capital and their likely effects over people's full life cycle. The subsequent section discusses how the Human Capital Index (HCI) can be used to quantify some of the likely impacts of the pandemic on children and youth.

3.1 TRANSMISSION OF THE COVID-19 SHOCK TO HUMAN CAPITAL

3.1.1 Health system disruptions

As governments scramble to respond to the immediate consequences of the pandemic, resources are likely to be diverted from other health efforts that nonetheless remain critical. In past health emergencies, substantial negative indirect effects have resulted from this crowding out of non-pandemic-related health services. For example, in the 2014–15 Ebola outbreak in West Africa, health facility closures, health worker deaths, and excess demand placed on the health system led to further loss of lives. In Ebola-affected areas, it was reported that maternal and delivery care dropped by more than

80 percent, malaria admissions for children under the age of 5 years fell by 40 percent, and vaccination coverage was also considerably reduced (Elston et al. 2017).

Some of these consequences are already apparent for COVID-19. The pandemic has interrupted vaccination programs in roughly 68 economies, and some 80 million children under the age of 1 year will go unvaccinated in low- and middle-income countries as a result (Nelson 2020; World Health Organization 2020). Supply-chain breakdowns combine with forced mobility restrictions under nonpharmaceutical interventions to complicate overall access to vaccines (Nelson 2020; World Health Organization 2020).

Children and pregnant mothers are not the only ones who will suffer from weakened service delivery capacities and curtailed access to services. During a pandemic, most people are more reluctant to seek medical care. During the SARS epidemic in Taiwan, China, people's fear of infection likely led to sharp drops in demand for access to medical care across the board (see Chang et al. 2004). In the current pandemic, many patients suffering from other illnesses will be unable to go for routine checkups, because of restricted movement and to avoid COVID-19 infection. Such service interruption will also likely lead to numerous deaths, many of them avoidable. For example, in high-burden countries, it is estimated that deaths due to tuberculosis, HIV, and malaria will increase by 20, 10, and 36 percent, respectively, over the coming five years.[2] A lesson is that, when determining how to reallocate resources for pandemic response, special attention must be given to maintaining coverage of key non-COVID-19 health care.[3]

3.1.2 School closures

By the end of April 2020, schools were closed or partly closed in roughly 180 economies, although schools are now slowly reopening in many jurisdictions.[4] Although the impact of school closures will depend on the effectiveness of mitigation from remote instruction, closures will likely result in a slowdown and loss of learning, and an increased likelihood of school dropouts, particularly for the most disadvantaged and for girls (see Azevedo et al. 2020).[5]

These human capital losses are not necessarily uniformly distributed across the population. As children learn from home, social inequalities become more salient. The closure of schools could widen existing gaps in education between children from more well-off homes and those who come from less well-off backgrounds, because poor households' access to technology and infrastructure is likely to be more limited. Additionally, learning from home requires more inputs from parents, and some parents' limited capacity to guide and support their children's learning could exacerbate inequalities.

Along with education, many children receive other services through their schools. These include meal programs, which tend to benefit poorer children. The suspension of school feeding programs could worsen food insecurity and malnutrition. The burden of making up the nutritional shortfall now falls on parents, many of whom are struggling economically because of the pandemic (Lancker and Parolin 2020).

3.1.3 Income effects, price effects, and food security

The emerging literature on containment strategies highlights the large benefits—in terms of lives saved and GDP losses averted—of testing and contact tracing (Acemoglu et al. 2020). Whereas countries such as Iceland and the Republic of Korea successfully implemented these strategies early on in the pandemic, most countries resorted to lockdowns and movement restriction (Hale et al. 2020). Voluntary mobility restrictions combined with government-driven lockdowns generate a significant drop in activity and aggregate demand, leading to a considerable reduction in incomes.

Nevertheless, the largest impacts to the economy are expected to come from reduced consumption due to people's avoidance of social interaction for fear of infection (Wren-Lewis 2020).

Projections show that the resulting economic fallout will be massive and potentially worse than that of the 2008–09 financial crisis (Wren-Lewis 2020). Lockdowns force many nonessential businesses to close and will further disrupt supply chains. Coupled with inherent uncertainty due to the pandemic, these closures and disruptions may prompt many people to cut back on expenses, which in turn may trigger more businesses to close and more people to lose their jobs (International Monetary Fund 2020). The ensuing economic decline is likely to undo years of gains in the fight to eradicate extreme poverty. Accordingly, the World Bank has projected an increase in international extreme poverty for the first time since 1998 (Mahler et al. 2020a).

Closures and decreased economic activity result in higher unemployment and income losses for many households. Households in countries that rely on remittances or seasonal migrants for income report that contributions from these sources have fallen considerably, and many households report that they expect to lose their remittances altogether. The fall in household incomes is likely to affect the poor disproportionately, because they often experience more fragile labor arrangements and, if inadequately covered by safety nets, are likely to fall through the cracks.

The income shock will probably be exacerbated by the initial price shock already observed in many countries. The pandemic has created a short-run demand shock, with consumers demanding different products. As movement restrictions dissuade people from venturing out in public, many activities that would typically happen in markets, restaurants, or other commercial settings end up taking place at home. Because manufacturing of goods for restaurants, hotels, and offices differs from manufacturing for home consumption, which has now increased, shortages can temporarily arise and prices increase as a short-run response (Hobbs 2020).

Concerns about localized food availability may not be unfounded. Because of mobility restrictions, many farmers may experience labor shortages, which can reduce yields and further strain the supply of staple foods.[6] Small-scale farmers may also choose to avoid going to markets to sell their goods, because they fear contagion. Mobility restrictions and labor shortages may also prevent farmers from transporting their goods to market, which will likely affect the availability of more perishable crops, such as fruits and vegetables. If these products cannot reach markets in time, they may simply rot in the fields, because many farmers lack adequate storage facilities (Tesfaye, Habte, and Minten 2020).

Given that many households will experience a fall in their incomes, they will likely face food insecurity. This situation will affect the poorest households most, because they devote a larger share of their incomes to food expenditures. Households will respond to such events by limiting their food intake or relying more on cheaper staple foods, reducing dietary diversity and further worsening the nutrition of millions of people.[7] Evidence of such scenarios is already emerging. For example, in Senegal, 86 percent of respondents to a telephone survey reported a drop in their incomes, and more than 33 percent indicated that they restrict their meals four to seven days a week (Le Nestour and Moscoviz 2020). In Nigeria, respondents report fear for their health and their financial future, with many also experiencing increased prices of major food items and loss of employment (Lain et al. 2020). In Uganda, households on average report a 60 percent reduction in total household incomes and a drop in food expenditures of roughly 50 percent per adult equivalent. Evidence from Uganda also points toward temporary coping mechanisms used by households, many of which increased borrowing, dipped into their savings, or invested more of their time in household enterprises (Mahmud and Riley, forthcoming).[8]

Despite the pandemic's severe direct health impacts, the largest effects on human capital will probably come through indirect channels. But indirect does not mean insignificant. Emerging results for a large set of rapid response phone surveys fielded by the World Bank speak to indirect consequences of the pandemic that may permanently weaken countries' human capital for generations (see box 3.1).

Box 3.1: Rapid response phone surveys reveal immediate impacts of COVID-19 on the poor

Although the impacts of the COVID-19 (coronavirus) pandemic are cross-cutting, they are particularly damaging for the poor and vulnerable. Policy makers need timely and relevant information on the impacts of the crisis as well as on the effectiveness of their policy measures to save lives, support livelihoods, and maintain human capital. To track the socioeconomic impacts of the pandemic, the World Bank rolled out a rapid response phone survey (RRPS) in more than 100 economies. Traditional face-to-face surveys are hindered by social distancing protocols and mobility restrictions, whereas RRPSs overcome these limitations. RRPSs can be deployed rapidly, implemented at low cost, used to regularly collect longitudinal information, and adapted swiftly to changing circumstances. Preliminary results are available for Ethiopia, Kenya, Mongolia, Myanmar, Nigeria, Tajikistan, and Uzbekistan.

Severe mobility restrictions imposed to limit the spread of the pandemic have severely disrupted economic activities. Many workers—especially in the services sector but also in agriculture, for example, in Ethiopia and Myanmar—lost employment. In Kenya, the unemployment rate tripled, while in Myanmar, Nigeria, Tajikistan, and Uzbekistan more than one in five households lost all employment. Despite some signs of recovery in employment, especially in Ethiopia, Nigeria, Tajikistan, and Uzbekistan, more than half of households report income losses in the remaining economies. Mainly because of the loss of income, food insecurity increased, often substantially. It tripled in Nigeria and doubled in Tajikistan compared to the previous year.

In addition, access to education has been severely limited in most economies, particularly for rural and poor households. In all of these economies, schools were closed and replaced with remote learning activities. Although RRPS questions across countries are not strictly comparable, the survey finds that access and utilization of remote learning activities vary widely. During the pandemic, almost all children are engaged in remote learning activities in Uzbekistan, 7 out of 10 children are learning remotely in Kenya and Mongolia, 6 out of 10 in Nigeria, and only 3 out of 10 in Ethiopia and Tajikistan. The types of learning activities also differ, for example, with Kenyan children mainly studying independently, whereas in Uzbekistan almost 9 out of 10 children report using educational television programs. In most economies, children living in rural or poor households are more affected by school closures because those children have more limited access to remote learning.

Access to medical services seems less affected, with 10 percent, over 16 percent, and 25 percent of households unable to obtain medical treatment in Mongolia, Uzbekistan, and Kenya, respectively.

Source: World Bank Global Poverty team and https://www.worldbank.org/en/topic/poverty/brief/high-frequency-monitoring-surveys.

3.2 THE COVID-19 HUMAN CAPITAL SHOCK: A LIFE-CYCLE PERSPECTIVE

The accumulation of human capital is the result of a dynamic process whose dimensions complement each other over time. Depending on an individual's stage in life, the impact of the pandemic on this process may come through different channels and have a differential impact. Setbacks during certain stages of the life cycle—chiefly early childhood—can have especially damaging and long-lasting effects. For example, economic hardship can force families to prioritize immediate consumption needs, forgoing spending on health or education. Because demand for investing in human capital rises with incomes (Bardhan and Udry 1999), a fall in incomes could worsen human capital accumulation for many people, especially the most disadvantaged.[9] Figure 3.1 depicts schematically how some of these shocks can affect the process of human capital accumulation over the life cycle. Across the top of the figure are some typical age-specific markers for human capital development, some of which enter as components into the HCI.

3.2.1 From conception to age 5

During childhood, the link between parental income and child health is particularly strong (Almond 2006). For example, reduced nutrition in pregnant mothers could have a substantial impact on children in utero, including long-lasting impacts on chronic health conditions and cognitive attainment in adulthood (see Almond and Currie 2011). The evidence shows that this is the case for children born during a pandemic but also for children born during conflict[10] and economic hardship (Rosales-Rueda 2018). For example, children who were in utero during the 1918 influenza pandemic had lower educational attainment and income during adulthood. The effect was even more salient among children of infected mothers (see Almond 2006). Much about the current virus remains to be learned. At the moment, the main

Figure 3.1: Human capital accumulation across the life cycle, key stages and metrics

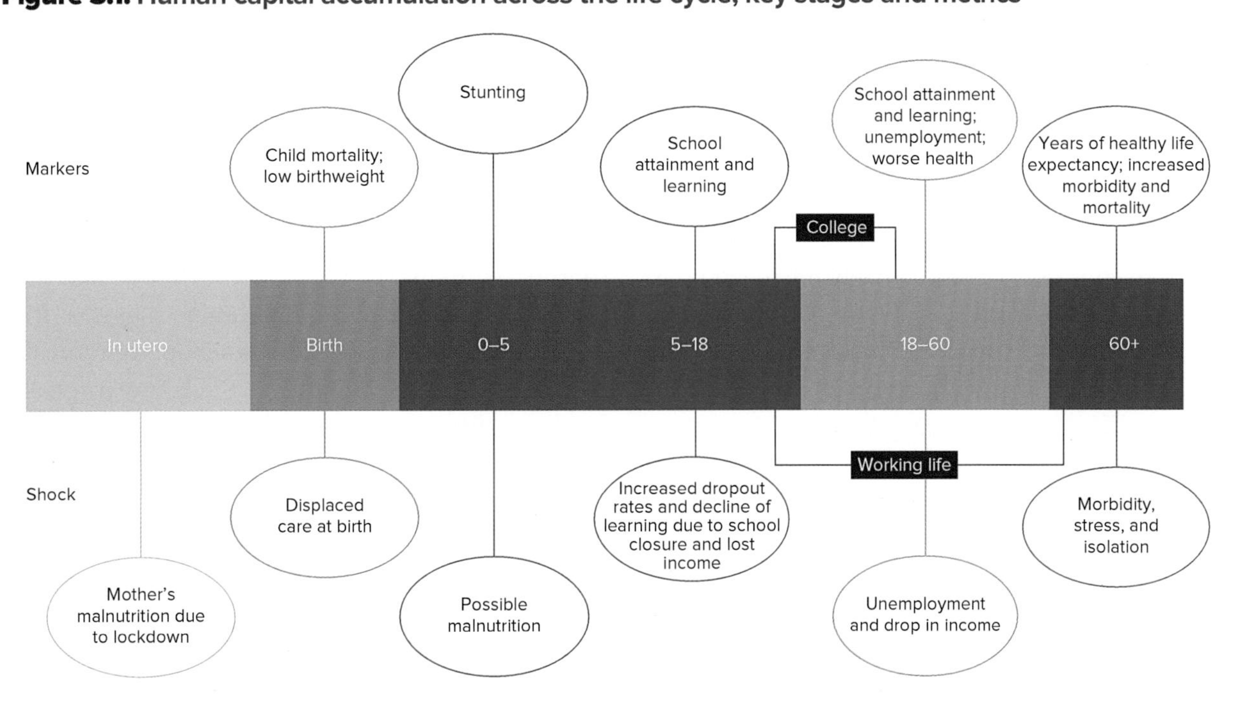

Source: Corral and Gatti 2020.

transmission channel affecting the fetus's human capital is expected to be through the disruption of health care and through lower household income.[11]

Birthweight is often interpreted as a key observable component of a child's initial endowment (Datar, Kilburn, and Loughran 2010). Children who were in utero during the 2008–09 recession were born with relatively lower birthweight, particularly in families at the bottom of the income distribution (Finch, Thomas, and Beck 2019). This was the case for children born in those California regions that suffered unusually elevated unemployment rates after the 2008–09 recession (Finch, Thomas, and Beck 2019). Similarly, in Ecuador during the 1998 El Niño floods, children who were in utero and especially in the third gestational trimester were much more likely to be born with low birthweight, and these children showed substantially reduced stature five and seven years afterward (see Rosales-Rueda 2018). These health effects were attributed to drops in household income following the devastation of El Niño. Similar outcomes can unfortunately be expected from the COVID-19 shock. Because low birthweight is associated with increased likelihood of malnutrition and with developmental delay, COVID-19-induced income effects may substantially affect human capital attainment for generations to come (see Black, Devereux, and Salvanes 2007; Lahti-Pulkkinen et al. 2018).

Child mortality is unfortunately also likely to increase, for two reasons. The first is the disruption in maternal and child health services due to COVID-19. Early simulated values project an increase of child mortality of up to 45 percent due to health service shortfalls and reductions in access to food in 118 low-income and middle-income countries (Roberton et al. 2020). Second, economic downturns have been associated with significant increases in child mortality, with a more marked increase in lower-income countries. A meta-analysis of studies for developing countries suggests that a 10 percent increase in GDP per capita is related to a decrease in infant mortality of 4.5 percent.[12] Recent estimates also show that the relationship between income and child mortality is likely higher in low-income countries, suggesting that short-term aggregate income shocks translate into an increase in child mortality of 1.3 deaths per 1,000 children among low-income countries, given a 10 percent decrease in per capita GDP.[13]

Stunting rates are also likely to increase because of the COVID-19 shock. Common factors related to stunting are maternal nutrition during pregnancy and nutrition during infancy, both of which will likely worsen if families have less disposable income (see Galasso and Wagstaff 2019). A fall in aggregate GDP could also lead to weakened health infrastructure and less funding for nutritional interventions and services (see Mary 2018). Existing estimates of elasticities suggest that a 10 percent increase in GDP leads to a decrease in stunting that may range from 2.7 to 7.3 percent.[14] Nevertheless, aggregate elasticities may obscure the fact that many of these shocks will disproportionately affect the poor and disadvantaged. Attention must be paid to ensure that these groups have access to any available support mechanisms that may mitigate such impacts.

3.2.2 The school years

With almost all economies having imposed some type of school closure in response to the pandemic, students in many settings are likely to suffer learning shocks. Evidence suggests that any interruption in children's schooling typically worsens learning outcomes. Such interruptions include disruptions caused by epidemics, conflict, natural disasters, and even scheduled school vacations. US students' achievement scores appear to decline by about a month's worth, on average, during the regular three-month summer break (Cooper et al. 1996).[15]

Historical experiences illustrate the impacts of large-scale school closures during a public health emergency. Studying the effects of the 1916 polio pandemic on educational attainment in the United States, Meyers and Thomasson (2017) find that young people ages 14–17 during the pandemic later showed reduced overall educational attainment compared to slightly older peers. Even short-term school closures appeared to have lasting impacts on children's educational attainment, though the study finds such effects only among children who were of legal working age during the school closures.

Increased dropout rates are one factor linking emergency school closures to future losses in lifetime educational attainment. In general, as children age, the opportunity cost of staying in school increases, which may make it harder for households to justify sending older children back to school after a forced interruption, especially if households are under financial stress. Again, such effects are not restricted to public health emergencies. Among agricultural households in Tanzania, income shocks, even transitory ones, have led to increased child labor and reduced school attendance (Beegle, Dehejia, and Gatti 2006).

Evidence from natural disasters confirms that interruptions and trauma in the neurodevelopmental process can adversely affect academic performance. Four years after bushfires in Australia, children from areas that were heavily affected by the fires performed worse in reading and numeracy than did their peers from less-affected areas (Gibbs et al. 2019). The case of the bushfires underscores the importance of continued support to affected populations, because a longer-term learning divergence was found even though students did not display any differences in learning outcomes immediately after the disaster.

Further indication of the damage caused by school interruptions can be gleaned from outcomes after the 2005 earthquake in Pakistan. Areas near the fault line were devastated, 80 percent of homes were destroyed, and schools suffered considerable damage. Cash transfers played an important mitigating role: four years after the earthquake, households near the fault line were indiscernible, in welfare terms, from those farther away from the fault line. Enrollment rates for children residing near the fault line were not affected. Despite the apparent return to normalcy, however, test scores for children living 10 kilometers away from the fault line were 0.24 standard deviations below those of children residing 40 kilometers away.[16]

Many countries have adopted distance learning as a means to mitigate learning losses during protracted school closures. Remote teaching strategies include not only online learning but also radio and TV programs and text nudges in those countries where digital connectivity is limited. These strategies make it less likely that negative effects of similar magnitude to other interruptions will be replicated; however, the effectiveness of these measures has yet to be determined.

The most recent global projections on the impact of school closures linked to COVID-19 suggest that, using the HCI metric of learning-adjusted years of schooling (LAYS; see box 1.1 in chapter 1), closures will result in almost 0.6 years lost. These numbers reflect the loss of schooling that comes from potential dropouts due to the loss of income,[17] as well as the adjustment in quality due to worsened learning because of inefficient remote teaching methods (Azevedo et al. 2020). The lost schooling in the face of a mitigation strategy that has medium efficiency translates to a yearly loss of over US$872 in 2011 purchasing power parity US dollars, reaching a loss of US$16,000 in lifetime earnings in present value terms at a discount rate of 3 percent and assuming a 45-year work life (Azevedo et al. 2020).[18] As children head back to school, countries with an already overextended education system may grapple with increased demand for public education, because household income losses have prompted many parents to turn to public schools rather than private. In June 2020, registration in public schools in the coastal zone of Ecuador, for example, increased by 6.5 percent, bringing some 120,000 additional students into the public system. This increase occurred despite the government's offering of a 25 percent subsidy on monthly private school tuition for parents who had lost jobs (Olsen and Prado 2020). With limited numbers of qualified teachers available, migration of students from private to public schools could worsen learning outcomes across many countries.

Thus, the impacts of school closures extend far beyond initial enrollment drops. For girls, school closures may also lead to increased exposure to pregnancy and sexual abuse. In many countries this outcome could be worsened by policies that prevent "visibly pregnant girls" from attending school (Bandiera et al. 2019). Both shorter- and longer-term impacts are likely to affect disadvantaged families most, further widening inequalities in learning and human capital accumulation between socioeconomic groups.

Finally, a drastic change in the day-to-day lives of children and adolescents is likely to affect their mental health. The pandemic may worsen existing mental health issues by provoking or exacerbating social isolation, economic uncertainty, and fear (Golberstein, Wen, and Miller 2020). A recent study among Ecuadorian teenagers (ages 14 to 18) found that one in six teenagers reported suffering from depression, and many cited household finances and social isolation as concerns (Asanov et al. 2020). The use of digital technology, particularly with voice and video, can ameliorate the loneliness faced by many teens and children, but these technologies are not available to all (Galea, Merchant, and Lurie 2020).

3.2.3 School-to-work transition and tertiary education

The pandemic is also disrupting human capital accumulation for students currently in tertiary education. Almost all students currently enrolled in tertiary education are experiencing a new learning modality (Bassett and Arnhold 2020). With students in low- and middle-income economies less likely to have internet access, between-country inequalities in learning will worsen. Within economies, those at the bottom of the income distribution will also be more affected, because they lack access to the necessary materials for remote learning. This disparity will again exacerbate existing inequalities in human capital accumulation.

Two opposing forces may influence tertiary enrollment rates. Pandemic-induced high unemployment rates are likely to reduce the opportunity cost of attending college. At the same time, the recession will affect many households economically, and funds for attending college may not be available. After the 2008–09 financial crisis, enrollment rates for tertiary education in the United States went up. Because of a substantial decrease in family incomes, however, students shifted away from four-year private colleges toward two-year public institutions (Dunbar et al. 2011).[19]

Those who graduate from college now are also likely to suffer short- to medium-term wage losses. Evidence from Canada suggests that graduating during a recession is linked to significant initial earning loss due to less desirable job placements but that this penalty fades over some 8 to 10 years (Oreopoulos, von Wachter, and Heisz 2012). Nevertheless, the average effect hides substantial heterogeneity. Recent graduates with the lowest predicted earnings are likely to suffer the largest losses and often do not recover the lost ground after 10 years.[20] Starting at a lower-paying job or at a less-desirable firm that does not make full use of an individual's existing human capital may well lead to a lag in skill accumulation and result in a persistent disadvantage.

Women who graduate from high school during the pandemic may choose to respond differently than their male peers to the shock and forgo college in the short term. They are also less likely to join the workforce because of the depressed wages. Evidence from the United States suggests that women, but not men, graduating from high school are more likely to skip college during recessions because of the lower observed returns to education and because the cost of more schooling increases (Hershbein 2012). For some, the alternative of child rearing may be more attractive in the short term, as was the case during the 2008–09 global recession. For others, disruptions in supply chains may lead to unintended pregnancies because many women will lose access to modern contraceptives.[21]

Finally, the depressed wages and fewer legal employment options available during a recession mean that crime also becomes more attractive. The longer the recession lasts, the more likely that acquired human capital depreciates and crime becomes a worthwhile option. This effect is heightened for those who have lower human capital levels and are less attached to the labor market.[22]

3.2.4 Working life

Together with its effects on the economy, the pandemic has affected labor markets dramatically. According to the International Labour Organization, working hours during the first quarter of 2020 declined by the equivalent of 130 million full-time jobs. The organization expects that the results will be even worse in the second quarter of 2020, with the number climbing to 305 million full-time jobs (International Labour Organization 2020). The pandemic and lockdown measures are affecting workers worldwide but are having particularly dramatic impacts for informal workers. Informal work often happens in crowded places, so that lockdown measures—when enforced strictly—make continuing with these jobs impossible (International Labour Organization 2020). Informal workers also often fall through the cracks of social protection systems, lacking access to unemployment and health insurance (Packard et al. 2019).

Unemployment stints, even short ones, tend to leave a lasting mark on individuals' earnings. For many, the current shock will be the second "unprecedented" economic shock of their working lifetime. Workers who have longer tenures in a company, if dismissed, are likely to face a considerable erosion of skills, because many skills they have accumulated may be particular to that employer. If these workers find employment in the future, and their new job requires different skills, they are likely to experience a considerable wage penalty (Poletaev and Robinson 2008). Those who lose a job during a mass layoff event are likely to experience large and persistent earning losses, roughly equivalent to 1.7 years of their earnings before dismissal (Davis and von Wachter 2011).

Evidence also suggests that those who have lost jobs during the pandemic could suffer far more than lost earnings. One study finds that US workers who were employed in a firm for at least six years and were then dismissed during a recession had higher mortality rates than similar workers who had not been displaced. The estimates suggest an average decrease in life expectancy for the dismissed workers of between 1.0 and 1.5 years, likely due to increased chronic stress (Sullivan and von Wachter 2009).

The pandemic and the nonpharmaceutical interventions taken to control it are also likely affecting women more than men. The sectors typically most affected by lockdowns have high shares of female employment (Alon et al. 2020). School closures will likely contribute to heavier workloads for many women, mostly because women are likely to be responsible for childcare in the absence of alternatives. These pressures may limit women's paid work (Wenham, Smith, and Morgan 2020). Established gender norms are also likely to prevail when a family member falls ill from COVID-19, with women in the household expected to care for the sick. Conversely, the current shift to flexible working arrangements could benefit some workers, including women, and could promote gender equality in the labor market in some settings (Alon et al. 2020).

Beyond work, interpersonal violence is also on the rise, leaving many women more exposed because of the lockdown (van Gelder et al. 2020). Evidence of this increase has already surfaced. For example, in Argentina, lockdown restrictions were directly linked to a 28 percent increase in calls to the domestic violence hotline. Additionally, also in Argentina, women whose partners were also in quarantine were more likely to report an increase in interpersonal violence due to increased exposure to the perpetrator (Perez-Vincent et al. 2020).[23] There also is evidence of this effect in India, where domestic violence complaints increased most in regions that implemented a stricter lockdown (Ravindran and Shah 2020).

3.2.5 Older adults

The risk of adverse health effects from COVID-19 increases significantly with age and comorbidities, making the elderly especially vulnerable. Residing in a long-term care facility also substantially increases risk. For example, preliminary analysis of April 2020 COVID-19 exposure data in Italy indicated that 44 percent of infections during this period were contracted in nursing homes or homes for the disabled (COVID-19 Task Force 2020). In the United States, as of mid-May 2020, nursing home residents accounted for about one-third of COVID-19 fatalities (see CDC 2020; Yourish et al. 2020). Although such findings are alarming, they probably underestimate actual infection and case fatality rates among older adults, because there is evidence that, especially at the beginning of national epidemics, deaths from COVID-19 went unrecorded in many long-term care facilities.

An immediate priority for countries fighting COVID-19 is to protect the elderly and those with significant comorbidities. Prevention, control, appropriate staffing, coordination, management, reporting, communication, and planning are all needed to safeguard older adults living in residential facilities.[24] In the longer run, the vulnerabilities revealed by COVID-19 point to the need to increase human capital resilience. Doing so could mean not only rethinking policies and services for today's elders but also supporting younger generations to prepare for a healthy longevity in the future. This support will involve stepping up prevention of noncommunicable diseases such as cardiovascular diseases, obesity, and diabetes.

3.3 USING THE HCI TO SIMULATE THE IMPACT OF THE PANDEMIC

The HCI is designed to capture the human capital a child born today can expect to attain by age 18. Given that the future is uncertain, the best approximation of human capital accumulation for a child born today is based on the currently observed outcomes of older cohorts. Despite uncertainty about how long it will take for the world to arrive at a post-COVID-19 "new normal" (and what the world will look like then), for the purpose of the long-term outcomes captured by the HCI, the pandemic is mostly a transitory shock. For example, although school closures affect school-age children now, they are unlikely to affect children who are born today, assuming that the pandemic has been controlled and school is in session by the time those children are ready to start school.

The disruption to health systems and shocks to family income will, however, affect young children's survival and healthy development (stunting) now. In turn, this health outcome will affect their learning and schooling. Because all the data for the 2020 HCI were collected before the virus struck, it serves as a pre-COVID-19 baseline, and the HCI construct can be used to simulate the direct and indirect impacts of the pandemic on young children's human capital.[25] Over time, it can be used to track the actual changes in human capital outcomes as the pandemic evolves.

The rest of this section discusses an example of a simulation of the effects of the pandemic shock on the future human capital of young children under 5 years. Then it uses the HCI to simulate how the pandemic—through school closures and shock to family income—will affect the future human capital of children who are currently in school.

3.3.1 Shock to children under 5

COVID-19 is seemingly not as directly damaging to the health of children or pregnant mothers as previous pandemics have been (Almond and Currie 2011).[26] The associated economic shock, however, is expected to be harmful for the youngest children and children in utero, because considerable drops in family income can translate into food insecurity, in turn leading to increased child mortality and stunting. An additional shock is the decrease in coverage of essential health interventions for pregnant mothers and young children. This decrease is due to health services disruptions. These shocks too will affect child mortality and child health. Mapping them into changes in human capital as measured by the HCI requires estimates of how mortality and stunting change in response to shocks to GDP per capita, as well as to reductions in health services.

Because child health (captured by worsened stunting rates) and educational outcomes are closely intertwined, the shock is also expected to affect the amount of education this cohort of children will attain in the future as well as how much education they can retain. Take a reduction in GDP per capita of 10 percent—a pessimistic scenario. An elasticity of stunting to income of −0.6 would imply an increase in stunting of 6 percent. For example, for a country like Bangladesh, where the pre-COVID-19 stunting rate was 31 percent, an income shock of this magnitude could increase stunting by 1.85 percentage points. Children who are stunted are less likely to stay in school and learn, so this increase in stunting could in turn lead to a drop in expected years of school of 0.03 years, and a drop in harmonized test scores (HTSs) of 1.16 points.[27] With about 10 years of schooling and HTS of 370, the losses due to an increase in stunting could amount to nearly 1 percent of the HCI. Add in the likely increase in child mortality due to health service disruptions, and the income drop would further drive down the HCI by an additional 0.10 to 0.47 percent, depending on the assumptions. Altogether, a decline in income of 10 percent could lead to a decline in the HCI ranging from 1.13 to 1.50 percent.

Annex 3A reports the methodology of the simulation in more detail. For each economy, the percentage decline in income due to COVID-19 is estimated as the difference between projections of per capita GDP growth made in June 2020 and the pre-COVID-19 projections made in late 2019. The calculations described above are then applied to simulate the likely effects on human capital as measured by the HCI for each economy. Averaged across all economies, the projected shock would result in an HCI loss of 0.44 percent. This outcome is worse for low- and lower-middle-income economies (losses of 0.73 and 0.64 percent, respectively), mostly because the stunting rates are highest for this group (table 3.1).[28] Although the loss may not seem large, it will likely set back children within the affected cohort for years to come, leading to accumulated losses. For example, by 1960, the cohort of adults who were in utero during the 1918 influenza pandemic had 0.1 fewer years of education than those adults born in the year before or after the pandemic. When comparing the wages of the same groups in 1960, those who were in utero during the influenza pandemic had wages that were 2.2 percent lower than those of the neighboring cohorts (Almond 2006). These losses build up over time and leave affected cohorts at a considerable disadvantage.

3.3.2 Schooling and learning

Through school closures, the human capital of the current cohort of school-age children is being heavily affected by the pandemic: at its peak, nearly

Table 3.1: Simulated drop in Human Capital Index due to the pandemic's impacts on children 5 and under

	HCI 2020	Percent drop in HCI	Percentage point difference between June 2020 and AM19 GDP per capita growth projections
World Bank income group			
High income	0.707	−0.17	−6.23
Upper-middle income	0.560	−0.42	−7.77
Lower-middle income	0.480	−0.64	−5.36
Low income	0.375	−0.73	−4.34
Global	0.561	−0.44	−6.16

Source: World Bank calculations based on the 2020 update of the Human Capital Index (HCI).

Note: Calculations are based on the methodology presented in annex 3A. Projected GDP changes are from the June version of the *Global Economic Prospects* and the 2019 Macro Poverty Outlook (Annual Meetings of 2019 [AM19]). The simulation assumes a four-month interruption to health system access. The access scenario comes from Roberton et al. (2020) and assumes considerable reductions in the availability of health workers and supply due to pandemic-driven reallocations. The scenario also assumes reduced demand due to fears of infection and movement restrictions as well as economic pressure. The scenario from Roberton et al. (2020) does not include additional child deaths due to wasting.

1.6 billion children worldwide were out of school.[29] The simulation framework proposed by Azevedo et al. (2020) quantifies the effects of this shock on the global stock of schooling and learning through three channels: during closures children (1) lose out on opportunities to learn, (2) may forget what they have previously learned, and (3) may drop out because of household income losses.

According to the 2020 HCI, before COVID-19 the global average of the expected years of school was 11.2 years, which, when adjusted for learning, translated into 7.8 LAYS. To simulate the effect of closures on learning, the simulation starts by assuming a value of learning gained in one year of schooling. This value is proxied by HTS points per year.[30] To determine how much of this learning will be lost as a result of closures, the simulation assumes three scenarios: optimistic, intermediate, and pessimistic, corresponding to three, five, and seven months of school closures, respectively. The three scenarios also differ on the assumed effectiveness of the mitigation measures put in place by governments, which vary by income group.[31] The three components are used to project HTS points lost because of school closures under the assumption that the losses due to school closures are not recuperated.[32]

Expected years of school are also projected to fall because the income shock will likely cause many children to drop out of school.[33] COVID-19 could lead an additional 6.8 million children to drop out of school around the world. Sixty percent of these dropouts will be children between 12 and 17 years of age, who are likely to leave school permanently because of losses in household income. Overall, the number of out-of-school children is likely to increase by 2 percent.

Take, for example, an upper-middle-income economy like Peru, and assume a drop in GDP per capita of 10 percent. The drop in GDP and rise in the rate of dropouts will result in a small loss in expected years of school (0.005).[34] School closures and the limited capacity of economies to deliver education during the closures lead to an additional loss to years of school. Assuming, in the optimistic scenario, that schools are closed for 3 months out of a 10-month school year, without any mitigation, students would lose 0.3 years of school. Assuming instead, in this scenario, a mitigation effectiveness of 0.4, only 60 percent of that period would be lost, leading to a loss of only 0.18 school years (0.3*(1.0 – 0.4)). A further dimension of loss comes from the drop in learning. Children in upper-middle-income economies like Peru gain 40 HTS points in a school year. With students missing out on 0.18 years of school, they are also losing 7.2 HTS points (40*0.3*(1 – 0.4)). Putting it all together means a loss of 0.27 LAYS.

Figure 3.2 depicts the combined losses in learning and expected years of schooling for different country income groups. Under the intermediate scenario of a five-month closure, COVID-19 could lead to a loss of 0.56 years of school, adjusted for quality. This scenario means that school closures due to COVID-19 could bring the average learning that students achieve during their lifetime down to 7.3 LAYS.[35] In the optimistic scenario, the projected loss is 0.25 years of schooling and, in the pessimistic scenario, 0.87 years.

Across the globe, the extent of this shortfall will vary. In high-income economies, where children were expected to complete 10.3 LAYS before the pandemic, the simulations suggest that COVID-19 could lower LAYS to 10.1 in the optimistic scenario and 9.2 in the pessimistic scenario. At the other end of the spectrum, children in low-income economies were expected to complete 4.3 LAYS before COVID-19. The optimistic scenario suggests that this value would fall to 4.1 years, whereas the pessimistic scenario foresees a decline to 3.8 years.

Putting these losses in LAYS in the context of the HCI implies a 4.5 percent drop in human capital for children of school age, which is on the order of the average gains in human capital made in the past decade (table 3.2).

What is known about the virus itself continues to evolve, making many behavioral patterns

Figure 3.2: Learning-adjusted years of schooling lost because of COVID-19 school closures and income shock

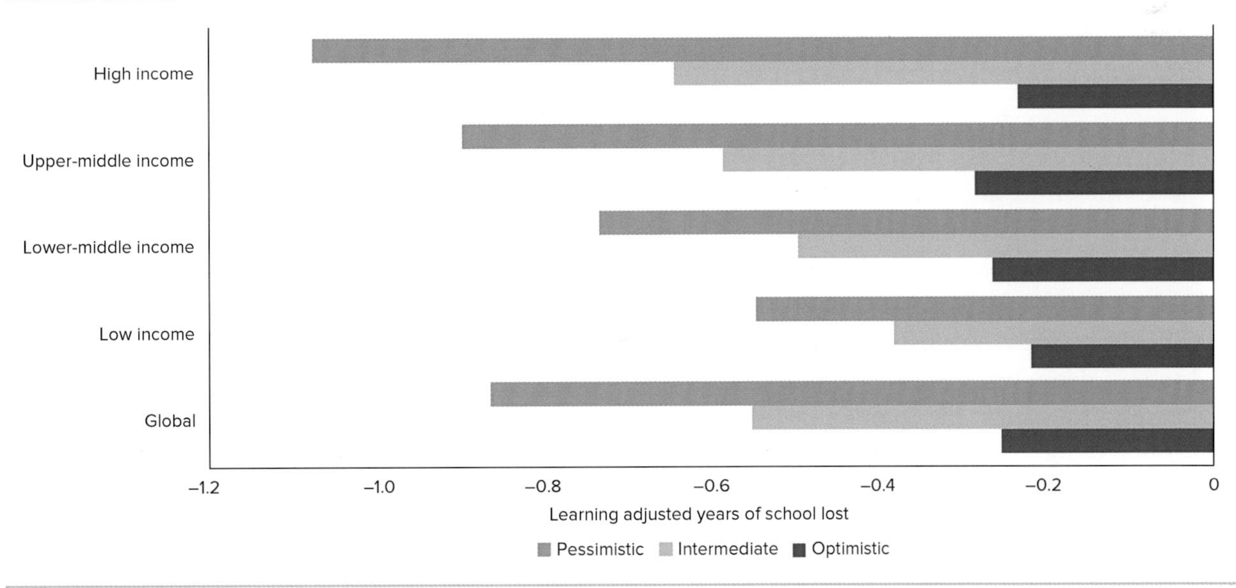

Source: Azevedo et al. 2020.

Note: Results based on latest available learning-adjusted school years for 174 economies (unweighted average). Coverage of 99 percent of the population ages 4–17 years using the methodology from Azevedo et al. (2020). Projected GDP changes are from the June version of the *Global Economic Prospects*. School closure length for each scenario: seven months for pessimistic, five months for intermediate, and three months for optimistic. Mitigation effectiveness also differs by scenario and income group. Refer to Azevedo et al. (2020) for full details.

Table 3.2: Human Capital Index shock to children currently in school during the pandemic

	Percent drop in HCI based on GDP per capita projected change as of June 2020	Percent drop in HCI if GDP per capita for all economies dropped by 10 percent
World Bank income group		
High income	−5.17	−5.34
Upper-middle income	−4.71	−5.04
Lower-middle income	−4.00	−4.54
Low income	−3.07	−3.66
Global	−4.45	−4.82

Source: World Bank calculations based on the 2020 update of the Human Capital Index (HCI) and on Azevedo et al. 2020.

Note: The calculation is based on the method presented in annex 3B. Projected GDP changes are from the June 2020 version of the *Global Economic Prospects*.

Table 3.3: Human capital loss of the workforce in 2040

	HCI drop based on GDP per capita projected change as of June 2020	HCI drop if GDP per capita for all economies dropped by 10 percent
World Bank income group		
High income	−0.011	−0.012
Upper-middle income	−0.009	−0.009
Lower-middle income	−0.007	−0.008
Low income	−0.005	−0.006
Global	−0.0084	−0.0093

Source: World Bank calculations based on the 2020 update of the Human Capital Index (HCI) and on Azevedo et al. 2020.

Note: The calculation is based on the methodology presented in annexes 3A and 3B. Projected GDP changes are from the June 2020 version of the *Global Economic Prospects*.

difficult to predict. For instance, parental concerns about child and family safety will likely dominate household decision-making around sending children back to schools when they reopen. Hence, any estimates of dropouts that consider only the relationship between incomes and school dropouts are likely to underestimate the extent to which the pandemic will affect children's schooling and learning. Additionally, these numbers ignore the possibility of remediating these losses.

3.3.3 The long-run HCI losses to the cohort

In 20 years, roughly 46 percent of the workforce in a typical country (people ages 20 to 65) will be composed of individuals who were either in school or under the age of 5 during the COVID-19 pandemic.[36] Assume that the 2020 HCI summarizes well the human capital children under the age of 5 could have achieved, and that the 2010 HCI is the best representation of the human capital children who are currently in school could have achieved. With the HCI losses as calculated in the earlier sections, the HCI of the workforce in 20 years' time in the typical economy would be lower by almost 1 HCI point (0.01) because of COVID-19 today.[37]

As an example, assume that an economy's HCI for children under 5 is expected to fall by 1 percent and that those children represent 15 percent of the workforce in 2040. Also assume that the losses due to school closures are 4 percent and that those school-age children will be 30 percent of the workforce by 2040. If the economy's HCI in 2010 was 0.54 and for 2020 is 0.56, then the HCI of that economy's workforce in 2040 will be 0.007 lower than it would have been in the absence of the pandemic.[38]

Given that children who are currently in school will be a larger share of the 2040 workforce than will those currently under 5, and that the losses for the former are larger in high-income economies, the fall is expected to be largest among high- and upper-middle-income economies. Those economies are also the ones that have the highest levels of HCI and thus are projected to lose more (table 3.3). The results shown here are meant to inspire action and show that, without remediation, an entire generation could be left behind.

ANNEX 3A. COVID-19 SHOCK TO THE UNDER-5 COHORTS

The starting point for this simulation is a version of the HCI calculated with stunting only.[39] Assuming that changes in stunting, through its relationship to height, are sufficient to capture the health component of the index, the relevant HCI equation in log terms can be written as

$$\ln HCI = \ln(Survival) + \phi\left(EYS \times \frac{HTS}{625} - 14\right) + \gamma_{Stuning}(-Stunting\ Rate) \quad (3A.1)$$

The changes in HCI for the under-5 cohorts are driven by the income shock and reduction in health care access. Consequently, the three pathways for the pandemic shock are as follows:

1. The income shock affects under-5 mortality rates.
2. The income shock also leads to an increase in stunting rates. In turn, a change in stunting rates is expected to be related to a change in the years of school completed by affected children. It is also likely to be related to a change in cognition, proxied by HTS.
3. An additional shock is due to the reduced access to health services, whether from fear of contagion or from the lockdown measures. This shock is expected mostly to affect under-5 mortality.

In sum, both the fall in access to health services and the income shock will lead to an increase in child mortality and will worsen stunting. Because more children will be stunted when they reach school age, it is also likely that this outcome will decrease educational outcomes.

Income shock

The income shock ($\Delta y/y$) used in the simulations comes from the World Bank Global Economic Prospects (World Bank 2020). The values come from the difference between projected GDP per capita growth for 2020 used in the Macro Poverty Outlook from the World Bank Annual Meetings of 2019 (before COVID-19), and the GDP per capita growth projections made in June 2020.

Stunting

The effect of the income shock on stunting is

$$\Delta lnHCI = -\gamma_{Stunting}\frac{\partial Stunting}{\partial y}\Delta y \quad (3A.2)$$

where $\gamma_{Stunting} = 10.2 \times 0.034 = 0.35$ as discussed in appendix A. Although a direct value of $\frac{\partial Stunting}{\partial y}$ is not available, this value is replaced with an elasticity from Ruel, Alderman, and the Maternal and Child Nutrition Study Group (2013):

$$\frac{\partial Stunting}{\partial y}\frac{y}{Stunting} = -0.6 \quad (3A.3)$$

Inserting equation (3A.3) into equation (3A.2) yields the following expression for the direct effect of an income-induced increase in stunting on the HCI:

$$\Delta lnHCI = -\gamma_{Stunting} \frac{\partial Stunting}{\partial y} \frac{y}{Stunting} \frac{\Delta y}{y} Stunting \quad (3A.4)$$

For economies missing stunting data, the average rate for its income group is applied.

Education

The effect of the income shock on education of a child born today is expected to come through the effect on stunting:

$$\Delta lnHCI = \frac{\phi}{625}\left(\frac{\partial EYS}{\partial Stunting}\frac{\partial Stunting}{\partial y} HTS + \frac{\partial HTS}{\partial Stunting}\frac{\partial Stunting}{\partial y} EYS\right)\Delta y \quad (3A.5)$$

where $\phi = 0.08$ and $\frac{\partial EYS}{\partial Stunting} = -1.594$ *years of education*, and $\frac{\partial HTS}{\partial Stunting} = -0.625$ standard deviations.

Inserting equation (3A.3) into equation (3A.5) gives us the effect of the income shock on education, operating through increased stunting:

$$\Delta lnHCI = \frac{\phi}{625}\left(\frac{\partial EYS}{\partial Stunting}\frac{\partial Stunting}{\partial y}\frac{y}{Stunting} HTS + \frac{\partial HTS}{\partial Stunting}\frac{\partial Stunting}{\partial y}\frac{y}{Stunting} EYS\right) \frac{\Delta y}{y} Stunting \quad (3A.6)$$

Mortality

The negative income shock increases child mortality, with the following effect on the HCI:

$$\Delta \ln HCI = \frac{\partial \ln survival}{\partial U5MR}\frac{\partial U5MR}{\partial y}\Delta y \quad (3A.7)$$

where $\frac{\partial \ln survival}{\partial U5MR}$ is equal to $\frac{-1}{1-U5MR}$. Although a direct value of $\frac{\partial U5MR}{\partial y}$ is not available, this value is replaced with a semielasticity from Ma et al. (2020):[40]

$$\frac{\partial U5MR}{\partial y} y = -0.013 \quad (3A.8)$$

Inserting equation (3A.8) into equation (3A.7) yields:

$$\Delta lnHCI = \frac{\partial \ln Survival}{\partial U5MR}\frac{\partial U5MR}{\partial y} y \frac{\Delta y}{y} \quad (3A.9)$$

An additional shock to mortality is assumed to come from the change in access to health services measured in months of disrupted access:

$$\Delta lnHCI = \frac{\partial \ln Survival}{\partial U5MR}\frac{\partial U5MR}{\partial Access}\Delta\ Access \quad (3A.10)$$

Although a direct value of $\frac{\partial U5MR}{\partial Access}$ is not available, this value is replaced with a monthly access change to the elasticity of the under-5 mortality rate from Roberton et al (2020).[41]

$$\frac{\partial U5MR}{\partial\ Access}\frac{Access}{U5MR} = 0.136 \quad (3A.11)$$

This value suggests a monthly relative increase in under-5 mortality of 13.6 percent given a one-month lack of access. Because the values that enter the index are annual, this value is extrapolated to the year and inserted into equation (3A.9):

$$\Delta lnHCI = \frac{\partial \ln Survival}{\partial U5MR}\frac{\partial U5MR}{\partial Access}\frac{Access}{U5MR}\frac{\Delta\ Access}{Access} U5MR \quad (3A.12)$$

Under the baseline scenario, a 3-month change in the access to care is assumed; thus, in equation (3A.12), access is equal to 12 months and $\Delta Access$ is equal to 3 months.

HCI

Putting all these pieces together returns the total HCI change due to the pandemic:

$$\Delta lnHCI = \frac{\partial \ln Survival}{\partial U5MR}\frac{\partial U5MR}{\partial Access}\frac{Access}{U5MR}\frac{\Delta Access}{Access} U5MR + \frac{\partial \ln Survival}{\partial U5MR}\frac{\partial U5MR}{\partial y}\frac{y}{U5MR}\frac{\Delta y}{y} U5MR + \frac{\phi}{625}\left(\frac{\partial EYS}{\partial Stunting}\frac{\partial Stunting}{\partial y}\frac{y}{Stunting} HTS + \frac{\partial HTS}{\partial Stunting}\frac{\partial Stunting}{\partial y}\frac{y}{Stunting} EYS\right) \frac{\Delta y}{y} Stunting - \gamma_{Stunting}\frac{\partial Stunting}{\partial y}\frac{y}{Stunting}\frac{\Delta y}{y} Stunting \quad (3A.13)$$

Note how the first component, the one related to access, enters independently from the income shock.

ANNEX 3B. COVID-19 SHOCK TO SCHOOL-AGE COHORTS

The shock to children who are presently in school is derived as in Azevedo et al. (2020), but using the data for the 2020 HCI. The shock to children operates through two channels: the income channel, leading to increased dropouts, and the school closure channel, leading to loss in learning and in school years. Recall that LAYS at the pre-COVID-19 baseline (0) is

$$LAYS_0 = EYS_0 \times \frac{HTS_0}{625}$$

The changes in income, how well governments can deliver education while schools are closed, and how long schools are closed are all expected to decrease LAYS. The number of out-of-school children is assumed to increase because of the income shock. These changes are calculated for each welfare quintile using data from 130 household surveys using the latest available Global Monitoring Database, separately for children ages 4–11 and 12–17. The shock from the GDP per capita growth projections is used to arrive at a new welfare value, which is achieved by assuming the shock is uniform across the distribution; thus, the shape of the distribution is maintained but is just shifted to the left. The shift of the household welfare of children moves children across welfare quintiles, and the quintile thresholds are the same as those from the original welfare distribution. Finally, the quintile's share of out-of-school children is used to get the new total number of out-of-school children.[42] In essence, when household income drops, children move down the welfare quintiles (because the thresholds are maintained). With more children in lower welfare quintiles with higher shares of out-of-school children, there will be an overall increase in the share of out-of-school children, because the denominator (total number of children in the specific school-age bracket) stays the same.

The first component of the change in LAYS is the years of school lost due to students who drop out due to the income shock (D).

When children go to school, they experience in-person learning, assumed to be the most efficient learning mode. With school closures, children will experience different, less efficient, learning. The length of school closures differs according to different scenarios: three months, five months, and seven months for the optimistic, intermediate, and pessimistic scenarios, respectively. The effectiveness of different remote learning strategies deployed, and the scenarios, are linked to the economy's income group (see table 3B.1).

The second component of the change in LAYS is the share of the school year that is lost because of the closure and the alternative learning modality (S):

$$S = (1 - Mitigation) \times Closure_{Share\ of\ School\ Year}$$

HTSs are assumed to change over a school year by a certain amount (p); the amount is dependent on the economy's income group (see table 3B.2). The learning of these children is compromised by

Table 3B.1: Mitigation effectiveness, by scenario and income group

	Low income	Lower-middle income	Upper-middle income	High income
Optimistic	0.2	0.28	0.4	0.6
Intermediate	0.1	0.14	0.2	0.3
Pessimistic	0.05	0.07	0.1	0.15

Source: Azevedo et al. 2020.

Table 3B.2: School productivity (HTS points gained per school year)

	Points
High income	50
Upper-middle income	40
Lower-middle income	30
Low income	20

Source: Azevedo et al. 2020.
Note: HTS = harmonized test score.

the closures and the limited effectiveness of the deployed learning modality.

The final component to the change in LAYS is the amount of learning that takes place under the remote learning scenario (H):

$$H = S \times p$$

The change in LAYS is then:

$$\Delta LAYS = LAYS_1 - LAYS_0$$

$$\Delta LAYS = LAYS_1 - EYS_0 \times \frac{HTS_0}{625}$$

where $LAYS_1$ is equal to

$$LAYS_1 = \left(EYS_0 - S - D\right)\frac{\left(HTS_0 - H\right)}{625}$$

NOTES

1. Simulations suggest that, in Ireland, 400,000 households may see a drop in their disposable income of 20 percent or more (Beirne et al. 2020). In Italy, simulations show that disposable income losses will be considerable and more pronounced for the poorest. Italian households in the poorest quintile are projected to lose 40 percent of their income (Figari and Fiorio 2020).
2. Hogan et al. (2020) find that for HIV the largest impact is from interruption of antiretroviral therapy, for tuberculosis the impact is due to reduction of timely diagnosis and treatment, and for malaria the impact reflects the interruption of prevention programs.
3. Roberton et al. (2020) suggest that maintaining key childbirth interventions like parenteral administration of uterotonics, antibiotics, anticonvulsants, and clean birth environments could lead to 60 percent fewer maternal deaths. Maintaining coverage of antibiotics for neonatal sepsis and pneumonia and oral rehydration solution for diarrhea would reduce child deaths by 41 percent. These results are likely contingent on modeling assumptions.
4. From the United Nations Educational, Scientific and Cultural Organization's COVID-19 web page, "Education: From Disruption to Recovery," at https://en.unesco.org/covid19/educationresponse.
5. Girls' educational outcomes during a crisis tend to fall more than do those of boys. This is particularly the case if parents' perception of returns on investments for boys are greater than for girls (Rose 2000).
6. This effect was observed during the 2014–15 Ebola outbreak in West Africa (see de la Fuente, Jacoby, and Lawin 2019). A similar effect is now seen in India, where nonavailability of migrant labor has interrupted harvesting activities (see Saha and Bhattacharya 2020).
7. Women will often sacrifice their own consumption needs in order to ensure sufficient nutrition for other household members (see Quisumbing et al. 2011).
8. When surveyed, Ugandan households had yet to resort to selling productive assets to cope with the losses in income, perhaps in the hope that the income shortfall will be short-lived.
9. In some cases, the substitution effect (the relative change in prices of activities) dominates the income effect (the drop in purchasing power). For example, Miller and Urdinola (2010) present evidence of how child health improved among children of coffee farmers in Colombia during a decline in the price of coffee. Because the fall in coffee prices made time spent farming less valuable, parents devoted more time to their children, which translates into better outcomes for children. Schady (2004) provides evidence that, in Peru,

children exposed to a crisis in the late 1980s completed on average one additional year of schooling.

10. For example, Bundervoet and Fransen (2018) find that children exposed to the Rwandan genocide while in utero suffered lower educational outcomes. The longer the exposure in utero, the poorer the educational outcomes.
11. Savasi et al. (2020) find that 12 percent of the 77 patients in their study (in Italy) had a preterm delivery. By contrast, Philip et al. (2020) find a reduction in preterm births in Ireland, and a reduction in very low birthweights, falling from 3.77 cases per 1,000 births to 2.17 cases.
12. O'Hare et al. (2013) obtain this estimate through meta-analysis from a systematic literature search of studies and find a pooled elasticity of income on infant mortality of −0.95.
13. Ma et al. (2020) find that, in low-income countries, a lockdown will potentially lead to 1.17 children's lives lost per COVID-19 fatality averted, due to the economic contraction, significantly higher than in lower-middle- and upper-middle-income countries (where it would stand at 0.48 and 0.06, respectively). Two factors account for this outcome: the younger demographic structure and the higher estimated elasticity of child mortality to GDP changes in low-income countries. The authors also assume that under-5 mortality is not affected by income shocks in high-income countries.
14. Mary (2018) suggests that the decrease may be 2.7 percent, whereas Mary, Shaw, and Paloma (2019) estimate it to be 7.3 percent, and Ruel, Alderman, and the Maternal and Child Nutrition Study Group (2013) suggest 6 percent. It is worth noting that these analyses concentrated mostly on low- and middle-income economies.
15. More recent research has called this result into question (see von Hippel and Hamrock 2019 for a more nuanced discussion); however, a summer break is not the same as a break during the school year.
16. Andrabi, Daniels, and Das (2020) posit that this difference in test scores is equivalent to 1.5 school grades. To arrive at this value, the authors note that the average 15-year-old has accumulated 5.6 grades and linearly gains 0.17 standard deviations in performance per grade level in the test the authors use. This result, in the context of harmonized test scores used in the HCI, translates to a drop of 24 points.
17. The simulation by Azevedo et al. (2020) implicitly assumes that income effects outweigh substitution effects that may arise in these cases. Nonetheless, substitution effects may be larger, and enrollment could increase. Shafiq (2010) presents two cases in which enrollment may increase: (1) falling wages make child labor less attractive, and (2) parents place a higher preference on education, perhaps because less-educated workers bear the brunt of the crisis.
18. Values are obtained for 157 economies. Authors model different mitigation strategies taken during remote learning, vary the length of school closures, and assume children will drop out of school because of the income shock. The yearly losses range from US$127 in low-income economies to US$1,865 in high-income economies.
19. A similar dynamic was observed in Peru, where the opportunity costs of going to school decreased by a considerable amount because wages dropped substantially. Thus, children exposed to the crisis completed more years of education (Schady 2004).
20. Rothstein (2020) finds evidence that those who graduated during the 2008–09 financial crisis had lower wages and employment than earlier cohorts. The author shows that market conditions at the time of labor market entry matter greatly for cohorts' employment probabilities.
21. Roughly 47 million women in 114 low- and middle-income economies could lose access to contraceptives in the scenario of a six-month lockdown or disruptions (UNFPA 2020).

22. Bell, Bindler, and Machin (2017) find that cohorts graduating into a recession are 10.2 percent more likely to commit criminal activity than cohorts entering the labor market in nonrecession times.
23. The authors of the study also note a considerable increase (of 57 percent) in the number of calls related to psychological violence.
24. Such facilities include long-term care homes, residential care homes, nursing homes, welfare homes, and others.
25. See appendix A for details on the methodology of the HCI.
26. In early 1919, roughly one-third of all newborns had mothers who had been infected by influenza while pregnant. The 1918 pandemic was disproportionately deadly to those between 25 and 35 (Almond 2006).
27. These calculations are based on the literature review in Galasso and Wagstaff (2019). The authors find that children who are stunted obtain 1.594 years less education, and score 0.625 standard deviations lower on standardized tests.
28. For economies for which stunting data are not available and that are thus not used in the calculation of the HCI, the income group's average stunting rate is applied to the individual economy to simulate the possible losses due to the pandemic.
29. This section was contributed by Joao Pedro de Azevedo based on Azevedo et al. (2020). The results presented in this section use the 2020 HCI numbers as baseline values. For that reason, they will be slightly different from those in the original paper.
30. For high-income economies, the value is assumed to be 50 points in a year; 40 points for upper-middle-income economies; 30 points for lower-middle-income economies; and 20 points for low-income economies.
31. The authors assume that all governments offer some alternative learning modality. Estimates of their effectiveness are informed by existing multitopic household surveys. Thus, access and effectiveness of the implemented modalities differ by country income. Efficiency for lower-, lower-middle-, upper-middle-, and high-income economies under the pessimistic scenario is 5, 7, 10, and 15 percent, respectively. The values are doubled in the intermediate scenario and quadrupled under the optimistic scenario.
32. The outcome results from multiplying the HTS points per year by the share of the school year that is assumed to be lost, and 1 minus the efficiency of the mitigation measure in place.
33. The authors use household surveys for 130 economies to calculate economy-specific dropout income elasticities and welfare using cross-sectional variation by welfare quintiles. Refer to Azevedo et al. (2020) for details.
34. See Azevedo et al. (2020) for a detailed explanation on how the income shock is incorporated.
35. Intermediate scenario in Azevedo et al. (2020).
36. Roughly 34 percent of the workforce will be composed of individuals whose schooling was interrupted by the pandemic, and 12 percent of the workforce will be composed of individuals who were under the age of 5 during the pandemic.
37. To calculate the HCI loss by economy, the percentage change for each of the cohorts (presented in table 3.1 and table 3.2) is applied to the HCI of 2020 for the under-5 cohort and the HCI of 2010 for the cohort of 2010 to arrive at a value for HCI that is lost. Economies missing an HCI in 2010 were imputed the value of their income group. The economy's projected population shares are used to calculate each economy's HCI point loss among the workforce. The result supposes that on average those who are currently between the ages of 18 and 45 will not experience any ill health effects due to the pandemic, and thus in 20 years their human capital will be the same.
38. $HCI\ Loss = 0.56\ (-0.01)\ 0.15 + 0.54\ (-0.04)\ 0.3$.
39. Because the parameter $\gamma_{Stunting}$ embodies the best alternative of the link between stunting to adult height and from adult height to earnings,

the index can be expressed by relying just on stunting as a proxy for health.

40. The elasticities are disaggregated by income groups: it is assumed to be 0 for high-income economies, −0.003 for for upper-middle-income economies, −0.01 for lower-middle-income economies, and −0.013 for low-income economies. Ma et al. (2020) express these values as a 1 percent decrease in GDP per capita being associated with an increase of 0.13 under-5 deaths per 1,000 children (or an increase of 0.013 percentage points in under-5 mortality rates).
41. Roberton et al. (2020) offer three scenarios in which the effect ranges from 8.0 to 34.5 percent.
42. For countries without a household survey, the overall change in out-of-school rates for the country's income group is used.

REFERENCES

Acemoglu, D., V. Chernozhukov, I. Werning, and M. D. Whinston. 2020. "Optimal Targeted Lockdowns in a Multi-Group SIR Model." NBER Working Paper 27102, National Bureau of Economic Research, Cambridge, MA.

Almond, D. 2006. "Is the 1918 Influenza Pandemic Over? Long-Term Effects of In Utero Influenza Exposure in the Post-1940 US Population." *Journal of Political Economy* 114 (4): 672–712.

Almond, D., and J. Currie. 2011. "Killing Me Softly: The Fetal Origins Hypothesis." *Journal of Economic Perspectives* 25 (3): 153–72.

Alon, T., M. Doepke, J. Olmstead-Rumsey, and M. Tertilt. 2020. "The Impact of COVID-19 on Gender Equality." NBER Working Paper 26947, National Bureau of Economic Research, Cambridge, MA.

Andrabi, T., B. Daniels, and J. Das. 2020. "Human Capital Accumulation and Disasters: Evidence from the Pakistan Earthquake of 2005." RISE Working Paper Series 20/039, Research on Improving Systems of Education (RISE) Programme, Oxford.

Asanov, I., F. Flores, D. J. Mckenzie, M. Mensmann, and M. Schulte. 2020. "Remote-Learning, Time-Use, and Mental Health of Ecuadorian High-School Students during the COVID-19 Quarantine." Policy Research Working Paper 9252, World Bank, Washington, DC.

Azevedo, J. P., A. Hazan, D. Goldemberg, S. A. Iqbal, and K. Geven. 2020. "Simulating the Potential Impacts of COVID-19 School Closures on Schooling and Learning Outcomes: A Set of Global Estimates." Policy Research Working Paper 9284, World Bank, Washington, DC.

Bandiera, O., N. Buehren, M. P. Goldstein, I. Rasul, and A. Smurra. 2019. "The Economic Lives of Young Women in the Time of Ebola: Lessons from an Empowerment Program." Policy Research Working Paper 8760, World Bank, Washington, DC.

Bardhan, P., and C. Udry. 1999. *Development Microeconomics.* Oxford: Oxford University Press.

Bassett, M. R., and N. Arnhold. 2020. "COVID-19's Immense Impact on Equity in Tertiary Education." *Education for Global Development* (blog), April 30, 2020. https://blogs.worldbank.org/education/covid-19s-immense-impact-equity-tertiary-education.

Beegle, K., R. H. Dehejia, and R. Gatti. 2006. "Child Labor and Agricultural Shocks." *Journal of Development Economics* 81 (1): 80–96.

Beirne, K., K. Doorley, M. Regan, B. Roantree, and D. Tuda. 2020. "The Potential Costs and Distributional Effect of COVID-19 Related Unemployment in Ireland." Budget Perspectives 2021 Paper 1, Economic & Social Research Institute, Dublin.

Bell, B., A. Bindler, and S. Machin. 2017. "Crime Scars: Recessions and the Making of Career Criminals." *The Review of Economics and Statistics* 100 (3): 392–404.

Black, S. E., P. J. Devereux, and K. G. Salvanes. 2007. "From the Cradle to the Labor Market? The Effect of Birth Weight on Adult Outcomes." *The Quarterly Journal of Economics* 122 (1): 409–39.

Bundervoet, T., and S. Fransen. 2018. "The Educational Impact of Shocks in Utero: Evidence from Rwanda." *Economics & Human Biology* 29 (C): 88–101.

CDC (Centers for Disease Control and Prevention). 2020. "Coronavirus Disease 2019 (COVID-19)." https://www.cdc.gov/coronavirus/2019-ncov/index.html.

Chang, H.-J., N. Huang, C.-H. Lee, Y.-J. Hsu, C.-J., Hsieh, and Y.-J. Chou. 2004. "The Impact of the SARS Epidemic on the Utilization of Medical Services: SARS and the Fear of SARS." *American Journal of Public Health* 94 (4): 562–64.

Cooper, H., B. Nye, K. Charlton, J. Lindsay, and S. Greathouse. 1996. "The Effects of Summer Vacation on Achievement Test Scores: A Narrative and Meta-Analytic Review." *Review of Educational Research* 66 (3): 227–68.

Corral, P., and R. Gatti. 2020. "Accumulation Interrupted: COVID-19 and Human Capital among the Young." In *COVID-19 in Developing Economies* edited by S. Djankov and U. Panizza. London: Centre for Economic Policy Research.

COVID-19 Task Force (Task Force COVID-19 del Dipartimento Malattie Infettive e Servizio di Informatica, Istituto Superiore di Sanità). 2020. "Epidemia COVID-19." Aggiornamento nazionale, April 2020.

Datar, A., R. Kilburn, and D. S. Loughran. 2010. "Endowments and Parental Investments in Infancy and Early Childhood." *Demography* 47 (1): 145–62.

Davis, S. J., and T. M. von Wachter. 2011. "Recessions and the Cost of Job Loss." NBER Working Paper 17638, National Bureau of Economic Research, Cambridge, MA.

de la Fuente, A., H. G. Jacoby, and K. G. Lawin. 2019. "Impact of the West African Ebola Epidemic on Agricultural Production and Rural Welfare: Evidence from Liberia." Policy Research Working Paper 8880, World Bank, Washington, DC.

Dunbar, A., D. Hossler, D. Shapiro, J. Chen, S. Martin, V. Torres, D. Zerquera, and M. Ziskin. 2011. "National Postsecondary Enrollment Trends: Before, during, and after the Great Recession." Signature Report, National Student Clearinghouse.

Elston, J. W. T., C. Cartwright, P. Ndumbi, and J. Wright. 2017. "The Health Impact of the 2014–15 Ebola Outbreak." *Public Health* 143 (February): 60–70.

Figari, F., and C. V. Fiorio. 2020. "Welfare Resilience in the Immediate Aftermath of the COVID-19 Outbreak in Italy." EUROMOD Working Papers EM6/20, EUROMOD at the Institute for Social and Economic Research, University of Essex.

Finch, B. K., K. Thomas, and A. N. Beck. 2019. "The Great Recession and Adverse Birth Outcomes: Evidence from California, USA." *SSM–Population Health* 9: 100470.

Galasso, E., and A. Wagstaff. 2019. "The Aggregate Income Losses from Childhood Stunting and the Returns to a Nutrition Intervention Aimed at Reducing Stunting." *Economics and Human Biology* 34: 225–38.

Galea, S., R. M. Merchant, and N. Lurie. 2020. "The Mental Health Consequences of COVID-19 and Physical Distancing: The Need for Prevention and Early Intervention." *JAMA Internal Medicine* 180 (6): 817–18.

Gibbs, L., J. Nursey, J. Cook, G. Ireton, N. Alkemade, M. Roberts, H. C. Gallagher, R. Bryant, K. Block, R. Molyneaux, and D. Forbes. 2019. "Delayed Disaster Impacts on Academic Performance of Primary School Children." *Child Development* 90 (4): 1402–12.

Golberstein, E., H. Wen, and B. F. Miller. 2020. "Coronavirus Disease 2019 (COVID-19) and Mental Health for Children and Adolescents." *JAMA Pediatrics*, April 14, 2020. https://jamanetwork.com/journals/jamapediatrics/fullarticle/2764730.

Hale, T., N. Angrist, E. Cameron-Blake, L. Hallas, B. Kira, S. Majumdar, A. Petherick, T. Phillips, H. Tatlow, and S. Webster. 2020. "Oxford COVID-19 Government Response Tracker." Blavatnik School of Government, University of Oxford.

Hershbein, B. J. 2012. "Graduating High School in a Recession: Work, Education, and Home Production." *B.E. Journal of Economic Analysis & Policy* 12 (1).

Hobbs, J. E. 2020. "Food Supply Chains during the COVID-19 Pandemic." *Canadian Journal of Agricultural Economics/Revue Canadienne d'agroeconomie* 68 (2): 171–76.

Hogan, A., B. Jewell, E. Sherrard-Smith, J. Vesga, O. Watson, C. Whittaker, A. Hamlet, J. Smith, K. Ainslie, M. Baguelin, S. Bhatt, A. Boonyasiri, N. Brazeau, L. Cattarino, G. Charles, L. Cooper, H. Coupland, G. Cuomo-Dannenburg, A. Dighe, and T. Hallett. 2020. "Report 19: The Potential Impact of the COVID-19 Epidemic on HIV, TB and Malaria in Low- and Middle-Income Countries." *Lancet Global Health*, July 13, 2020. https://www.thelancet.com/journals/langlo/article/PIIS2214-109X(20)30288-6/fulltext.

International Labour Organization. 2020. "As Job Losses Escalate, Nearly Half of Global Workforce at Risk of Losing Livelihoods." Press Release, April 29, 2020. https://www.ilo.org/global/about-the-ilo/newsroom/news/WCMS_743036/lang--en/index.htm.

International Monetary Fund. 2020. "Global Prospects and Policies." Chapter 1 in *World Economic Outlook, April 2020: The Great Lockdown*. Washington, DC: International Monetary Fund.

Lahti-Pulkkinen, M., S. Bhattacharya, K. Räikkönen, C. Osmond, J. E. Norman, and R. M. Reynolds. 2018. "Intergenerational Transmission of Birth Weight across Three Generations." *American Journal of Epidemiology* 187 (6): 1165–73.

Lain, J., J. Perng, T. Vishwanath, M. A. Azad, G. O. Siwatu, A. Palacio-Lopez, K. McGee, A. Amankwa, and I. Contreras. 2020. "COVID-19 from the Ground Up: What the Crisis Means for Nigerians." Findings from the Nigeria COVID-19 National Longitudinal Phone Survey Round 1, April–May 2020, World Bank, Washington, DC.

Lancker, W. V., and Z. Parolin. 2020. "COVID-19, School Closures, and Child Poverty: A Social Crisis in the Making." *Lancet Public Health* 5 (5): e243–e244.

Le Nestour, A., and L. Moscoviz. 2020. "Five Findings from a New Phone Survey in Senegal." Center for Global Development (blog), April 24, 2020. https://www.cgdev.org/blog/five-findings-new-phone-survey-senegal.

Ma, L., G. Shapira, D. de Walque, Q.-T. Do, J. Friedman, and A. A. Levchenko. 2020. "The Intergenerational Dilemma of COVID-19 Lockdown Policies." Unpublished manuscript.

Mahler, D. G., C. Lakner, A. Castaneda, and H. Wu. 2020a. "The Impact of COVID-19 (Coronavirus) on Global Poverty: Why Sub-Saharan Africa Might Be the Region Hardest Hit." *Data Blog*, April 20, 2020. https://blogs.worldbank.org/opendata/impact-covid-19-coronavirus-global-poverty-why-sub-saharan-africa-might-be-region-hardest.

Mahler, D. G., C. Lakner, A. Castaneda, and H. Wu. 2020b. "Updated Estimates of the Impact of COVID-19 on Global Poverty." *Data Blog*, June 8, 2020. https://blogs.worldbank.org/opendata/updated-estimates-impact-covid-19-global-poverty.

Mahmud, M., and E. Riley. Forthcoming. "Household Response to an Extreme Shock: Evidence on the Immediate Impact of the Covid-19 Lockdown on Economic Outcomes and Well-being in Rural Uganda." *World Development*.

Mary, S. 2018. "How Much Does Economic Growth Contribute to Child Stunting Reductions?" *Economies* 6 (4): 55.

Mary, S., K. Shaw, and S. G. Paloma. 2019. "Does the Sectoral Composition of Growth Affect Child Stunting Reductions?" *Development Policy Review* 37 (2): 225–44.

Meyers, K., and M. Thomasson. 2017. "Paralyzed by Panic: Measuring the Effect of School Closures during the 1916 Polio Pandemic on Educational Attainment." NBER Working Paper 23890, National Bureau of Economic Research, Cambridge, MA.

Miller, G., and B. P. Urdinola. 2010. "Cyclicality, Mortality, and the Value of Time: The Case of Coffee Price Fluctuations and Child Survival in

Colombia." *Journal of Political Economy* 118 (1): 113–55.

Nelson, R. 2020. "COVID-19 Disrupts Vaccine Delivery." *Lancet Infectious Diseases* 20 (5): 546.

O'Hare, B., I. Makuta, L. Chiwaula, and N. Bar-Zeev. 2013. "Income and Child Mortality in Developing Countries: A Systematic Review and Meta-analysis." *Journal of the Royal Society of Medicine* 106 (10): 408–14.

Olsen, A. S., and J. Prado. 2020. "COVID-19 y la transición de la educación privada a la pública en Ecuador." *Enfoque Educación* (blog), June 30, 2020. https://blogs.iadb.org/educacion/es/covid-19-y-la-transicion-de-la-educacion-privada-a-la-publica-en-ecuador/.

Oreopoulos, P., T. von Wachter, and A. Heisz. 2012. "The Short-and Long-Term Career Effects of Graduating in a Recession." *American Economic Journal: Applied Economics* 4 (1): 1–29.

Packard, T., U. Gentilini, M. Grosh, P. O'Keefe, R. Palacios, D. Robalino, and I. Santos. 2019. *Protecting All: Risk Sharing for a Diverse and Diversifying World of Work*. Washington, DC: World Bank.

Perez-Vincent, S., E. Carreras, M. A. Gibbons, T. E. Murphy, and M. Rossi. 2020. "COVID-19 Lockdowns and Domestic Violence: Evidence from Two Studies in Argentina." Working Papers 143. Universidad de San Andres, Departamento de Economia.

Philip, R. K., H. Purtill, E. Reidy, M. Daly, M., Imcha, D. McGrath, N. H. O'Connell, and C. P. Dunne. 2020. "Reduction in Preterm Births during the COVID-19 Lockdown in Ireland: A Natural Experiment Allowing Analysis of Data from the Prior Two Decades." *MedRxiv*, June 5, 2020. https://www.medrxiv.org/content/10.1101/2020.06.03.20121442v1.

Poletaev, M., and C. Robinson. 2008. "Human Capital Specificity: Evidence from the Dictionary of Occupational Titles and Displaced Worker Surveys, 1984–2000." *Journal of Labor Economics* 26 (3): 387–420.

Quisumbing, A., R. Meinzen-Dick, J. Behrman, and L. Basset. 2011. "Gender and the Global Food-Price Crisis." *Development in Practice* 21 (4–5): 488–92.

Ravindran, S., and M. Shah. 2020. "Unintended Consequences of Lockdowns: COVID-19 and the Shadow Pandemic." NBER Working Paper 17638, National Bureau of Economic Research, Cambridge, MA.

Roberton, T., E. D. Carter, V. B. Chou, A. R. Stegmuller, B. D. Jackson, Y. Tam, T. Sawadogo-Lewis, and N. Walker. 2020. "Early Estimates of the Indirect Effects of the COVID-19 Pandemic on Maternal and Child Mortality in Low-Income and Middle-Income Countries: A Modelling Study." *Lancet Global Health,* May 12, 2020. https://www.thelancet.com/journals/langlo/article/PIIS2214-109X(20)30229-1/fulltext.

Rosales-Rueda, M. 2018. "The Impact of Early Life Shocks on Human Capital Formation: Evidence from El Niño Floods in Ecuador." *Journal of Health Economics* 62: 13–44.

Rose, E. 2000. "Gender Bias, Credit Constraints and Time Allocation in Rural India." *Economic Journal* 110 (465): 738–58.

Rothstein, J. 2020. "The Lost Generation? Labor Market Outcomes for Post Great Recession Entrants." NBER Working Paper 27516, National Bureau of Economic Research, Cambridge, MA.

Ruel, M. T., H. Alderman, and the Maternal and Child Nutrition Study Group. 2013. "Nutrition-Sensitive Interventions and Programmes: How Can They Help to Accelerate Progress in Improving Maternal and Child Nutrition?" *Lancet* 382 (9891): 536–51.

Saha, T., and S. Bhattacharya. 2020. "Consequence of Lockdown amid Covid-19 Pandemic on Indian Agriculture." *Food and Scientific Reports* 1 Special Issue: 47–50.

Savasi, V. M., F. Parisi, L. Patanè, E. Ferrazzi, L. Frigerio, A. Pellegrino, A. Spinillo, S. Tateo, M. Ottoboni, P. Veronese, F. Petraglia, P. Vergani, F. Facchinetti, D. Spazzini, and I. Cetin. 2020. "Clinical Findings and Disease Severity in Hospitalized Pregnant Women with Coronavirus Disease 2019 (COVID-19)." *Obstetrics & Gynecology* 136 (2): 252–58.

Schady, N. R. 2004. "Do Macroeconomic Crises Always Slow Human Capital Accumulation?" *World Bank Economic Review* 18 (2): 131–54.

Shafiq, M. N. 2010. "The Effect of an Economic Crisis on Educational Outcomes: An Economic Framework and Review of the Evidence." *Current Issues in Comparative Education* 12 (2): 5.

Sullivan, D., and T. von Wachter. 2009. "Job Displacement and Mortality: An Analysis Using Administrative Data." *Quarterly Journal of Economics* 124 (3): 1265–306.

Tesfaye, A., Y. Habte, and B. Minten. 2020. "COVID-19 Is Shifting Consumption and Disrupting Dairy Value Chains in Ethiopia." *IFPRI Blog*, June 1, 2020. https://www.ifpri.org/blog/covid-19-shifting-consumption-and-disrupting-dairy-value-chains-ethiopia.

UNFPA (United Nations Population Fund). 2020. "Impact of the COVID-19 Pandemic on Family Planning and Ending Gender-based Violence, Female Genital Mutilation and Child Marriage." Interim Technical Note, April 27, UNFPA.

van Gelder, N., A. Peterman, A. Potts, M. O'Donnell, K. Thompson, N. Shah, and S. Oertelt-Prigione. 2020. "COVID-19: Reducing the Risk of Infection Might Increase the Risk of Intimate Partner Violence." *EClinicalMedicine* 21: 100348.

von Hippel, P. T. , and C. Hamrock. 2019. "Do Test Score Gaps Grow before, during, or between the School Years? Measurement Artifacts and What We Can Know in Spite of Them." *Sociological Science* 6: 43–80.

Wenham, C., J. Smith, and R. Morgan. 2020. "COVID-19: The Gendered Impacts of the Outbreak." *Lancet* 395 (10227): 846–48.

World Bank. 2020. *Global Economic Prospects, June 2020*. Washington, DC: World Bank.

World Health Organization. 2020. "At Least 80 Million Children under One at Risk of Diseases Such as Diphtheria, Measles and Polio as COVID-19 Disrupts Routine Vaccination Efforts, Warn Gavi, WHO and UNICEF." News Release, World Health Organization, May 22, 2020. https://www.who.int/news/item/22-05-2020-at-least-80-million-children-under-one-at-risk-of-diseases-such-as-diphtheria-measles-and-polio-as-covid-19-disrupts-routine-vaccination-efforts-warn-gavi-who-and-unicef.

Wren-Lewis, S. 2020. "The Economic Effects of a Pandemic." In *Economics in the Time of COVID-19*, edited by Richard Baldwin and Beatrice Weder di Mauro, 109–112. London: Centre for Economic Policy Research.

Yourish, K., K. K. R. Lai, D. Ivory, and M. Smith. 2020. "One-Third of All U.S. Coronavirus Deaths Are Nursing Home Residents or Workers." *New York Times*, May 11, 2020.

4 UTILIZING Human Capital

The World Bank's Human Capital Index (HCI) captures the size of the income gains when today's better-educated and healthier children become tomorrow's more productive workers. Specifically, a child born today can expect to be HCI × 100 percent as productive as a future worker as she would be if she enjoyed complete education and full health. But this expectation implicitly assumes that, when today's child becomes a future worker, she will be able to find a job—which may not be the case in economies with low employment rates. Moreover, even if today's child is able to find employment in the future, she may not have a job in which she can fully use her skills and cognitive abilities to increase her productivity. In these cases, human capital can be considered *underutilized,* because it is not being used to increase productivity to the extent it could be. For example, unemployed future workers may be underutilizing their human capital, as are those out of the labor force. Likewise, engineers driving taxis are underutilizing their human capital because, even though they are employed, they do not hold jobs in which their education increases their productivity.

In addition, a gender gap—which is not apparent in the human capital dimensions captured by the HCI—emerges and deepens during the working years. In many countries, women face worse jobs and income opportunities compared to men, even with the same human capital. As such, simply considering the HCI by sex may give a partial view in terms of realizing the potential of human capital investments.

This chapter introduces two Utilization-Adjusted Human Capital Indexes (UHCIs) that, as their name suggests, adjust the HCI for labor market underutilization of human capital.[1] The UHCIs are designed to complement the main HCI, and not to replace it, in part because these two measures have different purposes: the HCI is an index of the supply of a factor of production (in the future), whereas the UHCIs are a hybrid between an index of factor supply (capturing investment in human capital) and a utilization index (capturing how efficiently that human capital is used in production). Moreover, there are numerous challenges in defining and measuring utilization in a consistent way across diverse economic contexts. As such, the UHCIs should be viewed as a first attempt to address utilization in a simple way consistently across economies, and should be applied with caution in policy analysis.

Importantly, the HCI and UHCI measure only the effect of human capital on labor market earnings and future gross domestic product (GDP) per capita. But this effect is only one benefit of human capital. In many other domains, human capital improves well-being and economic development. Parents with more education have children with better human capital outcomes, and women with more human capital are more empowered. Even outside the categories of better employment (defined later in the chapter), human capital can still increase productivity—for example, smallholder farmers might use fertilizer more efficiently—but the increase is just less dramatic than for other employment types. As such, incomplete utilization should not be interpreted as a lack of gains from human capital investments, but rather as an indication that private labor market gains are smaller than they could be.

The two UHCIs take different approaches to measuring utilization. In the *basic* UHCI, utilization is measured as the fraction of the working-age population that is employed. Although simple and intuitive, this measure cannot capture underutilization resulting from a mismatch between the skills and cognitive abilities required to do a job, and the skills and cognitive abilities of the people employed to do it. The *full* UHCI measure adjusts for this mismatch by introducing the concept of *better employment*, which includes the types of jobs that are common in high-productivity countries.

Despite different methodologies, the basic and full measures produce broadly similar utilization rates. Utilization rates are U-shaped in per capita income across economies, first declining with income at lower income levels and then rising at higher income levels. This feature of utilization rates implies that UHCIs are low in the poorest economies, where the HCI is also low on average, but remain low over a wider range of lower-middle-income economies where rising HCIs are offset by declining utilization.

Moreover, both UHCIs reveal starkly different gender gaps from those using the HCI. Girls have a slight advantage over boys in human capital early in life, resulting in a higher HCI for girls on average. But female utilization rates are typically lower than those for males, resulting in lower UHCIs. Although gender gaps in human capital in childhood and adolescence (especially in education) have closed in the last two decades, large challenges remain to realizing these investments in terms of income opportunities for women.

4.1 METHODOLOGY AND THE BASIC UHCI MEASURE

Both the basic and full UHCIs have a simple form, the utilization rate multiplied by the HCI:

$$UHCI = Utilization\ Rate \times HCI \tag{4.1}$$

For the basic UHCI, this multiplicative form stems from its connection to economic growth. In the long run, GDP is proportional to the number of workers (employment) multiplied by the productivity boost that each worker gets from her human capital.[2] The basic UHCI inherits this multiplicative form, where the HCI captures the productivity boost from human capital, and the utilization rate captures employment.[3]

The HCI is derived to measure the effect of human capital on future GDP per capita so that projected future per capita GDP will be approximately $1/HCI$ times higher in a "complete education and full health" scenario than in a "status quo" scenario (Kraay 2018). This definition implicitly assumes that utilization rates of human capital—such as employment prospects—are the same in the complete education and full health scenario as in the status quo scenario.

Both UHCI measures are derived in a similar way, in keeping with the economic interpretation of the HCI. For the UHCIs, however, utilization rates are now different in the status quo and full human capital scenarios. Specifically, both UHCIs are derived as future GDP per capita under the "status quo" relative to future GDP per capita with "full health, complete education, and complete utilization," as in equation (4.2). This means that, in the long run, GDP per capita will be 1/UHCI times higher in a world of complete utilization, full health, and complete education than in the status quo.[4]

$$UHCI = \frac{Future\ GDP\ per\ Capita\left(Status\ Quo\right)}{Future\ GDP\ per\ Capita\ \left(Complete\ Utilization, Full\ Health, Complete\ Education\right)} \tag{4.2}$$

For the basic UHCI, the utilization rate is simply the employment rate of the working-age population. This rate is current employment L, relative to a measure of potential employment under full utilization L^*, the maximum theoretical employment. The standard definition of the potential labor force is the working-age population, individuals aged 15–64 years. This definition is also adopted for L^*.[5] Employment L is defined as the number of people aged 15–64 who are in paid employment (or are self-employed) to be consistent with the definition of the potential labor force.

As mentioned earlier, the basic UHCI takes the simple multiplicative form in equation (4.1) because, in a standard production function, long-run GDP per capita is proportional to human capital per worker h multiplied by employment L per capita (see box 4.1 for a derivation). Future GDP per capita under the status quo—in the numerator of equation (4.2)—is proportional to hL, and future GDP per capita under complete utilization and complete human capital is proportional to h^*L^* (h^* is complete human capital per worker) in the denominator of equation (4.2). Because the proportionality factors are the same, and so cancel out, this expression can be rearranged as $HCI = h/h^*$ multiplied by the basic utilization rate $Util\ (basic) = L/L^*$.

A natural concern is that, in economies with low basic utilization rates, human capital, as measured by the HCI, will have less effect on economic growth. This is not the case, however.[6] In the framework of the basic UHCI, an increase in human capital alone has the same effect on

Box 4.1: Deriving the basic Utilization-Adjusted Human Capital Index

Future gross domestic product (GDP) per capita of the next generation y in the status quo world is given by a Cobb-Douglas production function:

$$y = AK^{1-\beta}(hL)^{\beta}/N \qquad \text{(B4.1.1)}$$

where h represents human capital per worker under current policies, and L represents the number of workers under status quo employment rates. A is total factor productivity, K is the amount of physical capital, and N is the future population. Total factor productivity and the future population are assumed to grow at the same trend rates in all scenarios.

In an alternative world, there is complete human capital per worker, denoted by h^*, and complete employment of potential workers, denoted by L^*. Long-run GDP per capita in this complete human capital–complete employment world is denoted y^*. As in Kraay (2018), the production function can be rearranged in terms of the physical capital-to-output ratio $\overline{K}/\overline{Y}$, which is constant in the long run. Then, future GDP per capita under the status quo relative to the complete human capital–complete utilization scenario is given by:

$$\begin{aligned}\frac{y}{y^*} &= \frac{A^{1/\beta}\left(\overline{K}/\overline{Y}\right)^{(1-\beta)/\beta} h\ L/N}{A^{1/\beta}\left(\overline{K}/\overline{Y}\right)^{(1-\beta)/\beta} h^*\ L^*/N} \\ &= \frac{L}{L^*}\times\frac{h}{h^*} \\ &= \mathit{Utilization\ (basic)}\times \mathit{HCI} \\ &= \mathit{UHCI\ (basic)}\end{aligned} \qquad \text{(B4.1.2)}$$

long-run economic growth as in the HCI, but economies can do better by also increasing utilization (it is not one or the other).[7]

The main data source for the basic utilization measure is "Employment-to-population by sex and age (%) – Annual," for youth and adults aged 15–64, from the International Labour Organization (ILO), using the latest period available.[8] The secondary data source is the World Bank's Global Jobs Indicators Database (JOIN), which has employment data based on the same population age group, with a sample skewed toward low- and middle-income economies.[9] Data are generally taken from the most recent source if both are available.[10] The median year of the data is 2017, with 95 percent of economies having data from the 2010s. The basic utilization measure is available for 185 economies. The measurement of the full UHCI is discussed later in the chapter.

4.2 THE BASIC UHCI IN THE DATA

Basic utilization rates are not strongly correlated with the HCI (correlation coefficient of 0.45), which means that UHCI scores will differ from those of the HCI (figure 4.1). Employment rates average about 0.6, which suggests that the UHCI will, on average, be about 60 percent of the value of the HCI (figure 4.2), but with substantial variation across economies.

Employment rates (basic utilization) are approximately U-shaped in log per capita income (figure 4.3).[11] High-income economies have the highest utilization rates (about 0.7 for the group as a whole), which is unsurprising because it is difficult to have high per capita incomes with few people working. Low-income economies have utilization rates of about 0.6 on average, though many low-income economies—like Burundi (BDI in the figures), Madagascar (MDG), and Mozambique (MOZ)—also have extremely high employment rates of about 0.8. High employment rates among low-income economies are likely because most people are so poor that they need to work outside the home to survive. Lower-middle-income economies have the lowest utilization rates, at about 0.55, mostly because slightly higher incomes make it feasible for people (especially women) not

Figure 4.1: Employment to population (basic utilization) and Human Capital Index

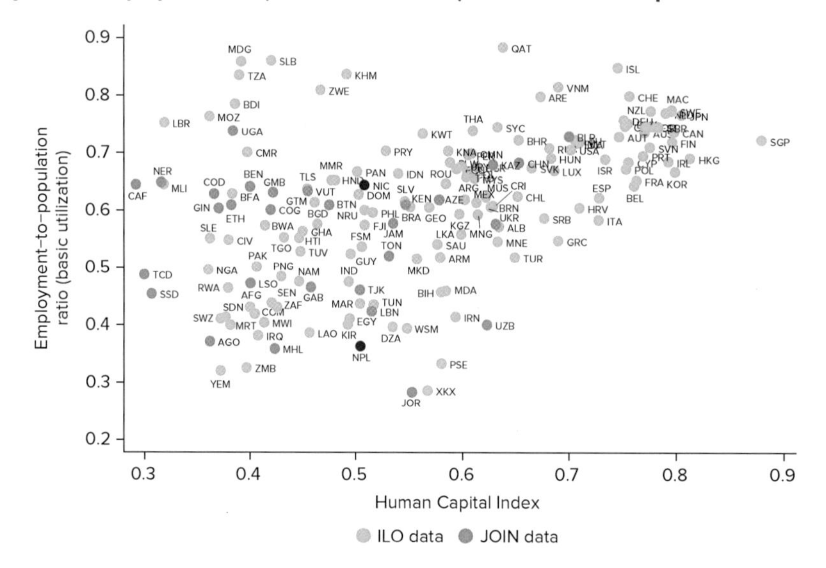

Source: World Bank calculations based on the 2020 update of the Human Capital Index (HCI), the World Development Indicators, the International Labour Organization, and the Global Jobs Indicators Database.

Note: Based on 169 economies with available data. Nepal (NPL) and Nicaragua (NIC) are in red.

Figure 4.2: Basic UHCI vs. Human Capital Index

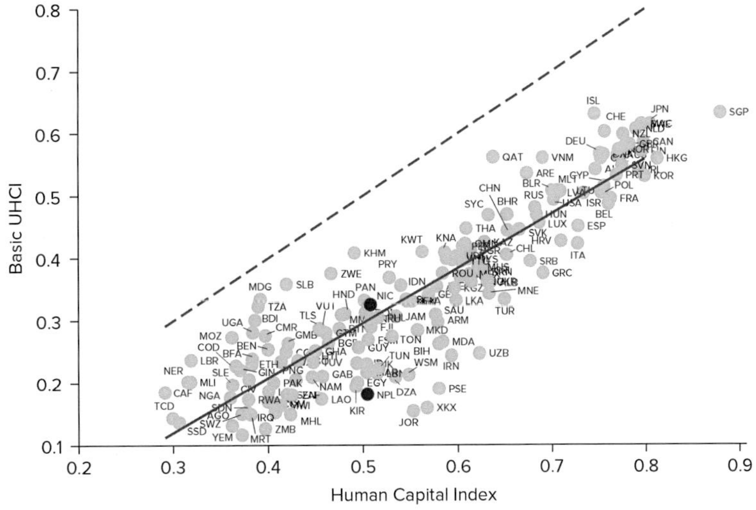

Source: World Bank calculations based on the 2020 update of the Human Capital Index (HCI), the World Development Indicators, the International Labour Organization, and the Global Jobs Indicators Database.

Note: Based on 169 economies with available data. Nepal (NPL) and Nicaragua (NIC) are in red. Dashed line is 45-degree diagonal, and solid line is a fitted model where $y = -0.14 + 0.88x$. UHCI = Utilization-Adjusted Human Capital Index.

Figure 4.3: Employment to population (basic utilization) and per capita income

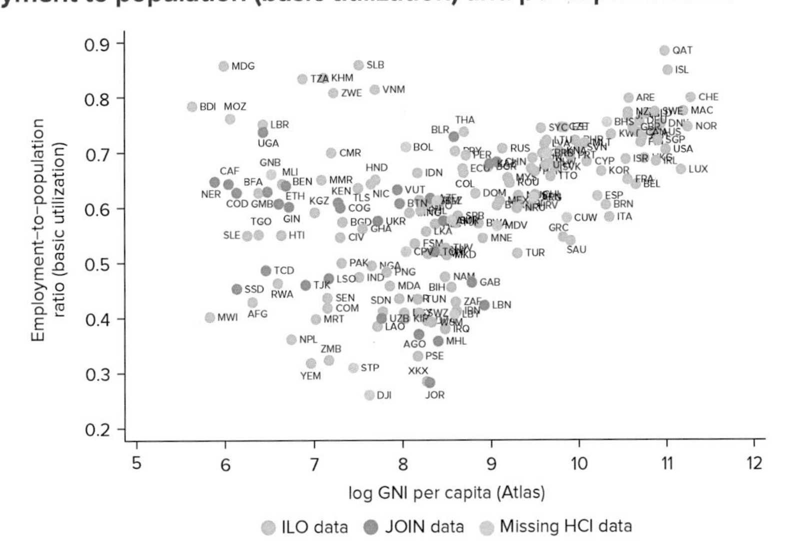

Source: World Bank calculations based on the World Development Indicators, the International Labour Organization, and the Global Jobs Indicators Database.

Note: Based on 182 economies with available data. Working-age population is 15–64 years of age. GNI = gross national income; HCI = Human Capital Index.

to work outside the home (see section 4.7 titled "Disaggregation by Sex" for a discussion).

Employment rates vary widely among low- and middle-income economies. Whereas many low-income economies have high employment rates of about 0.8, others—including Afghanistan (AFG), Malawi (MWI), and Nepal (NPL)—have employment rates of about 0.4. In part, this disparity may reflect the 2013 change in the ILO definition of employment to exclude own-use production workers (mostly subsistence agriculture), which has been applied in some countries but not in others.[12] These measurement issues also motivate using a more specific definition of employment in the full UHCI (discussed in the next section).

To understand the implications of differences between the UHCI and HCI for long-run economic growth, consider the example of two economies, Nepal and Nicaragua. These economies have similar scores for the HCI (0.5) but very different employment rates (figure 4.1, red dots). The employment rate in Nicaragua is about 0.65, which is above the median, against that in Nepal, 0.37, which is around the fifth percentile. These disparate employment rates mean that the basic UHCI score of Nepal (0.18) is much lower than that of Nicaragua (0.33) (figure 4.2, red dots). As mentioned previously, the increase in long-run per capita income moving to full human capital is 1/HCI times that in the status quo, and long-run per capita income moving to full human capital and complete utilization is 1/UHCI that in the status quo. An HCI score of 0.5 for both economies implies that long-run per capita incomes would double moving to full human capital. Moving to full human capital and complete utilization of that human capital, however, results in long-run GDP per capita that is 3.0 times the status quo in Nicaragua, but 5.4 times the status quo in Nepal.[13]

The basic UHCI is fairly flat over a wide range of log income before increasing (figure 4.4). Specifically, the UHCI is almost flat moving from low income (0.23) to lower-middle income (0.26), as higher HCI scores are largely offset by lower utilization rates. But the UHCI then increases rapidly to upper-middle income (0.32) and high income (0.51), as both human capital and utilization rates increase together.

4.3 THE FULL UHCI

One conceptual issue with the basic utilization measure (employment rate) is that it assumes that all jobs are the same in terms of their ability to utilize human capital. In practice, however, a large share of employment in developing countries is in jobs in which workers cannot fully use

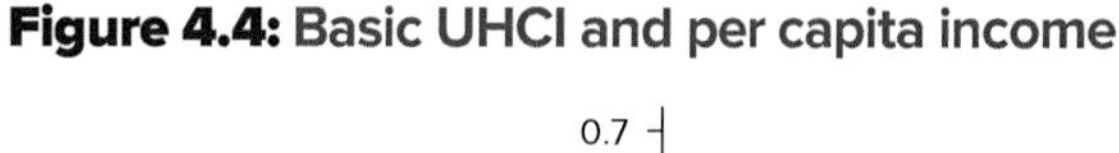
Figure 4.4: Basic UHCI and per capita income

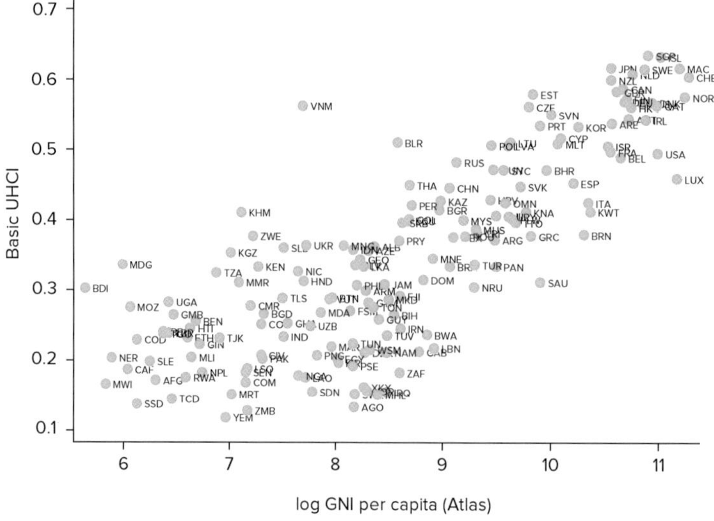

Source: World Bank calculations based on the World Development Indicators, the International Labour Organization, and the Global Jobs Indicators Database.

Note: Based on 182 economies with available data. Working-age population is 15–64 years of age. GNI = gross national income; UHCI = Utilization-Adjusted Human Capital Index.

their human capital. For example, in the poorest countries, about half of all workers work on family farms or as agricultural laborers, situations with low productivity (Merotto, Weber, and Reyes 2018). For the rest, about two-thirds of nonagricultural workers are self-employed or unpaid in family businesses. They include many small-scale traders selling household goods or food, with most of their time spent waiting for customers.

Although there is scope for human capital to increase productivity in these jobs, that scope is limited. Filmer and Fox (2014) compare the income of household enterprise owners of different education levels in four African countries. On average, the increase in income due to education, although positive, is much less than would be predicted given the number of years of schooling.[14] Most developing countries suffer from high rates of mismatch between the level of education required for a job and the education of the people doing it—such as the well-known anecdote of unemployed engineers driving taxis (see Battu and Bender 2020 for a survey).[15] The literature often refers to this mismatch as overeducation, though a more appropriate description is underutilization, because the lack of jobs and not the level of education causes the mismatch. In some regions, especially the Middle East and North Africa, underutilization is often associated with self-employment, for example, while waiting for a formal sector job (Gatti et al. 2013; Handel, Valerio, and Sanchez Puerta 2016).

To address this mismatch, the full UHCI introduces a concept of *better employment,* which is designed to capture the employment categories in which people can better use their human capital (subject to available data). More specifically, better employment is defined as nonagricultural employees, plus employers. This definition is not intended as a value judgment but rather is based on the types of jobs that are relatively rare in low-income countries but common in high-income countries—suggesting they are associated with higher productivity. The share of employment in better jobs (SEBJ) increases from about 20 percent in low-income countries to 80 percent in high-income countries (Merotto, Weber, and Reyes 2018). The main categories excluded from the definition are subsistence own-account/family agriculture, small-scale traders, and landless agricultural laborers, because these employment types are common only in low-income countries—suggesting they are more likely to have lower productivity. By using a more specific definition of employment, the full UHCI also avoids variation in utilization rates caused by differences in the definition of employment that affected the basic UHCI.

The definition of better employment is based on the way that the work is organized, rather than whether the job is formal or informal. For example, nonagricultural employees could be formal or informal.[16] Better employment involves work organized in a team consisting of at least an employer and an employee, and for which employees are paid (rather than working out of familial obligation). This arrangement allows a minimum degree of specialization and organization, which helps boost productivity and allows for people to use their skills.[17]

A second conceptual issue with the basic measure is that utilization should be relative to potential, which will depend on how much human capital there is to underutilize. That is, a doctor working as an agricultural laborer represents severely underutilized human capital, whereas the human capital of a worker with no education doing the same job is closer to being fully utilized. This distinction means that the utilization scores of countries with higher levels of human capital should be more heavily penalized by a lack of better employment.[18]

Putting these concerns together suggests that the full UHCI should depend on the better employment rate (BER)—as a share of the working-age population—rather than on the raw employment rate. But the full utilization rate is not simply the BER, because the BER fails to adjust for how much human capital there is to underutilize if people are not in jobs where they can fully use the human capital. Instead, utilization rates for those without better jobs should depend inversely on the HCI (relative to a natural minimum). The full utilization measure captures both concerns. The full UHCI is a weighted average of the country's HCI (for those in better employment) and the minimum HCI (for the rest) and is described further in box 4.2. The full UHCI can also be derived using the increase in long-run GDP per capita moving from the status quo to a world with full human capital and complete utilization in better employment (see Pennings 2020).[19]

In terms of data, the BER is constructed as the employment rate (as in the basic utilization measure) multiplied by the SEBJ. The measurement of the SEBJ requires data on the number of employers, nonagricultural employees, and total employment. The primary source is the ILO series "Employment by sex, status in employment, and economic activity (thousands)," using the most recent year available.[20] The secondary source is JOIN. At the time of writing, the public JOIN

Box 4.2: Definition of the full Utilization-Adjusted Human Capital Index

The full utilization rate is a weighted average of the utilization rates of those in better employment, and the utilization rate of the rest of the working-age population. Workers in better employment (with the better employment rate expressed as *BER*) are assumed to be as productive as their human capital allows—their human capital is fully utilized (utilization rate of 1). All others, a fraction (1 – *BER*) of the working-age population, are assumed to be only as productive as raw labor; hence, any excess human capital is underutilized.

In the HCI, raw labor has productivity of $HCI_{min} = 0.2$. This is the productivity of a worker with zero years of schooling and the worst possible health outcomes.[a] In contrast, the potential productivity of a worker in better employment is just *HCI*. Hence, the worker's productivity relative to potential, or utilization rate, is HCI_{min}/HCI. For example, in an economy with $HCI = 0.4$, workers without better employment will be half as productive as they could be if they were in better employment (0.2/0.4), so their utilization rate is 0.5. This result means that a shortage of better employment leads to more severe underutilization in countries with more human capital. The full utilization measure is given by:

$$Utilization\ (full\ measure) = BER \times 1 + (1 - BER) \times \frac{HCI_{min}}{HCI} \quad \text{(B4.2.1)}$$

The full UHCI is the full utilization measure multiplied by the HCI, as in equation (4.1) in the main text, meaning that the full UHCI is a weighted average of the HCI (for the share of the population in better employment) and the minimum HCI (for the rest of the working-age population):

$$UHCI\ (full\ measure) = BER \times HCI + (1 - BER) \times HCI_{min} \quad \text{(B4.2.2)}$$

[a] The minimum HCI score is derived by assuming zero years of schooling, complete stunting, and zero chance of adults surviving to age 60. $HCI_{min} = 1 \times e^{0.08\times(0-14)} \times e^{(0.65\times(0-1)+0.35\times(0-1))/2} \approx 0.2$. See Kraay (2018), equations 9–12. The probability of survival to age 5 is assumed to be 1, because it does not affect the growth calculations.

dataset provides a split by status in employment or economic activity, not both, so the SEBJ is calculated using an unpublished version constructed from the underlying microdata. The most recent data source is used if both the ILO data and JOIN are available. For many economies, both sources are missing data on the number of agricultural employees. In these cases, the number of agricultural employees is interpolated using ILO data on total agricultural employment (which is more widely available). The full utilization measure is available for 161 economies.

4.4 THE FULL UHCI IN THE DATA

The full utilization measure has the same U shape in log per capita income as the basic utilization measure, and similar mean values overall (0.62) and for each income level, though with less dispersion (figure 4.5). The U-shaped pattern, however, has quite different causes from those driving the basic utilization measure. For the full measure, the highest-income economies have about 70 percent of the working-age population in better employment (figure 4.6), which drives the high utilization rate. For low-income economies, only about 10 percent of the working-age population is in better employment, so the utilization rate for these economies is mostly determined by how much human capital there is to underutilize. In the 10 lowest-income economies, HCI ≈ 1/3, so HCI_{min}/HCI is about 0.2/0.33 = 0.6 (close to the full utilization rate for those economies in figure 4.5). The full utilization rate falls from low-income to middle-income economies, as higher rates of human capital mean that there is more human capital to underutilize (and the BER increases only slightly).

The full UHCI also has the same shape in per capita income as the basic UHCI (and similar mean values for each income level; figure 4.7). For the lowest-income economies, however, the UHCI value converges almost exactly to 0.2, with little variation (as against wide variation in the basic UHCI). The reason is that 0.2 is the minimum HCI score, which is the assumed productivity of raw labor for those without better employment.

Figure 4.5: Full utilization rate and per capita income

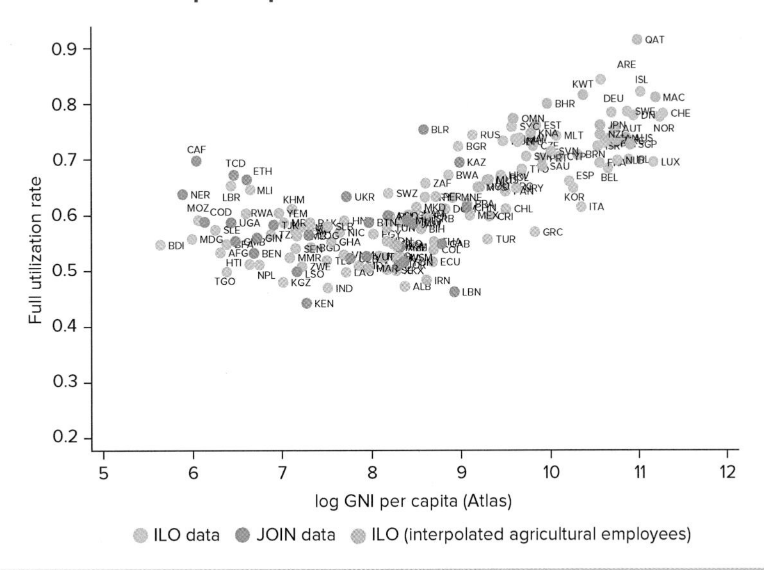

Source: World Bank calculations based on the 2020 update of the Human Capital Index (HCI), the World Development Indicators, the International Labour Organization, and the Global Jobs Indicators Database.

Note: Based on 161 economies with available data. GNI = gross national income.

Figure 4.6: Better employment rates and per capita income

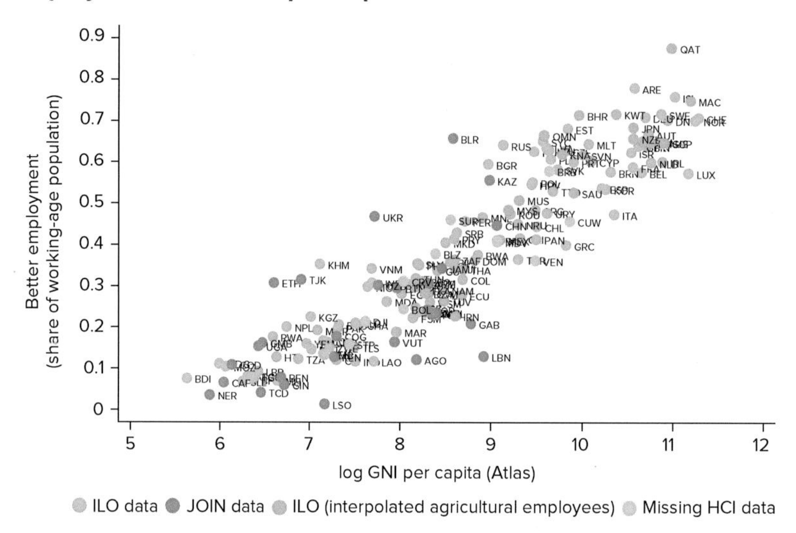

Source: World Bank calculations based on the World Development Indicators, the International Labour Organization, and the Global Jobs Indicators Database.

Note: Based on 171 economies with available data. GNI = gross national income; HCI = Human Capital Index.

Figure 4.7: Full UHCI and per capita income

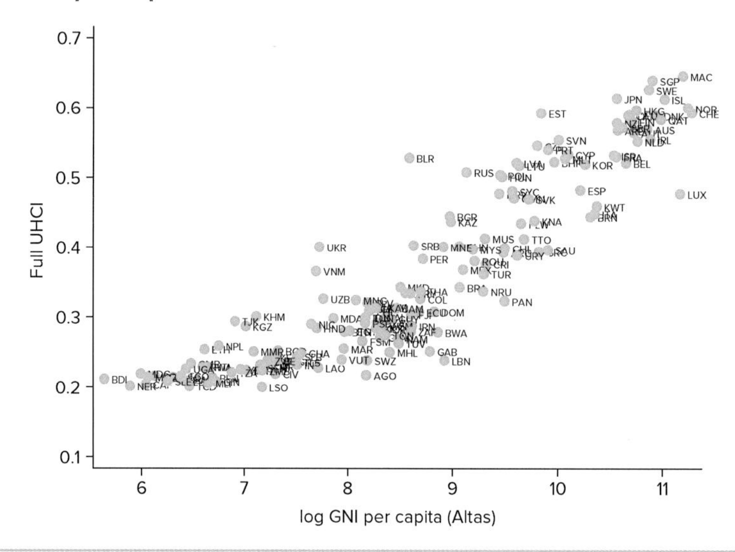

Source: World Bank calculations based on the 2020 update of the Human Capital Index (HCI), the World Development Indicators, the International Labour Organization, and the Global Jobs Indicators Database.

Note: Based on 161 economies with available data. GNI = gross national income; UHCI = Utilization-Adjusted Human Capital Index.

4.5 COMPARING THE UTILIZATION MEASURES

Although the full and basic utilization measures have the same U-shaped relationship with per capita income, they often differ substantially for individual economies (figure 4.8; correlation of only 0.6).[21] The strongest correlation is for high-income economies, because, in order to generate high per capita incomes, employment rates need to be high and those people working need to be productive. But, for lower-income economies, the drivers of

Figure 4.8: Basic utilization vs. full utilization

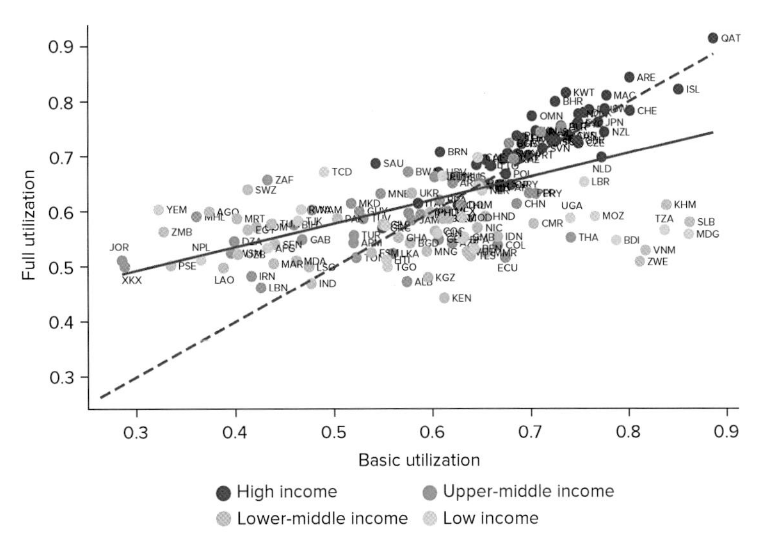

Source: World Bank calculations based on the 2020 update of the Human Capital Index (HCI), the World Development Indicators, the International Labour Organization, and the Global Jobs Indicators Database.

Note: Based on 161 economies with available data. Dashed line is 45-degree diagonal; solid line is a fitted model where $y = 0.37 + 0.43x$.

Figure 4.9: Basic UHCI vs. full UHCI

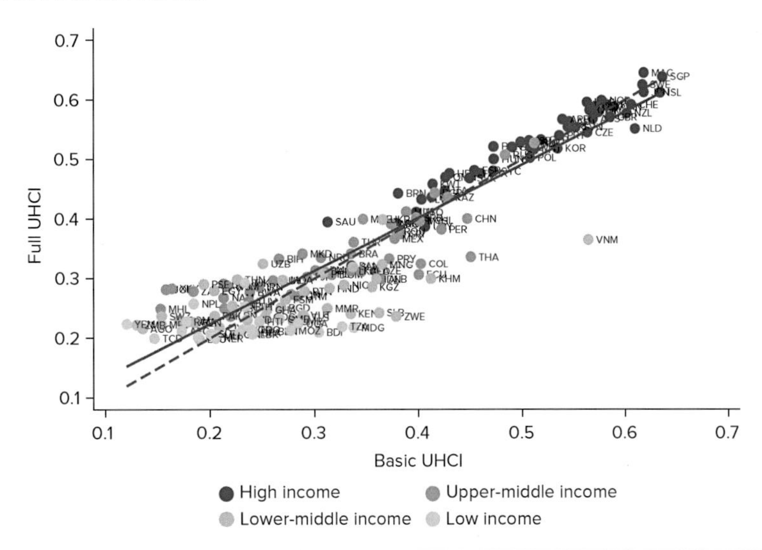

Source: World Bank calculations based on the 2020 update of the Human Capital Index (HCI), the World Development Indicators, the International Labour Organization, and the Global Jobs Indicators Database.

Note: Based on 161 economies with available data. Dashed line is 45-degree diagonal; solid line is a fitted model where $y = 0.05 + 0.89x$. UHCI = Utilization-Adjusted Human Capital Index.

high utilization vary across measures, and the similarity of average scores is coincidental. Specifically, employment rates (basic utilization) are often high in low-income economies because people cannot afford not to work, though the rates vary significantly because of the inconsistent cross-country classification of work in subsistence agriculture. In contrast, there is little variation in full utilization rates across low-income economies, because those economies have little human capital to underutilize.

For the UHCI, the scores of individual economies are very similar in the full and basic measures (figure 4.9; correlation 0.93). In part, this similarity is because full

Figure 4.10: Regional average UHCI or HCI

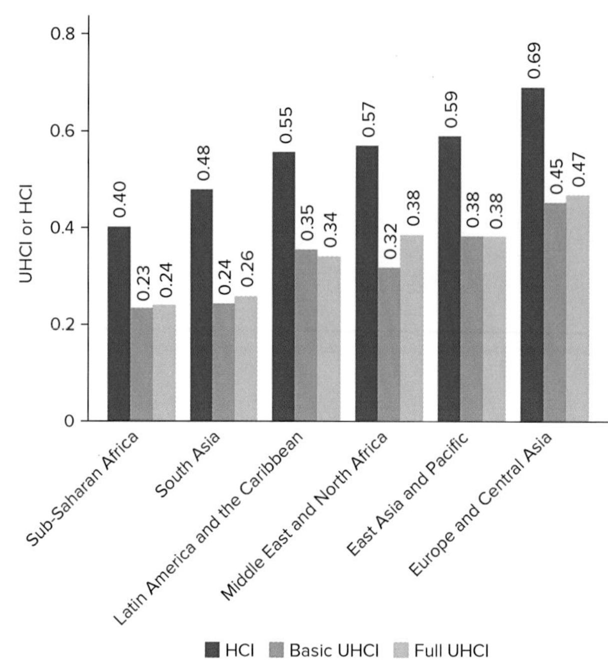

Source: World Bank calculations based on the World Development Indicators, the International Labour Organization, and the Global Jobs Indicators Database.

Note: Figure reports regional averages. HCI = Human Capital Index; UHCI = Utilization-Adjusted Human Capital Index.

and basic UHCI have the HCI as a common component. It is also because the differences between the two utilization measures occur mostly for countries with a low HCI, which mechanically shrinks any differences in utilization rates when forming the UHCI.[22]

4.6 DISAGGREGATION BY REGION

Regions line up similarly according to the UHCI and to the HCI (figure 4.10), though UHCI scores are lower. Sub-Saharan Africa has the lowest HCI (of about 0.40) and also the lowest UHCI (of about 0.23). South Asia has a similar UHCI, but a higher HCI (reflecting slightly lower utilization rates). Latin America and the Caribbean and the Middle East and North Africa are next, with HCI scores of about 0.56 and UHCI scores of about 0.35, though the Middle East and North Africa does relatively better for the full UHCI than for the basic UHCI, reflecting higher rates of wage employment. East Asia and Pacific scores marginally higher, followed by Europe and Central Asia.

4.7 DISAGGREGATION BY SEX

Many of the trends above are driven by differences in utilization rates by sex. Although the HCI is roughly equal across sex with a slight advantage for females relative to males, female utilization rates are typically lower than those for males (figure 4.11 and figure 4.12) leading the UHCI also to be lower for females than males (figure 4.13 and figure 4.14). Male and female UHCI scores increase proportionately, but with a constant gap for females (implying a larger percentage gap at low UHCI scores). The gender gap is larger for the basic measure than the full measure. Perhaps surprisingly, when women join the labor force, they often move rapidly into better employment (see Pennings 2020, figure 25A). More generally, female employment

Figure 4.11: Employment-to-population ratio (basic utilization) and per capita income

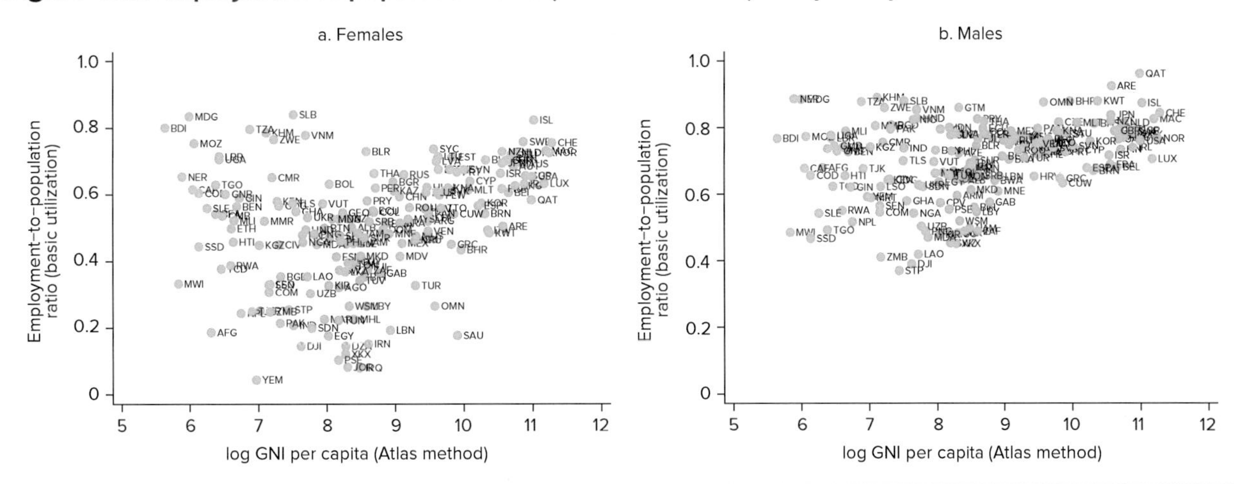

Source: World Bank calculations based on the 2020 update of the Human Capital Index (HCI), the World Development Indicators, the International Labour Organization, and the Global Jobs Indicators Database.

Note: Data for 182 economies. Working-age population is 15–64 years of age. GNI = gross national income.

Figure 4.12: Full utilization rate and per capita income

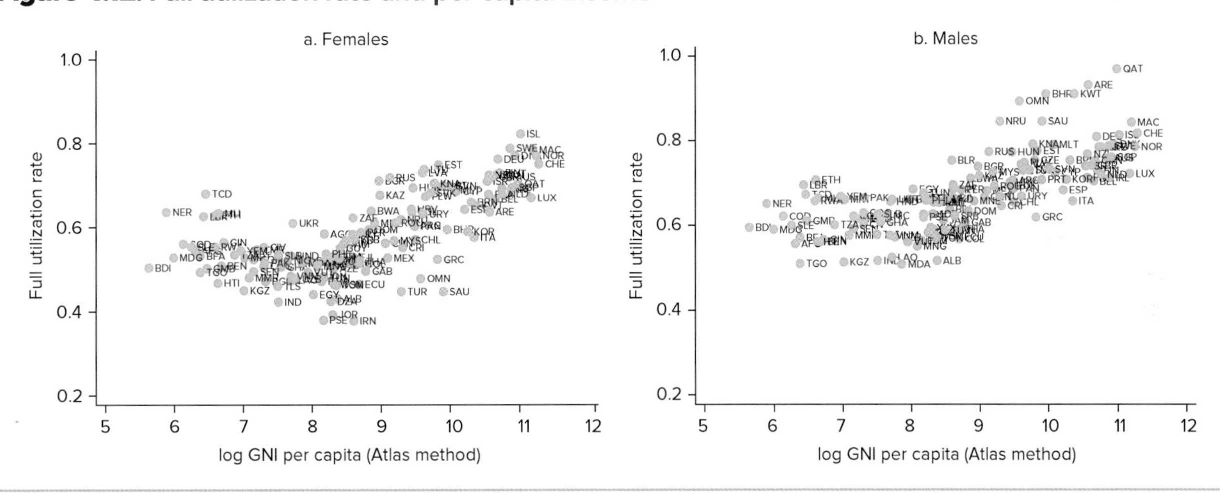

Source: World Bank calculations based on the 2020 update of the Human Capital Index (HCI), the World Development Indicators, the International Labour Organization, and the Global Jobs Indicators Database.

Note: GNI = gross national income.

rates are strongly U-shaped in the level of income, whereas male employment rates are much flatter (see Goldin 1995).[23] The largest gaps in utilization rates across sex (for both measures) are for several oil/gas producers: Bahrain, Kuwait, Oman, Qatar, and Saudi Arabia. These economies have very high male employment rates—almost all of which is represented by wage employment (perhaps due to migrant workers)—but low or average female utilization rates.

Figure 4.15 breaks down the HCI and UHCIs by gender and region. In almost all regions, the female HCI is higher than male HCI (equal for South Asia). The opposite is true, however, for the UHCI: in almost all regions the female UHCI is lower (for Europe and Central Asia, the full UHCI is similar for males and females). The largest gender gaps for the basic UHCI are in the Middle East and North Africa and in South Asia. In these two regions the female basic UHCI is very low, reflecting low

Figure 4.13: Basic UHCI and per capita income

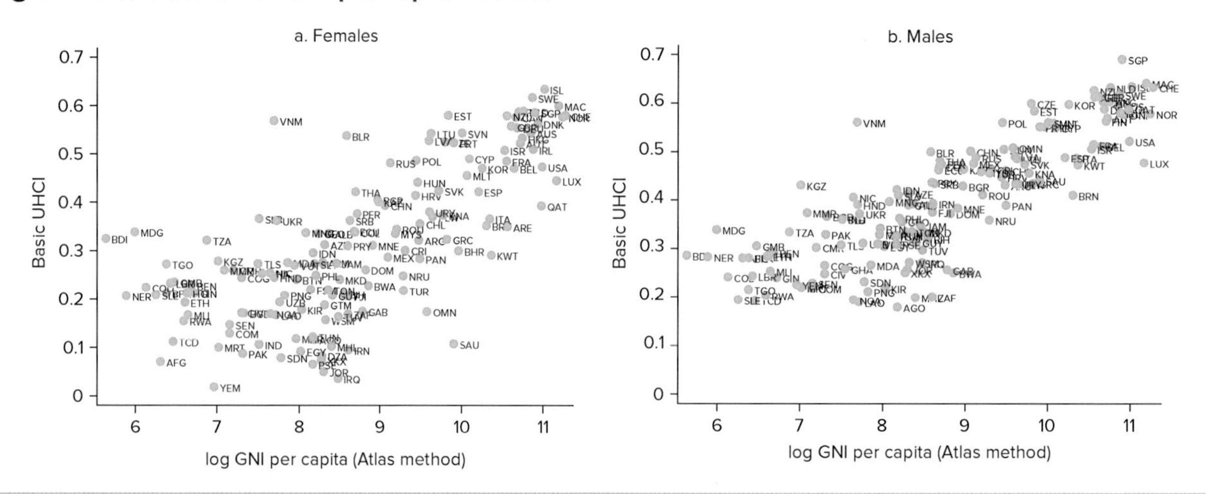

Source: World Bank calculations based on the 2020 update of the Human Capital Index (HCI), the World Development Indicators, the International Labour Organization, and the Global Jobs Indicators Database.

Note: Based on 148 economies with available data. GNI = gross national income; UHCI = Utilization-Adjusted Human Capital Index.

Figure 4.14: Full UHCI and per capita income

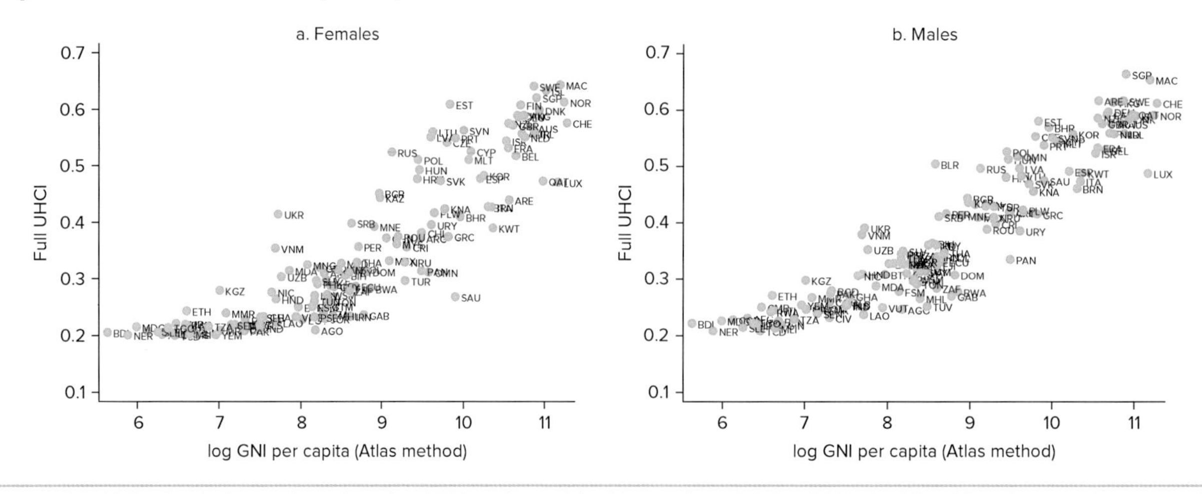

Source: World Bank calculations based on the 2020 update of the Human Capital Index (HCI), the World Development Indicators, the International Labour Organization, and the Global Jobs Indicators Database.

Note: Based on 138 economies (panel a) or 141 economies (panel b) with available data. GNI = gross national income; UHCI = Utilization-Adjusted Human Capital Index.

Figure 4.15: Gender gaps in HCI and UHCI, by region

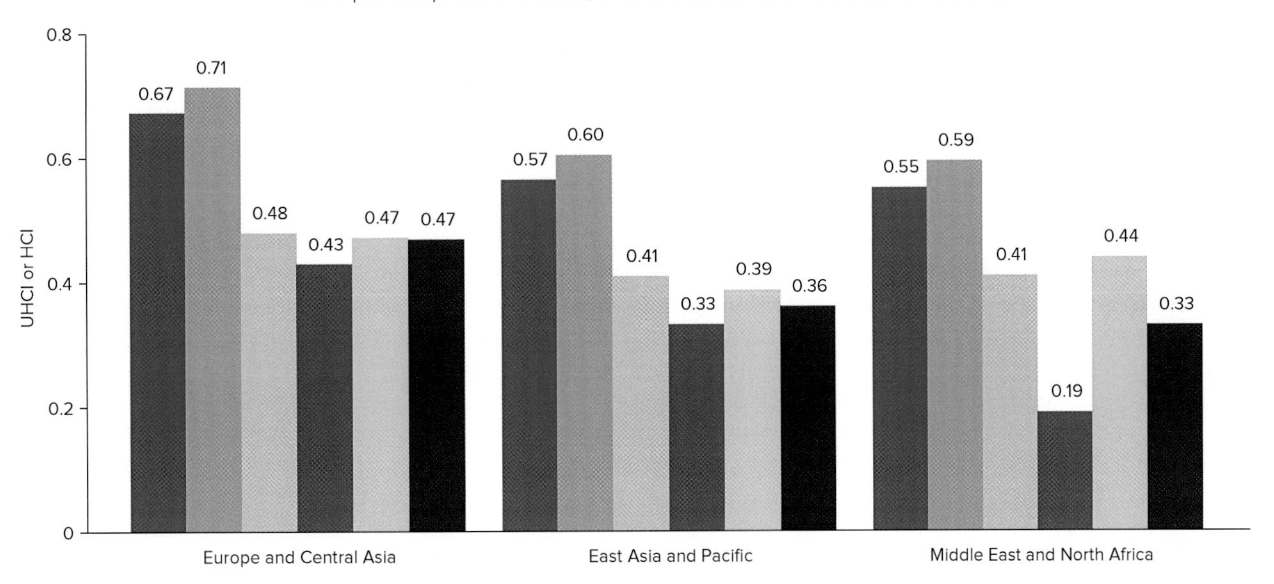

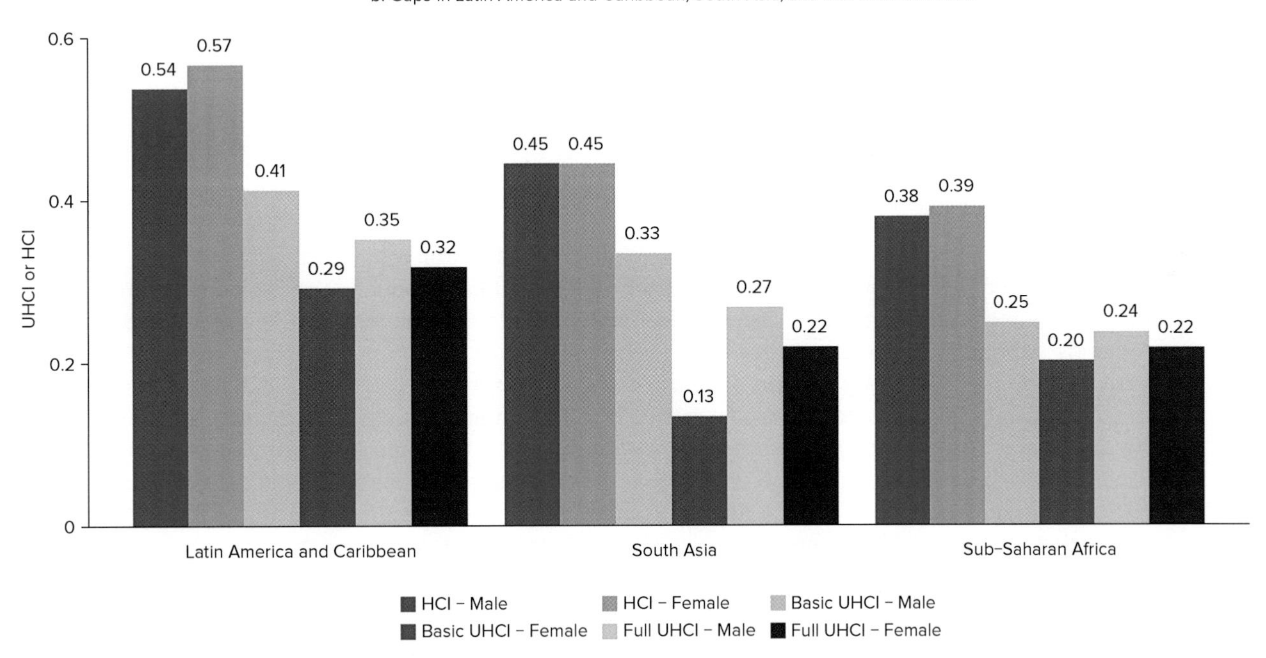

Source: World Bank calculations based on the 2020 update of the Human Capital Index (HCI), the World Development Indicators, the International Labour Organization, and the Global Jobs Indicators Database.

Note: HCI = Human Capital Index; UHCI = Utilization-Adjusted Human Capital Index.

Box 4.3: Closing gender gaps in human capital outcomes: Where do we go from here?

The Human Capital Index (HCI) approach implicitly assumes that human capital investments translate into productivity through labor market opportunities. How human capital is utilized in terms of paid work and labor markets, however, varies considerably. In particular, considerable and well-documented gaps exist in labor market opportunities between men and women. Globally, only 50 percent of women participate in the paid labor force, whereas 80 percent of men do. Across countries, the gender wage gap persists at about 20 percent, on average (International Labour Organization 2018). Women work in lower-paying occupations and jobs. Across the globe, only one in five firms has a female top manager.[a] Although these outcomes might in part reflect optimizing decisions within the family (for example, see Chioda 2016 for evidence from Latin America), evidence shows that various constraints explain some portion of these gaps, ranging from the lack of childcare and adequate leave policies to social norms that create barriers preventing women from working. These norms include those that put a disproportionate responsibility for domestic work and childcare on women, as well as those that result in occupational sex segregation, sexual harassment, and mobility restrictions. Women must also contend with differential constraints in access to finance and markets, a great divide in access to digital technology, and legal/regulatory barriers to start and grow firms.[b] All these factors result in wasted potential in terms of realizing economic gains from human capital investments in girls. Looking only at the sex-disaggregated HCI misses an important reality concerning gender gaps in how human capital is utilized.

For human capital to translate into productivity, *humans*, who own the *capital*, need to be employed in work where they can use their human capital. For example, in 2020, boys and girls growing up in Peru have the same HCI score of 0.6. Only 62 percent of women in Peru are employed, however, compared to 78 percent of men, resulting in a basic Utilization-Adjusted Human Capital Index that is 10 percentage points lower for females than for males (Pennings 2020).

Economies can act to enable women's full participation in labor market opportunities. Provision of affordable childcare options, parental leave policies, and flexible work options can accommodate women's entry into formal work and help women and men redistribute and balance demands at home and at work (Olivetti and Petrongolo 2017). Safe transport allows women to go to the workplace, and pay transparency can increase women's power to negotiate equal pay for equal work. Improved access to digital technology for women can unlock potential gains from the digital era. These range from accessing online education to expanded income-generating opportunities through flexible online gig work and e-commerce entrepreneurship (Alatas et al. 2019; Dammert, Galdo, and Galdo 2014; World Bank 2016). Resources need to be mobilized to ensure that women and men have equal access to livelihoods and economic opportunities.

Source: Prepared by Daniel Halim.

[a] World Bank Enterprise Surveys data retrieved from World Bank Gender Data Portal, https://datatopics.worldbank.org/gender/.

[b] In low- and middle-income countries, only 54 percent of women have access to mobile internet, compared with 74 percent of men (GSMA 2020).

employment rates driven by a variety of factors, including social norms. The full UHCI has smaller gender gaps, however, in part because of small gaps in how much human capital there is to underutilize. See box 4.3 for a discussion of closing gender gaps.

NOTES

1. This chapter was prepared by Steven Pennings (spennings@worldbank.org) with helpful comments from Roberta Gatti, Aart Kraay, Michael Weber, Kathleen Beegle, Paul Corral, and David Weil, as well as from other internal and external reviewers. See Pennings (2020) for an in-depth treatment. A data appendix is available for download at https://development-data-hub-s3-public.s3.amazonaws.com/ddhfiles/144347/uhci_dataappendix_sep2020.xlsx.
2. See box 4.1 for a derivation. More specifically, this relationship requires a Cobb-Douglas production function and the assumption that the capital-to-output ratio is constant in the long run (one of Kaldor's facts).
3. In the full UHCI, the utilization rate is defined as UHCI/HCI—and so satisfies equation (4.1) by construction—but still turns out to have an intuitive interpretation (see section 4.3 titled "The Full UHCI" later in the chapter).
4. Just like the HCI, the UHCI can also be interpreted in terms of productivity: a child born today can expect to be only UHCI × 100 percent as productive as she would be, on average, if she enjoyed complete education and full health, and if her future labor was fully utilized.
5. Naturally, no economies will have employment rates of 1. But this condition is consistent with the approach in the HCI, in which no economy has perfect test scores or 14 expected years of school.
6. In the full UHCI, discussed later in the chapter, economies with very low better employment rates will have GDP that is less sensitive to increases in human capital. But, even in those economies, improvements in human capital will still increase growth.
7. Technically, this is because the implicit assumption in the HCI is that basic utilization rates are constant across status quo and full human capital scenarios. A full employment assumption is not required.
8. Data from ILOSTAT, the ILO's labor statistics database (accessed December 13, 2019), https://www.ilo.org/shinyapps/bulkexplorer7/.
9. For more information on JOIN, see https://datacatalog.worldbank.org/dataset/global-jobs-indicators-database.
10. In some cases, the more recent data source of employment data is not used if it is missing data for the full UHCI.
11. For lower-income countries, the U-shape is mostly driven by several outliers with extremely high utilization rates.
12. In Malawi, a household survey in 2005 reported employment rates of 0.8, twice the most recent figure (from 2017). Likewise, in Nepal a household survey in 2008 reported employment rates of 0.84, also about twice the most recent figure (also from 2017). The difference is likely due to exclusion of own-use production workers in 2017, though this exclusion is not well documented.
13. For the average low-income economy, long-run incomes in the complete utilization and human capital scenario would be about 4.5 times those of the status quo ($1/0.22 \approx 4.5$), compared with 2.5 times that with complete human capital alone ($1/0.4 \approx 2.5$).
14. On average, those with a complete secondary education were earning only 60 percent more than those with no education, which is the equivalent of less than six years with an 8 percent return to education. Omitted variables such as parental income and ability mean that the six years is likely an overstatement.
15. Another cause of the mismatch can be poor education quality, with the result that those with a qualification cannot perform the functions required. In this case, the reason the engineer is driving a taxi is that he or she is not able to perform the tasks of an engineer because of poor-quality education. Handel, Valerio, and Sanchez Puerta (2016) find that, in 12 low- and middle-income countries, the overeducation/underutilization rate is 36 percent. Overeducation/underutilization rates vary across countries and can depend on how the rates are measured.
16. The definition of formal employment varies across countries, but it generally refers to the coverage of the worker with respect to benefits

like unemployment insurance, pensions, sick leave, or annual leave.

17. Better employment differs from "decent work" (ILO) and "good jobs for development" (World Bank 2012).
18. A final technical issue is that some of the increase in GDP in the basic UHCI comes from utilizing people's time rather than utilizing their human capital. The full UHCI also addresses this concern (see Pennings 2020).
19. It is important to acknowledge that the definition of better employment and the full UHCI are stylized for simplicity and cross-country data availability. In reality, many people without better jobs can partially use their human capital to increase productivity beyond that of raw labor. For example, education is positively correlated with high-yield-variety seed choice among Indian farmers (Foster and Rosenzweig 2010). Moreover, healthier people may be more productive laborers. Assuming that only educational human capital (not health human capital) is underutilized outside better employment results in the same U-shaped pattern in per capita gross national income, but with higher utilization rates (and UHCI) for low-income economies (not reported). Moreover, there are many examples of people without better jobs using their human capital to its full extent, such as self-employed professionals; however, the availability of cross-country employment data limits the amount of nuance possible in this regard.
20. Data from ILOSTAT (accessed February 20, 2020) (defined using ICSE-93).
21. This low correlation is driven by a number of economies on the left side of figure 4.8 in the Middle East and North Africa and elsewhere, where a high fraction of total employment is classified as better employment (such as wage employment), and a number of economies, often in East Asia and Pacific, with lower rates of wage employment on the right side of figure 4.8. Some of these East Asia and Pacific economies are also penalized in the full measure by having a high HCI that increases the potential to underutilize human capital.
22. The one exception is Vietnam, which has a high employment rate, but a low fraction of that is in better jobs. These differences remain prominent in the full UHCI because of Vietnam's high HCI score.
23. Klasen (2019) shows that the U-shaped pattern of female employment rates is mostly due to region fixed effects, and not to the development path for an individual country.

REFERENCES

Alatas, V., A. Banerjee, R. Hanna, B. A. Olken, R. Purnamasari, and M. Wai-Poi. 2019. "Does Elite Capture Matter? Local Elites and Targeted Welfare Programs in Indonesia." *AEA Papers and Proceedings* 109: 334–39.

Battu, H., and K. Bender. 2020. "Educational Mismatch in Developing Countries: A Review of the Existing Evidence." In *The Economics of Education: A Comprehensive Overview (2nd Ed)*, edited by S. Bradley and C. Green. Academic Press.

Chioda L. 2016. *Work and Family: Latin American and Caribbean Women in Search of a New Balance*. Latin American Development Forum. Washington, DC: World Bank.

Dammert, A. C., J. C. Galdo, and V. Galdo. 2014. "Preventing Dengue through Mobile Phones: Evidence from a Field Experiment in Peru." *Journal of Health Economics* 35: 147–61.

Filmer, D., and L. Fox. 2014. *Youth Employment in Sub-Saharan Africa*. Washington, DC: World Bank.

Foster, A., and M. Rosenzweig. 2010. "The Microeconomics of Technology Adoption." *Annual Review of Economics* 2: 395–424.

Gatti, R., M. Morgandi, R. Grun, S. Brodmann, D. Angel-Urdinola, J. M. Moreno, D. Marotta, M. Schiffbauer, and E. Mata Lorenzo. 2013. *Jobs for Shared Prosperity: Time for Action in the Middle East and North Africa*. Washington, DC: World Bank.

Goldin, C. 1995. "The U-Shaped Female Labor Force Function in Economic Development and Economic History." In *Investment in Women's Human Capital and Economic Development*, edited by T. P. Schultz, 61–90. University of Chicago Press.

GSMA. 2020. "The Mobile Gender Gap Report 2020." GSMA Connected Women, London. https://www.gsma.com/mobilefordevelopment/wp-content/uploads/2020/05/GSMA-The-Mobile-Gender-Gap-Report-2020.pdf.

Handel, M., A. Valerio, and M. Sanchez Puerta. 2016. "Accounting for Mismatch in Low- and Middle-Income Countries: Measurement, Magnitudes, and Explanations." Directions in Development Series. Washington, DC: World Bank.

International Labour Organization. 2018. "Global Wage Report 2018/19: What Lies behind Gender Pay Gaps." Geneva: International Labour Office.

Klasen, S. 2019. "What Explains Uneven Female Labor Force Participation Levels and Trends in Developing Countries?" *World Bank Research Observer* 34 (2).

Kraay, A. 2018. "Methodology for a World Bank Human Capital Index." Policy Research Working Paper 8593, World Bank, Washington, DC.

Merotto, D., M. Weber, and A. Reyes. 2018. "Pathways to Better Jobs in IDA Countries: Findings from Jobs Diagnostics." Jobs Series No. 14, World Bank, Washington, DC.

Olivetti, C., and B. Petrongolo. 2017. "The Economic Consequences of Family Policies: Lessons from a Century of Legislation in High-Income Countries." *Journal of Economic Perspectives* 31 (1): 205–30.

Pennings, S. 2020. "The Utilization-Adjusted Human Capital Index (UHCI)." Policy Research Working Paper 9375, World Bank, Washington, DC.

World Bank. 2012. "What Matters Most for School Health and School Feeding: A Framework Paper." SABER Working Paper 3, Systems Approach for Better Education Results, World Bank, Washington, DC.

World Bank. 2016. *World Development Report 2016: Digital Dividends*. Washington, DC: World Bank.

5 Informing Policies to Protect and Build HUMAN CAPITAL

The Human Capital Index (HCI) 2020 update arrives at a time when policy makers across the world face urgent choices. Strategic decisions made now have the power to protect and strengthen countries' human capital and, with it, their economic future.

In addition to documenting pre-COVID-19 (coronavirus) changes in human capital across 174 economies, the HCI 2020 update establishes a baseline for tracking the pandemic's effects on human capital. A further task for the update has been identifying pathways through which COVID-19 can influence human capital outcomes in the short and longer terms. Using the HCI methodology to quantify the gaps that will likely emerge in health, skills, and knowledge because of COVID-19, this analysis underscores the urgency of protecting and sustaining the recovery of human capital, which will be a cornerstone of countries' postcrisis recovery and future economic growth.

Good measurement and data are essential to shape well-targeted and cost-effective policies and to design course corrections when needed. To underscore this point, this report's final pages map short-term and longer-range agendas for strengthening the measurement of human capital, and link these agendas to policy changes necessary to protect human capital in the wake of COVID-19.

5.1 GOOD MEASUREMENT: NECESSITY, NOT LUXURY

As the COVID-19 crisis continues to unfold, good data and measurement are more vital than ever. Yet fiscal constraints and numerous competing priorities raise the risk of delays to investments in measurement when, in fact, measurement enables effective action.

Better measurement and transparent information can be transformational in safeguarding and strengthening human capital. By generating a shared understanding among diverse actors, measurement can shine a light on constraints that limit progress in human capital. Through this process, effective measurement can facilitate political consensus based on facts and mobilize support for reforms. Measurement also enables policy makers to target support to those who are most in need, which is often where interventions yield the highest payoffs. As policy implementation moves forward, measurement provides feedback to guide course corrections.

If measurement can improve policy results around human capital in ordinary times, its importance is multiplied during a crisis. Governments that can access and use relevant data in real time are better able to act in a coordinated way on multiple fronts. In the case of COVID-19, they can monitor the evolution of disease transmission and continuously update control strategies while responding to the immediate and long-term effects of the economic crisis on households and communities. Measuring how well children are growing, whether they are learning, and how financial stress and insecurity are affecting their development is a necessity, not a luxury. It is essential to design and target policies that can remediate the pandemic's negative impacts. At a time when demand for government spending is surging, and fiscal space is limited, data and their transparent communication are vital to ensure accountability for how scarce resources are used.

The power of measurement to support transformative action in difficult situations extends beyond public health emergencies. For example, data are especially important in countries affected by fragility or conflict, though measurement is far more difficult to carry out in these settings. Insecurity and the lack of robust institutions hinder data collection and, in turn, the ability of governments to take action informed by evidence. Fortunately, innovative methods have recently enabled some progress in understanding human capital dynamics in fragile contexts (box 5.1).

5.2 BEYOND THE HCI

The HCI offers a bird's-eye view of human capital across economies. By benchmarking the productivity costs of shortfalls in health and education, the index has spurred new conversations within governments, bringing discussion on human capital accumulation to the level where decisions about resource allocation are actually made. This is an important achievement.

As a measurement tool, however, the HCI has substantial limitations. For example, it does not speak to distributional or geographical differences within economies. And although it focuses on what matters—outcomes—it does not chart the specific pathways that each economy needs to follow to accelerate progress in human capital. Much greater depth in measurement and research is needed to better understand the dynamics of human capital accumulation, including across socioeconomic groups and geography, and how policies can affect it. Some key measurement improvements can be achieved in the short term (for example, on test scores, see box 5.2). Longer-term efforts will demand a more sustained commitment from economies and development partners.

5.2.1 A short-term measurement agenda

Because of the dramatic changes in household incomes and service delivery driven by COVID-19, there is an immediate need to measure the pandemic's welfare impacts. Social distancing, however, is limiting the way in which traditional surveys are collected by enumerators who visit families. Phone surveys have helped respond to this challenge by reaching households remotely.[1]

Phone surveys are relatively inexpensive, an important consideration at a moment when resources are especially scarce and countries face many competing priorities. Such surveys are well suited for gathering information about behaviors (including access to health services and uptake of remote learning arrangements) or outcomes (such as income and consumption) subject to rapid change. They are likely to return more reliable and informative data when they build on existing information bases, pointing to the importance of triangulating with existing data collection initiatives.

Facility phone surveys are a complement to household phone surveys. They can document, for example, how prepared health facilities are to manage COVID-19 patients and can identify bottlenecks in the delivery of routine health services, including immunization and maternal and child health services. Administrative data can also be used to monitor many aspects of service provision—at a low marginal cost because these data already exist in most countries. These data could provide valuable insights but are often poorly linked, of varying quality, and inaccessible to groups outside of government. Big data can be similarly leveraged to guide action. For example, data from mobile phone records have been used to monitor mobility (which is important for modulating disease containment), to nudge behavior, and to improve service delivery, including delivering educational content. Digital technology and data can be harnessed to provide social protection benefits more equitably and efficiently, both immediately and in the longer run.

Box 5.1: Innovative data collection in fragile contexts: Examples from West Africa and the Middle East and North Africa

Epidemics affect people's health, and they also disrupt livelihoods and well-being through school closures, workers placed on furlough, restrictions on transportation and gatherings, and closing of international borders. As such, at the height of the Ebola epidemic in West Africa, in addition to assessing the impact of the disease on people's health, it was also important to measure and monitor the epidemic's socioeconomic impact. Given the nature of the epidemic, however, it was impossible and unethical to deploy enumerators to the field for data collection in face-to-face interviews at households and in communities. In 2014, capitalizing on the proliferation of mobile phone networks, and building on the experiences of the mobile phone survey initiative called Listening to Africa, high-frequency mobile phone interventions were designed and implemented to provide rapid monitoring of the socioeconomic impacts of the Ebola crisis in Liberia and Sierra Leone.

Two nationally representative surveys, each conducted in Liberia and Sierra Leone when the crisis broke out, were used as the baseline for anchoring estimates in a representative dataset. In Liberia, researchers drew on the country's Household Income and Expenditure Survey, which had to curtail fieldwork in August 2014. In Sierra Leone, they used the Labor Force Survey, which had completed fieldwork in July 2014. These existing surveys provided a database of phone numbers and household characteristics, which eventually became the sample frame for the phone survey. Data were then collected through call centers, either nationally or internationally, to reach over two thousand respondents in each country. Although phone surveys cannot replace face-to-face household surveys in all contexts, the experience in Liberia and Sierra Leone illustrates substantial benefits of such innovation in specific circumstances and for specific data collection needs, particularly the ability to collect timely data in volatile and high-risk environments.

Implementing surveys in a rapidly evolving context involves myriad challenges, including the lack of a relevant and reliable sample frame. For example, excluding displaced populations from national sample frames threatens the representativeness of socioeconomic surveys and consequently provides a skewed understanding of the country. As the size of forcibly displaced populations increases globally, it is urgent to devise strategies to include these populations in nationally representative surveys. The sampling procedure undertaken for the Syrian Refugee and Host Community Surveys, implemented over 2015–16 in the Kurdistan region of Iraq, in Jordan, and in Lebanon, offers valuable insights on overcoming survey-implementation challenges to obtain representative estimates in challenging contexts. In the absence of updated national sample frames for host communities, and given the lack of comprehensive mapping of forcibly displaced populations, geospatial segmenting was used to create enumeration areas where they did not exist. Data collected by humanitarian agencies, including the United Nations High Commissioner for Refugees and the International Organization for Migration, were used to generate sample frames for displaced populations.

Source: Based on Hoogeveen and Pape 2020.

Box 5.2: Leveraging national assessments to obtain internationally comparable estimates of education quality

The Human Capital Index (HCI) highlights the need for regular and globally comparable measurement of learning to assess the quality of an economy's education system. Although most data on education quality included in the HCI currently come from assessments designed to be comparable across economies and over time using psychometric methods, those assessments are often infrequent and do not yet cover all economies.

Leveraging national learning assessments can help bridge the gaps in learning data. Most economies regularly conduct some form of assessment that can be augmented with short modules of globally benchmarked and validated items to construct globally comparable measures of education quality (Birdsall, Bruns, and Madan 2016; UNESCO 2018). Despite the lack of a comprehensive bank of globally benchmarked items, some items from international assessments can be incorporated into national assessments as linking items. These linking items provide commonality with international assessments, enabling learning outcomes to be placed on a global scale (Kolen and Brennan 2004). For instance, the 2021 National Assessment for Secondary Schools will enable Bangladesh to produce globally comparable learning outcomes. To allow comparison of national education quality on a global scale, the following countries have recently fielded or are planning to include linking items from international assessments in their national assessments.

Nigeria. Besides conducting an Early Grade Reading Assessment in 2014 for 4 of its 37 states, Nigeria had only sparse learning data until recently. The HCI 2018 emphasized the need for a nationally representative and internationally comparable assessment of learning outcomes in Nigeria. The Nigerian National Learning Assessment (NLA 2019), supported by the World Bank, is the first nationally representative learning assessment conducted in Nigeria using an internationally recognized methodology. The NLA 2019 measures student learning at grades 4 and 8 in the core subjects of mathematics, English, and science, and includes linking items to allow comparison on an international scale. Once fully harmonized with international assessments, the NLA 2019 will allow for inclusion in a future HCI of a nationally representative and globally comparable learning measure for Nigeria.

Sri Lanka. In 2009, the national assessment included linked Trends in International Mathematics and Science Study (TIMSS) items. Subsequent national assessments in Sri Lanka have maintained linking items with TIMSS to allow international comparability. The resulting score is used in the World Bank's HCI.

Uzbekistan. Before 2019, no internationally comparable learning outcomes data were available for Uzbekistan. The launch of the 2018 HCI galvanized the government toward measurement of education quality; in 2019, with World Bank support, the country conducted its first nationally representative and internationally comparable assessment (using TIMSS linking items) for grade 5 students in mathematics. That assessment is now part of the country's 2020 HCI.

Relatively few linking items are currently available from international assessments, necessitating a cautious approach informed by individual economy contexts: ensuring that the selected linking items align with the economy's national grade-level curriculum, are translated according to the protocols of the international assessment, are piloted in the economy, and are not too easy or too difficult for the target population; that similar testing conditions are arranged as for international assessments; and that a sufficient number of items is selected to provide reliable internationally comparable estimates of education quality in the economy.

5.2.2 Tackling long-term measurement needs

In addition to solutions that can be deployed rapidly, economies need strategies to improve the measurement of human capital in the longer run.

The HCI update offered an opportunity for economies to take stock of their data on human capital outcomes. In this process, the World Bank engaged with counterparts in several fruitful collaborations to improve the quality of data used to calculate the HCI. For example, thanks to close collaboration with the Ministry of Human Resource Development in India, it was possible to significantly improve upon publicly available data for school enrollment and arrive at a measure of expected years of school (EYS) constructed on the basis of actual age-specific enrollment rates, which capture enrollment more precisely.[2]

Despite improvements, many gaps in the measurement of internationally comparable key dimensions of human capital persist (box 5.2). For example, establishing well-functioning vital registry systems to record such basic events as births and deaths is still a work in progress: less than 70 percent of economies record such events, and progress to fill these gaps has been slow (box 5.3). The quality of school enrollment data, which in the index are based on administrative records, is highly variable in low- and middle-income economies, particularly at the lower- and upper-secondary levels. Finally, benchmarking learning outcomes internationally has been a challenge, both across economies and especially over time. This difficulty has significantly constrained the coverage of the long-run analysis of changes in measured human capital. These challenges are heightened in fragile situations: in some cases, data to inform various HCI components simply do not exist; in others, data are too old and likely do not sufficiently capture the rapid deterioration of human capital that can occur in fragile contexts. In addition, comparable data, including over time, for refugees, displaced persons, and host populations, are extremely limited.

An upcoming *World Development Report* will focus on data and provide a comprehensive description of the complex and rapidly evolving measurement landscape. But it is worth noting here the areas in which better-funded and coordinated data collection and use could improve the understanding of human capital accumulation and effective interventions to accelerate it.

One such area concerns the long-term consequences of interventions that have proved successful in the short run. For example, there is well-established evidence that conditional cash transfers have improved a variety of health and education outcomes within a few years of program inception. Relatively little evidence exists, however, on whether and how the increased time spent in school thanks to the transfers has led to better learning outcomes and improved labor market opportunities. Similarly, long-term evidence on the efficacy of some types of interventions often relies on small pilots that were not followed by countrywide scale-up, and questions therefore remain about the generalizability of promising findings.

Administrative data can allow for the tracking of critical outcomes over time by, for example, linking educational assessments and hospital records to taxation records, social security contributions, or health insurance via unique identifiers. The benefits of user-friendly administrative data systems are vast, because such systems can inform policy choices about the design of cost-effective interventions, allow regular monitoring of key outcomes, and support decision-making in real time, all at low marginal cost. Within an economy, however, administrative data are collected by a variety of ministries and other entities, often resulting in a patchwork of systems that does not favor integration and optimal use. Taking advantage of these data requires expertise that is scarce

Box 5.3: Data quality and freshness in the components of the Human Capital Index

The Human Capital Index (HCI) has proved a useful tool for policy dialogue, largely because it incorporates human capital outcomes that are easily recognizable, consistently measured across the world, and salient to policy makers. However, even the basic index components suffer from significant data gaps and quality issues.

The child and adult survival measures used in the index are based on data on birth and death rates by age group. These data come primarily from national vital registries that are mandated to record vital events like births and deaths. As such, vital statistics are essential to the measurement of demographic indicators like life expectancy and to identifying health priorities for the population. They can also help target health interventions and monitor their progress. Coverage of vital registries varies widely: only 68 percent of economies register at least 90 percent of births (see map B5.3.1), and only 55 percent cover at least 90 percent of deaths.[a] Birth registration has increased by only 7 percentage points (from 58 percent to 65 percent) in the past decade (UNICEF 2013); in Sub-Saharan Africa, only eight countries have birth registration coverage above 80 percent.[b]

Stunting serves as an indicator for prenatal, infant, and early childhood health environments. The Joint Malnutrition Estimates (JME) database that compiles global stunting data reports data for 152 economies, 33 of which have data that are more than 5 years old.[c] In 10 economies, the most recent survey is over 10 years old.

Gaps also remain in education data. The expected years of school measure is based on enrollment data that national governments provide to the United Nations Educational, Scientific and Cultural Organization Institute for Statistics. Of the 174 economies in the HCI 2020 sample, 22 economies rely on primary enrollment data from 2015 or earlier. Because primary enrollment data are typically the most consistently reported, the issue of data freshness is of even greater concern for other levels of school. Significant gaps also exist in time series data on enrollment rates. Of the 103 economies included in the 2010 HCI sample, 22 economies were missing primary enrollment rates for 2010. Data gaps are more numerous at other levels of schooling—over 30 economies were missing secondary-level enrollment data for 2010, and 42 economies were missing these data at the preprimary level.

Finally, the latest update to the Global Dataset on Education Quality that produces harmonized test scores covers 98.7 percent of the school-age population. Of the 174 economies with an HCI, 14 rely for test score data on Early Grade Reading Assessments that are not representative at the national level. Sixty-five economies (roughly 37 percent of the sample) rely on test score data from 2015 or earlier.

Significant gaps exist in sex-disaggregated data across HCI components. The JME reports disaggregated stunting data for only 56 percent of the 887 surveys that are part of the database. Whereas sex-disaggregated enrollment rates are reasonably complete at the primary level, they are missing at the lower-secondary level for 29 of the 174 economies in the HCI 2020 sample. Sixteen economies in this sample are also missing disaggregated test score data. As a result of these gaps, 21 of the 174 economies in the 2020 sample do not have sex-disaggregated HCI scores. These gaps in disaggregated data span all regions and income groups.[d]

(continued next page)

Box 5.3: Data quality and freshness in the components of the Human Capital Index *(Continued)*

The credible and consistent measurement of human capital outcomes is essential to identifying priority areas for policy intervention, informing the design of those policies, and tracking their effectiveness over time. Collection of high-quality data can doubtless be a costly undertaking, but countries can explore more cost-effective ways of monitoring their citizens' health and education outcomes. For instance, instead of bearing the costs of participating in an international assessment, Uzbekistan incorporated assessment items into its national learning assessment that would allow for linking with the Trends in International Mathematics and Science Study (see box 5.2).

Map B5.3.1: Coverage of live births registration

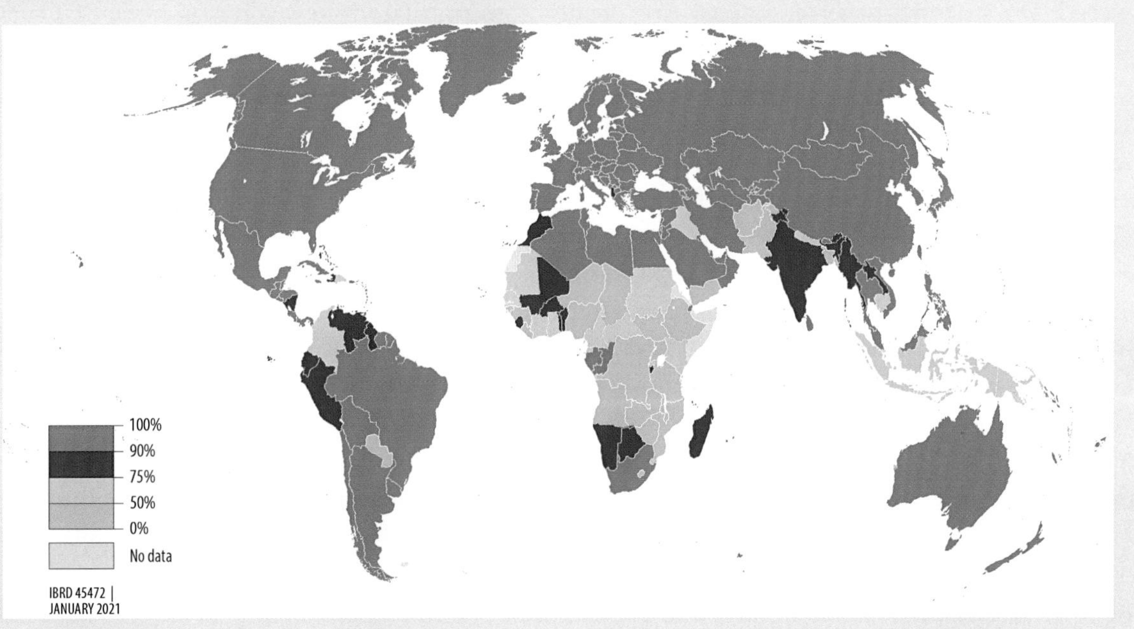

Source: United Nations Statistics Division.

Note: Boundaries and names shown and the designations used in this map do not imply official endorsement or acceptance by the United Nations or the World Bank.

[a] See the United Nations Statistics Division web page, "Coverage of Birth and Death Registration," https://unstats.un.org/unsd/demographic-social/crvs/#coverage. For countries without robust vital registries, the United Nations Interagency Group for Child Mortality Estimation and the United Nations Population Division (that reports on adult mortality) fill data gaps using population censuses, household surveys, and sample registrations combined with model life tables. All these data must then be modeled to produce mortality rates.

[b] "Coverage of Birth and Death Registration" web page.

[c] For more information on the JME database, see https://data.unicef.org/resources/jme-report-2020/.

[d] Of the 21 economies missing a sex-disaggregated HCI score, 13 are from Sub-Saharan Africa; 2 each from East Asia and the Pacific, Latin America and the Caribbean, and South Asia; and 1 each from the Middle East and North Africa and Europe and Central Asia. Of those 21 economies, 3 are high-income, 4 are upper-middle-income, 7 are lower-middle-income, and 6 are low-income.

in many economies. Finally, legitimate privacy concerns also restrict access and can make data linking incomplete or impossible.

A related concern involves understanding the production function of health and education outcomes from the service delivery perspective. This issue is essential for designing effective interventions and systems for quality health care and education. It is even more pressing in a post-COVID-19 world, where extensive remediation will be needed to compensate for the losses to human capital caused by the shock. Many basic questions remain unanswered. Do students have textbooks? Are health centers stocked with the necessary drugs?

Beyond assessing fundamental inputs, countries need answers on how to improve the quality of services. They need to understand, for example, whether teachers actually master the curriculum they are teaching and if physicians diagnose diseases accurately and treat them appropriately. Selection mechanisms and incentives also matter for the quality of services. For example, pay for performance has been widely introduced and requires evaluation. How can it best be managed and at what level? Private sector financing and delivery also have the potential to improve service quality. But how can countries make sure that quality improves while services remain affordable? Rapid advances in information and communications technology likewise hold promise to improve service delivery. Reliable strategies to make such improvements are not obvious, however, and will differ across country contexts. Additionally, quality reflects management capacities and choices. What management interventions improve service delivery in cost-effective ways? And how can countries measure the quality of management in the social sectors?

Administrative data can answer some of these questions but cannot provide insights into behaviors and competencies. Surveys such as those conducted by the Service Delivery Indicators (SDI) initiative can help. SDI surveys are nationally representative facility surveys that measure the quality of services received by average citizens in primary health care centers and primary schools.[3] SDI surveys collect data on critical inputs and provider performance and, in the case of schools, children's learning. These types of data allow governments and service providers to identify gaps in service provision, link financing inputs with health and education outcomes, and understand the margins along which social sector spending fails to translate into quality services. SDI surveys are important platforms for innovation and research, including measuring the quality of management in schools and hospitals.

The analysis of delivery systems needs to advance in parallel with a deeper understanding of how human capital accumulates through the life course. For example, evidence points to the nodal importance of early childhood years for lifelong cognitive, physical, and socioemotional development. Very few economies, however, make systematic measurement of skills in early years a priority. Even when those measures are available, the evolution of health status, cognitive abilities, and noncognitive skills during early childhood is not well understood. Similarly, measuring skills—cognitive and noncognitive—among adolescents and adults is still rare in most economies.

Advancing this long-term measurement agenda will require purposeful investments. In turn, funding measurement is a way to increase the efficiency and impact of future policy action across multiple domains. By supporting the political economy of reform processes and guiding policy choices toward cost-effective solutions, better measurement and data use are investments that pay off.

5.3 BUILDING, PROTECTING, AND EMPLOYING HUMAN CAPITAL IN A POST-COVID-19 WORLD

Governments are now working under intense pressure to roll out policies across multiple sectors in response to COVID-19. Measurement is essential to ensure that these policies are strategically designed and well implemented, and that they get results. What might effective policy solutions look like in the domains most important for human capital? A companion paper to the HCI 2020 update (World Bank 2020b) discusses policy responses to COVID-19 in detail; what follows are some of the broad directions these responses may adopt.

5.3.1 A data-driven health sector response

The immediate priority for countries fighting COVID-19 remains containment and elimination of the novel coronavirus. Global efforts, such as improvements in testing and access to a safe and effective vaccine, will need to accompany local measures to test, trace, and isolate carriers of infection; to support the use of nonpharmaceutical interventions such as masks and social distancing; and to implement targeted lockdowns when necessary. Strengthening public health surveillance capacity will be essential to the timeliness and effectiveness of these interventions. Robust surveillance requires the ability to collect, analyze, and interpret relevant health-related data and use these data to plan, implement, and evaluate control actions. With most pandemics being of zoonotic origin, closer coordination between health and the agriculture sector will be instrumental to prevent future outbreaks, in keeping with a "one health" approach.

Complementing strong surveillance, it is essential to step up health care for COVID-19 patients while maintaining the delivery of core health services. COVID-19 highlights the need to invest in primary health care with strong frontline delivery systems. In low- and middle-income countries, priority measures to strengthen primary care may focus on reproductive and child health and nutrition; infectious disease control programs for HIV, tuberculosis, and malaria; and community-based health promotion and disease prevention. In middle- and higher-income countries, a focus on improving healthy longevity, addressing noncommunicable diseases, and linking primary care practitioners systematically to disease surveillance networks will go a long way toward increasing resilience. In the face of widening health disparities, it is essential to ensure that disadvantaged households and communities have access to quality and affordable care. In the past, disruptions to the health and economic status quo have sometimes enabled countries to introduce bold health system reforms (see McDonnell, Urrutia, and Samman 2019). In that sense, these difficult times may offer an unexpected opportunity in many countries to renew the commitment to universal health coverage (World Bank 2020c).

5.3.2 Preventing losses in learning

Along with more and better investments in health, economies need a broad range of interventions in other sectors to get human capital accumulation back on track, both in the short and longer terms (World Bank 2020a). Because of school closures and economic hardships, the current generation of students stands to lose significantly in terms of learning and noncognitive skills now, and in terms of earnings later in life. Strategies to remediate schooling losses will require designing and implementing school reopening protocols adapted to the specificities of the pandemic. At a minimum, protocols will involve protective equipment and supplies, health screening, and social distancing. Tailored teaching and learning resources, especially for disadvantaged children, are urgently needed in many settings to make up for lost learning (World Bank 2020b).

Deeper reforms will need to follow so that countries can sustain access to schooling and promote children's learning at all stages: from cognitive stimulation in the early years to nurturing relevant skills in childhood and adolescence. Building blocks for success will include better-prepared teachers, better-managed schools, and incentives that are aligned across the many stakeholders in education reform. The efforts that economies have made in providing continuity with remote learning during the pandemic could carry benefits beyond the current emergency. Appropriately structured online learning can facilitate the acquisition of those competencies, such as collaboration and higher-order cognitive skills, that are increasingly essential in the changing world of work (Reimers and Schleicher 2020). To shape resilient education systems, economies will need to draw lessons from this worldwide distance learning experience and expand the infrastructure for online and remote learning.

5.3.3 Reinforcing resilience among vulnerable people and communities

In the face of sharp declines in income, support to poor and vulnerable households is essential to mitigate COVID-19's impact and to sustain access to services and food security. In the first phase of the pandemic response, the consensus on social assistance programs has been to cast the net wide, to avoid excluding any of those in need. In the medium term, these interventions need to be reassessed and complemented or replaced by policy measures geared toward an inclusive and sustainable economic recovery with support for employment and livelihoods (including with active labor market policies that help match workers to new jobs and upgrade their skills), as well as assistance to small and microenterprises (World Bank 2020d). In parallel, strengthening social services, including counseling, will help mitigate impacts on mental health and disruptions in people's social networks.

COVID-19 has exacerbated many forms of inequality, notably gender gaps. School closures and a reduction in health services can interrupt the trajectories of adolescent girls at a critical life juncture. With women-owned firms primarily concentrated in informal or low-paying sectors, the lack of basic formal social protection deprives women and their families of buffers against economic shocks, exactly at a time when they are being hit the hardest. Risks of gender-based violence can also be heightened during times of crisis, isolation, and confinement (World Bank 2020d). These effects are amplified in fragile settings.

Deepening inequalities make targeting interventions to the most disadvantaged—and particularly to children in their early years—an imperative, to prevent setbacks that are likely to compromise lifetime health, education, and socioeconomic trajectories among the most vulnerable. These interventions should have an explicit gender angle to help progressively close the gaps now being magnified by COVID-19.

5.3.4 Coordinating action across sectors and adopting a whole-of-society approach

COVID-19 has underscored the interdependence of multiple sectors that are fundamental for human capital accumulation. These sectors include health, education, infrastructure, water and sanitation, information technology, and others. Complex links connect these domains. For example, proper hygiene contributes to limiting diffusion of the virus. In turn, reduced transmission is often a precondition to reopening of schools. Digital technologies enable educational continuity when schools cannot physically reopen, but many poor and marginalized communities lack access to digital tools. These links point to the need for ambitious investments in many economies to expand access to water, sanitation, and digitalization as key enablers of human capital accumulation.

Connections across sectoral and social boundaries emphasize the value of policy approaches that engage diverse stakeholders. Nurturing a nation's human capital is everybody's business. If a child accumulates strong human capital during her critical years of growth and development, it is because a large network of people and institutions has contributed to the process. Parents decide what to feed a child, when to take her to the doctor, and whether and for how long to send her to school. Families make these choices within communities that transmit norms and that may provide a safety net to households in need. In turn, communities rely on services that, in many contexts, are provided largely by the private sector, including nongovernmental organizations. Finally, governments provide public goods, address externalities, and ensure equity. Wise public policy choices, informed by measurement, facilitate the shared achievement of human capital and make it more than the sum of its parts.

The COVID-19 crisis has put all the links in this network under strain, not least the governments themselves. Under these conditions, progress depends on leadership that recognizes the importance of building a future in which all children can reach their potential. In the months and years ahead, with limited fiscal space, protecting core spending for human capital will challenge policy makers in many economies, regardless of their levels of income. Yet, by making these investments with a view to the future, economies can emerge from the COVID-19 crisis prepared to do more than restore the human capital that has been lost. Ambitious policies informed by rigorous measurement can take human capital beyond the levels previously achieved, opening the way to a more prosperous and inclusive future.

NOTES

1. Some of the emerging messages from these surveys are summarized in chapter 3 of this report.
2. EYS, conceptually, is just the sum of enrollment rates by age from age 4 to age 17. Because age-specific enrollment rates are seldom available, however, data on enrollment rates by level of school are used to approximate enrollment rates for the age bracket. In India, enrollment rates provided and used for EYS calculation are age-specific and thus there is no need to approximate the values.
3. For more information on SDI, see https://www.sdindicators.org/.

REFERENCES

Birdsall, N., B. Bruns, and J. Madan. 2016. "Learning Data for Better Policy: A Global Agenda." CGD Policy Paper 096, Center for Global Development, Washington, DC.

Hoogeveen, J., and U. Pape, eds. 2020. *Data Collection in Fragile States: Innovations from Africa and Beyond*. Washington, DC: World Bank.

Kolen, M. J., and R. L. Brennan. 2004. *Test Equating, Scaling, and Linking: Methods and Practices*. Second Edition. Springer-Verlag.

McDonnell, A., A. Urrutia, and E. Samman. 2019. "Reaching Universal Health Coverage: A Political Economy Review of Trends across 49 Countries." ODI Working Paper No. 570, Overseas Development Institute, London.

Reimers, F., and A. Schleicher. 2020. "Schooling Disrupted, Schooling Rethought: How the COVID-19 Pandemic Is Changing Education." OECD, Paris.

UNESCO. 2018. "TCG4 Measurement Strategies." TCG4/23, United Nations Educational, Scientific and Cultural Organization Institute for Statistics, Dubai.

UNICEF (United Nations Children's Fund). 2013. "A Passport to Protection: A Guide to Birth Registration Programming." UNICEF, New York.

World Bank. 2020a. "The Effect of the H1N1 Pandemic on Learning. What to Expect with Covid-19?" World Bank, Washington, DC.

World Bank. 2020b. "Protecting the Poor and Vulnerable: Social Response Framework for COVID-19." Unpublished. Social Protection and Jobs Global Practice, World Bank, Washington, DC.

World Bank. 2020c. "COVID-19 and Health Systems: Just the Beginning." Unpublished. World Bank, Washington, DC.

World Bank. 2020d. "Protecting People and Economies: Integrated Policy Responses to COVID-19." COVID-19 Coronavirus Response, World Bank, Washington, DC.

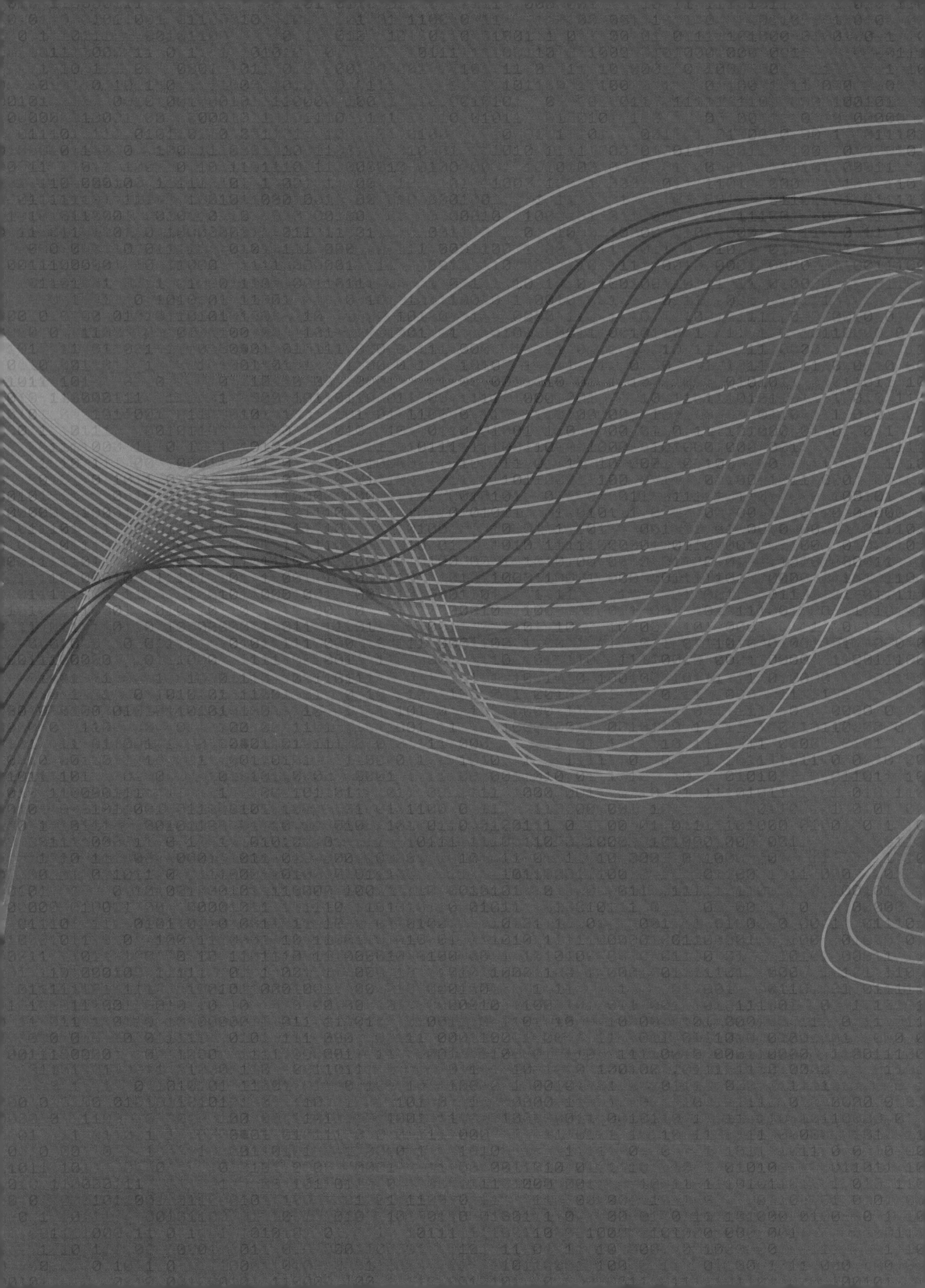

APPENDIXES

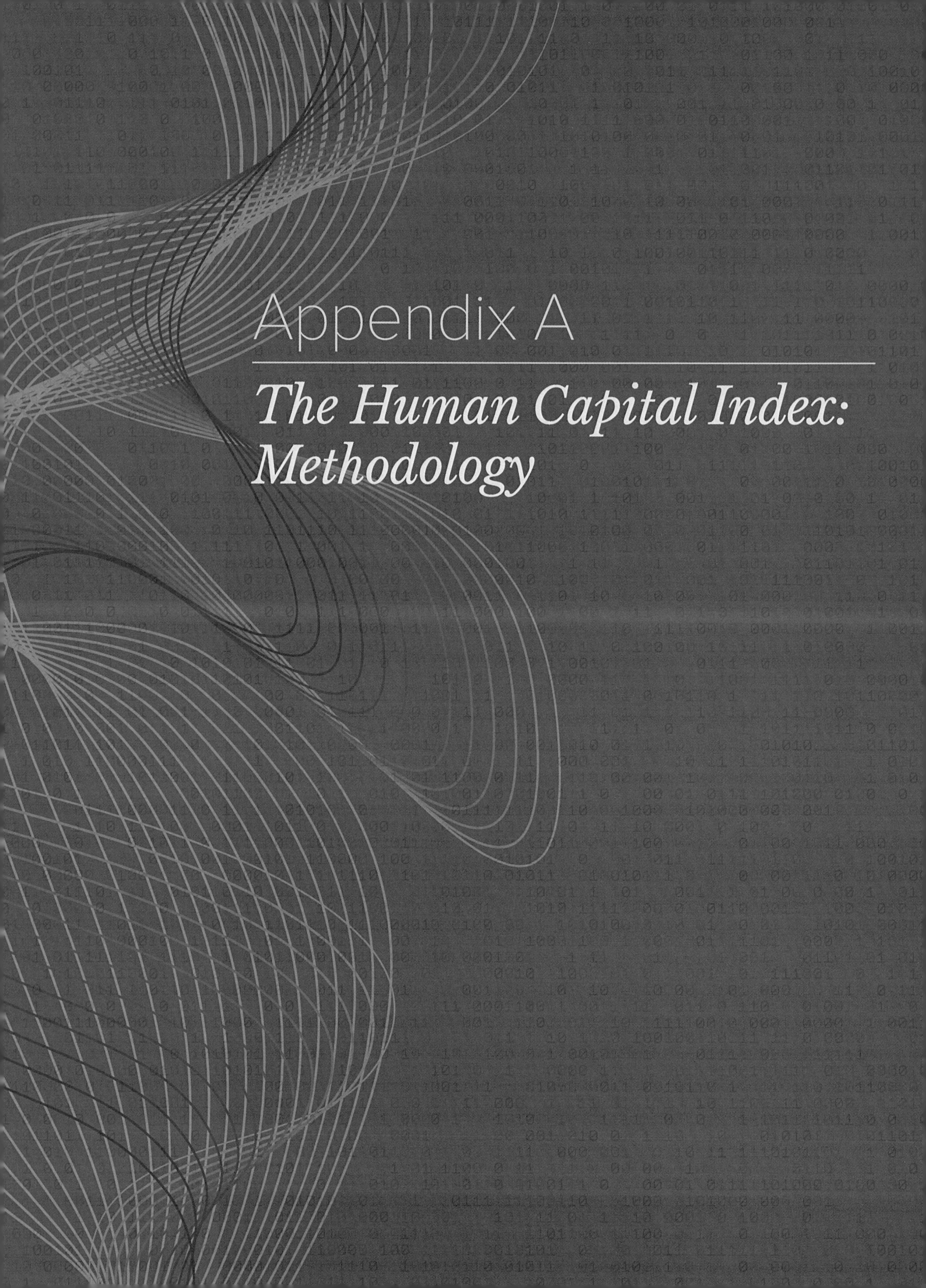

Appendix A

The Human Capital Index: Methodology

1. COMPONENTS OF THE HUMAN CAPITAL INDEX

The Human Capital Index (HCI) measures the human capital that a child born today can expect to attain by age 18, given the risks of poor health and poor education that prevail in the country where she lives. The HCI follows the trajectory from birth to adulthood of a child born today.[1] In the poorest countries in the world, there is a significant risk that the child will not survive to her fifth birthday. Even if she does reach school age, there is a further risk that she will not start school, let alone complete the full cycle of 14 years of school from preschool to grade 12 that is the norm in rich countries. The time she does spend in school may translate unevenly into learning, depending on the quality of the teachers and schools she experiences. When she reaches age 18, she carries with her the lasting effects of poor health and nutrition from her childhood that limit her physical and cognitive abilities as an adult.

The HCI quantitatively illustrates the key stages in this trajectory and their consequences for the productivity of the next generation of workers, with three components:

Component 1: Survival. This component of the index reflects the unfortunate reality that not all children born today will survive until the age when the process of human capital accumulation through formal education begins. It is measured using the under-5 mortality rate (figure A1.1, panel a), with survival to age 5 as the complement of the under-5 mortality rate.

Component 2: School. This component of the index combines information on the quantity and quality of education:

- The *quantity of education* is measured as the number of years of school a child can expect to obtain by age 18 given the prevailing pattern of enrollment rates (figure A1.1, panel b). The maximum possible value is 14 years, corresponding to the maximum number of years of school obtained as of her 18th birthday by a child who starts preschool at age 4. In the data, expected years of school (EYS) range from about 4 to close to 14 years.

- The *quality of education* reflects work at the World Bank to harmonize test scores from major international student achievement testing programs into a measure of harmonized test scores.[2] Harmonized test scores are measured in units of the Trends in International Mathematics and Science Study (TIMSS) testing program and range from about 300 to about 600 across economies (figure A1.1, panel c).

Harmonized test scores are used to convert EYS into learning-adjusted years of schooling (LAYS). LAYS are obtained by multiplying EYS by the ratio of harmonized test scores to 625, corresponding to the TIMSS benchmark of advanced achievement.[3] For example, if EYS in a country is 10 and the average harmonized test score is 400, then the country has 10(400/625) = 6.4 LAYS. The distance between 10 and 6.4 represents a learning gap equivalent to 3.6 years of school.

Component 3: Health. There is no single broadly accepted, directly measured, and widely available summary measure of health that can be used in the same way that EYS is used as a standard measure of educational attainment. Instead, two proxies for the overall health environment are used:

- *Adult survival rate* is measured as the share of 15-year-olds who survive until age 60. This measure of mortality serves as a proxy for the range of nonfatal health outcomes that a child born today would experience as an adult if current conditions prevail into the future.

- *Healthy growth among children under age 5* is measured as the fraction of children who are not stunted, that is, as 1 minus the share of children under 5 whose height-for-age is more than two standard deviations below the World Health Organization Child Growth Standards' median. Stunting serves as an indicator for the prenatal, infant, and early childhood health environments, summarizing the risks to good health that children born today are likely to experience in their early years, with important consequences for health and well-being in adulthood.

Data on these two health indicators are shown in figure A1.1., panels d and e. Data for all the components of the HCI 2020 by economy are reported in table C8.1 in appendix C.

1.1 Aggregation methodology

The components of the HCI are combined into a single index by first converting them into contributions to productivity.[4] Multiplying the component contributions to productivity gives the overall HCI, which is measured in units of productivity relative to a benchmark corresponding to complete education and full health.

In the case of survival, the relative productivity interpretation is stark: children who do not survive childhood never become productive adults. As a result, expected productivity as a future worker of a child born today is reduced by a factor equal to the survival rate, relative to the benchmark where all children survive.

In the case of education, the relative productivity interpretation is anchored in the large empirical literature measuring the returns to education at the individual level. A rough consensus from this literature is that an additional year of school raises earnings by about 8 percent.[5] This evidence can be used to convert differences in LAYS across countries into differences in worker productivity. For example, compared with a benchmark where all children obtain a full 14 years of school by age 18, a child who obtains only 10 years of education can expect to be 32 percent less productive as an adult (a gap of 4 years of education, multiplied by 8 percent per year).

In the case of health, the relative productivity interpretation is based on the empirical literature measuring the economic returns to better health at the individual level. The key challenge in this literature is that there is no unique directly measured summary indicator of the various aspects of health that matter for productivity. This literature often uses proxy indicators for health, such as adult height (see, for example, Case and Paxson 2008; Horton and Steckel 2011). It does so because adult height can be measured directly and reflects the accumulation of shocks to health through childhood and adolescence. A rough consensus drawn from this literature is that an improvement in health associated with a 1 centimeter increase in adult height raises productivity by 3.4 percent.

Converting this evidence on the returns to one proxy for health (adult height) into the other proxies for health used in the HCI (stunting and adult survival) requires information on the relationships between these different proxies (for details, see Kraay 2018; Weil 2007).

For stunting, there is a direct relationship between stunting in childhood and future adult height because growth deficits in childhood persist to a large extent into adulthood, together with the associated health and cognitive deficits. Available evidence suggests that a reduction in stunting rates of 10 percentage points increases attained adult height by approximately 1 centimeter, which increases productivity by (10.2 × 0.1 × 3.4) percent, or 3.5 percent.

For adult survival, the empirical evidence suggests that, if overall health improves, both adult height and adult survival rates increase in such a way that adult height rises by 1.9 centimeters for every 10-percentage-point improvement in adult survival. This increase implies that an improvement in health that leads to an increase in adult survival rates of 10 percentage points is associated with an improvement in worker productivity of 1.9 × 3.4 percent, or 6.5 percent.

In the HCI, the estimated contributions of health to worker productivity based on these two alternative proxies are averaged if both are available and are used individually if only one of the two is available. The contribution of health to productivity is expressed relative to the benchmark of full health, defined as the absence of stunting, and a 100 percent adult survival rate. For example, compared with a benchmark of no stunting, poor health reduces worker productivity by 30 × 0.34 percent, or 10.2 percent, in a country where the stunting rate is 30 percent. Similarly, compared with the benchmark of 100 percent adult survival, poor health reduces worker productivity by 30 × 0.65 percent, or 19.5 percent, in a country where the adult survival rate is 70 percent. The average of the two estimates of the effect of health on productivity is used in the HCI.

The overall HCI is constructed by multiplying the contributions of survival, school, and health to relative productivity, as follows:

$$HCI = Survival \times School \times Health, \tag{A1.1}$$

with the three components defined as

$$Survival \equiv \frac{1 - Under\ 5\ Mortality\ Rate}{1} \tag{A1.2}$$

$$School \equiv e^{\phi\left(Expected\ Years\ of\ School \times \frac{Harmonized\ Test\ Score}{625} - 14\right)} \tag{A1.3}$$

$$Health \equiv e^{\left(\gamma_{ASR} \times (Adult\ Survival\ Rate - 1) + \gamma_{Stunting} \times (Not\ Stunted\ Rate - 1)\right)/2} \tag{A1.4}$$

The components of the index are expressed here as contributions to productivity relative to the benchmark of complete high-quality education and full health. The parameter $\phi = 0.08$ measures the returns to an additional year of school. The parameters $\gamma_{ASR} = 0.65$ and $\gamma_{Stunting} = 0.35$ measure the improvements in productivity associated with an improvement in health, using adult survival and stunting as proxies for health. The benchmark of complete high-quality education corresponds to 14 years of school and a harmonized test score of 625. The benchmark of full health corresponds to 100 percent child and adult survival and a stunting rate of 0 percent.

These parameters serve as weights in the construction of the HCI. The weights are chosen to be the same across economies, so that cross-country differences in the HCI reflect only cross-country differences in the component variables. This choice facilitates the interpretation of the index. It is also a pragmatic choice because estimating country-specific returns to education and health for all economies included in the HCI is not feasible.

As shown in figure A1.1, panel a, child survival rates range from about 90 percent in the highest-mortality economies to near 100 percent in the lowest-mortality economies. This range implies a loss of productivity of 10 percent relative to the benchmark of no mortality. LAYS range from about 3 years to nearly 14 years. This gap in LAYS implies a gap in productivity relative to the benchmark of complete education of $e^{\phi(3-14)} = e^{0.08(-11)} = 0.4$; that is, the productivity of a future worker in economies with the lowest LAYS is only 40 percent of what it would be under the benchmark of complete education. For health, adult survival rates range from 50 to 95 percent, and the share of children not stunted ranges from about 45 percent to 95 percent. Using adult survival rates indicates a gap in productivity of $e^{\gamma_{ASR}(0.5-1)} = e^{0.65(-0.5)} = 0.72$. Thus, based on adult survival rates as a proxy for health, the productivity of a future worker is only 72 percent of what it would be under the benchmark of full health. Using the share of children not stunted leads to a gap in productivity of $e^{\gamma_{Stunting}(0.45-1)} = e^{0.35(-0.55)} = 0.82$. The productivity of a future worker using the stunting-based proxy for health is therefore only 82 percent of what it would be under the benchmark of full health.

Figure A1.1: Components of the Human Capital Index, relative to GDP per capita

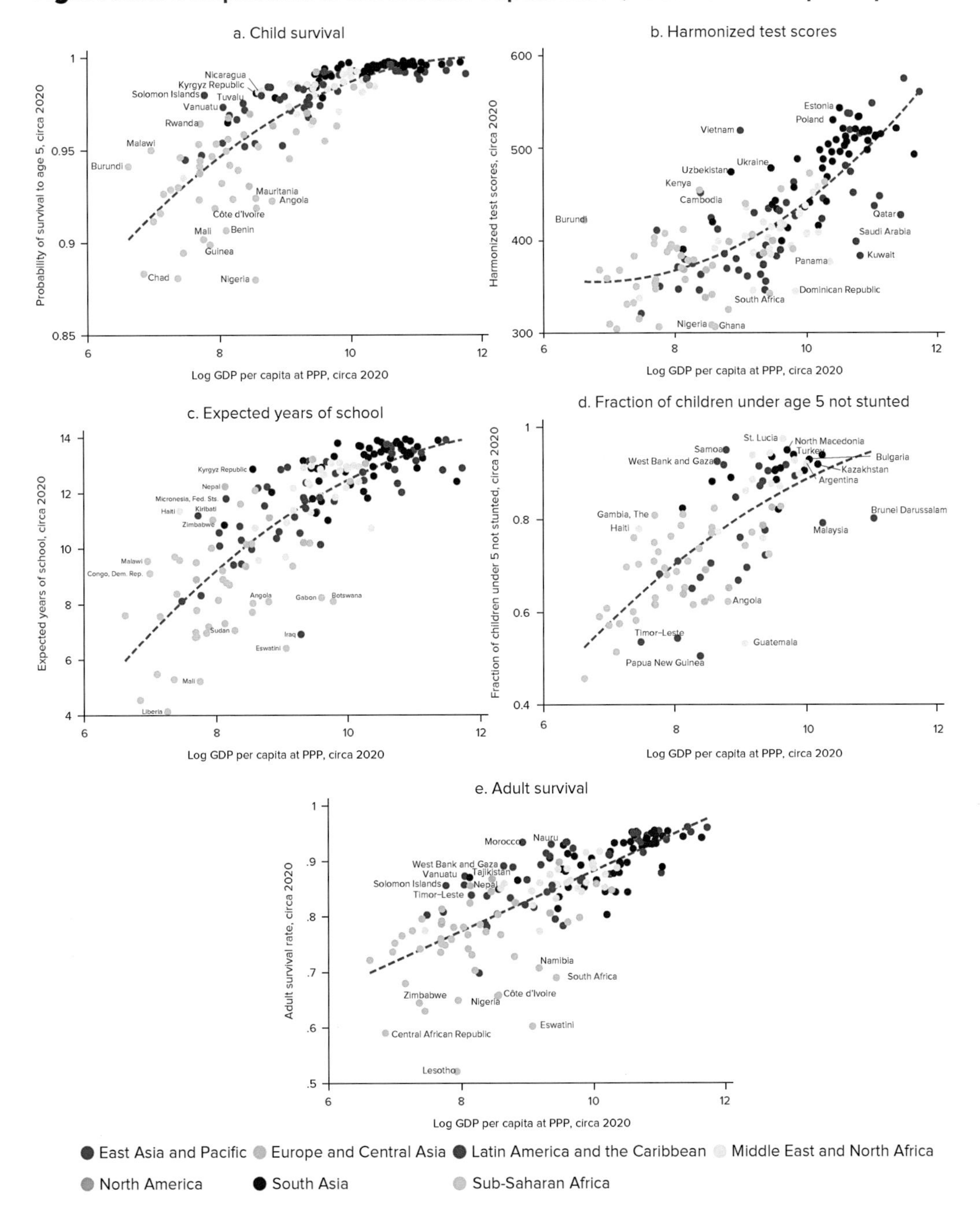

Source: World Bank calculations based on the 2020 update of the Human Capital index (HCI).

Note: The figure reports the most recent cross-section of 174 economies for the five HCI components as used to calculate the 2020 HCI. Each panel plots the country-level averages for each component on the vertical axis and GDP per capita in PPP on the horizontal axis. The dashed line illustrates the fitted regression line between GDP per capita and the respective component. Scatter points above (below) the fitted regression line illustrate economies that perform better (worse) in the outcome variable than their level of GDP would predict. Economies above the 95th and below the 5th percentile in distance to the fitted regression line are labeled. PPP = purchasing power parity.

2. THE HCI

The HCI scores for 174 countries are presented in figure 2.1 in the main text. HCI data are available at www.worldbank.org/humancapital. The HCI is, on average, higher in rich economies than in poor economies and ranges from about 0.3 to about 0.9. The units of the HCI have the same interpretation as the components measured in terms of relative productivity. Consider an economy such as Morocco, which has an HCI of about 0.5. If current education and health conditions in Morocco persist, a child born today will be only half as productive as she could have been if she enjoyed complete education and full health.

All the components of the HCI are measured with some error, and this uncertainty naturally has implications for the precision of the overall HCI. To capture this imprecision, the HCI estimates for each economy are accompanied by upper and lower bounds that reflect the uncertainty in the measurement of the components of the HCI (figure A2.1). These bounds are constructed by recalculating the HCI using lower- and upper-bound estimates of the HCI components. The resulting uncertainty intervals appear in figure A2.1 as vertical ranges around the value of the HCI for each economy.

The upper and lower bounds highlight to users that the estimated HCI values for all economies are subject to uncertainty, reflecting the corresponding uncertainty in the components. When these intervals overlap for two economies, it indicates that the

Figure A2.1: Human Capital Index with uncertainty intervals

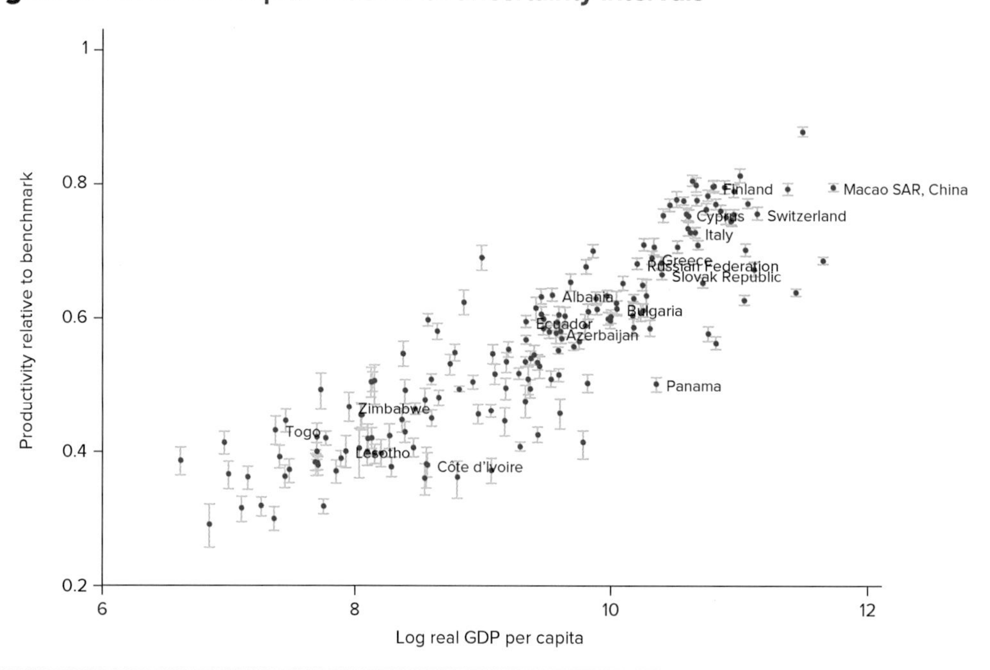

Source: World Bank calculations based on the 2020 update of the Human Capital Index (HCI).

Note: The figure plots the HCI (on the vertical axis) against log GDP per capita (on the horizontal axis). The dark blue dots represent country averages and the top (bottom) end of the vertical bars indicate the values for the upper (lower) bounds of the HCI.

differences in the HCI estimates for these two economies should not be overinterpreted because they are small relative to the uncertainty around the value of the index itself. The use of upper and lower bounds is intended to help move the discussion away from small differences in the HCI across economies and toward more useful discussions around the level of the HCI and what it implies for the productivity of future workers.

The HCI uses the returns to education and health to convert the education and health indicators into differences in worker productivity across economies. The higher the returns, the larger the resulting worker productivity differences. The size of the returns also influences the relative contributions of education and health to the overall index. For example, if the returns to education are high while the returns to health are low, then cross-country differences in education will account for a larger portion of cross-country differences in the index. Although varying the assumptions about the returns to education and health will affect the relative positions of economies on the index, in practice these changes are small because the health and education indicators are strongly correlated across economies (for more details, see Kraay 2018).

2.1 Connecting the HCI to future growth and income

The HCI can be connected to future aggregate income levels and growth following the logic of the development accounting literature. This literature typically adopts a simple Cobb-Douglas form for the aggregate production function, as follows:

$$y = Ak_p^{\alpha} k_h^{1-\alpha}, \tag{A2.1}$$

where y is gross domestic product (GDP) per worker; k_p and k_h are the stocks of physical and human capital per worker; A is total factor productivity; and α is the output elasticity of physical capital. To analyze how changes in human capital may affect income in the long run, it is useful to rewrite the production function as follows:

$$y = \left(\frac{k_p}{y}\right)^{\frac{\alpha}{1-\alpha}} A^{\frac{1}{1-\alpha}} k_h \tag{A2.2}$$

In this formulation, GDP per worker is proportional to the human capital stock per worker, holding constant the level of total factor productivity and the ratio of physical capital to output, $\frac{k_p}{y}$. This formulation can be used to answer the following question: By how much does an increase in human capital raise output per worker, in the long run after taking into account the increase in physical capital that is likely to be induced by the increase in human capital? Equation (A2.2) shows the answer: output per worker increases equiproportionately to human capital per worker, that is, a doubling of human capital per worker will lead to a doubling of output per worker in the long run.

Linking this framework to the HCI requires a few additional steps. First, assume that the stock of human capital per worker that enters the production function, k_h, is equal to the human capital of the average worker. Second, the human capital of the next generation, as measured in the HCI, and the human capital stock that enters the production function need to be linked. This linkage can be done by considering different scenarios. Imagine first a status quo scenario in which the expected years of learning-adjusted schooling and health as measured in the HCI today persist into the future. Over time, new entrants to the workforce with status quo health and education will replace current members of the workforce until eventually the entire workforce of the future has the expected years of learning-adjusted schooling and health captured in the current human capital index. Let $k_{h,NG} = e^{\phi s_{NG} + \gamma z_{NG}}$ denote the future human capital stock in this baseline scenario, where s_{NG} represents the number of quality-adjusted years of school of the next generation of workers, and γz_{NG} is shorthand notation for the contribution of the two health indicators to productivity in the HCI in equation (A1.4). Contrast this scenario with one in which the entire future workforce benefits from complete education and enjoys full health, resulting in a higher human capital stock, $k_h^* = e^{\phi s^* + \gamma z^*}$, where s^* represents the benchmark of 14 years of high-quality school, and z^* represents the benchmark of complete health.

Assuming that total factor productivity and the physical capital-to-output ratio are the same in the two scenarios, the eventual steady-state GDP per worker in the two scenarios is as follows:

$$\frac{y}{y^*} = \frac{k_{h,NG}}{k_h^*} = e^{\phi\left(S_{NG} - S^*\right) + \gamma\left(Z_{NG} - Z^*\right)} \tag{A2.3}$$

This expression is the same as the HCI in equations (A1.1)–(A1.4) except for the term corresponding to survival to age 5 (because children who do not survive do not become part of the future workforce), which creates a close link between the HCI and potential future growth. Disregarding the contribution of the survival probability to the HCI, equation (A2.3) shows that an economy with an HCI equal to x could achieve GDP per worker that would be $\frac{1}{x}$ times higher in the future if citizens enjoy complete education and full health (corresponding to $x = 1$). For example, an economy such as Morocco with an HCI value of about 0.5 could, in the long run, have future GDP per worker in this scenario of complete education and full health that is $\frac{1}{0.5} = 2$ times higher than GDP per worker in the status quo scenario. What this means in terms of average annual growth rates depends on how long the long run is. For example, under the assumption that it takes 50 years for these scenarios to materialize, then a doubling of future per capita income relative to the status quo corresponds to roughly 1.4 percentage points of additional growth per year.

The calibrated relationship between the HCI and future income described here is simple because it focuses only on steady-state comparisons. In related work, Collin and Weil (2018) elaborate on this relationship by developing a calibrated growth model that traces out the dynamics of adjustment to the steady state. They use this model to trace out trajectories for per capita GDP and for poverty measures for individual countries and global aggregates under alternative assumptions for the future path of human capital. They also calculate the equivalent increase in investment rates in physical capital that would be required to deliver the same increases in output associated with improvements in human capital.

NOTES

1. This appendix provides a summary of the methodology for the HCI. For additional details, see Kraay (2018), on which this appendix is based.
2. The methodology for harmonizing test scores is detailed in Altinok, Angrist, and Patrinos (2018) and Patrinos and Angrist (2018).
3. This methodology was introduced by World Bank (2018) and is elaborated on in Angrist et al. (2019).
4. This approach has been used extensively in the development accounting literature (for example, Caselli 2005; Hsieh and Klenow 2010). The approach for health closely follows Weil (2007). Galasso and Wagstaff (2016) apply a similar framework to measure the costs of stunting.
5. The seminal methodology is due to Mincer (1958). See Montenegro and Patrinos (2014) for recent cross-country estimates of the returns to schooling.

REFERENCES

Altinok, N., N. Angrist, and H. A. Patrinos. 2018. "Global Data Set on Education Quality (1965–2015)." Policy Research Working Paper 8314, World Bank, Washington, DC.

Angrist, N., S. Djankov, P. Goldberg, and H. A. Patrinos. 2019. "Measuring Human Capital." Policy Research Working Paper 8742, World Bank, Washington, DC.

Case, A., and C. H. Paxson. 2008. "Stature and Status: Height, Ability, and Labour Market Outcomes." *Journal of Political Economy* 116 (3): 499–532.

Caselli, F. 2005. "Accounting for Cross-Country Income Differences." In *Handbook of Economic Growth*, 1st ed., vol. 1, edited by P. Aghion and S. Durlauf, 679–741. North-Holland: Elsevier.

Collin, M., and D. Weil. 2018. "The Effect of Increasing Human Capital Investment on Economic Growth and Poverty: A Simulation Exercise." Policy Research Working Paper 8590, World Bank, Washington, DC.

Galasso, E., and A. Wagstaff. 2016. "The Economic Costs of Stunting and How to Reduce Them." Policy Research Note, World Bank, Washington, DC.

Horton, S., and R. Steckel. 2011. "Global Economic Losses Attributable to Malnutrition 1900–2000 and Projections to 2050." Assessment Paper: Malnutrition, Copenhagen Consensus on Human Challenges, Tewksbury, MA.

Hsieh, C. T., and P. Klenow. 2010. "Development Accounting." *American Economic Journal: Macroeconomics* 2 (1): 207–23.

Kraay, A. 2018. "Methodology for a World Bank Human Capital Index." Policy Research Working Paper 8593, World Bank, Washington, DC.

Mincer, J. 1958. "Investment in Human Capital and Personal Income Distribution." *Journal of Political Economy* 66 (4): 281–302.

Montenegro, C. E., and H. A. Patrinos. 2014. "Comparable Estimates of Returns to Schooling around the World." Policy Research Working Paper 7020, World Bank, Washington, DC.

Patrinos, H. A., and N. Angrist. 2018. “Global Dataset on Education Quality: A Review and Update (2000–2017).” Policy Research Working Paper 8592, World Bank, Washington, DC.

Weil, D. 2007. “Accounting for the Effect of Health on Economic Growth.” *Quarterly Journal of Economics* 122 (3): 1265–1306.

World Bank. 2018. *The Human Capital Project*. World Bank, Washington, DC.

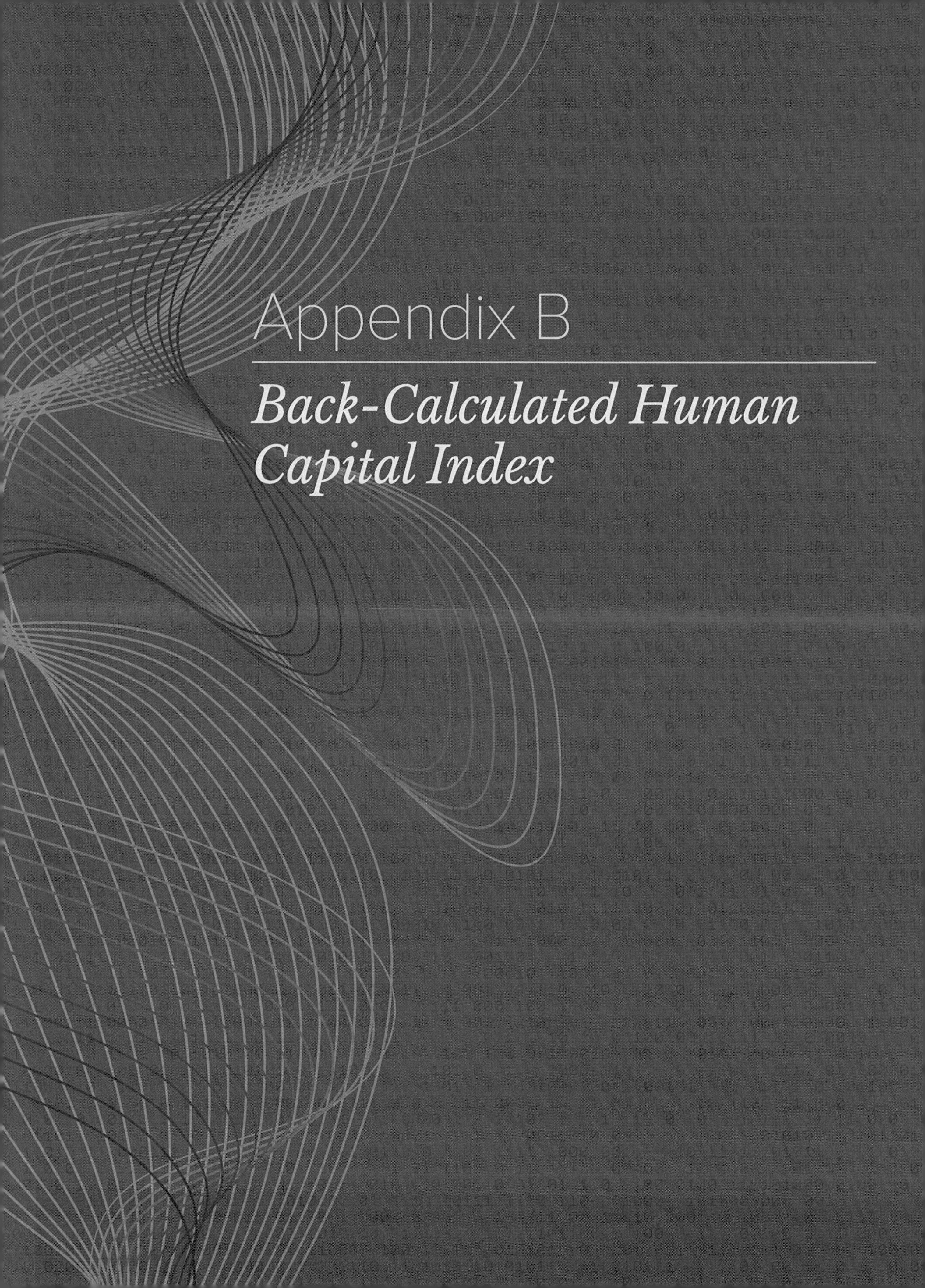

Appendix B

Back-Calculated Human Capital Index

The first iteration of the Human Capital Index (HCI) in 2018 made use of the best and most recently available data as of 2018. It was calculated for 157 economies. As is common with indicators, comprehensive revisions of the source data have been implemented since then. For example, gross domestic product series are revised quite often, as are international poverty numbers when improved harmonization of survey data is implemented (see Atamanov et al. 2019 for an example). Revisions to series incorporate the most recent and accurate data and also ensure temporal comparability.

In the case of the HCI, the index makes use of data from different institutions, and most of these institutions release their data annually and revise them periodically, as well as revising them for the past. Such revisions provide the opportunity to reflect these measurement improvements in a newly recalculated (back-calculated, actually) 2018 HCI. As a result, the back-calculated 2018 HCI will differ from the original 2018 HCI. Figure B.1 plots these two 2018 HCI versions. On the y-axis are displayed those economies for which it is now possible to generate a back-calculated 2018 HCI, mainly thanks to newly available harmonized test scores. Consequently, the number of economies with a back-calculated 2018 HCI is 167, 10 more than for the 2018 HCI. All economies are quite close to the 45-degree line. The global average for the back-calculated 2018 index is 0.565 as opposed to 0.567 for the 2018 HCI.[1]

When looking at individual components, however, the differences between the 2018 HCI and the back-calculated 2018 HCI are starker. This difference is particularly relevant for the expected years of school. With newer vintages of data from the United Nations Educational, Scientific and Cultural Organization's Institute for Statistics, many of the enrollment rates used in the previous round of the HCI have been updated, so data are added for years that are closer to 2018. Updating these data is further complicated because for some economies a preferred rate is now available (total net enrollment rate is preferred over adjusted net enrollment rate, which is preferred over net enrollment rate, which is preferred over gross enrollment rate).[2] For example, in most economies where expected years of school increased by at least half a year, the data come from a year that is closer to 2018, and in many cases there is a move to a preferred enrollment type.

Figure B.1: Comparing the 2018 and back-calculated 2018 Human Capital Indexes

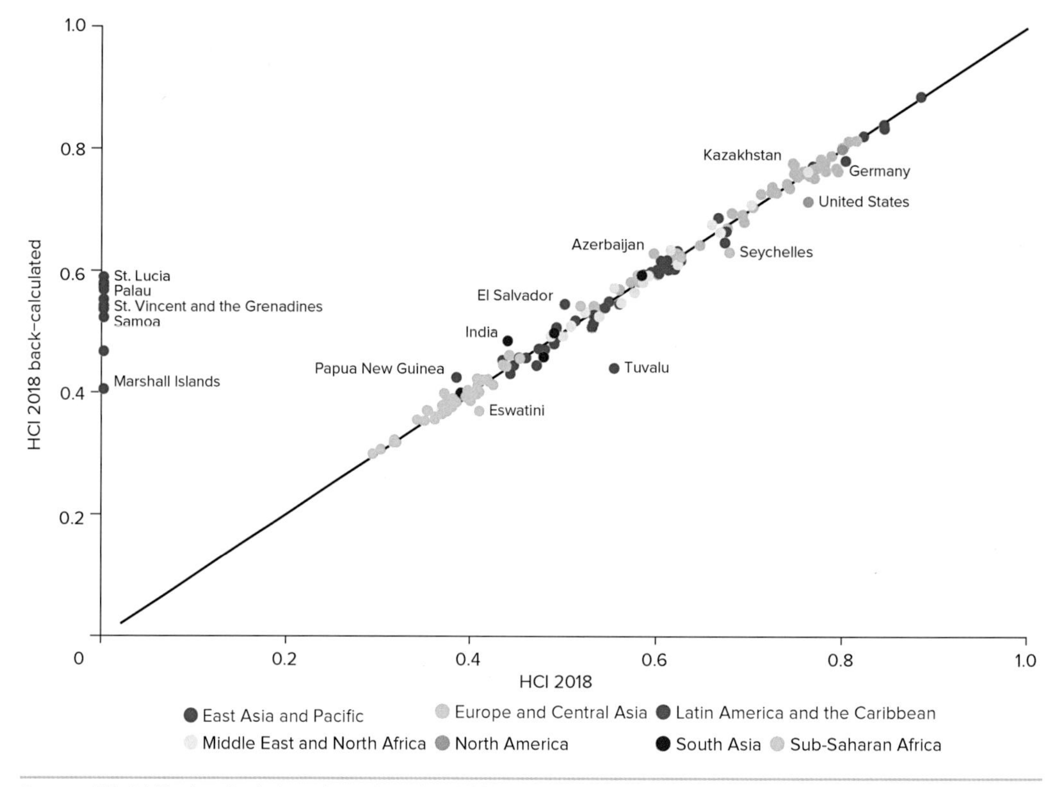

Source: World Bank calculations based on the 2020 update of the Human Capital Index and the 2018 Human Capital Index.

Note: The figure plots the HCI 2018 (on the horizontal axis) against the back-calculated HCI 2018 (on the vertical axis). The black line is a 45-degree line; points above (below) the line represent an increase (decrease) in HCI scores between the HCI 2018 and back-calculated HCI 2018. Economies not present in the 2018 HCI but present in the back-calculated HCI and displayed on the vertical axis are Antigua and Barbuda, Dominica, Federated States of Micronesia, Grenada, St. Kitts and Nevis, St. Lucia, the Marshall Islands, Palau, St. Vincent and the Grenadines, and Samoa. HCI = Human Capital Index.

The back-calculated HCI makes use of the most recent data available, which allows for an index that better reflects the human capital that a child born in that year could achieve in the country where she lives. The construction of each component for the 2018 back-calculated HCI is detailed in appendix C, and the back-calculated HCI 2018 scores by economy are reported in table C8.1.

NOTES

1. Tuvalu is one of the few outliers. The 2018 HCI makes use of stunting as a proxy for health, and the back-calculated 2018 HCI makes use of adult mortality. Stunting rates used in the 2018 HCI corresponded to a 2007 survey. The back-calculated 2018 HCI uses more recent adult mortality rates from 2012, from the World Health Organization, that were not previously available.
2. For details, see the description of the construction of the expected years of school variable in appendix C.

REFERENCE

Atamanov, A., R. Castaneda Aguilar, C. Diaz-Bonilla, D. Jolliffe, C. Lakner, D. Mahler, J. Montes, L. Morena Herrera, D. Newhouse, M. Nguyen, E. Prydz, P. Sangraula, S. Tandon, and J. Yang. 2019. "September 2019 PovcalNet Update: What's New." Global Poverty Monitoring Technical Note 10, World Bank, Washington, DC.

Appendix C

Human Capital Index Component Data Notes

1. UNDER-5 MORTALITY RATES

The probability of survival to age 5 is calculated as the complement of the under-5 mortality rate. The under-5 mortality rate is the probability that a child born in a specified year will die before reaching the age of 5, if subject to current age-specific mortality rates. It is frequently expressed as a rate per 1,000 live births, in which case it must be divided by 1,000 to obtain the probability of dying before age 5.

Under-5 mortality rates are calculated by the United Nations Interagency Group for Child Mortality Estimation (IGME) using mortality as recorded in household surveys and vital registries. The IGME compiles and assesses the quality of all available nationally representative data relevant to the estimation of child mortality, including data from vital registration systems, population censuses, household surveys, and sample registration systems. Globally, birth registration coverage remains inadequate, having increased by only 7 percentage points (from 58 percent to 65 percent) in the past decade (UNICEF 2013). In Sub-Saharan Africa, only eight countries have coverage of 80 percent or more for birth registration.[1]

The IGME assesses data quality, recalculates data inputs, and makes adjustments if needed by applying standard methods. It then fits a statistical model to these data to generate a smooth trend curve that averages over possibly disparate estimates from the different data sources for an economy. Finally, it extrapolates the model to a target year. Data are reported annually and cover 198 economies. The IGME estimates are disaggregated by gender and include uncertainty intervals corresponding to 95 percent confidence intervals.

2020 update

Under-5 mortality rates for the 2020 update of the Human Capital Index (HCI) come from the September 2019 update of the IGME estimates, available at the Child Mortality Estimates website (see also UNIGME 2019).[2] Data for the back-calculated 2018 HCI come from 2017. Data for the baseline comparator year of 2010 come from 2010. Because under-5 mortality rates are estimated by modeling all available child mortality data from vital registration systems, population censuses, household surveys, and sample registration systems, every new release of data from the IGME updates estimates for all the years in the time series. As a result, data for the same past year might differ slightly across updates.

Values for under-5 mortality rates used to produce the back-calculated HCI 2018 are aligned with but not the same as those used in the previous iteration of the HCI, as illustrated in figure C1.1. Data from the two vintages align along the 45-degree line. The figure highlights the four economies where under-5 mortality rates have changed by more than 10 deaths per 1,000 live births. The largest revisions were for Nigeria (which went from 100 to 122 deaths per 1,000 live births) and Guinea (which went from 86 to 103 deaths per 1,000 live births).

Figure C1.2 reports the most recent cross-section of under-5 mortality rates used to calculate the 2020 HCI. Child mortality rates range from about 0.002 (2 per 1,000 live births) in the richest countries to about 0.120 (120 per 1,000 live births) in the poorest countries.

Under-5 mortality rates tend to be slightly lower for girls than for boys, as reported in figure C1.3. In the figure, the solid dot indicates the country average, the triangle indicates the average for girls, and the horizontal bar indicates the average for boys. The average under-5 mortality rate for boys was 0.03 (30 deaths per 1,000 live births), compared to 0.025 for girls (25 deaths per 1,000 live births).

Figure C1.1: Comparing original and back-calculated 2018 under-5 mortality rates

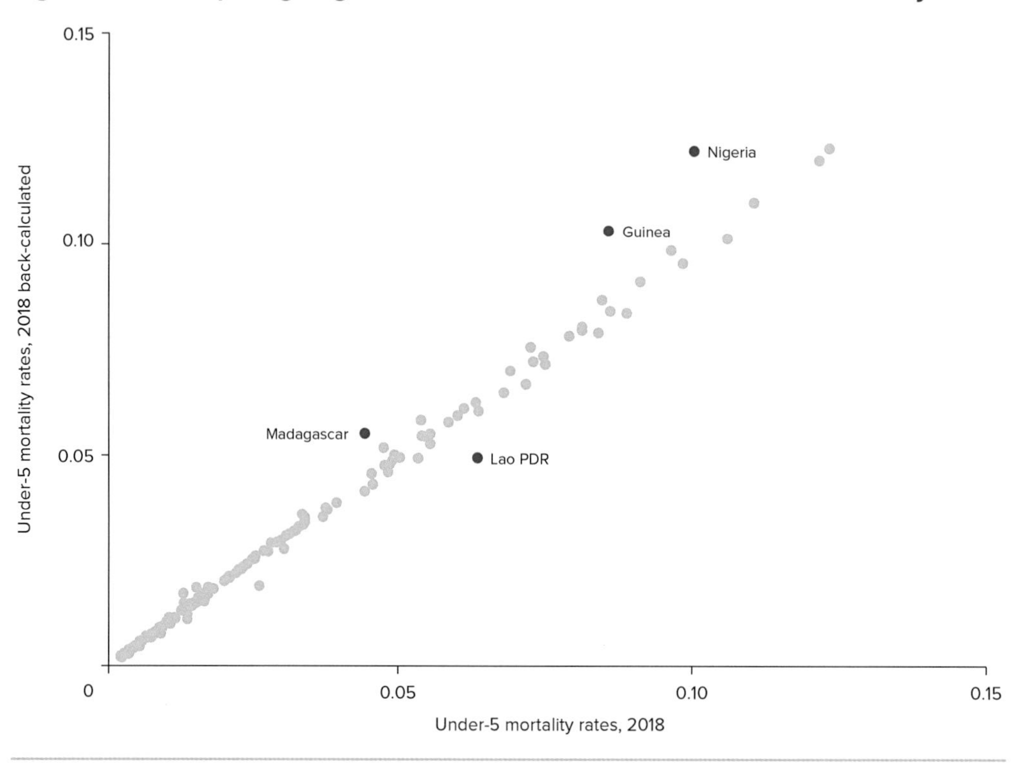

Source: World Bank calculations based on the 2020 update of the Human Capital Index (HCI).

Note: The figure plots the under-5 mortality rates as used in the 2018 HCI (on the horizontal axis) against the under-5 mortality rates used for the back-calculated 2018 HCI (on the vertical axis). Economies where under-5 mortality rates have changed by more than 10 deaths per 1,000 live births between 2018 and back-calculated 2018 are labeled.

Figure C1.2: Under-5 mortality rates, Human Capital Index 2020, relative to GDP per capita

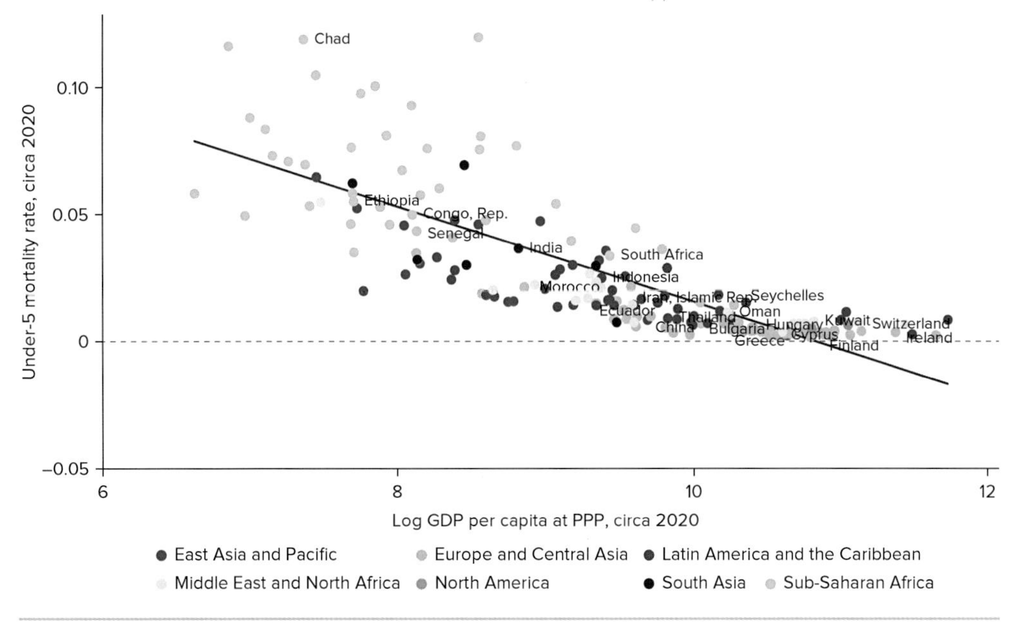

Source: World Bank calculations based on the 2020 update of the Human Capital Index (HCI).

Note: The figure plots under-5 mortality rates (on the vertical axis) against log GDP per capita at 2011 PPP US dollars (on the horizontal axis). PPP = purchasing power parity.

Figure C1.3: Sex-disaggregated under-5 mortality rates, relative to GDP per capita

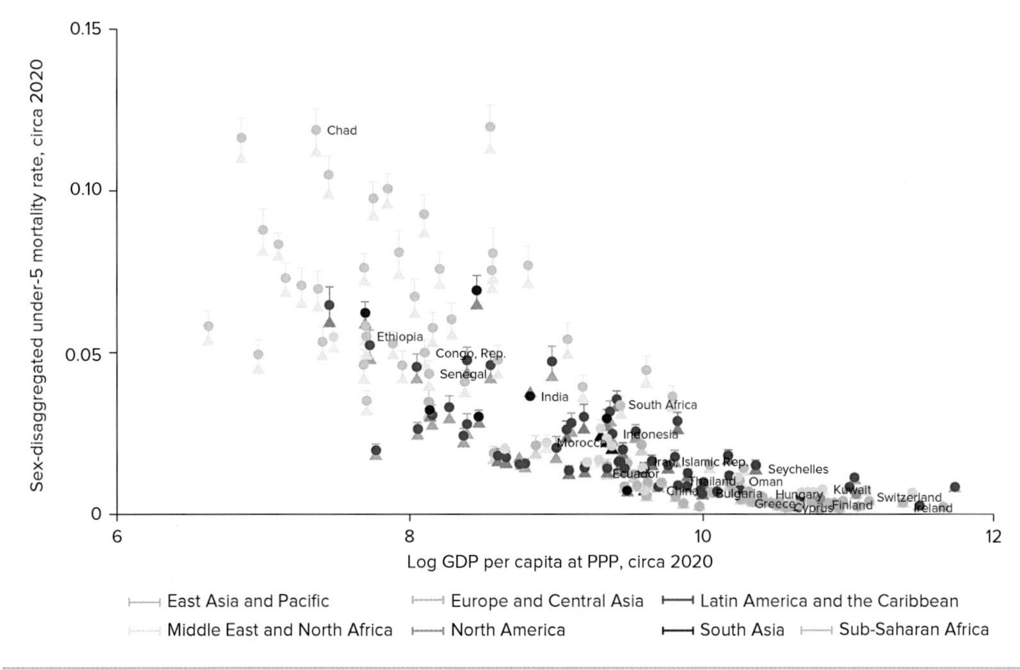

Source: World Bank calculations based on the 2020 update of the Human Capital Index (HCI).

Note: The figure plots sex-disaggregated under-5 mortality rates (on the vertical axis) against log GDP per capita (on the horizontal axis). The solid dot indicates the national average, the triangle shows the average value for girls, and the horizontal line shows the average value for boys. PPP = purchasing power parity.

Figure C1.4: Under-5 mortality rates, by income group and region

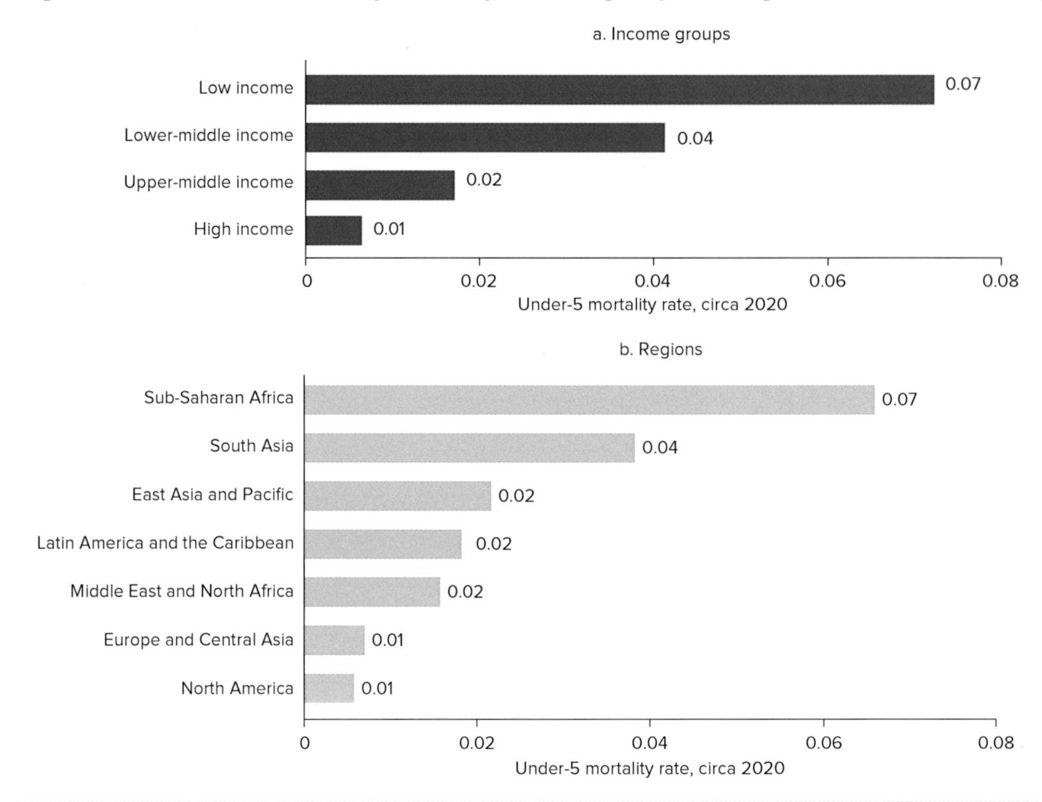

Source: World Bank calculations based on the 2020 update of the Human Capital Index (HCI).

Note: The figures plot regional and income group average values for under-5 mortality rates.

Figure C1.4 reports average child mortality rates by income group and by World Bank region. Mortality rates tend to be highest in low-income economies, and regional averages are highest in Sub-Saharan Africa and South Asia, reflecting that poor economies continue to bear a disproportionate burden of child mortality.

2. EXPECTED YEARS OF SCHOOL

The expected years of school (EYS) component of the HCI captures the number of years of school a child born today can expect to achieve by age 18, given the prevailing pattern of enrollment rates in her country.[3] Conceptually, EYS is simply the sum of enrollment rates by age from age 4 to 17. Because age-specific enrollment rates are not broadly or systematically available, more readily available data on enrollment rates by level of school are used to approximate enrollment rates in different age brackets. Preprimary enrollment rates approximate the enrollment rates for 4- and 5-year-olds, primary enrollment rates approximate for 6- to 11-year-olds, lower-secondary rates approximate for 12- to 14-year-olds, and upper-secondary rates approximate for 15- to 17-year-olds. Cross-country definitions in school starting ages and the duration of the various levels of school imply that these rates will be only approximations of the number of years of school a child can expect to complete by age 18.

Given that the objective is to obtain a close proxy to age-specific enrollment rates, the preferred measure is the total net enrollment rate (TNER). TNER measures the fraction of children in the theoretical age range for a given level of school who are in school at any level. For many countries, the TNER is not readily available for all levels and thus, in many instances, less preferred rates are used. The order of preference for the use of enrollment rates is the following:

1. *Total net enrollment rate* (TNER) measures the fraction of children in the theoretical age range for a given level of school who are in school at any level. Because there is no level before preprimary, TNER is not available, and ANER is the preferred measure.

2. *Adjusted net enrollment rate* (ANER) measures the fraction of children in the theoretical age range for a given level of school who are in that level or the level above.

3. *Net enrollment rate* (NER) measures the fraction of children in the theoretical age range for a given level of school who are in that level of school.

4. *Gross enrollment rate* (GER) measures the number of children of any age who are enrolled in a given level as a fraction of the number of children in that age range.

The conceptually appropriate enrollment rate to approximate enrollment rates by age brackets is the repetition-adjusted total net enrollment rate. The primary source for enrollment and repetition rates is the United Nations Educational, Scientific, and Cultural Organization's Institute for Statistics (UIS),[4] revised and supplemented with data provided by World Bank country teams that participated in an extensive data review process. When the resulting data on TNERs are incomplete, ANERs, NERs, or GERs are used instead in that order of priority. The same enrollment rate type is used for a given level of education over time.

Because EYS is constructed using primarily administrative data on enrollment rates, uncertainty intervals are not available for this component of the HCI. This does not imply that there is no measurement error; instead, the use of administrative data implies that there is no error due to modeling or sampling.[5] Consequently, uncertainty in the measurement of EYS is not reflected in the uncertainty intervals of the overall HCI.

EYS is calculated as follows:

$$EYS = \sum_{i}^{4} Rate_i Y_i; \quad i = preprimary, primary, lower\text{–}secondary, upper\text{–}secondary \qquad (C2.1)$$

where $Rate_i$ is the enrollment rate for the preferred enrollment type available for that level, and Y_i is the number of years corresponding to each level.[6]

Enrollment rates for 2020 and 2010

Temporal coverage for enrollment rates is not complete in the UIS public database. Consequently, the first step toward ensuring that the rates used are the most recent and accurate relies on getting inputs from World Bank specialists working on each economy to validate and provide more recent values when available.[7]

Enrollment rates for 2020 for each school level and for the four enrollment rate types (TNER, ANER, NER, and GER) are obtained from UIS.[8] Any inputs from World Bank teams working on specific economies are then added to the corresponding enrollment rates. Existing gaps for 2020 in enrollment rates for each level and economy are filled by setting the 2020 enrollment rate equal to the latest enrollment rate available for that enrollment rate type. This process is henceforth referred to as the *carryforward rule*. The rule is applied if the latest available enrollment rate is not older than 10 years.[9] This process ensures that the HCI of 2020 and the back-calculated HCI for 2018 are calculated compatibly with the first version of the HCI released in 2018. Additionally, enrollment rates are adjusted for repetition, when repetition rates are available; otherwise a repetition rate of 0 is assumed. Finally, enrollment rate types are chosen on the basis of the filled series (that is, using the 2020 rates when gaps have been filled) and according to the following order of preference: TNER, ANER, NER, and GER.[10]

In the current HCI update, an effort has been made to also populate an HCI for 2010 using data circa 2010.[11] Because data collection and availability generally improve over time, enrollment rates for 2010 and earlier are less likely to be available than more recent rates. This means that the rule from the first edition of the HCI used to obtain an EYS measure for 2020 and 2018 cannot be applied to obtain rates for 2010, because it is not possible to apply the carryforward rule for all economies for which comparable data over time for other components of the HCI are available circa 2010 and circa 2020. Moreover, to allow that (1) the preferred enrollment type is used for 2020 and (2) the enrollment rate type for a given school level in a given economy is the same over time, different rules are applied to fill in the year 2010 to ensure comparability over time and to maximize economy coverage.

The rules used to fill in gaps in enrollment values for 2010 rely on annualized growth rates and are implemented sequentially for each school level (that is, preprimary, primary, lower-secondary, and upper-secondary):

1. If a value is available for 2010 that comes from the same enrollment type as the value assigned to 2020, this value is used (provided the 2010 value has not already been used to fill in 2020 using the carryforward rule).[12]

2. If a 2010 value is not available in the enrollment type used to populate 2020, available data for that enrollment type are used to generate an annualized growth rate (agr) that is then applied to the most recent year before 2010 (Year) for which data are available to generate a value for 2010. Annualized growth rates are calculated between the years before and after 2010 that are closest to 2010 and for which non-missing values of the selected enrollment type are available.

$$Rate_{2010} = Rate_{Year}(1+agr)^{2010-Year} \quad (C2.2)$$

3. If no value is available for the chosen enrollment type before 2010, then annualized growth rates are obtained using GER, which are available for most economies. Annualized growth rates using GER are calculated using the same approach as outlined before, between the years before and after 2010 that are closest to 2010 and for which nonmissing values of GER are available. For example, if TNER is used to populate 2020 and its earliest value is for 2012, then an annualized growth rate is obtained from the GER. The annualized growth rate from the GER is calculated between the first rate available for 2010 or before, and the first rate available for or after 2012, because the TNER is available for 2012. This rate is then applied backward to the TNER of 2012 to obtain a value for 2010.

$$Rate_{2010} = Rate_{Year}(1+agr_{GER})^{2010-Year} \quad (C2.3)$$

The process described above yields a value for EYS in 2010 for 99 out of 114 eligible economies. For the remaining 15 economies, calculations to populate enrollment for 2010 are on a case-by-case basis in order to populate enrollment rates in 2010.

Disaggregation by sex

Disaggregation by sex is an important feature of the HCI. Although the rules presented in the previous section are meant to complete the EYS for both sexes, there are still adjustments required to ensure that EYS values for boys and girls are plausible. These adjustments are necessary because, although a certain enrollment type may be available as a combined series, it may lack sex-disaggregated information. In other instances, it may be necessary to adjust the disaggregated series because values for both girls and boys are above (or below) those of the combined enrollment rate.

To fill in the sex-disaggregated enrollment rates, the following rules are applied:

1. For every year for which rates for both genders and the aggregate are available, the male-to-female ratio and the population share of males and females are calculated.

2. For years that are missing a sex-disaggregated rate, the shares and ratios calculated in step 1 from the closest year available in the past (but not more than 10 years back) are used to impute missing values.

3. For the remaining years for which the disaggregated enrollment rates for the preferred enrollment type are still missing, the male and female shares and, where available, the male-to-female ratio from GER enrollment rates are used to impute a value.

It is still possible that the rules above, when applied, return inconsistent values, and it is necessary to adjust the disaggregated series when the male and female rates are both larger (or smaller) than the aggregate enrollment rate. In those cases, we adjust the disaggregated enrollment rate to the value that leaves the aggregate rate $Rate_{mf}$ at the same distance from each of the disaggregated rates.

$$Rate_f^* = Rate_{mf} + \frac{Rate_f - Rate_m}{2} \tag{C2.4}$$

$$Rate_m^* = Rate_{mf} + \frac{Rate_m - Rate_f}{2} \tag{C2.5}$$

2018 back-calculated EYS

Data for the 2020 update of EYS rely on data from UIS, which releases data in September of each year and completes the release in February of the following year. The February 2020 release of enrollment data from UIS is used for the update of EYS, effectively reporting enrollment data up to 2019.

The latest data release from UIS is complemented with rates obtained by World Bank staff.[13] The updated data provide an opportunity to update EYS values from the 2018 vintage of the HCI to the latest information available to arrive at a back-calculated EYS for 2018. Because the update allows for the calculation of EYS incorporating more recent data or data from a different enrollment type than what was used in the first vintage of the HCI, the EYS from the first vintage of the HCI is not comparable with the current vintage of the EYS.

Differences in the 2018 value of EYS between the 2018 vintage and the 2020 update may be due to a combination of three factors:

1. Data are updated in UIS, or by World Bank staff.

2. Data on enrollment from a more recent year are now available.

3. Different enrollment types have become available. In some cases, it will be possible to move to a more preferred enrollment type, whereas in others it is necessary to rely on a less preferred enrollment type. The latter may be the case if UIS has removed the series or if the series is too old.

The average absolute deviation between the back-calculated EYS and the 2018 vintage is 0.3 year; however, the changes may be substantial for specific countries (see figure C2.1).

Although the differences between vintages are considerable, they are mostly due to the fact that the EYS measure generated in this round relies on more preferred rates, newer data, or both. For the 2018 back-calculated EYS, the enrollment data for at least one of the levels for 131 economies come from a more recent year.[14] For 85 economies, the enrollment rates for all levels correspond to a more recent year. In 21 economies it is necessary to change to a less preferred series for at least one of the levels. This change occurs mostly when the series has been removed in the update of the source data. Conversely, in 20 economies, it is possible to calculate EYS for at least one level with a more preferred type of enrollment rate.

Figure C2.2 and figure C2.3 present details for economies in which EYS in the new data vintage has increased by at least half a year. In most economies where EYS increased by at least half a year, there is a move to a data point that is closer to 2018. The exception is Zimbabwe, where all the enrollment rates correspond to the same year and are for the same enrollment type. In the case of Zimbabwe, the difference is explained as being due to the change in the vintage of UIS data. The biggest change for Zimbabwe is observed for primary, for which the rate increased by almost 10 percentage points.

A different case can be observed for Côte d'Ivoire, where every data point comes from a more recent year. In this case, however, the difference is also complicated because the previous EYS was built with rates that did not come from UIS but were drawn from government sources by World Bank staff. In the case of Papua New Guinea, the change is due to two factors. Not only are more recent data used for all levels, but also the data used for all but primary are from a preferred series (figure C2.3). These three countries illustrate the multiple sources for the potential mismatch between the EYS value produced in 2018 and the updated 2018 back-calculated EYS.

Figure C2.1: Comparing original and back-calculated 2018 expected years of school

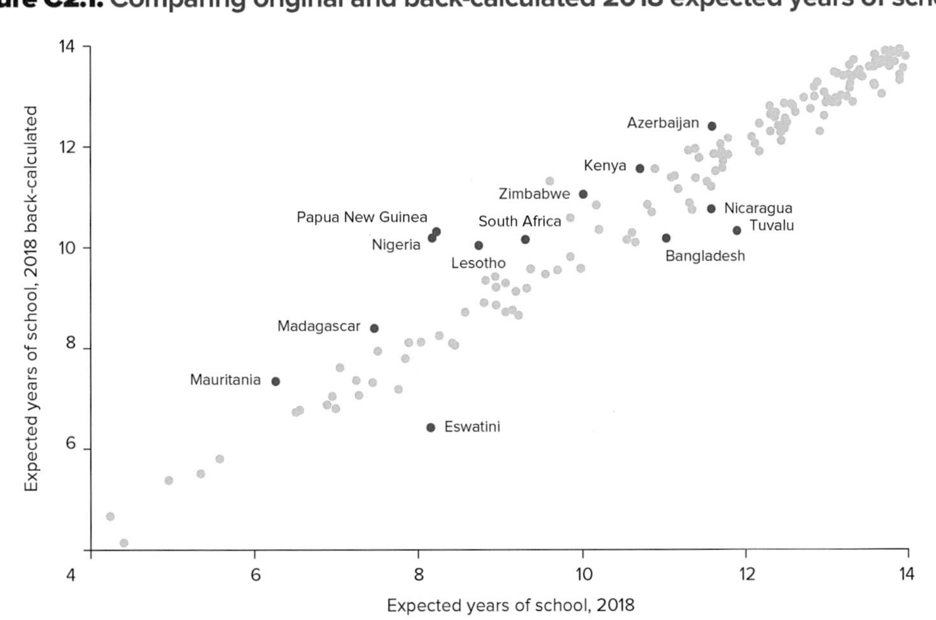

Source: World Bank calculations based on the 2020 update of the Human Capital Index (HCI).

Note: The figure plots the expected years of school as used in the 2018 HCI (on the horizontal axis), and the expected years of school used for the back-calculated 2018 HCI (on the vertical axis). Economies where expected years of school changed by 0.75 years or more between 2018 and back-calculated 2018 are labeled.

Figure C2.2: Vintage data year for back-calculated 2018 and original 2018, increase of 0.5 year or more in expected years of school

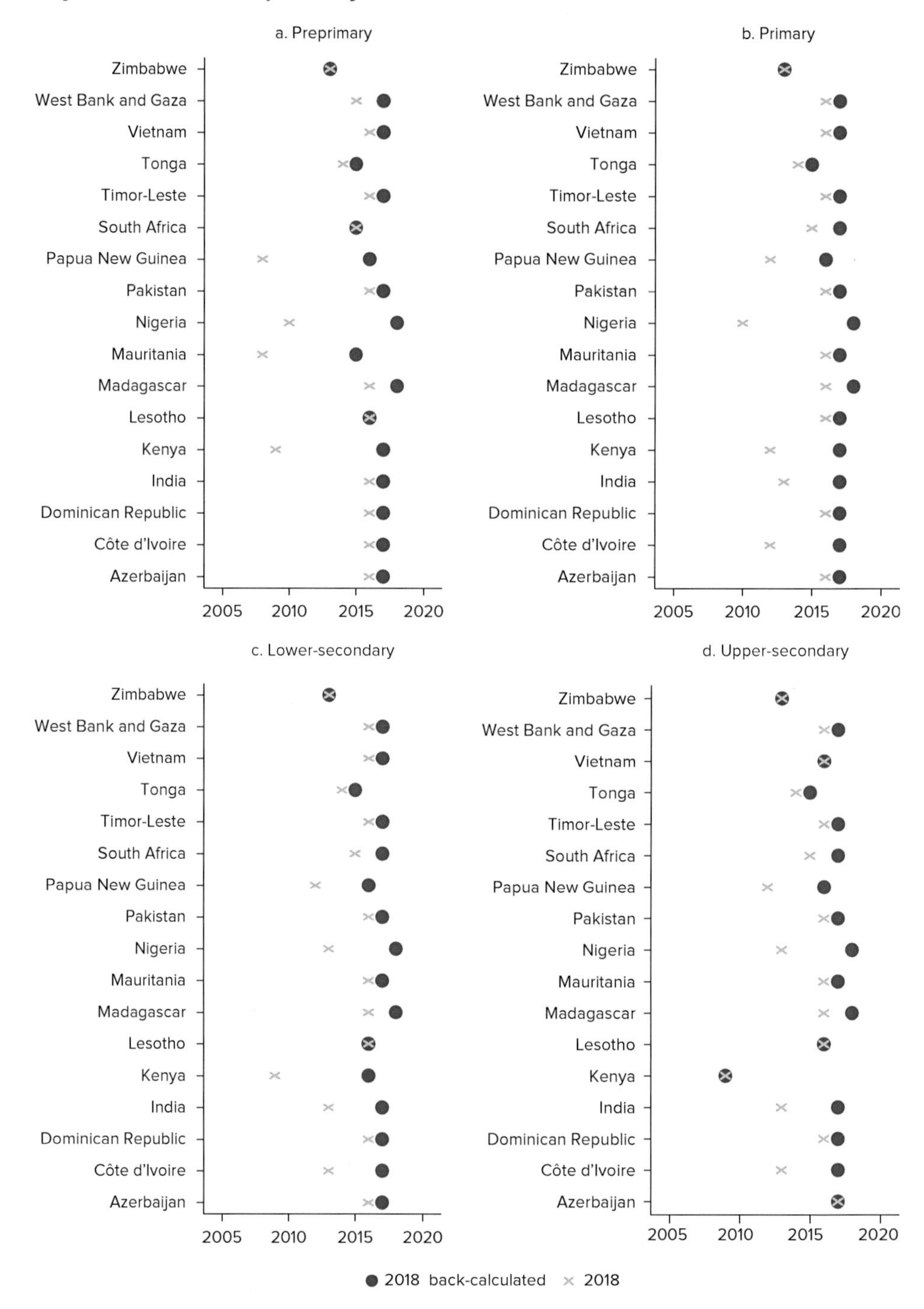

Source: World Bank calculations based on the 2020 update of the Human Capital Index (HCI).

Note: The panels plot the year of data used for calculation of expected years of school. Solid dot represents the data used for the back-calculated 2018 HCI, and x indicates the data used for the calculation of the 2018 HCI.

Figure C2.3: Enrollment type for back-calculated 2018 and original 2018, increase of 0.5 year or more in expected years of school

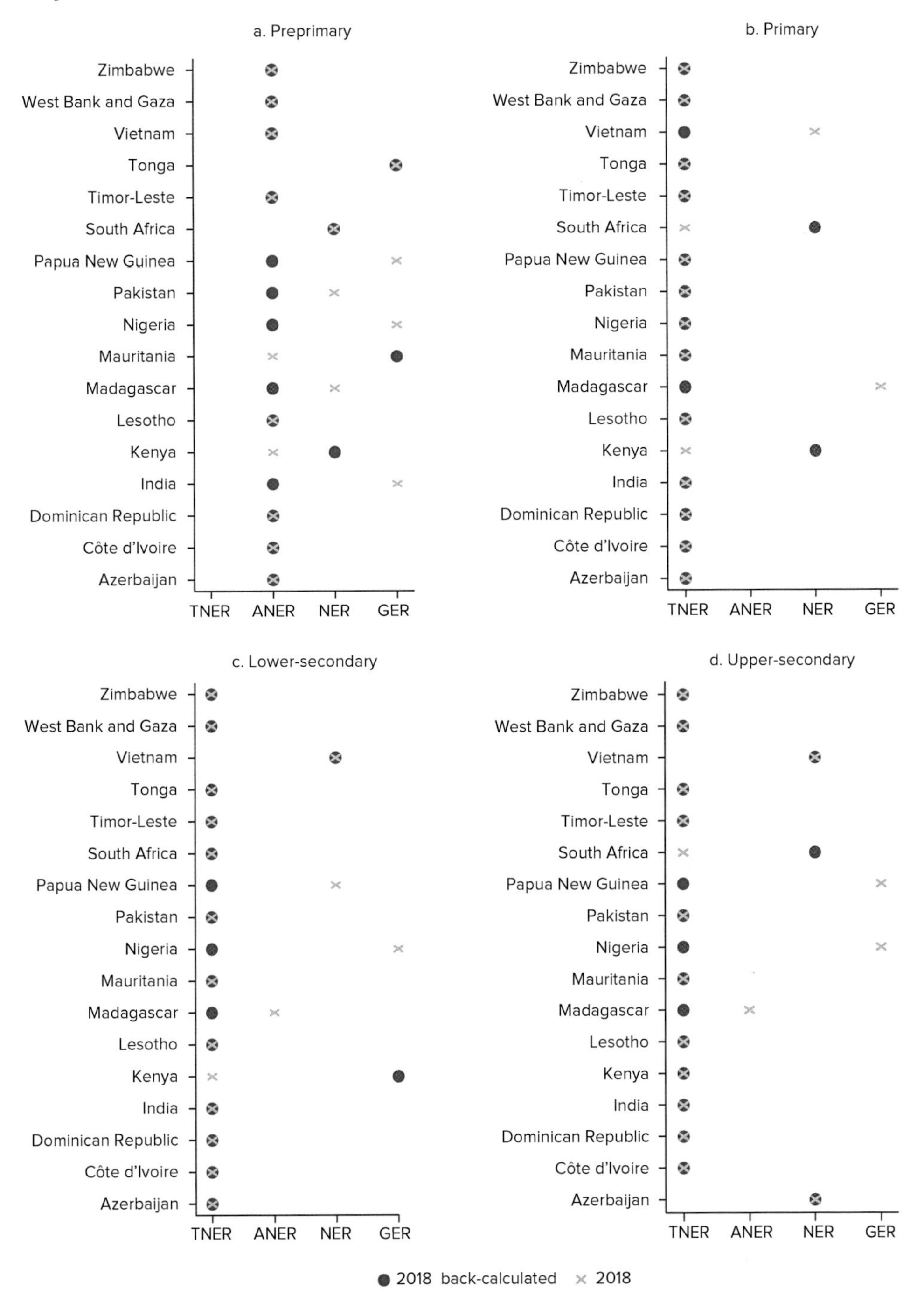

Source: World Bank calculations based on the 2020 update of the Human Capital Index (HCI).

Note: The panels plot the enrollment type used for calculation of expected years of school. Solid dot represents the data used for the back-calculated 2018 HCI, and x indicates the data used for the calculation of the 2018 HCI. ANER = adjusted net enrollment rate; GER = gross enrollment rate; NER = net enrollment rate; TNER = total net enrollment rate.

Figure C2.4 and figure C2.5 present details for countries in which the back-calculated 2018 EYS has decreased by at least half a year (figure C2.4 reports changes in year and figure C2.5 changes in enrollment types). Only in Tanzania is it necessary to move to an older rate, but it is to a preferable type (GER to TNER), and it is only one year older. In Bangladesh, the change in EYS is mostly driven by changes in preprimary and lower-secondary. For preprimary, the back-calculated rate relies on data from 2017 versus 2011, although it is for a less preferred rate (GER versus ANER). Meanwhile, for lower-secondary the rate for the back-calculated EYS is for a more recent year but a less preferred rate (ANER versus TNER). In this case, it is necessary to move to a less preferred rate because the TNER series is no longer available in the UIS data vintage for years after 2010.

In India, because the latest available TNER series in UIS is for 2013, World Bank staff have sourced more recent data. EYS is now built with age-specific enrollment profiles that make use of information from the updated Unified District Information System for Education (UDISE+) from the Ministry of Human Resource Development, as well as early childhood care and education enrollment from the Ministry of Women and Child Development and Entrepreneurship and population projections from the Ministry of Health and Family Welfare. The resulting EYS for the back-calculated HCI is 10.8 versus 10.2, which was used in the calculation for the 2018 HCI.

Figure C2.4 and figure C2.5 present selected evidence comparing 2018 EYS estimates used in the calculation of the 2018 HCI against those used in the 2020 update. For a more detailed look into the differences, table C7.1 presents enrollment data for all the economies where the absolute EYS change between the back-calculated 2018 and the 2018 versions of the index is greater than half a year.

2020 update

The 2020 EYS shows a high rank correlation to the EYS from 2018, as well as a strong positive relationship between the 2020 EYS and log gross domestic product per capita (figure C2.6). EYS tends to be slightly higher for girls than for boys, as reported in figure C2.7. In figure C2.7, the solid dot indicates the country average, the triangle indicates the average for girls, and the horizontal bar indicates the average for boys. The average EYS for boys was 11.3 compared to 11.4 for girls. Disparity in EYS between girls and boys is lower in richer countries.

Figure C2.8 reports average EYS by income group and by World Bank region. EYS tends to be lowest in low-income economies, and regional averages are lowest in Sub-Saharan Africa and South Asia, which suggests that much work remains to be done to close the gap in low-income economies.

Figure C2.4: Vintage data year for back-calculated 2018 and original 2018, decrease of 0.5 year or more in expected years of school

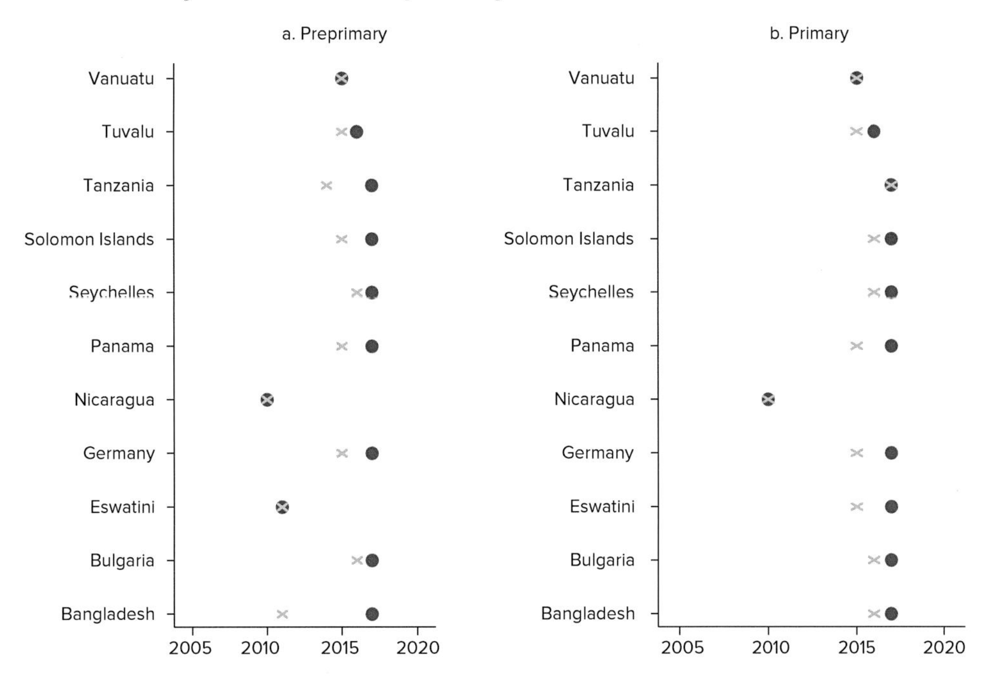

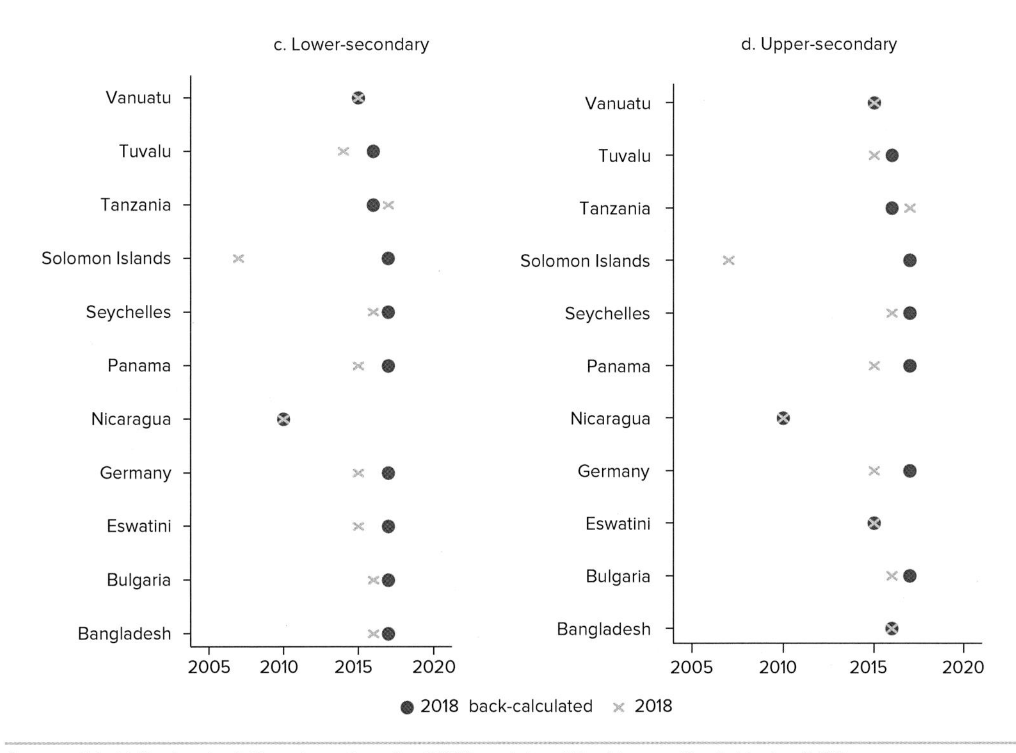

Source: World Bank calculations based on the 2020 update of the Human Capital Index (HCI).

Note: The panels plot the year of data used for calculation of expected years of school. Solid dot represents the data used for the back-calculated 2018 HCI, and x indicates the data used for the calculation of the 2018 HCI.

Figure C2.5: Enrollment type for back-calculated 2018 and original 2018, decrease of 0.5 year or more in expected years of school

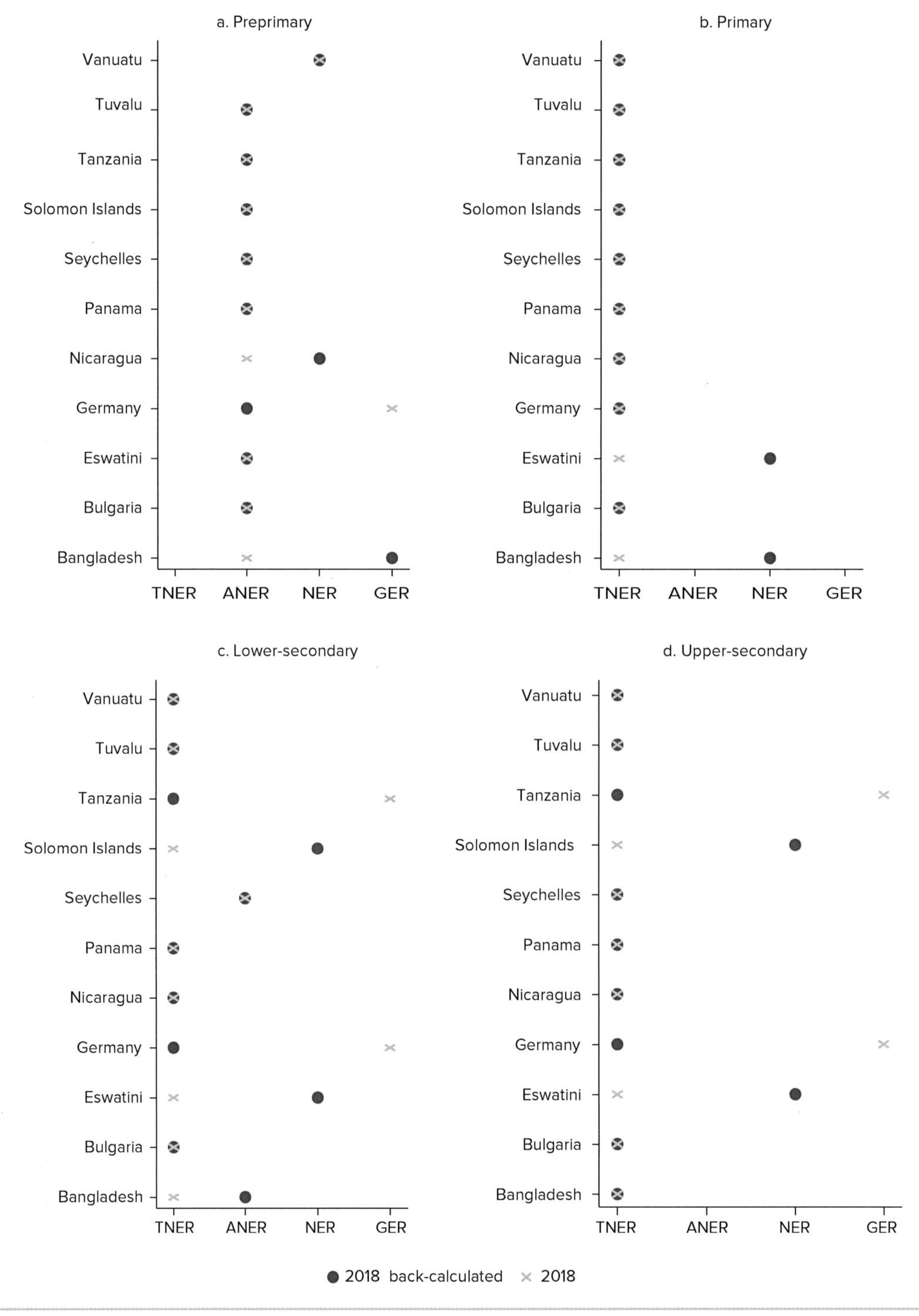

Source: World Bank calculations based on the 2020 update of the Human Capital Index (HCI).

Note: The panels plot the enrollment type used for calculation of expected years of school. Solid dot represents the data used for the back-calculated 2018 HCI, and x indicates the data used for the calculation of the 2018 HCI. ANER = adjusted net enrollment rate; GER = gross enrollment rate; NER = net enrollment rate; TNER = total net enrollment rate.

Figure C2.6: Expected years of school circa 2020, relative to GDP per capita

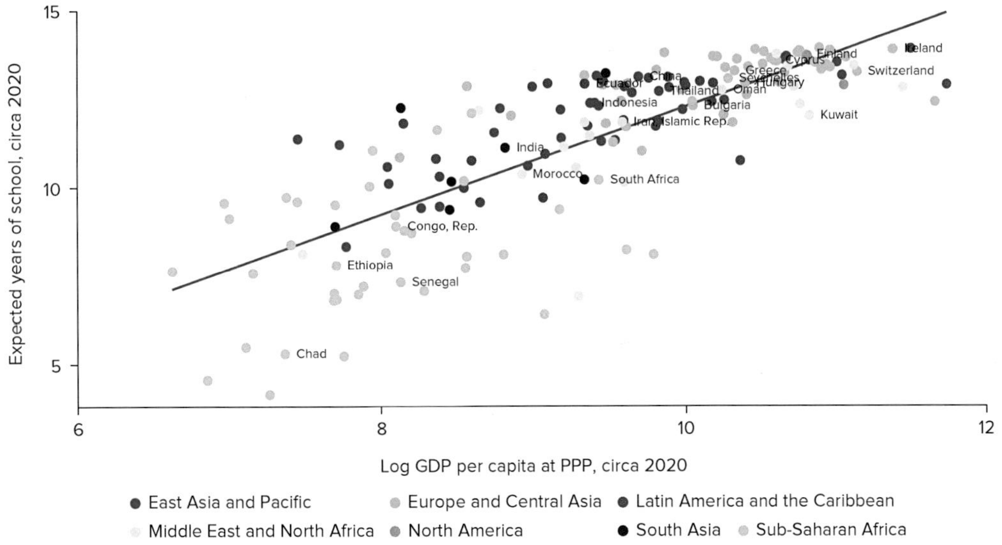

Expected years of school, circa 2020

15
10
5

Ireland
Switzerland
Finland
Cyprus
Greece
Seychelles
Hungary
Oman
Ecuador
China
Thailand
Indonesia
Bulgaria
Kuwait
Iran, Islamic Rep.
India
Morocco
South Africa
Congo, Rep.
Ethiopia
Senegal
Chad

6 8 10 12

Log GDP per capita at PPP, circa 2020

East Asia and Pacific
Europe and Central Asia
Latin America and the Caribbean
Middle East and North Africa
North America
South Asia
Sub-Saharan Africa

Source: World Bank calculations based on the 2020 update of the Human Capital Index (HCI).

Note: The figure plots expected years of school (on the vertical axis) against log GDP per capita at 2011 PPP US dollars (on the horizontal axis). PPP = purchasing power parity.

Figure C2.7: Sex-disaggregated expected years of school, relative to GDP per capita

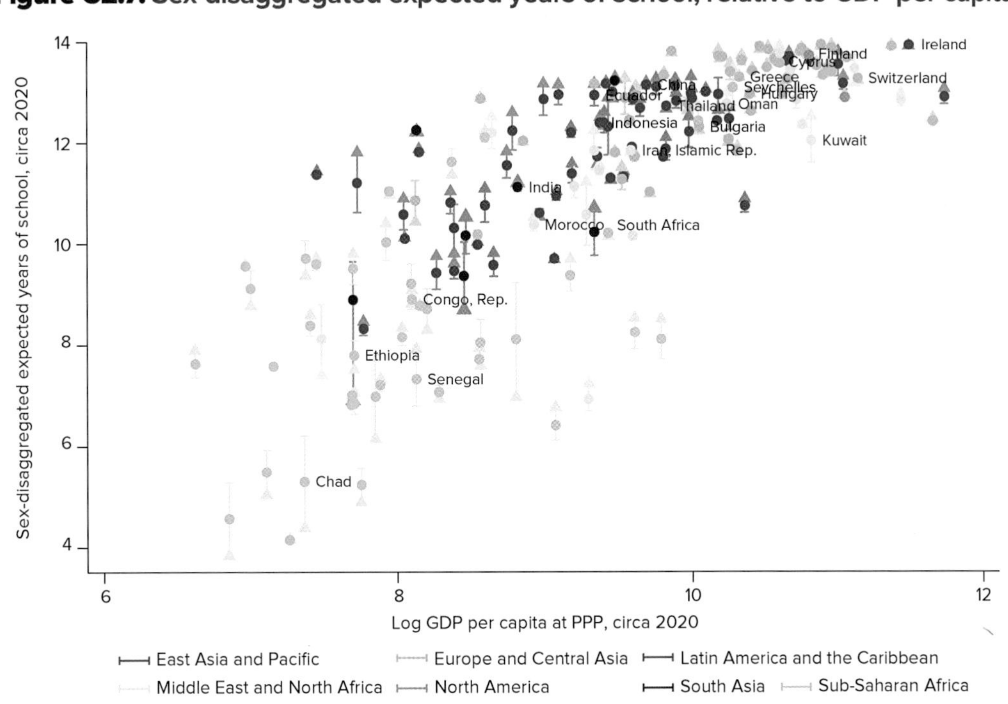

Source: World Bank calculations based on the 2020 update of the Human Capital Index (HCI).

Note: The figure plots sex-disaggregated expected years of school. The solid dot indicates the national average, the triangle shows the average value for girls, and the horizontal line shows the average value for boys. PPP = purchasing power parity.

Figure C2.8: Expected years of school, by income group and region

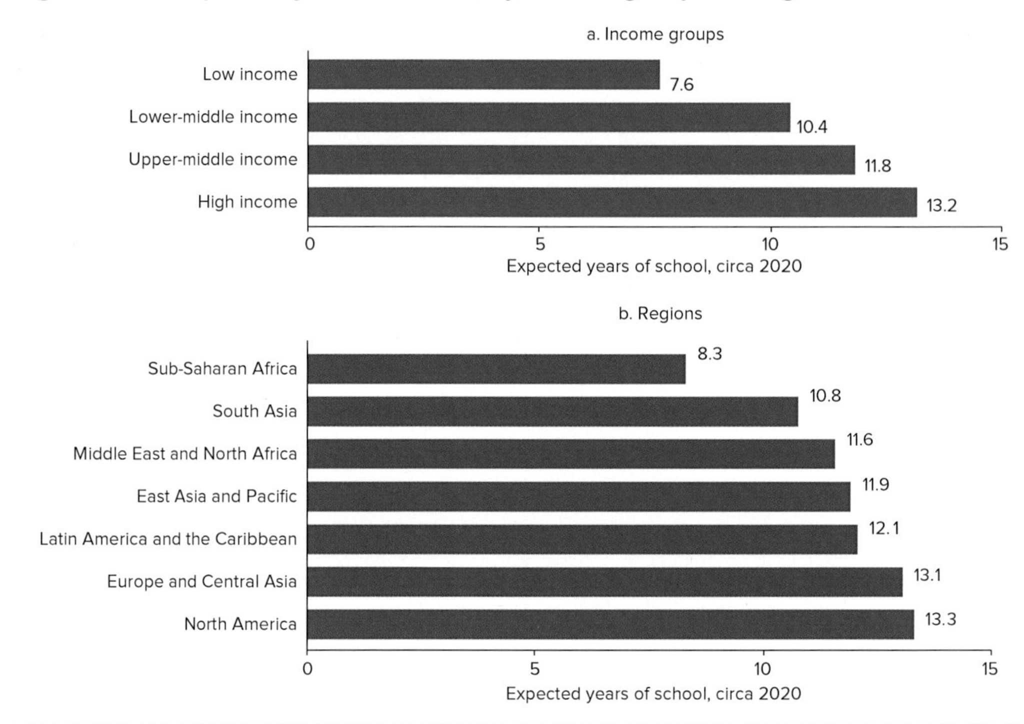

Source: World Bank calculations based on the 2020 update of the Human Capital Index (HCI).

Note: The figures plot regional and income group average values for expected years of school.

3. HARMONIZED TEST SCORES

The school quality adjustment is based on a large-scale effort to harmonize international student achievement tests from several multicountry testing programs to produce the Global Dataset on Education Quality. A detailed description of the test score harmonization exercise is provided in Patrinos and Angrist (2018), and the HCI draws on an updated version of this dataset as of January 2020.[15] The dataset harmonizes scores from three major international testing programs—the Trends in International Mathematics and Science Study (TIMSS) program, the Progress in International Reading Literacy Study (PIRLS), and the Programme for International Student Assessment (PISA)—as well as from four major regional testing programs—the Southern and Eastern Africa Consortium for Monitoring Educational Quality (SACMEQ), the Program for the Analysis of Education Systems (PASEC), the Latin American Laboratory for Assessment of the Quality of Education (LLECE), and the Pacific Island Learning and Numeracy Assessment (PILNA). It also incorporates Early Grade Reading Assessments (EGRAs) coordinated by the United States Agency for International Development.

The harmonization methodology relies on the production of an exchange rate between international student achievement tests and their regional counterparts, which can then be used to place tests on a common scale. Test scores are converted into TIMSS units as the numeraire, corresponding roughly to a mean of 500 and a standard deviation across students of 100 points. The exchange rate is based on the ratio of average economy scores in each program to the corresponding economy scores in the numeraire testing program for the set of economies participating in both the numeraire and the other testing program. For example, consider the set of economies that participate in both the PISA and the TIMSS assessments. The ratio of average PISA scores to average TIMSS scores for this set of economies provides a conversion factor for PISA into TIMSS scores that can then be used to convert the PISA scores of all economies into TIMSS scores. The exchange rate is calculated pooling all overlapping observations between 2000 and 2017 and is therefore constant over time. This ensures that within-country fluctuations in harmonized test scores over time for a given testing program reflect only changes in the test scores themselves and not changes in the conversion factor between tests.[16] The most recent update of the dataset also uses the 2000–17 period to calculate exchange rates, so that the rates between testing programs do not change between the 2018 and 2020 versions of the database.

2020 update

The 2020 update of the Global Dataset on Education Quality extends the database to 184 economies, drawing on a large-scale effort by the World Bank to collect learning data globally.

Updates to the database come from new data from PISA 2018, PISA for Development (PISA-D), PILNA, and EGRA. The database adds 20 new economies (8 using EGRAs, 8 using PILNA, 3 using PISA and PISA-D, and 1 using a national TIMSS-equivalent assessment). These additions bring the percentage of the global school-age population represented by the database to 98.7 percent. In addition, more recent data points have been added for 94 economies (75 from PISA 2018, 7 from PISA-D, 5 from EGRAs, and 7 from PILNA).

In most cases, the tests are designed to be nationally representative. There are, however, some notable cases in which they are not. In the case of China, extrapolations are needed to arrive at nationally representative estimates, because only a small number of relatively affluent regions have participated in PISA assessments. For India, the only internationally comparable assessment is the 2009 PISA. Instead, recent national assessment data and exchange rates with international benchmarks derived from the UIS Global Alliance to Monitor Learning (GAML) process are used to estimate a national harmonized test score (HTS). In a number of countries, EGRAs are not nationally representative and are identified as EGRANR in the data documentation.[17]

When economies participate in multiple testing programs, a hierarchy of tests is applied to determine which HTS to use. This hierarchy is based on the strength of the underlying test construction; the number of overlapping economies to produce the exchange rate; and consistency in administration, procedures, and documentation over time. The first HTS choice is an international test like the PISA, TIMSS, or PIRLS. The next-choice HTS is a regional test, like LLECE, SACMEQ, PASEC, and

PILNA (in that order). Finally, if neither an international nor a regional test is available, an economy is assigned an HTS that comes from an EGRA. The one exception to this rule is the Republic of Yemen, for which TIMSS data from 2007 and 2011 yield implausibly low scores and are replaced with EGRA data from 2011.

Uncertainty intervals for HTSs are constructed by bootstrapping. Patrinos and Angrist (2018) take 1,000 random draws from the distribution of subject-grade average test scores for each test in their dataset. They then form exchange rates and calculate HTSs in each bootstrapped sample. The 2.5th and 97.5th percentiles of the distribution of the resulting HTSs across bootstrapped samples constitute the lower and upper bounds of the uncertainty interval for the HTS. Test scores are harmonized by subject and grade and are then averaged across subjects and grades.[18]

HTSs for the 2020 HCI come from the most recently available test as of 2019, whereas data for the back-calculated 2018 HCI come from the most recent test available as of 2017. Data for the baseline comparator year of 2010 are populated for each economy using the test closest to 2010, typically with a minimum gap of five years between the test used to populate the 2010 and 2020 cross-sections. Some exceptions to this rule include Bahrain, Botswana, the Islamic Republic of Iran, Kuwait, Oman, and South Africa, for which data from the 2011 TIMSS or PIRLS are used to calculate the 2010 HCI, and data from the 2015 TIMSS or PIRLS are used to calculate the 2020 HCI. In addition, data for Timor-Leste come from a 2009 and 2011 EGRA, and data for Vietnam come from a 2012 PISA for the 2010 HCI and a 2015 PISA for the 2020 HCI.

In order to ensure the comparability of HTSs across time, we ensure that the 2010 and 2020 cross-sections are populated with scores that come from the same testing program. That is, if an economy has an HTS from a PISA test circa 2020, it must also have scores from another PISA test circa 2010 to be included in the over-time comparison. The five exceptions are Algeria, Morocco, North Macedonia, Saudi Arabia, and Ukraine. For Algeria, HTSs from the PIRLS or the TIMSS in 2007 are used to populate the 2010 HCI, and HTSs based on the PISA in 2015 are used to populate the 2020 HCI. For Morocco, North Macedonia, Saudi Arabia, and Ukraine, data from PIRLS or TIMSS in 2011 are used for the 2010 HCI, and data from PISA 2018 are used for the 2020 HCI. To maximize comparability with PISA, only scores from secondary-level schooling are considered for these five economies for the 2010 HCI. Applying these rules yields a sample of 103 economies with test scores in both 2010 and 2020.

Test scores used to produce the back-calculated HCI 2018 are similar to those used in the previous iteration of the HCI, as illustrated in figure C3.1. Data from the two vintages align almost perfectly along the 45-degree line because outcomes for these economies come from the same test and the same harmonization methodology. The figure also highlights the 10 economies for which test scores have changed because a more recent test was made available in the latest version of the database or, as in the case of China and India, because alternate methodologies were used to refine estimates of national average learning outcomes (see table C3.1 for details on changes in

Figure C3.1: Comparing original and back-calculated 2018 harmonized test scores

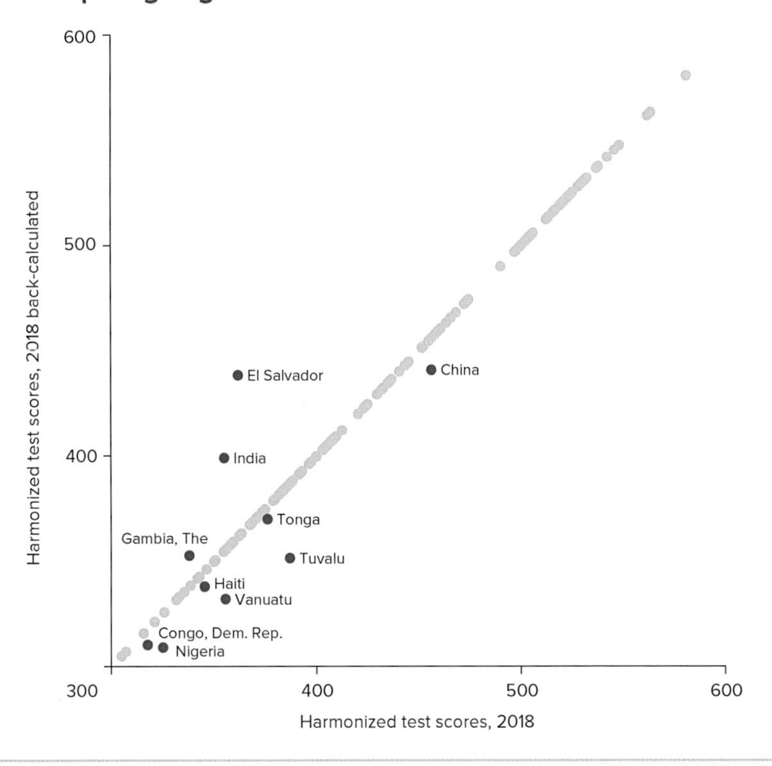

Source: World Bank calculations based on the 2020 update of the Human Capital Index (HCI).

Note: The figure plots the harmonized test scores as used in the 2018 HCI (on the horizontal axis), and the harmonized test scores used for the back-calculated 2018 HCI (on the vertical axis). Economies where harmonized test scores have changed between 2018 and back-calculated 2018 are labeled.

the source of test data). In the case of El Salvador, a choice guided by consultations with the country team was made to replace the previous test used (TIMSS/PIRLS from 2007) with a 2006 LLECE for reading to enhance comparability to the 2018 EGRA (not representative) used in 2020.

Figure C3.2 reports the most recent cross-section of test scores used to calculate the 2020 HCI. HTSs range from about 575 in the richest economies to about 305 in the poorest economies. To interpret these units, note that 400 corresponds to the benchmark of low proficiency in TIMSS at the student level, and 625 corresponds to advanced proficiency.

Test scores tend to be slightly higher for girls than for boys, as reported in figure C3.3. In the figure, the solid dot indicates the country average, the triangle indicates the average for girls, and the horizontal bar indicates the average for boys. Globally, the average HTS for boys was 420, compared with 430 for girls.

Figure C3.4 reports average test scores by income group and by World Bank region. Test scores tend to be lowest in low-income economies, and regional averages are lowest in South Asia and Sub-Saharan Africa.

Table C3.1: Source data for economies with different values in original 2018 and back-calculated 2018

Economy	2018 vintage			2020 vintage		
	Test	Year	Value	Test	Year	Value
China	PISA/PIRLS (Extrapolated)	2015	456	PISA/PIRLS (Extrapolated)	2015	441
Congo, Dem. Rep.	EGRANR	2012	318	EGRANR	2015	310
El Salvador	TIMSS/PIRLS	2007	362	LLECE	2006	438
Gambia, The	EGRA	2011	338	EGRA	2016	353
Haiti	EGRANR	2013	345	EGRA	2016	339
India	PISA	2009	355	NAS	2017	399
Malaysia	TIMSS	2015	468	TIMSS/PIRLS	2015	468
Nigeria	EGRANR	2010	325	EGRANR	2014	309
Tonga	EGRA	2014	376	PILNA	2015	370
Tuvalu[a]	EGRA	2016	387	EGRA	2016	351
Vanuatu	EGRA	2010	356	PILNA	2015	332

Source: World Bank calculations based on the 2020 update of the Human Capital Index (HCI).

Note: EGRA = Early Grade Reading Assessment; EGRANR = Non-nationally-representative Early Grade Reading Assessment; LLECE = Latin American Laboratory for Assessment of the Quality of Education; NAS = National Achievement Survey; PILNA = Pacific Island Learning and Numeracy Assessment; PIRLS = Progress in International Reading Literacy Study; PISA = Programme for International Student Assessment; TIMSS = Trends in International Mathematics and Science Study.

a. Data for Tuvalu from the 2016 EGRA were revised once student-level data were made available to the harmonized test score team.

Figure C3.2: Harmonized test scores, Human Capital Index 2020, relative to GDP per capita

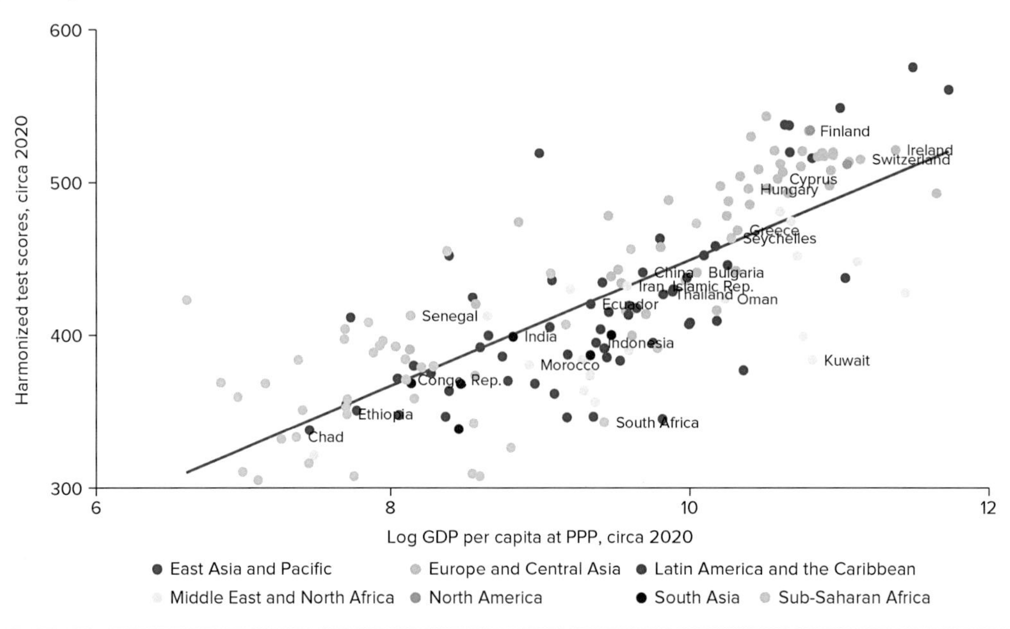

Source: World Bank calculations based on the 2020 update of the Human Capital Index (HCI).

Note: The figure plots harmonized test scores (on the vertical axis) against log GDP per capita at 2011 PPP US dollars (on the horizontal axis). PPP = purchasing power parity.

Figure C3.3: Sex-disaggregated harmonized test scores, relative to GDP per capita

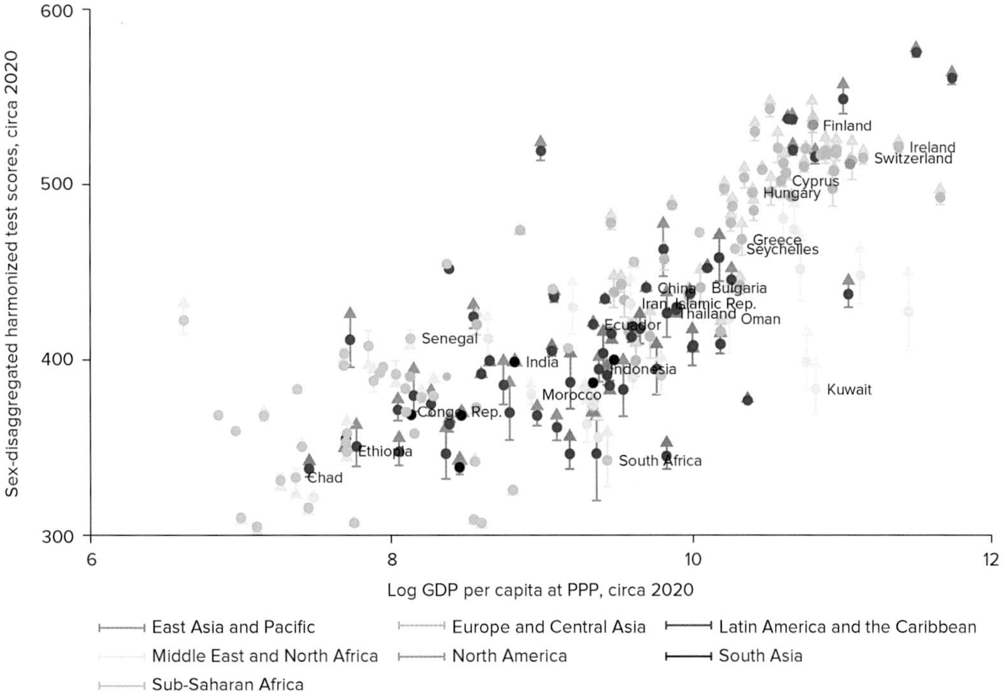

Source: World Bank calculations based on the 2020 update of the Human Capital Index (HCI).

Note: The figure plots sex-disaggregated harmonized test scores. The solid dot indicates the national average, the triangle shows the average value for girls, and the horizontal line shows the average value for boys. PPP = purchasing power parity.

Figure C3.4: Harmonized test scores, by income group and region

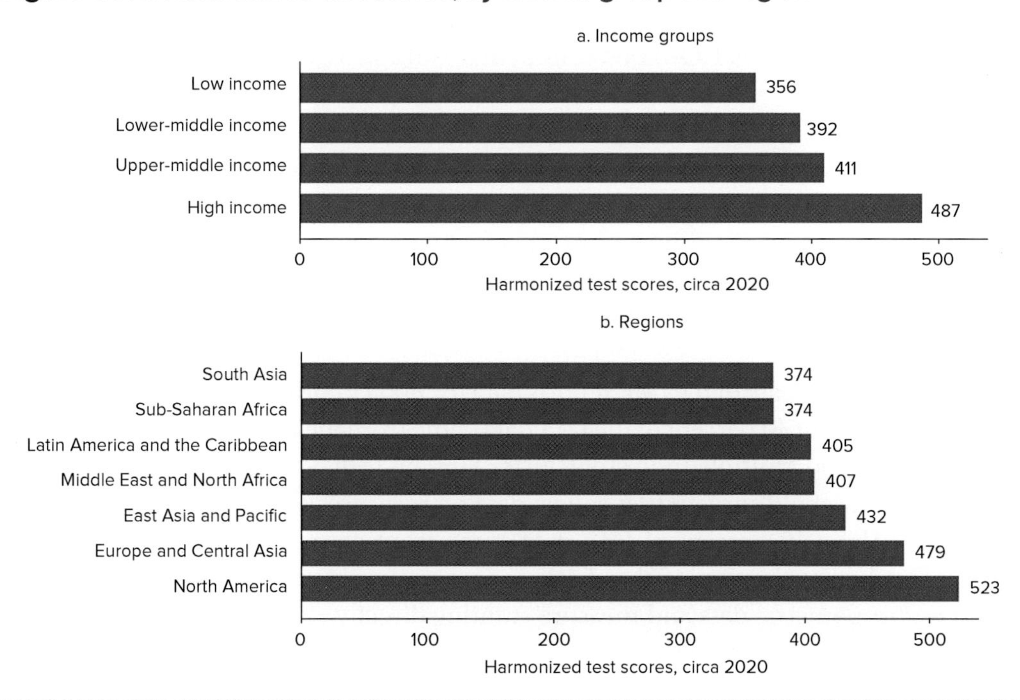

Source: World Bank calculations based on the 2020 update of the Human Capital Index (HCI).

Note: The figures plot regional and income-group average values for harmonized test scores.

4. UNDER-5 STUNTING RATES

The fraction of children under 5 not stunted is calculated as the complement of the under-5 stunting rate. The stunting rate is defined as the share of children under the age of 5 whose height is more than two reference standard deviations below the reference median for their ages. The reference median and standard deviations are set by the World Health Organization (WHO) for normal healthy child development (World Health Organization 2009). Child-level stunting prevalence is averaged across the relevant 0–5 age range to arrive at an overall under-5 stunting rate. The stunting rate is used as a proxy for latent health of the population, in addition to the adult survival rate, in countries for which stunting data are available.

Data on stunting rates are taken from the Joint Child Malnutrition Estimates (JME) database,[19] managed by the United Nations Children's Fund (UNICEF), WHO, and the World Bank (see UNICEF, World Health Organization, and World Bank 2020). The database reports the prevalence of stunting, wasting, and underweight, and is populated with estimates from survey data, gray literature, and reports from national authorities, reviewed by the JME interagency team. If required, data are reanalyzed to produce nationally representative estimates for the appropriate age cohort (0–5 years), comparable across economies and across time. Surveys presenting anthropometric data for age groups other than 0–59 months or 0–60 months are adjusted using national survey results—gathered as close in time as possible—from the same economy that include the age range 0–59/60 months. National rural estimates are adjusted similarly using another national survey for the same economy as close in time as possible with available national urban and rural data to derive an adjusted national estimate. Historical data that use different growth reference standards are reanalyzed to produce estimates based on WHO standards when raw data are available. If raw data are unavailable, estimates are converted to WHO-based prevalence using an algorithm developed by Yang and de Onis (2008).

The JME reports stunting rates from surveys and administrative data and is updated twice a year, in March and September. The HCI team supplements stunting data from the JME with data provided by country teams for five countries: Bhutan, Chile, Fiji, Indonesia, and Timor-Leste. It does so primarily to include more recent surveys that have not yet been incorporated in the JME.

The March 2020 update of the JME reports data for 152 economies and 887 country-year observations. About 50 percent of the JME data come from the Demographic and Health Surveys (DHS) and Multiple Indicator Cluster Surveys (MICS). Both are nationally representative household surveys that collect data on measures of population, health, and nutrition.[20] About 10 percent of JME data come from country nutrition surveillance programs, whereas the rest of the database is populated using national surveys that collect anthropometric data and measure stunting directly.

The JME database reports sex-disaggregated stunting rates for 56 percent of the surveys. It also reports 95 percent confidence intervals around estimates of stunting for about

40 percent of the observations, primarily those on which the JME team had access to record-level survey data. Absent better alternatives, the HCI team imputes confidence intervals for the remaining observations in the JME database using the fitted values from a regression of the width of the confidence interval on the stunting rate.

Surveys from low- and middle-income economies make up 90 percent of the JME database. High-income economies tend to have much lower average stunting rates (the national average for the 13 high-income economies in the JME sample is 6 percent) and are less likely to regularly monitor stunting through frequent surveys. Some high-income economies like Kuwait, Oman, and the United States continue frequent monitoring of stunting prevalence through national surveys. Inconsistent measurement is of greater concern in middle- or low-income economies where stunting rates continue to be elevated. The most recent survey for 33 economies in the JME database is more than 5 years old, and it is about 10 years old for 10 economies. Conversely, economies like Peru and Senegal elected to field DHS annually. The continuous DHS played a key role in Peru's national strategy for early childhood development, *Crecer*, which helped reduce the country's rate of chronic malnutrition from 28 percent in 2005 to 13 percent in 2016, with an even pace of change among rural and urban children (Marini and Rokx 2017). In the JME data, the average gap between surveys for economies with at least two surveys is 5.6 years, and it is 5.0 years when high-income economies are excluded.

2020 update

Stunting rates for the 2020 update of the HCI come from the March 2020 update of the JME database, available at the WHO website.[21] Relative to the 2018 edition of the HCI, this latest update to the database allows us to update stunting rates for 54 economies and to add stunting rates for Argentina, Bulgaria, and Uzbekistan, which did not have rates in the previous iteration of the HCI.

Stunting rates for the 2020 HCI come from the most recently available survey as of 2019, and data for the back-calculated 2018 HCI come from the most recent survey available as of 2017. Data for the baseline comparator year of 2010 are populated for each economy using the survey closest to 2010 that was fielded between 2005 and 2015. When populating the 2010 cross-section, we ensure a minimum gap of five years between the survey used to populate the 2010 and 2020 cross-sections. To maximize the overlap among the three cross-sections, we do not rely on stunting rates in the calculation of the HCI for high-income economies, even when stunting data are available for some of these economies. This is because stunting rates typically come from surveys that are 5–10 years old for these economies. Further, to ensure consistency across time periods, we use stunting data to calculate the HCI for an economy only if such data are available in both 2010 and 2020. This does not prevent the calculation of an HCI score for high-income economies or those economies missing stunting data in any period; we simply use the adult survival rate as the proxy for latent health in our calculations.

Values for stunting rates used to produce the back-calculated 2018 HCI are very similar to those used in the previous iteration of the HCI, as illustrated in figure C4.1, where data from the two vintages align almost perfectly along the 45-degree line. The figure highlights eight economies where stunting rates have changed by 3 percentage points or more in the back-calculated 2018 HCI versus the original 2018 HCI. This change is predominantly because the March 2020 update of the JME makes a more recent survey available or, in the case of Sierra Leone, because JME estimates have been updated following a reanalysis of survey data (see table C4.1).

Figure C4.2 reports the most recent cross-section of stunting rates used to calculate the 2020 HCI. Stunting ranges from about 2.5 percent in the richest economies in the sample to about 54 percent in the poorest economies.

The levels of stunting tend to be slightly lower for girls than for boys, as reported in figure C4.3. In the figure, the solid dot indicates the economy average, the triangle indicates the average for girls, and the horizontal bar indicates the average for boys. The average stunting rate is 24 percent for boys, compared with 22 percent for girls.

Figure C4.4 reports average stunting rates by income group and by World Bank region. Levels tend to be highest in low-income economies, and regional averages are highest in Sub-Saharan Africa and South Asia.

Figure C4.1: Comparing original and back-calculated 2018 stunting rates

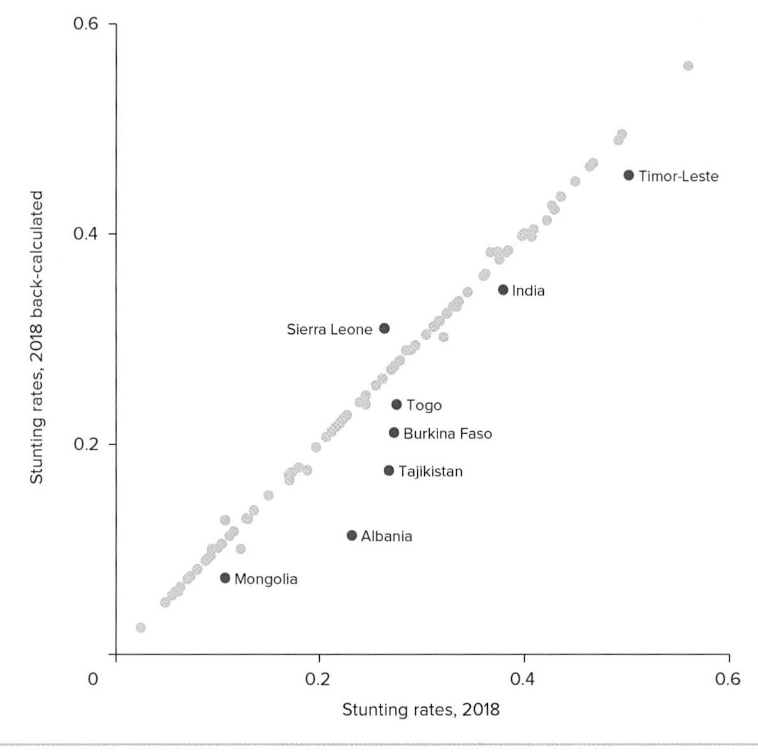

Source: World Bank calculations based on the 2020 update of the Human Capital Index (HCI).

Note: The figure plots the stunting rates as used in the 2018 HCI (on the horizontal axis), and the stunting rates used for the back-calculated 2018 HCI (on the vertical axis). Economies where stunting rates have changed by 3 percentage points between 2018 and back-calculated 2018 are labeled.

Table C4.1: Source data for economies with different values in 2018 and back-calculated 2018

Economy	2018 vintage			2020 vintage		
	Source	Year	Value	Source	Year	Value
Albania	DHS	2009	0.23	DHS	2017	0.11
Burkina Faso	SMART	2016	0.27	SMART	2017	0.21
India	DHS	2015	0.38	NNS	2017	0.35
Mongolia	MICS	2013	0.11	NNS	2016	0.07
Sierra Leone	MICS	2017	0.26	MICS	2017	0.31
Tajikistan	DHS	2012	0.27	DHS	2017	0.18
Timor-Leste	Timor-Leste Food and Nutrition Survey, Final Report 2015	2013	0.50	Timor-Leste Demographic and Health Survey 2016	2016	0.46
Togo	DHS	2014	0.28	MICS	2017	0.24

Source: World Bank calculations based on World Bank 2018 and the 2020 update of the Human Capital Index (HCI).

Note: DHS = Demographic and Health Surveys; MICS = Multiple Indicator Cluster Surveys; NNS = National Nutrition Survey; SMART = Standardized Monitoring and Assessment of Relief and Transition.

Figure C4.2: Stunting rates, Human Capital Index 2020, relative to GDP per capita

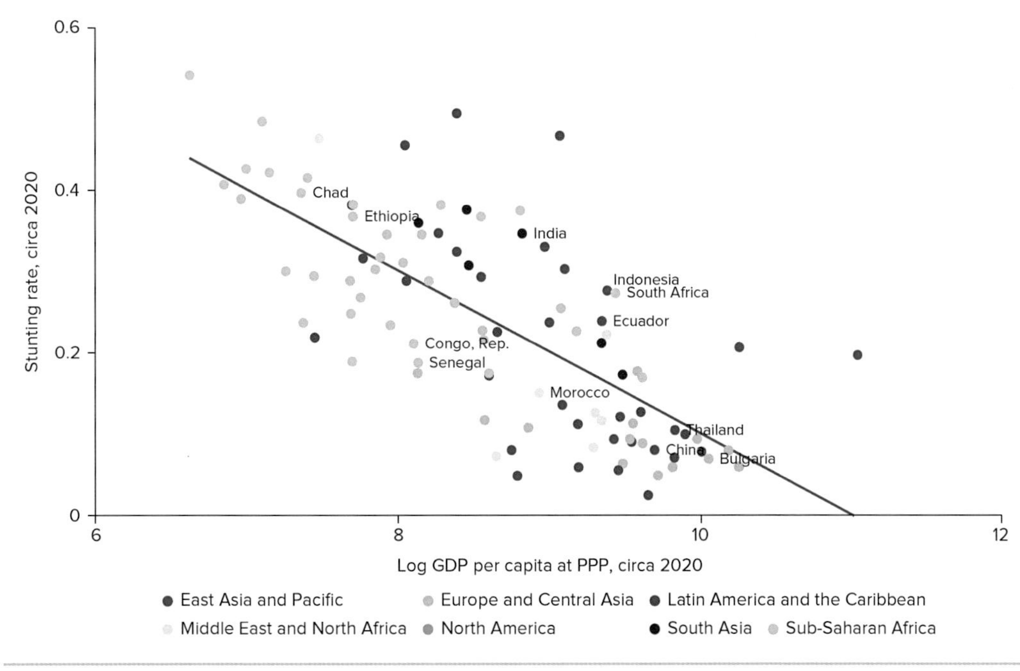

Source: World Bank calculations based on the 2020 update of the Human Capital Index (HCI).

Note: The figure plots stunting rates (on the vertical axis) against log GDP per capita at 2011 PPP US dollars (on the horizontal axis). PPP = purchasing power parity.

Figure C4.3: Sex-disaggregated stunting rates, relative to GDP per capita

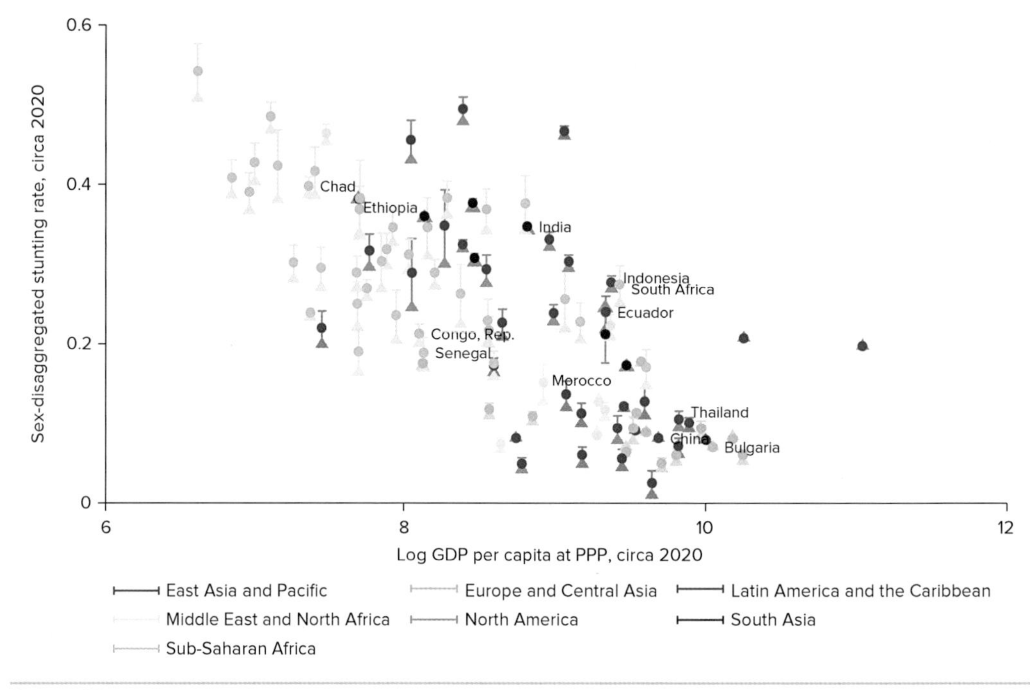

Source: World Bank calculations based on the 2020 update of the Human Capital Index (HCI).

Note: The figure plots sex-disaggregated stunting rates. The solid dot indicates the national average, the triangle shows the average value for girls, and the horizontal line shows the average value for boys. PPP = purchasing power parity

Figure C4.4: Stunting rates, by income group and region

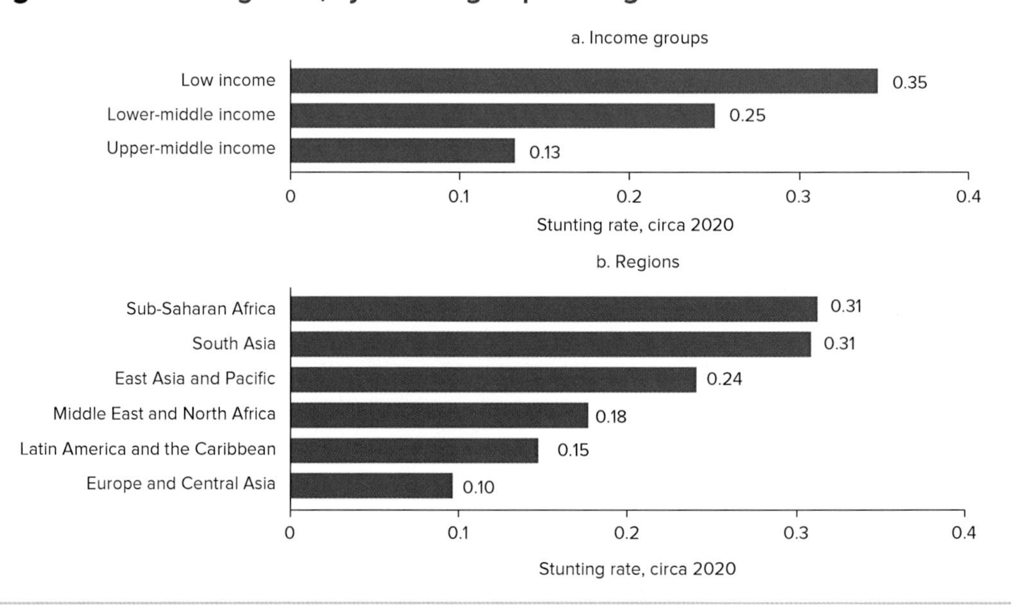

Source: World Bank calculations based on the 2020 update of the Human Capital Index (HCI).

Note: The figures plot regional and income-group average values for stunting. High-income-group economies are not included in these figures.

5. ADULT SURVIVAL RATES

The adult survival rate is calculated as the complement of the mortality rate for 15- to 60-year-olds. The mortality rate for 15- to 60-year-olds is the probability that a 15-year-old in a specified year will die before reaching the age of 60, if subject to current age-specific mortality rates. It is frequently expressed as a rate per 1,000 alive at 15, in which case it must be divided by 1,000 to obtain the probability that a 15-year-old will die before age 60.

Adult mortality rates are estimated on the basis of prevailing patterns of death rates by age and are reported by the United Nations Population Division (UNPD) for five-year periods. The five-year data are interpolated to arrive at annual estimates to calculate the HCI. The measurement of adult survival rates requires data on death rates by age. Although they are readily available in economies with strong vital registries, such data are missing or incomplete in roughly the poorest quarter of economies. In these economies, UNPD estimates death rates by age by linking the limited available age-specific mortality data with model life tables that capture the typical pattern in the distribution of deaths by age.

UNPD does not individually report adult mortality rates for economies with fewer than 90,000 inhabitants. For this reason, data from UNPD are supplemented with adult mortality rates from the Global Burden of Disease (GBD) project, managed by the Institute of Health Metrics and Evaluation (IHME). Data from this source are used for Dominica and the Marshall Islands. Data for Nauru, Palau, San Marino, St. Kitts and Nevis, and Tuvalu come from WHO.

Despite uncertainty on the primary estimates of mortality as well as the process for data modeling, uncertainty intervals are not reported in the UNPD data. Here we use uncertainty intervals reported in the GBD modeling process for adult survival rates.[22] The point estimates for adult survival rates in these two datasets are quite similar for most economies. The ratio of the upper (lower) bound to the point estimate of the adult survival rate in the GBD data is applied to the point estimate of the adult survival rate in the UNPD and WHO data to obtain upper (lower) bounds.

2020 update

Adult mortality rates for the 2020 update of the HCI come from the 2019 update of the UNPD World Population Prospects estimates, available at the World Population Prospects website.[23] The GBD data come from the 2017 update—the most recent available—and can be retrieved from the IHME data visualization site.[24] The WHO data are located on the UN Data platform.[25] Data for five-year periods from the UNPD are interpolated to arrive at annual estimates. Data from the GBD and WHO are carried forward up to 10 years to fill gaps in the series. UNPD adult mortality rates for the 2020 HCI come from the most recent available year, as of 2019, and data for the back-calculated 2018 HCI come from 2017. Data for the comparator year of 2010 come from 2010.

For economies with data from the GBD, the latest data from 2017 are used to populate the 2020 and back-calculated 2018 rates. For economies with data from WHO, the most recent estimate to populate the 2020 and back-calculated 2018 rates comes from 2012.

Because adult mortality rates are estimated by modeling all available data on adult mortality from vital registration systems, population censuses, household surveys, and sample registration systems combined with model life tables, every new release of data from UNPD and GBD updates estimates for all the previous years in the time series. As a result, data for the same year might differ slightly across updates.

Values for adult mortality rates used to produce the back-calculated 2018 HCI are similar to those used in the previous iteration of the HCI, as illustrated in figure C5.1, where data from the two vintages align closely along the 45-degree line for most economies. The figure highlights the 10 economies where adult mortality rates have changed by 30 deaths or more per 1,000 15-year-olds. The largest changes were for Angola (which went from 236 to 279 deaths per 1,000 15-year-olds) and Kazakhstan (which went from 203 to 158 deaths per 1,000 15-year-olds).

Figure C5.1: Comparing original and back-calculated 2018 adult mortality rates

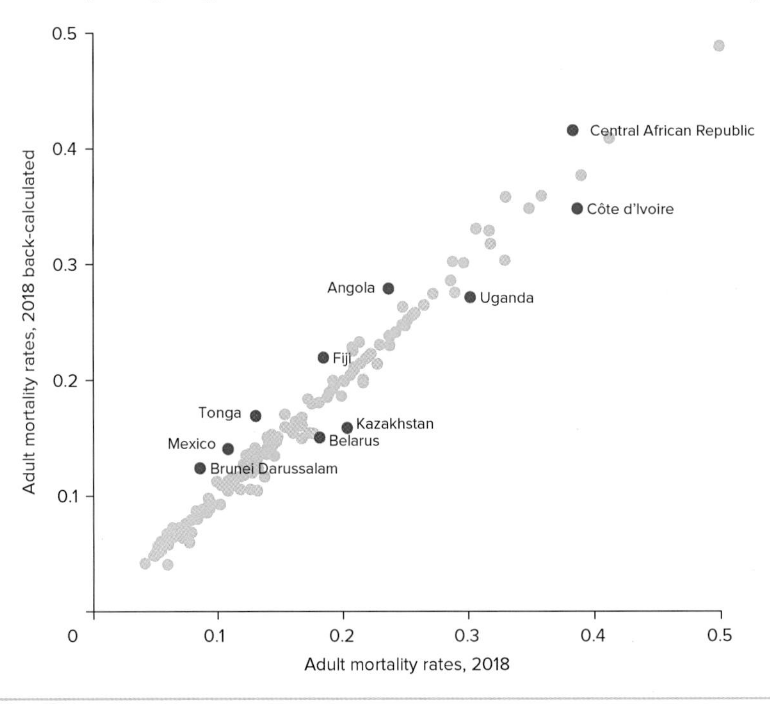

Source: World Bank calculations based on the 2020 update of the Human Capital Index (HCI).

Note: The figure plots adult rates as used in the 2018 HCI (on the horizontal axis), and the adult mortality rates used for the back-calculated 2018 HCI (on the vertical axis). Economies where adult mortality rates have changed by 30 deaths or more per 1,000 15-year-olds between 2018 and back-calculated 2018 are labeled.

Figure C5.2 reports the most recent cross-section of adult mortality rates used to calculate the 2020 HCI. Rates range from about 0.039 (39 deaths per 1,000 15-year-olds) in the richest economies to about 0.477 (477 deaths per 1,000 15-year-olds) in the poorest economies.

Adult mortality rates tend to be lower for women than for men, as reported in figure C5.3. In the figure, the solid dot indicates the country average, the triangle indicates the average for women, and the horizontal bar indicates the average for men. The average adult mortality rate for men was 0.183 (183 deaths per 1,000 15-year-olds), compared to 0.120 for women (120 deaths per 1,000 15-year-olds).

Figure C5.4 reports average adult mortality rates by income group and by World Bank region. Mortality rates tend to be highest in low-income ecomomies, and regional averages are highest in Sub-Saharan Africa and South Asia, reflecting that poor economies continue to bear a disproportionate burden of adult mortality.

Figure C5.2: Adult mortality rates, Human Capital Index 2020, relative to GDP per capita

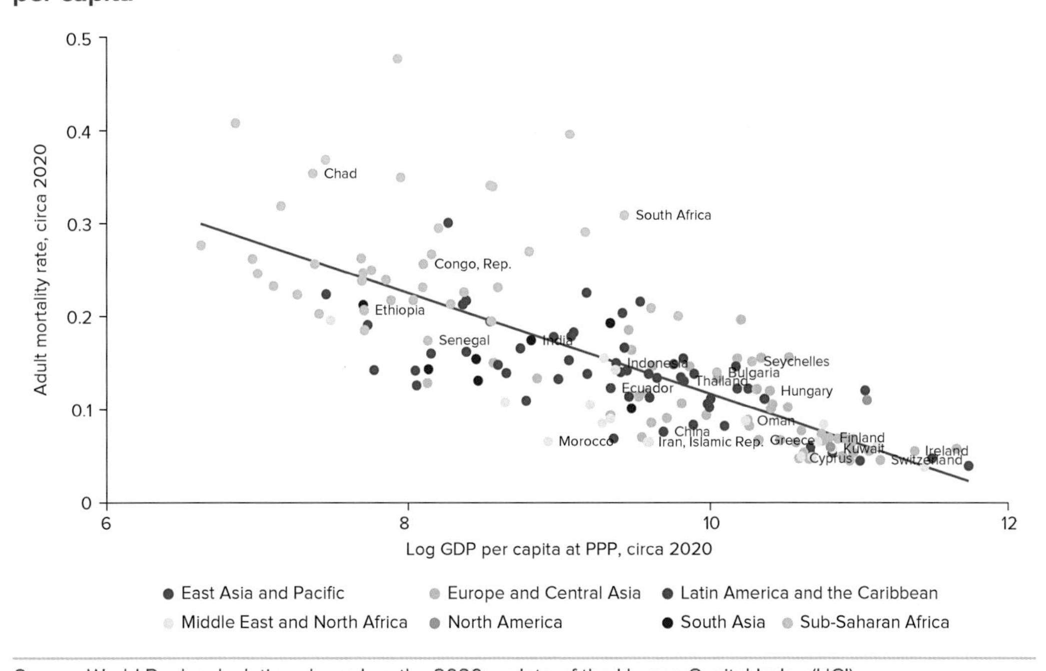

Source: World Bank calculations based on the 2020 update of the Human Capital Index (HCI).

Note: The figure plots adult mortality rates (on the vertical axis) against log GDP per capita at 2011 PPP US dollars (on the horizontal axis). PPP = purchasing power parity.

Figure C5.3: Sex-disaggregated adult mortality rates, relative to GDP per capita

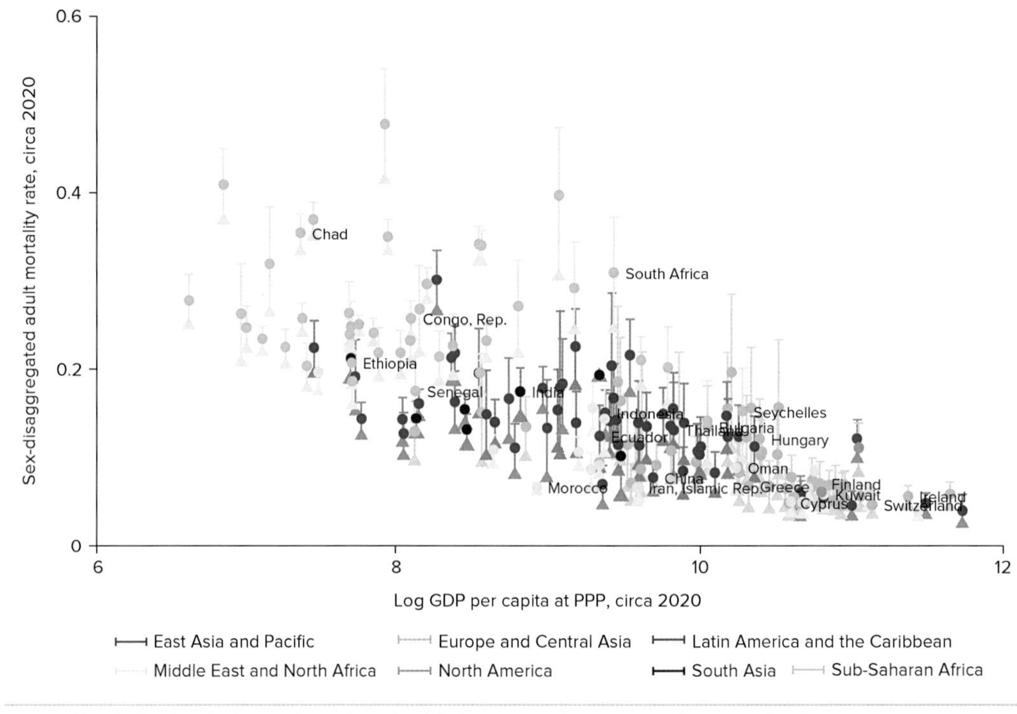

Source: World Bank calculations based on the 2020 update of the Human Capital Index (HCI).

Note: The figure plots sex-disaggregated adult mortality rates. The solid dot indicates the national average, the triangle is used to show the average value for women, and the horizontal line shows the average value for men.

Figure C5.4: Adult mortality rates, by income group and region

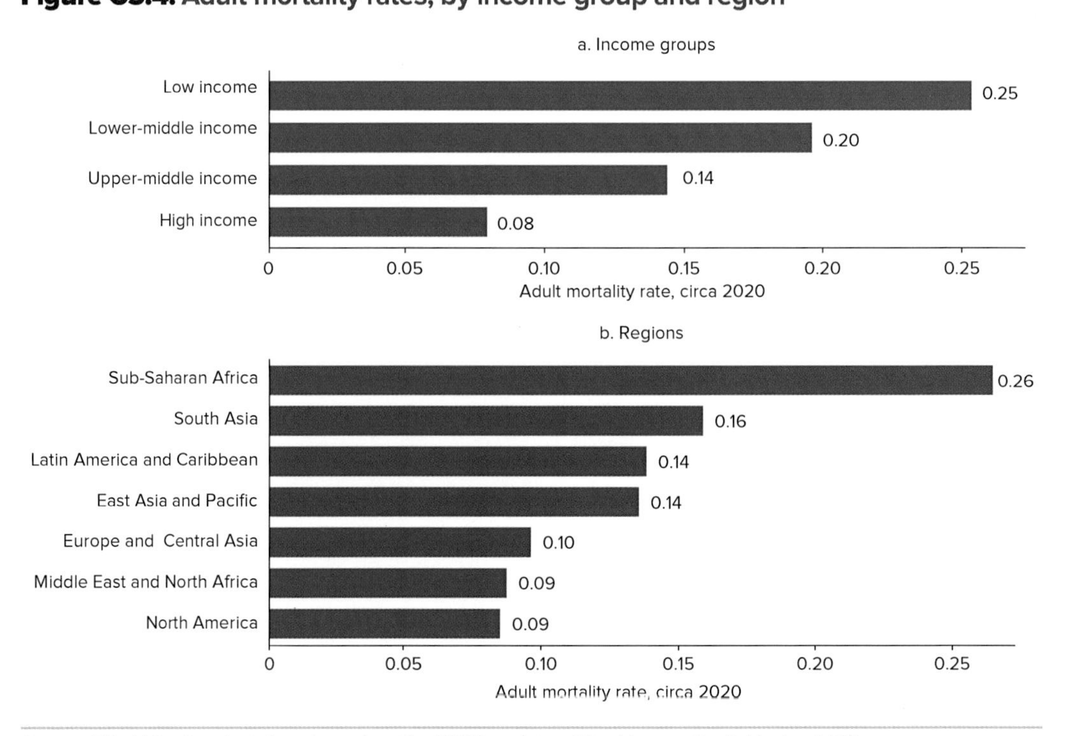

Source: World Bank calculations based on the 2020 update of the Human Capital Index (HCI).

Note: The figures plot regional and income group average values for adult mortality rates.

6. WORLD BANK–WIDE DATA REVIEW PROCESS AND QUALITY ASSESSMENT

Component data for the HCI 2020 update were subject to extensive World Bank-wide data review to ensure data quality. The review process was conducted between February and July 2020, and was split into two parts. The first part of the process (February to May 2020) focused on the enrollment data used to construct estimates of expected years of school and was conducted with World Bank Program Leaders for Human Development. The second part of the data review process (May to July 2020) focused on the other four index components—child mortality, harmonized test scores, stunting rates, and adult mortality. The enrollment data were validated separately because experience from the first edition of the HCI in 2018 suggested that those data required the most intensive review in terms of time and inputs needed from World Bank country teams, due to extensive gaps in the data as reported by UIS. All component data were reviewed for timeliness and completeness, with gaps filled and revisions made as needed.

7. SUPPLEMENTARY APPENDIX TABLES

Table C7.1: Data sources for every education level for economies with an absolute change in EYS of at least 0.5, original 2018 and back-calculated 2018

Economy	Level	2018				2018 back-calculated			
		EYS	Rate	Year	Source	EYS	Rate	Year	Source
Azerbaijan	Preprimary	11.6	24.9	2016	UIS (ANER)	12.4	61.3	2017	UIS (ANER)
	Primary		99.1	2016	UIS (TNER)		97.9	2017	UIS (TNER)
	Lower-secondary		93.8	2016	UIS (TNER)		99.4	2017	UIS (TNER)
	Upper-secondary		77.4	2017	WB Staff (NER)		77.5	2017	WB Staff (NER)
Bangladesh	Preprimary	11.0	59.7	2011	UIS (ANER)	10.2	41.7	2017	UIS (GER)
	Primary		92.8	2016	UIS (TNER)		92.5	2017	WB Staff (NER)
	Lower-secondary		86.8	2016	UIS (TNER)		69.2	2017	UIS (ANER)
	Upper-secondary		55.4	2016	UIS (TNER)		57.2	2016	UIS (TNER)
Bulgaria	Preprimary	12.9	95.4	2016	UIS (ANER)	12.3	84.0	2017	UIS (ANER)
	Primary		93.4	2016	UIS (TNER)		88.2	2017	UIS (TNER)
	Lower-secondary		90.7	2016	UIS (TNER)		87.6	2017	UIS (TNER)
	Upper-secondary		89.5	2016	UIS (TNER)		90.3	2017	UIS (TNER)
Congo, Dem. Rep.	Preprimary	9.2	7.9	2012	WB Staff (ANER)	8.5	4.0	2013	UIS (NER)
	Primary		72.1	2014	WB Staff (TNER)		72.1	2014	WB Staff (TNER)
	Lower-secondary		81.9	2014	WB Staff (TNER)		81.9	2014	WB Staff (TNER)
	Upper-secondary		74.9	2014	WB Staff (TNER)		53.0	2014	WB Staff (TNER)

(continued next page)

Table C7.1: Data sources for every education level for economies with an absolute change in EYS of at least 0.5, original 2018 and back-calculated 2018 (*Continued*)

Economy	Level	2018				2018 back-calculated			
		EYS	Rate	Year	Source	EYS	Rate	Year	Source
Côte d'Ivoire	Preprimary	7.0	21.2	2016	UIS (ANER)	7.6	22.2	2017	UIS (ANER)
	Primary		60.1	2012	WB Staff (TNER)		79.0	2017	UIS (TNER)
	Lower-secondary		61.5	2013	WB Staff (TNER)		49.6	2017	UIS (TNER)
	Upper-secondary		39.0	2013	WB Staff (TNER)		31.7	2017	UIS (TNER)
Dominican Republic	Preprimary	11.3	77.1	2016	UIS (ANER)	11.9	87.4	2017	UIS (ANER)
	Primary		84.9	2016	UIS (TNER)		90.2	2017	UIS (TNER)
	Lower-secondary		85.5	2016	UIS (TNER)		87.2	2017	UIS (TNER)
	Upper-secondary		69.8	2016	UIS (TNER)		71.7	2017	UIS (TNER)
Eswatini	Preprimary	8.2	17.0	2011	UIS (ANER)	6.4	18.9	2011	UIS (ANER)
	Primary		64.4	2015	UIS (TNER)		81.4	2017	WB Staff (NER)
	Lower-secondary		75.8	2015	UIS (TNER)		28.3	2017	WB Staff (NER)
	Upper-secondary		55.9	2015	UIS (TNER)		10.4	2015	WB Staff (NER)
Germany	Preprimary	13.9	100.0	2015	UIS (GER)	13.3	98.8	2017	UIS (ANER)
	Primary		99.4	2015	UIS (TNER)		99.0	2017	UIS (TNER)
	Lower-secondary		97.5	2015	UIS (GER)		92.9	2017	UIS (TNER)
	Upper-secondary		100.0	2015	UIS (GER)		87.6	2017	UIS (TNER)
India	Preprimary	10.2	12.9	2016	UIS (GER)	10.8	13.7	2018	WB Staff (ANER)
	Primary		97.2	2013	UIS (TNER)		88.7	2018	WB Staff (TNER)
	Lower-secondary		84.9	2013	UIS (TNER)		62.2	2018	WB Staff (TNER)
	Upper-secondary		51.0	2013	UIS (TNER)		30.3	2018	WB Staff (TNER)
Lesotho	Preprimary	8.7	36.0	2016	UIS (ANER)	10.0	42.4	2016	UIS (ANER)
	Primary		75.9	2016	UIS (TNER)		88.6	2017	UIS (TNER)
	Lower-secondary		64.3	2016	UIS (TNER)		70.1	2016	UIS (TNER)
	Upper-secondary		51.3	2016	UIS (TNER)		59.2	2016	UIS (TNER)
Madagascar	Preprimary	7.5	26.1	2016	UIS (NER)	8.4	60.7	2018	UIS (ANER)
	Primary		100.0	2016	UIS (GER)		72.5	2018	UIS (TNER)
	Lower-secondary		22.8	2016	UIS (ANER)		63.5	2018	UIS (TNER)
	Upper-secondary		8.7	2016	UIS (ANER)		31.1	2018	UIS (TNER)
Mauritania	Preprimary	6.3	5.5	2008	WB Staff (ANER)	7.4	10.5	2015	UIS (GER)
	Primary		65.5	2016	UIS (TNER)		76.5	2017	UIS (TNER)
	Lower-secondary		45.4	2016	UIS (TNER)		52.3	2017	UIS (TNER)
	Upper-secondary		28.5	2016	UIS (TNER)		32.9	2017	UIS (TNER)

(continued next page)

Table C7.1: Data sources for every education level for economies with an absolute change in EYS of at least 0.5, original 2018 and back-calculated 2018 (*Continued*)

Economy	Level	2018				2018 back-calculated			
		EYS	Rate	Year	Source	EYS	Rate	Year	Source
Nicaragua	Preprimary	11.6	88.3	2010	UIS (ANER)	10.8	55.6	2010	UIS (NER)
	Primary		90.6	2010	UIS (TNER)		88.7	2010	UIS (TNER)
	Lower-secondary		82.3	2010	UIS (TNER)		81.8	2010	UIS (TNER)
	Upper-secondary		63.5	2010	UIS (TNER)		62.4	2010	UIS (TNER)
Nigeria	Preprimary	8.2	41.8	2010	UIS (GER)	7.3	41.8	2010	UIS (GER)
	Primary		65.9	2010	UIS (TNER)		66.0	2010	UIS (TNER)
	Lower-secondary		52.5	2013	UIS (GER)		45.0	2016	UIS (GER)
	Upper-secondary		60.3	2013	UIS (GER)		38.6	2016	UIS (GER)
Pakistan	Preprimary	8.8	57.6	2016	UIS (NER)	9.3	43.4	2017	WB Staff (ANER)
	Primary		82.1	2016	UIS (TNER)		77.8	2017	WB Staff (TNER)
	Lower-secondary		53.8	2016	UIS (TNER)		71.4	2017	WB Staff (TNER)
	Upper-secondary		37.8	2016	UIS (TNER)		55.7	2017	WB Staff (TNER)
Panama	Preprimary	11.3	78.9	2015	UIS (ANER)	10.7	75.6	2017	UIS (ANER)
	Primary		87.4	2015	UIS (TNER)		84.0	2017	UIS (TNER)
	Lower-secondary		84.5	2015	UIS (TNER)		84.2	2017	UIS (TNER)
	Upper-secondary		66.1	2015	UIS (TNER)		55.6	2017	UIS (TNER)
Papua New Guinea	Preprimary	8.2	98.6	2008	UIS (GER)	10.3	71.4	2016	UIS (ANER)
	Primary		85.4	2012	UIS (TNER)		84.4	2016	UIS (TNER)
	Lower-secondary		15.6	2012	UIS (NER)		77.1	2016	UIS (TNER)
	Upper-secondary		22.0	2012	UIS (GER)		50.4	2016	UIS (TNER)
Seychelles	Preprimary	13.7	96.5	2016	UIS (ANER)	13.0	97.4	2017	UIS (ANER)
	Primary		99.8	2016	UIS (TNER)		97.2	2017	UIS (TNER)
	Lower-secondary		92.0	2016	UIS (ANER)		91.8	2017	UIS (ANER)
	Upper-secondary		99.9	2016	UIS (TNER)		83.7	2017	UIS (TNER)
Solomon Islands	Preprimary	9.2	65.4	2015	UIS (ANER)	8.7	55.7	2017	WB Staff (ANER)
	Primary		75.0	2016	UIS (TNER)		92.9	2017	UIS (TNER)
	Lower-secondary		69.0	2007	UIS (TNER)		37.0	2017	WB Staff (NER)
	Upper-secondary		44.8	2007	UIS (TNER)		28.4	2017	WB Staff (NER)
South Africa	Preprimary	9.3	21.9	2015	UIS (NER)	10.2	14.9	2015	UIS (NER)
	Primary		83.1	2015	UIS (TNER)		92.8	2017	WB Staff (NER)
	Lower-secondary		71.1	2015	UIS (TNER)		72.1	2017	UIS (TNER)
	Upper-secondary		58.4	2015	UIS (TNER)		70.8	2017	WB Staff (NER)

(continued next page)

Table C7.1: Data sources for every education level for economies with an absolute change in EYS of at least 0.5, original 2018 and back-calculated 2018 (*Continued*)

Economy	Level	2018				2018 back-calculated			
		EYS	Rate	Year	Source	EYS	Rate	Year	Source
Tanzania	Preprimary	7.8	45.0	2014	UIS (ANER)	7.2	54.7	2017	UIS (ANER)
	Primary		91.5	2017	WB Staff (TNER)		80.7	2017	UIS (TNER)
	Lower-secondary		38.7	2017	WB Staff (GER)		27.8	2016	UIS (TNER)
	Upper-secondary		6.9	2017	WB Staff (GER)		14.2	2016	UIS (TNER)
Timor-Leste	Preprimary	9.9	57.3	2016	UIS (ANER)	10.6	43.2	2017	UIS (ANER)
	Primary		68.9	2016	UIS (TNER)		82.4	2017	UIS (TNER)
	Lower-secondary		85.9	2016	UIS (TNER)		85.0	2017	UIS (TNER)
	Upper-secondary		66.6	2016	UIS (TNER)		74.3	2017	UIS (TNER)
Tonga	Preprimary	10.9	38.5	2014	UIS (GER)	11.6	45.8	2015	UIS (GER)
	Primary		98.7	2014	UIS (TNER)		98.9	2015	UIS (TNER)
	Lower-secondary		96.4	2014	UIS (TNER)		95.1	2015	UIS (TNER)
	Upper-secondary		43.3	2014	UIS (TNER)		62.0	2015	UIS (TNER)
Vanuatu	Preprimary	10.6	55.9	2015	UIS (NER)	10.1	49.7	2015	UIS (NER)
	Primary		83.6	2015	UIS (TNER)		77.8	2015	UIS (TNER)
	Lower-secondary		95.3	2015	UIS (TNER)		92.8	2015	UIS (TNER)
	Upper-secondary		54.9	2015	UIS (TNER)		55.5	2015	UIS (TNER)
Vietnam	Preprimary	12.3	89.6	2016	UIS (ANER)	12.8	99.7	2017	UIS (ANER)
	Primary		96.2	2016	WB Staff (NER)		97.9	2017	UIS (TNER)
	Lower-secondary		89.7	2016	WB Staff (NER)		96.7	2017	UIS (NER)
	Upper-secondary		68.1	2016	WB Staff (NER)		68.1	2016	WB Staff (NER)
West Bank and Gaza	Preprimary	11.4	64.7	2015	UIS (ANER)	12.0	64.4	2017	UIS (ANER)
	Primary		92.4	2016	UIS (TNER)		97.4	2017	UIS (TNER)
	Lower-secondary		87.7	2016	UIS (TNER)		92.7	2017	UIS (TNER)
	Upper-secondary		63.5	2016	UIS (TNER)		68.1	2017	UIS (TNER)
Zimbabwe	Preprimary	10.0	36.4	2013	UIS (ANER)	11.1	40.7	2013	UIS (ANER)
	Primary		87.9	2013	UIS (TNER)		97.6	2013	UIS (TNER)
	Lower-secondary		86.9	2013	UIS (TNER)		93.9	2013	UIS (TNER)
	Upper-secondary		46.7	2013	UIS (TNER)		52.2	2013	UIS (TNER)

Source: World Bank calculations based on World Bank 2018 and the 2020 update of the Human Capital Index.

Note: ANER = adjusted net enrollment rate; EYS = expected years of school; GER = gross enrollment rate; NER = net enrollment rate; TNER = total net enrollment rate; UIS = United Nations Educational, Scientific and Cultural Organization's Institute of Statistics; WB = World Bank.

Table C7.2: Data sources for every level of schooling for economies with a decrease in EYS between 2010 and 2020

Economy	Level	2010				2020			
		EYS	Rate	Year	Source	EYS	Rate	Year	Source
Austria	Preprimary	13.5	96.9	2010	UIS (ANER)	13.4	100.0	2017	UIS (ANER)
	Primary		96.5	2010	UIS (TNER)		97.0	2017	UIS (TNER)
	Lower-secondary		98.1	2010	UIS (TNER)		97.5	2017	UIS (TNER)
	Upper-secondary		93.1	2010	UIS (TNER)		89.4	2017	UIS (TNER)
Bulgaria	Preprimary	12.9	93.2	2010	UIS (ANER)	12.3	84.0	2017	UIS (ANER)
	Primary		99.2	2010	UIS (TNER)		88.2	2017	UIS (TNER)
	Lower-secondary		88.6	2010	UIS (TNER)		87.6	2017	UIS (TNER)
	Upper-secondary		81.1	2010	UIS (TNER)		90.3	2017	UIS (TNER)
Denmark	Preprimary	13.4	99.1	2010	UIS (ANER)	13.4	93.7	2017	UIS (ANER)
	Primary		98.6	2010	UIS (TNER)		98.9	2017	UIS (TNER)
	Lower-secondary		99.2	2010	UIS (TNER)		98.4	2017	UIS (TNER)
	Upper-secondary		85.3	2010	UIS (TNER)		87.9	2017	UIS (TNER)
Germany	Preprimary	13.3	96.8	2010	UIS (ANER)	13.3	98.8	2017	UIS (ANER)
	Primary		97.2	2010	UIS (TNER)		99.0	2017	UIS (TNER)
	Lower-secondary		94.5	2010	UIS (TNER)		92.9	2017	UIS (TNER)
	Upper-secondary		91.4	2010	UIS (TNER)		87.6	2017	UIS (TNER)
Greece	Preprimary	13.4	94.4	2010	UIS (ANER)	13.3	92.7	2017	UIS (ANER)
	Primary		96.4	2010	UIS (TNER)		98.0	2017	UIS (TNER)
	Lower-secondary		94.9	2010	UIS (TNER)		92.5	2017	UIS (TNER)
	Upper-secondary		95.4	2010	UIS (TNER)		92.5	2017	UIS (TNER)
Guatemala	Preprimary	10.3	85.5	2010	UIS (ANER)	9.7	85.1	2018	UIS (ANER)
	Primary		84.1	2011	UIS (TNER*)		81.3	2018	UIS (TNER)
	Lower-secondary		78.9	2010	UIS (TNER)		63.8	2018	UIS (TNER)
	Upper-secondary		38.3	2010	UIS (TNER)		40.6	2018	UIS (TNER)
Hungary	Preprimary	13.0	94.2	2010	UIS (ANER)	13.0	87.1	2017	UIS (ANER)
	Primary		96.5	2010	UIS (TNER)		96.2	2017	UIS (TNER)
	Lower-secondary		93.0	2010	UIS (TNER)		94.7	2017	UIS (TNER)
	Upper-secondary		85.7	2010	UIS (TNER)		86.8	2017	UIS (TNER)
Italy	Preprimary	13.6	99.6	2010	UIS (ANER)	13.3	93.9	2017	UIS (ANER)
	Primary		99.3	2010	UIS (TNER)		97.2	2017	UIS (TNER)
	Lower-secondary		95.2	2010	UIS (TNER)		95.9	2017	UIS (TNER)
	Upper-secondary		93.2	2010	UIS (TNER)		88.9	2017	UIS (TNER)
Japan	Preprimary	13.7	95.6	2010	WB Staff (ANER)	13.6	91.1	2015	WB Staff (ANER)
	Primary		99.4	2010	WB Staff (TNER)		98.8	2015	WB Staff (TNER)
	Lower-secondary		99.7	2010	WB Staff (TNER)		99.9	2015	WB Staff (TNER)
	Upper-secondary		94.7	2010	WB Staff (TNER)		96.4	2015	WB Staff (TNER)

(continued next page)

Table C7.2: Data sources for every level of schooling for economies with a decrease in EYS between 2010 and 2020 (*Continued*)

Economy	Level	2010				2020			
		EYS	Rate	Year	Source	EYS	Rate	Year	Source
Jordan	Preprimary	11.8	37.9	2010	WB Staff (NER)	11.1	36.5	2018	WB Staff (NER)
	Primary		97.2	2010	WB Staff (NER)		92.4	2018	WB Staff (NER)
	Lower-secondary		96.2	2010	WB Staff (NER)		92.4	2018	WB Staff (NER)
	Upper-secondary		78.8	2010	WB Staff (NER)		70.1	2018	WB Staff (NER)
Korea, Rep.	Preprimary	13.7	96.9	2013	WB Staff (ANER**)	13.6	95.9	2017	UIS (ANER)
	Primary		99.8	2010	UIS (TNER)		97.6	2017	UIS (TNER)
	Lower-secondary		99.8	2010	UIS (TNER)		94.4	2017	UIS (TNER)
	Upper-secondary		92.2	2010	UIS (TNER)		99.7	2017	UIS (TNER)
Kuwait	Preprimary	12.7	91.7	2012	UIS (ANER*)	12.0	81.2	2018	UIS (ANER)
	Primary		98.3	2010	UIS (TNER)		88.4	2018	UIS (TNER)
	Lower-secondary		92.7	2010	UIS (TNER)		92.1	2015	UIS (TNER)
	Upper-secondary		71.3	2010	UIS (TNER)		78.1	2015	UIS (TNER)
Luxembourg	Preprimary	12.8	95.1	2010	UIS (ANER)	12.4	98.2	2017	UIS (ANER)
	Primary		95.7	2010	UIS (TNER)		95.8	2017	UIS (TNER)
	Lower-secondary		89.4	2010	UIS (TNER)		84.7	2017	UIS (TNER)
	Upper-secondary		81.8	2010	UIS (TNER)		72.2	2017	UIS (TNER)
Moldova	Preprimary	12.0	92.6	2010	UIS (ANER)	11.8	93.3	2018	UIS (ANER)
	Primary		91.6	2010	UIS (TNER)		91.0	2018	UIS (TNER)
	Lower-secondary		87.5	2010	UIS (TNER)		85.0	2018	UIS (TNER)
	Upper-secondary		66.4	2010	UIS (TNER)		64.5	2018	UIS (TNER)
Panama	Preprimary	11.3	76.8	2010	UIS (ANER)	10.7	75.6	2017	UIS (ANER)
	Primary		91.4	2010	UIS (TNER)		84.0	2017	UIS (TNER)
	Lower-secondary		83.3	2010	UIS (TNER)		84.2	2017	UIS (TNER)
	Upper-secondary		60.5	2010	UIS (TNER)		55.6	2017	UIS (TNER)
Qatar	Preprimary	12.9	77.9	2013	UIS (ANER*)	12.8	92.4	2018	UIS (ANER)
	Primary		97.5	2010	UIS (TNER)		96.8	2018	UIS (TNER)
	Lower-secondary		96.6	2011	UIS (TNER*)		89.6	2018	UIS (TNER)
	Upper-secondary		86.8	2010	UIS (TNER)		83.0	2010	UIS (TNER)
Romania	Preprimary	12.7	78.8	2013	WB Staff (ANER**)	11.8	83.9	2018	WB Staff (ANER)
	Primary		95.8	2010	UIS (TNER)		89.5	2018	WB Staff (TNER)
	Lower-secondary		91.7	2010	UIS (TNER)		84.9	2018	WB Staff (TNER)
	Upper-secondary		86.3	2010	WB Staff (TNER)		74.4	2017	WB Staff (TNER)

(continued next page)

Table C7.2: Data sources for every level of schooling for economies with a decrease in EYS between 2010 and 2020 (*Continued*)

Economy	Level	2010				2020			
		EYS	Rate	Year	Source	EYS	Rate	Year	Source
Slovak Republic	Preprimary	12.7	84.7	2010	UIS (ANER)	12.6	82.3	2017	UIS (ANER)
	Primary		92.0	2010	UIS (TNER)		91.4	2017	UIS (TNER)
	Lower-secondary		93.2	2010	UIS (TNER)		93.5	2017	UIS (TNER)
	Upper-secondary		89.1	2010	UIS (TNER)		89.5	2017	UIS (TNER)
South Africa	Preprimary	10.2	11.1	2015		10.2	14.9	2015	UIS (NER)
	Primary		92.3	2010	WB Staff (NER)		93.1	2018	WB Staff (NER)
	Lower-secondary		79.0	2017	UIS (TNER*)		71.2	2017	UIS (TNER)
	Upper-secondary		69.7	2010	WB Staff (NER)		73.1	2018	WB Staff (NER)
Turkey	Preprimary	12.1	67.1	2013	WB Staff (ANER**)	12.1	67.6	2017	UIS (ANER)
	Primary		94.6	2010	UIS (TNER)		92.6	2017	UIS (TNER)
	Lower-secondary		96.6	2010	UIS (TNER)		90.4	2017	UIS (TNER)
	Upper-secondary		74.1	2010	UIS (TNER)		81.5	2017	UIS (TNER)
Ukraine	Preprimary	13.1	99.1	2010	UIS (GER)	12.9	83.9	2013	UIS (GER)
	Primary		90.7	2010	UIS (TNER)		91.9	2014	UIS (TNER)
	Lower-secondary		94.8	2010	UIS (TNER)		96.3	2014	UIS (TNER)
	Upper-secondary		94.4	2010	UIS (TNER)		94.1	2014	UIS (TNER)

Source: World Bank calculations based on the 2020 update of the Human Capital Index (HCI).

Note: ANER = adjusted net enrollment rate; EYS = expected years of school; GER = gross enrollment rate; NER = net enrollment rate; TNER = total enrollment rate; UIS = United Nations Educational, Scientific and Cultural Organization's Institute of Statistics; WB = World Bank.

*interpolated using the same series; **interpolated using GER.

8. HCI AND COMPONENT DATA

Table C8.1: Human Capital Index and components: 2020, 2018 back-calculated, and 2010

Economy	Components of HCI 2020						HCI		
	Probability of survival to age 5	Expected years of school	Harmonized test scores	Learning-adjusted years of schooling	Adult survival rate	Fraction of children under 5 not stunted	HCI 2020	HCI 2018 back-calculated	HCI 2010
Afghanistan	0.94	8.9	355	5.1	0.79	0.62	0.40	0.39	–
Albania	0.99	12.9	434	9.0	0.93	0.89	0.63	0.63	0.54
Algeria	0.98	11.8	374	7.1	0.91	0.88	0.53	0.53	0.53
Angola	0.92	8.1	326	4.2	0.73	0.62	0.36	0.36	–

(continued next page)

Table C8.1: Human Capital Index and components: 2020, 2018 back-calculated, and 2010 (*Continued*)

Economy	Components of HCI 2020						HCI		
	Probability of survival to age 5	Expected years of school	Harmonized test scores	Learning-adjusted years of schooling	Adult survival rate	Fraction of children under 5 not stunted	HCI 2020	HCI 2018 back-calculated	HCI 2010
Antigua and Barbuda	0.99	13.0	407	8.4	0.90	–	0.60	0.58	–
Argentina	0.99	12.9	408	8.4	0.89	0.92	0.60	0.62	0.59
Armenia	0.99	11.3	443	8.0	0.89	0.91	0.58	0.58	–
Australia	1.00	13.6	516	11.2	0.95	–	0.77	0.78	0.75
Austria	1.00	13.4	508	10.9	0.94	–	0.75	0.77	0.74
Azerbaijan	0.98	12.4	416	8.3	0.88	0.82	0.58	0.63	0.50
Bahrain	0.99	12.8	452	9.3	0.93	–	0.65	0.66	0.60
Bangladesh	0.97	10.2	368	6.0	0.87	0.69	0.46	0.46	–
Belarus	1.00	13.8	488	10.8	0.85	–	0.70	–	–
Belgium	1.00	13.5	517	11.2	0.93	–	0.76	0.76	0.75
Benin	0.91	9.2	384	5.7	0.77	–	0.40	0.40	0.37
Bhutan	0.97	10.2	387	6.3	0.81	0.79	0.48	–	–
Bosnia and Herzegovina	0.99	11.7	416	7.8	0.91	0.91	0.58	0.62	–
Botswana	0.96	8.1	391	5.1	0.80	–	0.41	0.41	0.37
Brazil	0.99	11.9	413	7.9	0.86	–	0.55	0.55	0.53
Brunei Darussalam	0.99	13.2	438	9.2	0.88	0.80	0.63	–	–
Bulgaria	0.99	12.3	441	8.7	0.87	0.93	0.61	0.67	0.64
Burkina Faso	0.92	7.0	404	4.5	0.76	0.75	0.38	0.38	0.32
Burundi	0.94	7.6	423	5.2	0.72	0.46	0.39	0.39	0.34
Cambodia	0.97	9.5	452	6.8	0.84	0.68	0.49	0.49	–
Cameroon	0.92	8.7	379	5.3	0.70	0.71	0.40	0.39	0.38
Canada	1.00	13.7	534	11.7	0.94	–	0.80	0.80	0.77
Central African Republic	0.88	4.6	369	2.7	0.59	0.59	0.29	–	–
Chad	0.88	5.3	333	2.8	0.65	0.60	0.30	0.30	0.29
Chile	0.99	13.0	452	9.4	0.92	–	0.65	0.67	0.63
China	0.99	13.1	441	9.3	0.92	0.92	0.65	0.65	–
Colombia	0.99	12.9	419	8.6	0.89	0.87	0.60	0.60	0.58
Comoros	0.93	8.2	392	5.1	0.78	0.69	0.40	0.40	–
Congo, Dem. Rep.	0.91	9.1	310	4.5	0.75	0.57	0.37	0.36	–
Congo, Rep.	0.95	8.9	371	5.3	0.74	0.79	0.42	0.42	0.41
Costa Rica	0.99	13.1	429	9.0	0.92	–	0.63	0.60	0.60

(continued next page)

Table C8.1: Human Capital Index and components: 2020, 2018 back-calculated, and 2010 (*Continued*)

	Components of HCI 2020						HCI		
Economy	Probability of survival to age 5	Expected years of school	Harmonized test scores	Learning-adjusted years of schooling	Adult survival rate	Fraction of children under 5 not stunted	HCI 2020	HCI 2018 back-calculated	HCI 2010
Croatia	1.00	13.4	488	10.4	0.92	–	0.71	0.73	0.69
Cyprus	1.00	13.6	502	10.9	0.95	–	0.76	0.75	0.69
Czech Republic	1.00	13.6	512	11.1	0.92	–	0.75	0.76	0.73
Côte d'Ivoire	0.92	8.1	373	4.8	0.66	0.78	0.38	0.37	0.30
Denmark	1.00	13.4	518	11.1	0.93	–	0.76	0.77	0.75
Dominica	0.96	12.4	404	8.0	0.86	–	0.54	0.55	–
Dominican Republic	0.97	11.9	345	6.6	0.84	0.93	0.50	0.51	–
Ecuador	0.99	12.9	420	8.7	0.88	0.76	0.59	0.60	0.53
Egypt, Arab Rep.	0.98	11.5	356	6.5	0.86	0.78	0.49	0.49	0.48
El Salvador	0.99	10.9	436	7.6	0.82	0.86	0.55	0.54	–
Estonia	1.00	13.5	543	11.7	0.90	–	0.78	0.77	0.73
Eswatini	0.95	6.4	440	4.5	0.60	0.74	0.37	0.37	0.31
Ethiopia	0.94	7.8	348	4.3	0.79	0.63	0.38	0.38	–
Fiji	0.97	11.3	383	7.0	0.78	0.91	0.51	–	–
Finland	1.00	13.7	534	11.7	0.93	–	0.80	0.81	0.82
France	1.00	13.8	510	11.3	0.93	–	0.76	0.76	0.76
Gabon	0.96	8.3	456	6.0	0.79	0.83	0.46	0.46	–
Gambia, The	0.94	9.5	353	5.4	0.75	0.81	0.42	0.40	0.37
Georgia	0.99	12.9	400	8.3	0.85	–	0.57	0.61	0.54
Germany	1.00	13.3	517	11.0	0.93	–	0.75	0.76	0.76
Ghana	0.95	12.1	307	6.0	0.77	0.82	0.45	0.44	–
Greece	1.00	13.3	469	10.0	0.93	–	0.69	0.69	0.71
Grenada	0.98	13.1	395	8.3	0.85	–	0.57	0.54	–
Guatemala	0.97	9.7	405	6.3	0.85	0.53	0.46	0.46	0.44
Guinea	0.90	7.0	408	4.6	0.76	0.70	0.37	0.37	–
Guyana	0.97	12.2	346	6.8	0.77	0.89	0.50	0.49	–
Haiti	0.94	11.4	338	6.1	0.78	0.78	0.45	0.44	–
Honduras	0.98	9.6	400	6.1	0.86	0.77	0.48	0.48	–
Hong Kong SAR, China	0.99	13.5	549	11.9	0.95	–	0.81	0.82	0.78
Hungary	1.00	13.0	495	10.3	0.88	–	0.68	0.71	0.69
Iceland	1.00	13.5	498	10.7	0.95	–	0.75	0.74	0.76
India	0.96	11.1	399	7.1	0.83	0.65	0.49	0.48	–

(*continued next page*)

Table C8.1: Human Capital Index and components: 2020, 2018 back-calculated, and 2010 (*Continued*)

Economy	Components of HCI 2020						HCI		
	Probability of survival to age 5	Expected years of school	Harmonized test scores	Learning-adjusted years of schooling	Adult survival rate	Fraction of children under 5 not stunted	HCI 2020	HCI 2018 back-calculated	HCI 2010
Indonesia	0.98	12.4	395	7.8	0.85	0.72	0.54	0.54	0.50
Iran, Islamic Rep.	0.99	11.8	432	8.2	0.93	–	0.59	0.59	0.56
Iraq	0.97	6.9	363	4.0	0.84	0.87	0.41	0.40	–
Ireland	1.00	13.9	521	11.6	0.94	–	0.79	0.81	0.77
Israel	1.00	13.8	481	10.6	0.95	–	0.73	0.76	0.72
Italy	1.00	13.3	493	10.5	0.95	–	0.73	0.75	0.75
Jamaica	0.99	11.4	387	7.1	0.86	0.94	0.53	0.54	–
Japan	1.00	13.6	538	11.7	0.95	–	0.80	0.84	0.82
Jordan	0.98	11.1	430	7.7	0.89	–	0.55	0.55	0.56
Kazakhstan	0.99	13.7	416	9.1	0.84	0.92	0.63	0.78	0.59
Kenya	0.96	11.6	455	8.5	0.77	0.74	0.55	0.54	–
Kiribati	0.95	11.2	411	7.4	0.81	–	0.49	0.47	–
Korea, Rep.	1.00	13.6	537	11.7	0.94	–	0.80	0.83	0.82
Kosovo	0.99	13.2	374	7.9	0.91	–	0.57	0.57	–
Kuwait	0.99	12.0	383	7.4	0.94	–	0.56	0.56	0.57
Kyrgyz Republic	0.98	12.9	420	8.7	0.85	0.88	0.60	0.59	–
Lao PDR	0.95	10.6	368	6.3	0.82	0.67	0.46	0.46	–
Latvia	1.00	13.6	504	11.0	0.84	–	0.71	0.74	0.68
Lebanon	0.99	10.2	390	6.3	0.93	–	0.52	0.52	–
Lesotho	0.92	10.0	393	6.3	0.52	0.65	0.40	0.40	0.34
Liberia	0.93	4.2	332	2.2	0.78	0.70	0.32	0.32	–
Lithuania	1.00	13.8	496	11.0	0.84	–	0.71	0.73	0.69
Luxembourg	1.00	12.4	493	9.8	0.94	–	0.69	0.69	0.70
Macao SAR, China	0.99	12.9	561	11.6	0.96	–	0.80	0.76	0.65
Madagascar	0.95	8.4	351	4.7	0.80	0.58	0.39	0.39	0.39
Malawi	0.95	9.6	359	5.5	0.74	0.61	0.41	0.41	0.36
Malaysia	0.99	12.5	446	8.9	0.88	0.79	0.61	0.63	0.58
Mali	0.90	5.2	307	2.6	0.75	0.73	0.32	0.32	–
Malta	0.99	13.4	474	10.2	0.95	–	0.71	0.71	0.68
Marshall Islands	0.97	9.4	375	5.7	0.70	0.65	0.42	0.40	–
Mauritania	0.92	7.7	342	4.2	0.80	0.77	0.38	0.37	–
Mauritius	0.98	12.4	473	9.4	0.86	–	0.62	0.62	0.60

(continued next page)

Table C8.1: Human Capital Index and components: 2020, 2018 back-calculated, and 2010 (*Continued*)

Economy	Components of HCI 2020						HCI		
	Probability of survival to age 5	Expected years of school	Harmonized test scores	Learning-adjusted years of schooling	Adult survival rate	Fraction of children under 5 not stunted	HCI 2020	HCI 2018 back-calculated	HCI 2010
Mexico	0.99	12.8	430	8.8	0.86	0.90	0.61	0.61	0.59
Micronesia, Fed. Sts.	0.97	11.8	380	7.2	0.84	–	0.51	0.47	–
Moldova	0.98	11.8	439	8.3	0.84	0.94	0.58	0.58	0.56
Mongolia	0.98	13.2	435	9.2	0.80	0.91	0.61	0.62	–
Montenegro	1.00	12.8	436	8.9	0.91	0.91	0.63	0.62	0.59
Morocco	0.98	10.4	380	6.3	0.93	0.85	0.50	0.49	0.47
Mozambique	0.93	7.6	368	4.5	0.68	0.58	0.36	0.36	–
Myanmar	0.95	10.0	425	6.8	0.80	0.71	0.48	0.47	–
Namibia	0.96	9.4	407	6.1	0.71	0.77	0.45	0.45	0.39
Nauru	0.97	11.7	347	6.5	0.93	–	0.51	–	–
Nepal	0.97	12.3	369	7.2	0.86	0.64	0.50	0.50	–
Netherlands	1.00	13.9	520	11.5	0.95	–	0.79	0.80	0.80
New Zealand	0.99	13.7	520	11.4	0.94	–	0.78	0.77	0.78
Nicaragua	0.98	10.8	392	6.7	0.85	0.83	0.51	0.51	–
Niger	0.92	5.5	305	2.7	0.77	0.52	0.32	0.32	–
Nigeria	0.88	10.2	309	5.0	0.66	0.63	0.36	0.35	–
North Macedonia	0.99	11.0	414	7.3	0.91	0.95	0.56	0.54	0.54
Norway	1.00	13.7	514	11.2	0.94	–	0.77	0.77	0.77
Oman	0.99	12.8	424	8.6	0.91	–	0.61	0.61	0.55
Pakistan	0.93	9.4	339	5.1	0.85	0.62	0.41	0.40	–
Palau	0.98	11.7	463	8.7	0.87	–	0.59	0.57	–
Panama	0.98	10.7	377	6.5	0.89	–	0.50	0.51	0.51
Papua New Guinea	0.95	10.3	363	6.0	0.78	0.51	0.43	0.42	–
Paraguay	0.98	11.3	386	7.0	0.86	0.94	0.53	0.53	0.51
Peru	0.99	13.0	415	8.6	0.89	0.88	0.61	0.59	0.55
Philippines	0.97	12.9	362	7.5	0.82	0.70	0.52	0.55	–
Poland	1.00	13.4	530	11.4	0.89	–	0.75	0.76	0.70
Portugal	1.00	13.9	509	11.3	0.93	–	0.77	0.78	0.74
Qatar	0.99	12.8	427	8.8	0.96	–	0.64	0.63	0.59
Romania	0.99	11.8	442	8.4	0.88	–	0.58	0.59	0.60
Russian Federation	0.99	13.7	498	10.9	0.80	–	0.68	0.73	0.60
Rwanda	0.96	6.9	358	3.9	0.81	0.62	0.38	0.38	–

(continued next page)

Table C8.1: Human Capital Index and components: 2020, 2018 back-calculated, and 2010 (*Continued*)

Economy	Components of HCI 2020						HCI		
	Probability of survival to age 5	Expected years of school	Harmonized test scores	Learning-adjusted years of schooling	Adult survival rate	Fraction of children under 5 not stunted	HCI 2020	HCI 2018 back-calculated	HCI 2010
Samoa	0.98	12.2	370	7.2	0.89	0.95	0.55	0.52	–
Saudi Arabia	0.99	12.4	399	7.9	0.92	–	0.58	0.58	0.55
Senegal	0.96	7.3	412	4.8	0.83	0.81	0.42	0.42	0.39
Serbia	0.99	13.3	457	9.8	0.89	0.94	0.68	0.76	0.65
Seychelles	0.99	13.1	463	9.7	0.85	–	0.63	0.63	0.57
Sierra Leone	0.89	9.6	316	4.9	0.63	0.71	0.36	0.35	–
Singapore	1.00	13.9	575	12.8	0.95	–	0.88	0.89	0.85
Slovak Republic	0.99	12.6	485	9.8	0.90	–	0.66	0.68	0.68
Slovenia	1.00	13.6	521	11.4	0.93	–	0.77	0.79	0.75
Solomon Islands	0.98	8.3	351	4.7	0.86	0.68	0.42	0.43	–
South Africa	0.97	10.2	343	5.6	0.69	0.73	0.43	0.42	0.43
South Sudan	0.90	4.7	336	2.5	0.68	0.69	0.31	0.31	–
Spain	1.00	13.0	507	10.5	0.95	–	0.73	0.74	0.71
Sri Lanka	0.99	13.2	400	8.5	0.90	0.83	0.60	0.59	–
St. Kitts and Nevis	0.99	13.0	409	8.5	0.88	–	0.59	0.57	–
St. Lucia	0.98	12.7	418	8.5	0.87	0.98	0.60	0.59	–
St. Vincent and the Grenadines	0.98	12.3	391	7.7	0.83	–	0.53	0.54	–
Sudan	0.94	7.1	380	4.3	0.79	0.62	0.38	0.38	–
Sweden	1.00	13.9	519	11.6	0.95	–	0.80	0.80	0.76
Switzerland	1.00	13.3	515	10.9	0.95	–	0.76	0.77	0.77
Tajikistan	0.97	10.9	391	6.8	0.87	0.82	0.50	0.54	–
Tanzania	0.95	7.2	388	4.5	0.78	0.68	0.39	0.39	–
Thailand	0.99	12.7	427	8.7	0.87	0.89	0.61	0.62	0.58
Timor-Leste	0.95	10.6	371	6.3	0.86	0.54	0.45	0.45	0.41
Togo	0.93	9.7	384	6.0	0.74	0.76	0.43	0.42	0.37
Tonga	0.98	11.6	386	7.1	0.83	0.92	0.53	0.52	–
Trinidad and Tobago	0.98	12.4	458	9.1	0.85	–	0.60	0.60	0.55
Tunisia	0.98	10.6	384	6.5	0.91	0.92	0.52	0.51	0.53
Turkey	0.99	12.1	478	9.2	0.91	0.94	0.65	0.63	0.63
Tuvalu	0.98	10.8	346	6.0	0.79	–	0.45	0.44	–

(continued next page)

Table C8.1: Human Capital Index and components: 2020, 2018 back-calculated, and 2010 (*Continued*)

Economy	Components of HCI 2020						HCI		
	Probability of survival to age 5	Expected years of school	Harmonized test scores	Learning-adjusted years of schooling	Adult survival rate	Fraction of children under 5 not stunted	HCI 2020	HCI 2018 back-calculated	HCI 2010
Uganda	0.95	6.8	397	4.3	0.74	0.71	0.38	0.38	0.34
Ukraine	0.99	12.9	478	9.9	0.81	–	0.63	0.64	0.63
United Arab Emirates	0.99	13.5	448	9.6	0.94	–	0.67	0.68	0.62
United Kingdom	1.00	13.9	520	11.5	0.93	–	0.78	0.78	0.77
United States	0.99	12.9	512	10.6	0.89	–	0.70	0.71	0.69
Uruguay	0.99	12.2	438	8.6	0.89	–	0.60	0.60	0.59
Uzbekistan	0.98	12.0	474	9.1	0.87	0.89	0.62	–	–
Vanuatu	0.97	10.1	348	5.6	0.87	0.71	0.45	0.44	–
Vietnam	0.98	12.9	519	10.7	0.87	0.76	0.69	0.69	0.66
West Bank and Gaza	0.98	12.2	412	8.0	0.89	0.93	0.58	0.57	–
Yemen, Rep.	0.95	8.1	321	4.2	0.80	0.54	0.37	0.37	–
Zambia	0.94	8.8	358	5.0	0.73	0.65	0.40	0.39	–
Zimbabwe	0.95	11.1	396	7.0	0.65	0.77	0.47	0.46	0.41

Source: World Bank calculations based on the 2020 update of the Human Capital Index (HCI).

Notes: This table reports the components and overall index scores for the HCI 2020, the back-calculated HCI 2018 and the HCI 2010. The HCI ranges between 0 and 1. The index is measured in terms of the productivity of the next generation of workers relative to the benchmark of complete education and full health. An economy in which a child born today can expect to achieve complete education and full health will score a value of 1 on the index. – indicates missing data.

NOTES

1. United Nations Statistics Division web page, "Coverage of Birth and Death Registration," http://unstats.un.org/unsd/demographic/CRVS/CR_coverage.htm.
2. For more information, see http://www.childmortality.org/.
3. This section borrows heavily from the technical appendix of Kraay (2018).
4. The main source for enrollment data from UIS is administrative data. Data are collected by UIS on an annual basis from official national statistical authorities. The data are released in September of every year and include national data for the school or reference year ending in the previous year. The national data are then updated in February, which completes the UIS publication of educational data for the data collection effort of the previous reference year.
5. An important agenda concerns the frequent and substantial discrepancies between household survey–based measures of school enrollment and administrative records. D'Souza, Gatti, and Kraay (2019) briefly discuss these discrepancies.

6. $Y_i = 2$ for preprimary, $Y_i = 6$ for primary, $Y_i = 3$ for lower-secondary, and $Y_i = 3$ for upper-secondary.
7. For the 2020 update, this process was conducted between January 29 and April 29, resulting in revised enrollment rates for all levels, which are available in individual economy files at https://www.worldbank.org/en/publication/human-capital.
8. See http://data.uis.unesco.org/.
9. The exceptions to this rule are Fiji, Kenya, and Kiribati, for which the most recent data available are from before 2010.
10. Note that one level of schooling may use TNER whereas another may use NER. For a given level of education, however, the same enrollment type is used over time.
11. This effort is made for all economies for which the same test is available in or close to the specified year.
12. Exceptions are Qatar preprimary and primary, for which the same value of 2010 is used.
13. World Bank staff working in each economy obtain these data from local government sources, for example, the Ministry of Education or National Statistics Office.
14. The flip side is that for 15 economies at least one of the enrollment rates used comes from an older year than was available in 2018's EYS, mostly because UIS revises the series and in some instances may remove years from the series.
15. For the latest updates on the harmonized test scores, see Angrist et al. (2019).
16. The one exception to this is the 2007 and 2014 PASEC rounds, which were not designed to be intertemporally comparable and in which different overlapping countries were used to construct the exchange rate in the two periods.
17. For the 2020 HCI, 13 economies have an HTS that comes from a nonrepresentative EGRA: Bangladesh, Central African Republic, the Democratic Republic of Congo, Ethiopia, Iraq, Jamaica, Lao PDR, Liberia, Mali, Myanmar, Nigeria, Pakistan, and South Sudan.
18. See Patrinos and Angrist (2018) for further details.
19. See JME (UNICEF-WHO-World Bank Joint Child Malnutrition Estimates) (database), 2020 edition, UNICEF, New York, https://data.unicef.org/resources/jme/.
20. The DHS program has fielded over 400 surveys across 90 economies, and over 300 MICS have been carried out in more than 100 economies.
21. See https://www.who.int/publications-detail/jme-2020-edition.
22. See Global Burden of Disease (GBD), database, Institute for Health Metrics and Evaluation (IHME), Seattle, http://www.healthdata.org/gbd.
23. See https://population.un.org/wpp/.
24. See http://www.healthdata.org/results/data-visualizations.
25. See https://data.un.org/.

REFERENCES

Angrist, N., S. Djankov, P. Goldberg, and H. A. Patrinos. 2019. "Measuring Human Capital." Policy Research Working Paper 8742, World Bank, Washington, DC.

D'Souza, R., R. Gatti, and A. Kraay. 2019. "A Socioeconomic Disaggregation of the World Bank Human Capital Index." Policy Research Working Paper 9020, World Bank, Washington, DC.

Kraay, A. 2018. "Methodology for a World Bank Human Capital Index." Policy Research Working Paper 8593, World Bank, Washington, DC.

Marini, A., and C. Rokx. 2017. "Standing Tall: Peru's Success in Overcoming Its Stunting Crisis." World Bank, December 11, 2017. https://www.worldbank.org/en/news/video/2017/12/11/standing-tall-perus-success-in-overcoming-its-stunting-crisis.

Patrinos, H. A., and N. Angrist. 2018. "Global Dataset on Education Quality: A Review and Update (2000–2017)." Policy Research Working Paper 8592, World Bank, Washington, DC.

UNICEF (United Nations Children's Fund). 2013. "A Passport to Protection: A Guide to Birth Registration Programming." UNICEF, New York.

UNICEF (United Nations Children's Fund), WHO (World Health Organization), and World Bank. 2020. *Levels and Trends in Child Malnutrition: Key Findings from the 2020 Edition*. Geneva: World Health Organization.

UNIGME (United Nations Interagency Group for Child Mortality Estimation). 2019. "Levels and Trends in Child Mortality, Report 2019." United Nations Children's Fund, New York.

World Bank. 2018. "The Human Capital Project." World Bank, Washington, DC.

World Health Organization. 2009. "The WHO Multicentre Growth Reference Study (MGRS)." World Health Organization, Geneva.

Yang, H., and M. de Onis. 2008. "Algorithms for Converting Estimates of Child Malnutrition Based on the NCHS Reference into Estimates Based on the WHO Child Growth Standards." *BMC Pediatrics* 8 (19).

ECO-AUDIT

Environmental Benefits Statement

The World Bank Group is committed to reducing its environmental footprint. In support of this commitment, we leverage electronic publishing options and print-on-demand technology, which is located in regional hubs worldwide. Together, these initiatives enable print runs to be lowered and shipping distances decreased, resulting in reduced paper consumption, chemical use, greenhouse gas emissions, and waste.

We follow the recommended standards for paper use set by the Green Press Initiative. The majority of our books are printed on Forest Stewardship Council (FSC)–certified paper, with nearly all containing 50–100 percent recycled content. The recycled fiber in our book paper is either unbleached or bleached using totally chlorine-free (TCF), processed chlorine–free (PCF), or enhanced elemental chlorine–free (EECF) processes.

More information about the Bank's environmental philosophy can be found at http://www.worldbank.org/corporateresponsibility.